Knowledge and Learning

Knowledge and Learning

An Interdisciplinary Theory with Application to Teaching

By Steffen E. Palko

Fort Worth, Texas

Copyright © 2025 by Steffen E. Palko

Library of Congress Control Number: 2025018747

TCU Box 298300
Fort Worth, Texas 76129
www.tcupress.com

Cover illustration by Ekaterina Glazkova

To Betsy and my children for their support and understanding.

Contents

Preface ix

1. The Neuroscience of Memory 1
Cognitive Neuroscience of Memory
  Cellular Memory Mechanisms
  Structure of Memory
  Influence of Other Cortical Regions on Memory Creation
Cognitive Psychology of Memory

2. Nonlinear Systems and the Nature of Perception 22
Nonlinear Systems Theory
  Basic Nonlinear System Properties
  Bifurcations in Nonlinear Systems
  Self-Organization in Nonlinear Systems
  Chaos
Perception

3. Theory of Knowledge 43
Philosophic Background
  Ancient Greek Philosophy
  Modern Philosophy
Theory of Language
Theory of Knowledge
A Note on Postmodern Philosophy

4. Construction of Knowledge   103
Associative Learning
Consciously Constructed Knowledge
   Human Executive Function
   Human Executive Function and Teacher Scaffolding
Inductive Learning
   Metaphors, Analogies, and Other Literary Devices
   Induction and Interpretations of Classical Literature
   Inductive Reasoning
Deductive Learning
   Deductive Learning Models
   Research Paradigms
   Principles of Learning Applicable to Deductive Learning
Reflective Abstraction and Trial and Error
   Trial and Error
   Reflective Abstraction
Learning through Application
   Direct Application
   Contextual Teaching and Learning
   Applied Learning and Writing Instruction
Learning through Dialectic Process and Emergence
A Note on Creativity
A Note on Technology

5. Applications   264
Educator's Toolbox
   Theory of Knowledge Summary
   First Principles of Learning
   Inventory of Active Verbs Associated with Knowledge-Construction Methods
Creating and Designing Lessons and Instructional Experiences
Auditing and Improving Existing Lessons
Curriculum Design

Reference List   317

About the Author   325

Preface

I have had a lifelong dedication to the field of education. My education was what allowed me to go from the bottom rung of the socioeconomic ladder to a much loftier station later in life. My direct involvement with educational institutions began in the 1980s, primarily in a policy role. I served in the following positions at the local level:

- Management team member for Paschal High School (Fort Worth Independent School District)
- School board trustee of the Fort Worth Independent School District (eight years)
- Chairman of the Tarrant County Workforce Development Board (adult education)
- Member and chairman of the advisory board: TCU College of Education, TCU MBA program, University of Texas at Arlington's College of Education
- Education committee member of Performing Arts Fort Worth
- Trustee for Brite Divinity School

I served in the following positions at the state level:

- Chairman of the Texas Business and Education Coalition
- Advisory board member of the University of Texas at Austin's Petroleum Engineering Department

And I served in the following positions at the national level:

- Commissioner of the US Department of Labor, Secretary's Commission on Achieving Necessary Skills (SCANS)
- Chairman of the National Assessment of Vocational Education, US Department of Education
- Member of the board of directors for GED Testing Service
- Trustee for the Committee for Economic for Development (CED), leading several educational policy efforts

From these experiences, I learned what policy can do and what it cannot do. At its best, policy sets direction, expresses goals, delineates criteria to be used to assess goal attainment, and provides support, such as money and other resources, to assist in the achievement of policy objectives. Policy does not directly solve problems. Those who are subject to the policy, the practitioners, solve the problems and attain the goals. While leadership is critically important, organizational success is still contingent upon the motivation, commitment, education, training, experience, and expertise of those charged with carrying out the functions and everyday activities of the institution. For example, no matter how enlightened and well-crafted policy is, success in an institution like the Fort Worth Independent School District is ultimately dependent on the efficacy of the interaction among the fifty-six hundred teachers and their eighty-three thousand students. It is the collective consequence of many individual efforts.

After twenty years in an active policy role, I became frustrated with the lack of progress in public education. I became increasingly convinced that the next step for me was helping teachers achieve more success through better understanding of the nature of knowledge and learning, improved curriculum, and better instructional delivery methods. In 2005, I retired from my position as president of XTO Energy to pursue a doctoral degree in education. From 2009 to 2021, I taught education and leadership courses as a professor in TCU's College of Education. This book is the culmination my effort to determine ways to assist educators in achieving greater success.

When I began my career as an engineer, I had the benefit of first principles to assist my efforts to solve problems and to create designs. I had the principles of physics, chemistry, thermodynamics, fluid dynamics, and electromagnetism. Because of the complexity of the human brain and the consequent complexity of human behavior, educators have not enjoyed this luxury. This book is my attempt to remedy that situation. It is the culmination of sixteen years of effort to achieve this goal.

In trying to derive a set of first principles, I came to the realization that I had to first answer the metaphysical question What is knowledge? and the epistemological questions What can humans know and How do they go about knowing it? The first three chapters of this book describe my efforts to answer what knowledge is and what humans can know. I derive a theory of knowledge using results from cognitive science (chapter 1), nonlinear systems theory (chapter 2), and from results in philosophy and theory of language (chapter 3). Results from educational research are incorporated throughout the chapters. Chapter 4 is my answer to how humans acquire knowledge. I define nine different knowledge-construction methods and derive eighteen first principles of learning. I illustrate how to develop lessons using the nine knowledge-construction methods and the principles of learning applicable to the different methods. Chapter 5 demonstrates the application of the principles of learning and the theory of knowledge to lesson design, lesson improvement, and curriculum design.

Two principles that guided my efforts were the philosophic concepts of coherence and correspondence. The results I obtained from the different disciplines had to **cohere** with one another; they had to collectively consist of a body of knowledge or a set of beliefs that taken together indicate and point to a single unified theory of knowledge. In short, the final results had to be logically consistent and free of contradictions.

The results also had to **correspond** to, accurately relate, and describe research results and the experience of practitioners in the real world.

This book is designed to be a textbook for undergraduate and graduate school students pursuing degrees in the fields of education and educational leadership. It can also be a useful resource for corporate and institutional trainers. In fact, it can be of use and a benefit to anyone interested in knowledge and learning. Parents, policymakers, researchers, and anyone with a role in teaching and learning should benefit from the content presented.

I endeavored to make the articulations clear and comprehensible in order to make the book accessible to a wide audience. The arguments and presentations are not overly scholarly and erudite. An adage in publishing says that every equation in a book reduces the readership by one half. I have enough equations in this book to reduce the readership to zero. In my defense, I offer the following explanation: with a couple of exceptions, the level of the math is Algebra 1. The lessons and curricula demonstrated in the book are from the traditional content areas of language arts, social studies, mathematics, and science. There are also art history examples. With the exception of the section on bifurcation in nonlinear systems, which is crucial to understanding human perception, the book is written so that math-adverse individuals can skip the mathematical sections and examples without losing a conceptual understanding of the book's content and theory. All the chapters should be of interest to the general reader except chapter 5. This chapter is designed for those who have responsibility for creating lessons, auditing and improving lessons, and designing curriculum.

It is my earnest hope that this book will help the reader not only have a better understanding of the nature of knowledge and learning but also become more successful educators and educational leaders.

The Neuroscience of Memory

Cognitive Neuroscience of Memory

Cellular Memory Mechanisms

The human faculties of perception, logic, and reason and for affective responses to stimuli all rely on and utilize the human capacity for memory. Memories of past experiences constitute our knowledge of the world we live in. As such, any theory of knowledge must incorporate, correspond to, and cohere with the science of memory as rendered by cognitive neuroscience and cognitive psychology.

Every conscious human experience—every sight, sound, smell, and thought—is the activation of some set of cells called neurons in the brain. These neurons are said to "represent" those sights, sounds, smells, and thoughts. The idea of representation is illustrated by figure 1.1. By activating different lights on a message board, words are "represented" on the board.

Figure 1.1 Example of representation

In similar fashion, the state of objects and actions in the outside world is represented by the activation of *neurons* in the brain. The internal states of our body are represented by the activation of the neurons that are part of the feeling- and emotion-processing system.

There are over two billion neurons in the brain, many with over ten thousand connections to other neurons, yielding a complex nonlinear system with over one trillion connections.

Before embarking on a description of how neurons become activated, it is beneficial to review the physical forces involved in the activation. The first is electrical attraction and repulsion. All atoms have two types of charged particles: positively charged particles, called *protons*, in the nucleus of the atom and negatively charged particles, called *electrons*, outside of the nucleus. Opposite charges attract and like charges repel. In an atom, the charges are balanced and the electrons are attracted and held to the atom by the positively charged protons. This is illustrated in figure 1.2.

Figure 1.2a Structure of an atom

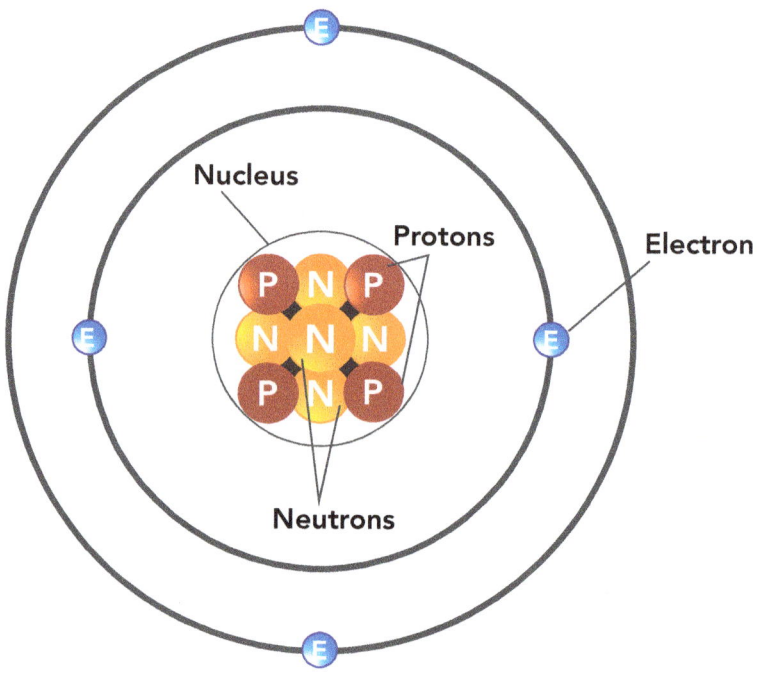

A sodium atom, for example, is initially balanced with respect to charges and has one electron in its outer shell. A chlorine atom is balanced and has seven electrons in its outer shell. When sodium atoms and chlorine atoms come into contact, they combine to form salt, the molecule NaCl. The single electron from the outer shell of the sodium atom moves over to complete the outer shell of the chlorine atom (eight electrons), and the molecule is held together by the electrical attraction between the now net negatively charged chlorine atom and the now net positively charged sodium atom. This is called an *ionic bond*. When the salt (NaCl) is dissolved in a solvent like water, these atoms retain their net-charged nature: +1 for sodium and –1 for chlorine. These net-charged, or electrically imbalanced, atoms are called *ions*.

Another force involved in neuron activation is the force associated with diffusion. Diffusion is the movement of something, like atoms or molecules, from a region of higher concentration to a region of lower concentration until a state of dynamic equilibrium is reached. The driving force is chemical potential energy, or what is called Gibbs free energy. This process is illustrated in figure 1.3.

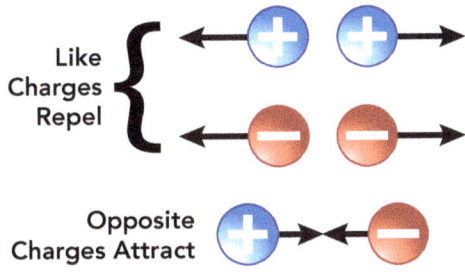

Figure 1.2b Interaction of charges

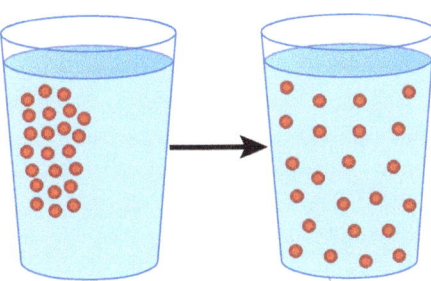

Figure 1.3a Diffusion

Figure 1.3b Diffusion of ink in water

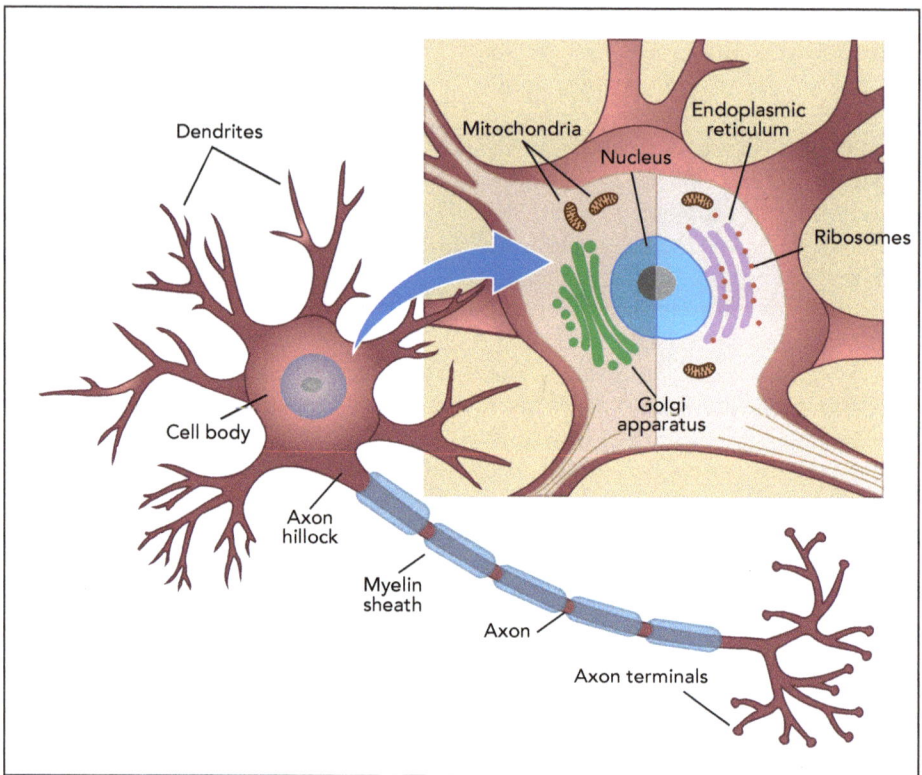

Figure 1.4 Parts of a neuron

A neuron has all of the organelles or parts that other living cells have. For example, it has a nucleus with DNA that can produce RNA, which is read by an organelle called a *ribosome* that produces protein molecules that the cell requires, after reading the RNA. A neuron, however, is specialized for electrical activation and receiving and sending information. Information is received in extensions called *dendrites* and sent from extensions called *axons*. An illustration of a neuron is shown in figure 1.4.

Every neuron is activated (turned on) by another neuron, except those at the sensory interface, which are activated by physical properties of some external object or action. Those neurons that sense changes in internal body states also respond to physical properties.

The message that a neuron receives from another neuron at its dendrites is to turn on (activate) or to not turn on. This message is communicated by an organic molecule called a neurotransmitter. Neurotransmitters released by the axons of an activated neuron travel across the gap (synapse) between the sending axon and the dendrite of the receiving neuron and lodge in the receptors of ion channels in the dendrite. When they lodge in the channel, they cause the channel to twist open and allow ions to enter the receiving neurons. It is the influx of ions that activates the receiving neuron.

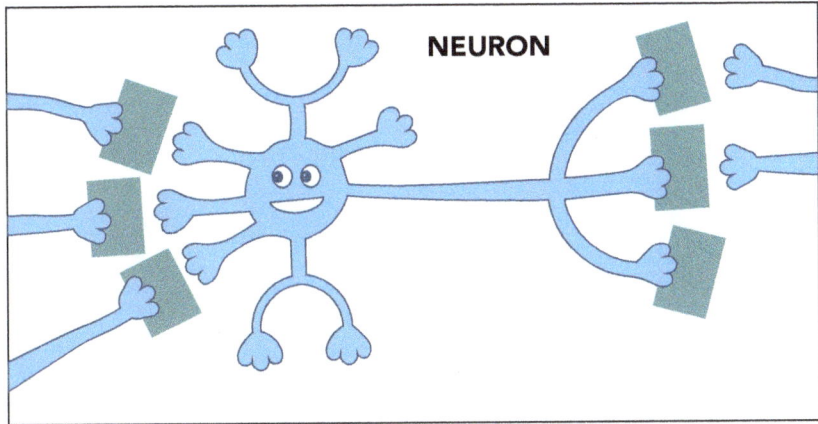

Figure 1.5 Communication between neurons

The size of the channels determines what kind of ions can pass through; for example, sodium ions versus chlorine ions. Some neurotransmitters act to open channels, like glutamate, which is the principal neurotransmitter involved in the memory system, and some act to inhibit or prevent activation, like GABA, which is the principal inhibitory neurotransmitter in the memory system.

A resting neuron that is not in the process of being activated has a potential energy across its initially closed membrane of around −65 millivolts. Its interior is more negatively charged than its exterior. This potential is produced by sodium-potassium pumps in the membrane of the neuron that intake potassium ions and pump out sodium ions, creating a high concentration of sodium outside the cell and a net negative charge inside the cell. As shown in figure 1.6, the chemical ATP powers the process.

When a neurotransmitter like glutamate twists the ion channel open, the combined force of diffusion and electrical attraction causes sodium to enter the neuron, which depolarizes the cell, activating it and changing the voltage (potential energy) across its membrane. The change in voltage is called an *action potential*. When the concentration of positive ions becomes sufficient, a current (movement) of positive ions will flow down the axon of the neuron and activate the release of neurotransmitters from the axon of the neuron to the dendrites of another connected neuron. It is in this manner that activations are passed from neuron to neuron. Figure 1.7 shows the activation process schematically.

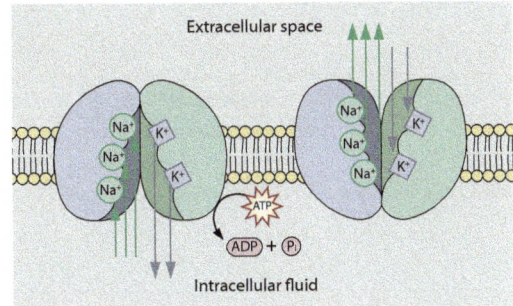

Figure 1.6 Ion transport across the neuronal membrane

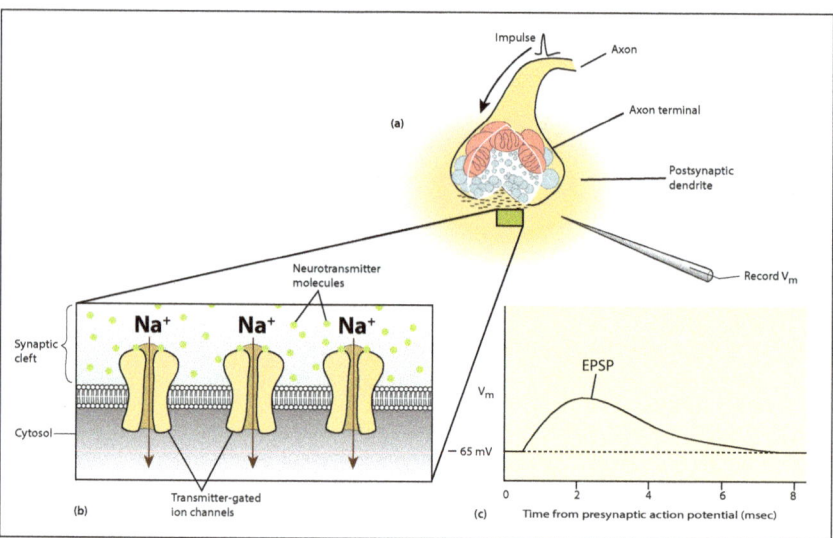

Figure 1.7 Neuron activation

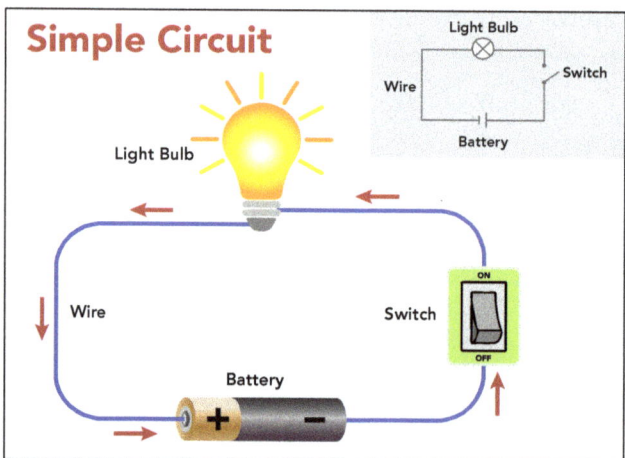

Figure 1.8 Simple circuit analogy

The neuron activation process can be illustrated using a simple analogy of a circuit. You can see this in figure 1.8.

We can think of the lightbulb as a neuron that can be switched on and off (activated/deactivated). The battery is analogous to the voltage and positive-charge differential that exists across the membrane of the neuron. The switch is analogous to a neurotransmitter. In the simple circuit, the lightbulb turns on when the switch is closed and a current begins to flow in the circuit. Analogously, when the neurotransmitter causes an ion channel to open, sodium ions move into the neuron because of the charge and concentration difference. The neuron is activated, and a current of ions begins to flow to the axon of the neuron. When the current reaches the end of the axon, it will cause the release of neurotransmitters that will activate neurons whose dendrites are connected to the axon.

Neurons can record memories. They form a memory of which neurons have activated them in the past. Neurons with the capacity to form memories have additional ion channels called *NMDA receptors*. The previously discussed ion channels that open and allow sodium ions to pass through when the neurotransmitter glutamate attaches are called *AMPA receptors*.

Glutamate binds to both types of receptors; however, the NMDA receptors have a magnesium ion (Mg2+) lodged in their channels that blocks the flow of ions into the neuron. The size of the channel in an NMDA receptor is such that it allows calcium ions to flow into the neuron when the magnesium ion is removed. For the NMDA receptor to open, there must be a sufficient inflow of sodium ions through the AMPA receptors to create enough positive charge inside the neuron (depolarization) to pop the magnesium ion out through the repelling force between positive ions. There is, therefore, a threshold level of neuron activation by sodium ions from AMPA receptors before the magnesium ion pops out and calcium ions begin to flow into the neuron. This process is schematically illustrated in figure 1.9.

The influx of calcium ions activates protein kinases in the neuron that catalyze (bring about) several reactions. They can bring about the addition of phosphate ions to strengthen and stabilize receptors that are active. They can also bring about the insertion of additional AMPA receptors into dendrites that are active, which increases the strength of connection between active connected neurons. This process is schematically illustrated in figure 1.10.

If calcium concentrations are high enough for long enough, protein kinases will activate a transcription factor (CREB) that interacts with the DNA in the nucleus to release RNA that will result in the production of stable and permanent changes in the strength of the connections at the active synapses. The released RNA can also result in

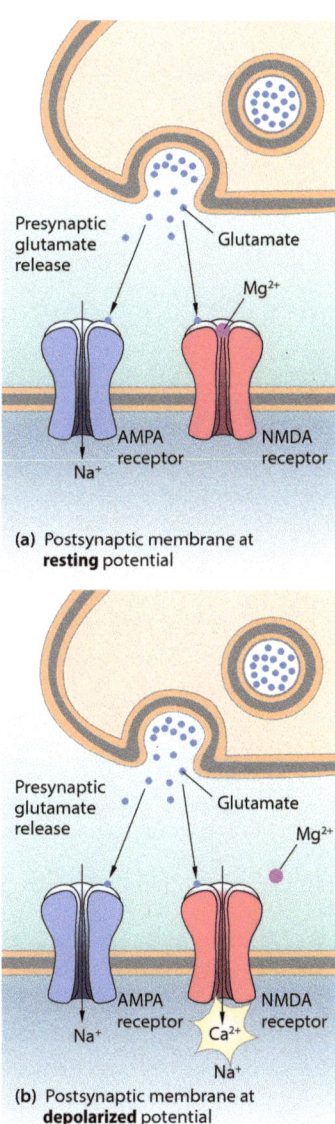

Figure 1.9 Opening of an NMDA receptor

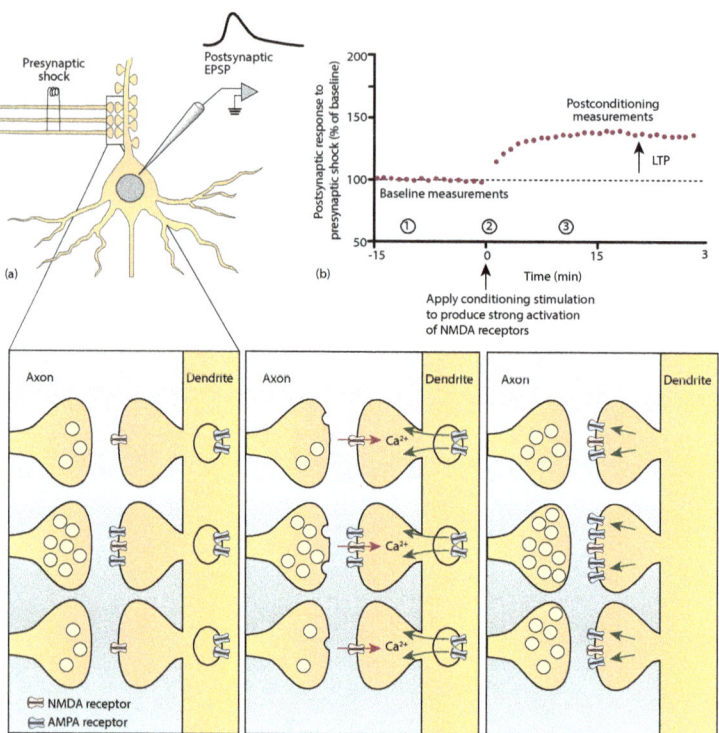

Figure 1.10 Calcium-catalyzed insertion of AMPA receptors

the production of additional dendrites to increase the strength of connection between neurons even further. The change brought about by the calcium ions is called *long-term potentiation*. It is important to note that the changes that increase the strength of connection occur only in those dendrites and AMPA receptors that are active when calcium ions enter the neuron. This consequence is expressed in the colloquial version of Hebb's rule: neurons that fire together wire together, those that fire out of sync lose their link. Through the processes described, neurons that activate together are strongly connected, while through another process, called *long-term depression*, neurons that do not activate together become disconnected.

Getting a neuron to a sufficient level of depolarization or sodium ion concentration to dislodge magnesium ions and facilitate the memory process can occur in several different ways. A particularly strong input from a connected neuron or a series of inputs in quick succession can bring it about. The most common way sufficient input can be achieved is the reception of input from the axons of several different neurons. These processes are illustrated in figure 1.11.

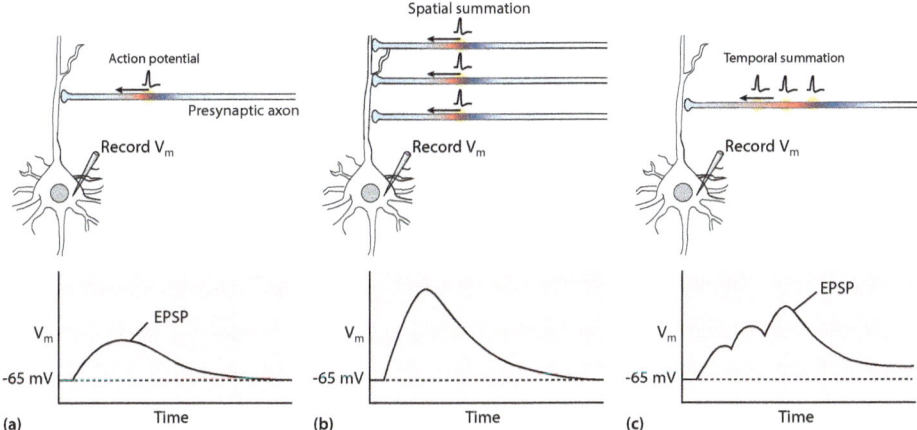

Figure 1.11 Different ways of achieving sufficient depolarization

Structure of Memory

In an excellent 2009 paper, neuroscientist Joaquin Fuster summarized his research and that of others regarding the structural configuration of the human memory system. Fuster described two large hierarchical memory components: a frontal cortex component that represents motor, procedural, and executive function memories and knowledge and a dispersed component that represents sensory stimuli, more complex multimodal perceptual memories in the association areas of the cerebral cortex, and even more complex semantic and conceptual memories in progressively higher levels of the posterior cortex. Fuster's findings can be summarized by four principles:

1. A memory or item of knowledge consists of a widespread neural network of connections, formed by experience, that joins distributed cell populations. **The memory code is a relational code.**

2. A complex memory, such as an autobiographical memory, is widely dispersed, linking neuron assemblies and smaller networks in noncontiguous areas of the cortex; the lower-level assemblies and networks represent the more concrete aspects of memory or knowledge.

3. Memory networks differ widely in content, complexity, source, temporal origin, and level of abstraction because of the combinatorial power of cortex neurons. Representations range from concrete sensations, or actions, to semantic or conceptual knowledge and complete plans of action.

4. Memory networks overlap and interlink through common nodes. A neuron or neural assembly can be part of many networks and, therefore, multiple memories or items of knowledge.

Fuster's model recognizes specialized regions, such as those for processing faces and words, but emphasizes the convergence of connections toward the top to more categorical and abstract representations. Integration takes place everywhere (particularly at the top) between widely dispersed elements with both hierarchical and heterarchical connections.

What Fuster describes is a productive, semantic feature–based, nonlinear system with hierarchical as well as heterarchical connections that are created through experience. In its initial formation, all memory is essentially associative. All memory is distributed and intermixed, enabling the characteristics of a productive system. A productive system is one where more complex entities are created by different combinations of simpler entities. Two familiar examples are language and LEGO bricks. In language, twenty-six letters can be flexibly combined to produce the approximately two hundred thousand words of a typical language. In turn, these words can be flexibly combined to create an unlimited number of ideas. In a LEGO set, a limited number of bricks can be flexibly combined to produce many different objects. Figure 1.12 is a schematic illustration of Fuster's model. As the model illustrates, a given neuron, or set of neurons lower in the connection hierarchy, can be part of different memories or items of knowledge as per principal four, described earlier.|

Strengthening of connections between neurons through the process described previously, between the representations of associated semantic features of objects and actions, in such a hierarchical system, results in higher-level neurons or neural assemblies being increasingly abstract, schematic, and categorical (Schwartz, Weaver, and Kaplan 1999). Neuron cell groups that have simultaneous firing patterns during experience will grow increasingly interconnected and begin to function as a unit (long-term potentiation). Conversely, neuron cells that have firing patterns at different times will become increasingly distinct and end up as members of different neural circuits. This is the process that Hebb (1949) referred to as *recruitment* and *fractionation*. The same process of recruitment and fractionation occurring higher in the hierarchy can develop neural representations that stand for classes of objects. With additional cortical depth we could expect neural representations not only for classes of objects but also for classes of classes, and so on (Schwartz, Weaver, and Kaplan 1999).

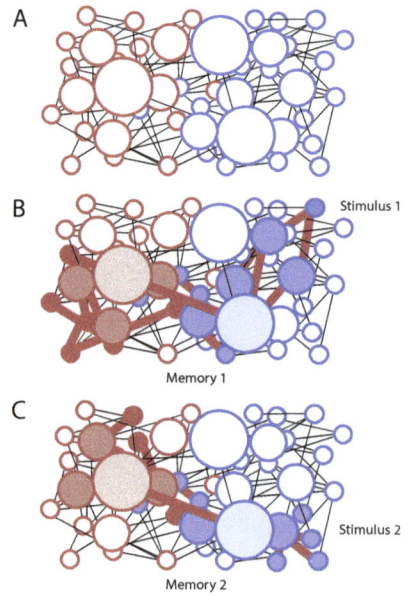

Figure 1.12 Model of the hierarchical and productive structure of memory circuits

To express the preceding in simpler terms, let's say a person is experiencing an object like a tree. Different sets of neurons will represent various elements of the semantic features of the tree (semantic features being those physical properties detected by the senses). Various neurons or assemblies of neurons might represent the shape and size characteristics of tree parts, like the trunk, the branches, and the leaves. Other neurons and neuron assemblies might represent features like texture and weight, if tree parts were touched. Since all these neuron and neuron assemblies are activating at the same time, the connection between the neurons representing the various semantic features of the tree will grow stronger. Each time a tree is experienced, the same sets of neurons are activated simultaneously, so in time the connections will continue to increase in strength, and one will have "knowledge" of trees in memory. That knowledge is the collection of semantic features that were similar across the different events in which trees were experienced, or in neuron terms, those collections of neurons that were activated simultaneously during each experience. As stated earlier, since the different tree experiences are using the same neural assemblies to represent semantic features that are similar across the events, the neural assemblies are in effect abstracting those features across the different events. The connective structure, as described by Fuster, coupled with the cellular mechanisms for memory creation implements the faculty of abstraction and the process of inductive generalization. As Schwartz, Weaver, and Kaplan (2009) state, it creates neural representations that stand for classes of objects/actions and even classes of classes.

Influence of Other Cortical Regions on Memory Creation

The creation of autobiographical (episodic) memories involves the medial temporal lobe structures of the hippocampus, entorhinal cortex, perirhinal cortex, and parahippocampal cortex. Sensory information that has been processed into the final form we experience in sensory images is represented in the association area of each sensory modality. In creating a memory of episodic experience, activations from each sensory association area enter the perirhinal cortex. These activations provide information about "what" an item of experience is, In other words, information about the attributes and characteristics of the item. Information from the polymodal sensory association area, which contains converged information from different sensory processing areas, and from the parietal lobe spatial-processing areas, which contain information about "where" an item is located and what it is associated with, enters the posterior parahippocampal cortex. These streams of information enter but remain segregated in the entorhinal cortex and then converge in the hippocampus (Gazzaniga, Ivry, and Mangun 2009). This convergence facilitates relationship, combination, and conjunction of perceptual input (Squire 1992). This is schematically illustrated in figure 1.13.

Functional MRI studies of source memory (remember the item and context in which it was experienced or learned) versus recognition memory (item seems familiar) show that correct recollection and attribution of source activates the hippocampus and the posterior parahippocampal cortex. If an item was simply familiar (recognition memory)

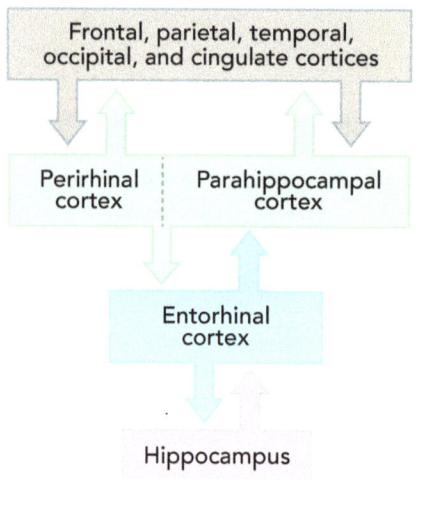

Figure 1.13
Medial temporal lobe connections

to a subject, activation is limited to proximal areas outside the hippocampus—the entorhinal cortex and perirhinal cortices. Strength of activation correlates with the level of the subject's familiarity with the item (Montaldi et al. 2006).

Diana, Yonelinas, and Ranganath (2010) have proposed a model that binds item and context for the operation of the medial temporal lobe memory structures. In this model, the perirhinal cortex represents item information, and the parahippocampal cortex represents context information, or things peripheral to the principal target of encoding. The hippocampus itself binds item and context information. According to the model, familiarity and recollection are not the dominant paradigm or organizing principle; it is the type of information characterizing a retrieval cue. Familiarity is associated with the retrieval of item representations supported by the perirhinal cortex. Retrieval of context details is supported by the parahippocampal cortex, and recollection is associated with the retrieval of item-context binding supported by the hippocampus. Functional MRI on healthy subjects revealed perirhinal cortex activation associated with successful retrieval of item details and parahippocampal cortex/hippocampus activation associated with successful recollection of source (Diana, Yonelinas, and Ranganath 2010).

The structures of the medial temporal lobe are not the repository of long-term memory. The medial temporal lobe structures reactivate the original cortex areas that provided input during encoding. This is accomplished through feedback projections from medial temporal lobe structures to the areas that provided the input. During retrieval of visual information, such as pictures, the regions of the neocortex that were activated during perception of the pictures become reactivated. Similarly, during retrieval of sounds, the areas activated during perception are reactivated (Wheeler, Peterson, and Buckner 2000). The areas reactivated are not the lower-level sensory regions but the highly processed association areas where inputs are processed to the point of identity. The continuing reactivation process, as it proceeds through time, is described as interleaving. When memory items are repeatedly re-instantiated by the medial temporal lobe, they potentiate through the Hebbian process in the reactivated areas of the neocortex and often become independent of the medial temporal lobe structures. The effects of this process are seen in patients who have experienced damage to the medial temporal lobe structures.

Typically, retrograde amnesia does not extend beyond two years, and all declarative memories more than two years old remain intact. Obviously, the ability to form new memories is greatly impaired. Older memories, hence, result from the accumulation of synaptic changes in the cortex resulting from multiple reinstatements of memories. Eventually, the cortical representations achieve a state of self-sufficiency and become independent. The interleaving or slow rate of change of the cortex prevents interference between old memories and new information. New information does not immediately override and interfere with an existing knowledge base but is instead gradually added to it (LeDoux 2002). Conversely, newly formed memories are quite fluid and susceptible to change. This has extensive and obvious implications for classroom instruction. For example, for effective learning, new information should be experienced numerous times and preferably in multiple contexts. New information does not immediately override existing information structures and previously formed paradigms. In addition, new learning is flexible, potentially unstable, and susceptible to change with the receipt of new information.

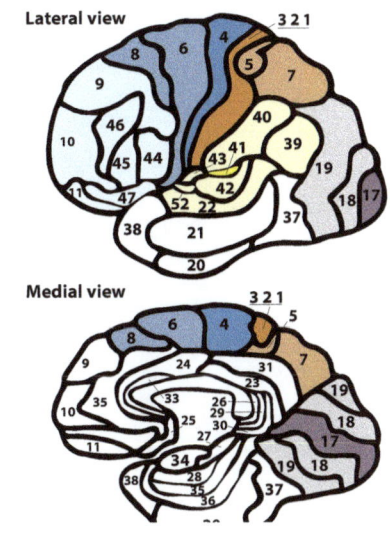

Figure 1.14
Brodmann region designations

In several sections of this book, I will be referring to different areas of the brain that carry out different functions. Figure 1.14 is a depiction by Korbinian Brodmann, created in 1909, of the brain subdivided into regions. Brodmann's subdivisions were based on changes in the structure of the cells from region to region. The Brodmann region designations are commonly used in neuroscience literature to refer to different brain areas.

Descriptions can also refer to the following subdivisions and have location designations such as the following:

1. Dorsal – upper

2. Ventral – lower

3. Anterior – front

4. Posterior – back

5. Superior – top

6. Inferior – bottom

7. Medial – middle

8. Lateral – farther from the middle

9. Prefrontal – anterior portion of frontal

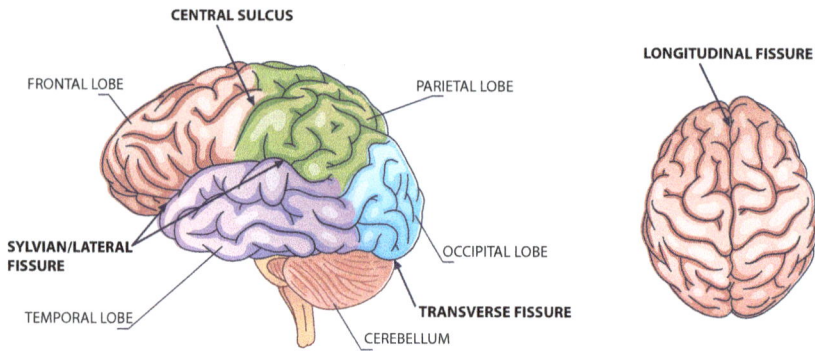

Figure 1.15 Alternative brain-location designations

A description like dorsolateral frontal cortex would refer to the upper area (dorso) away from the midline longitudinal fissure (lateral) portion of the frontal lobe (see figure 1.15).

The brain's memory system behaves like a connected system. In addition to the sensory-processing association areas and the medial temporal lobe structures previously discussed, the system includes extensive connections to the frontal and prefrontal cortex, structures of the diencephalon, and other subcortical structures, such as the amygdala. A disruption in any part of the circuit will disrupt the formation and consolidation of long-term memories. The frontal lobes are importantly involved in the temporal organization of memory (Gazzaniga, Ivry, and Mangun 2009). Individuals with frontal lobe lesions are impaired in their ability to organize and segregate events in memory—an ability termed *recency memory* (Milner 1995). Such an individual might remember the ingredients involved in preparing dishes for a meal but be unable to organize their actions into a proper temporal (time) sequence. The specific area implicated appears to be the dorsolateral prefrontal cortex (Brodmann area 46). Interestingly, this same area is also indicated to support working memory. A laterality effect is in evidence contingent upon the type of stimulus used to evoke a response. With word stimuli, the deficit is associated with left hemisphere lesions to the dorsolateral prefrontal cortex, and with visual stimuli, such as drawings, the deficit is associated with lesions to the right dorsolateral prefrontal cortex (Gazzaniga, Ivry, and Mangun 2009).

An additional functionality supported by the prefrontal cortex is the consolidation of source memory (context: time, place, and various associated items in an episode). In comparison tests with healthy patients, those with prefrontal cortex lesions exhibit differentiated performance between recall and source memory tasks: lesioned patients perform as well as unlesioned subjects on recall tasks but perform poorly on source memory tasks (Jankowsky, Shimamura, and Squire 1989). Even in healthy patients, a double dissociation is in evidence between item memory and source memory (Glisky, Polster, and Routhuieaux 1995). High temporal lobe function is associated with good performance on item memory tests, while higher frontal lobe functionality is correlated with better performance on source memory tests. The level of functionality was determined by separate neuropsychological testing.

When memory encoding and consolidation activities involve semantic processing or thinking about the meaning of the information to be coded, the inferior frontal gyrus (ventrolateral prefrontal cortex, Brodmann areas 45/47) is activated. When stimulus material is verbal or symbolic, the left inferior frontal gyrus is active. When stimulus material is visual, activation is bilateral (Wagner et al. 1998). If an encoding task requires organizing information within working memory, the middle frontal gyrus (dorsolateral prefrontal cortex, Brodmann area 46) becomes activated (Ranganath and Blumenfeld 2005). In summary, when memory-encoding and consolidation tasks require active constructions such as temporal ordering, assembly of contexts, semantic processing, or organization and manipulation in working memory, the required functionalities of different areas of the frontal cortex are enlisted. If we consider that the executive function areas of the frontal and prefrontal cortex also support the manipulation of input from both perceptual areas and long-term memory in the active, conscious construction of rules and their subsequent translation into programs of action, the results described earlier are not surprising. Support of these activities would suggest the likelihood that they play a role in the encoding, consolidation, and retrieval of long-term memory when these executive functionalities are required for memory construction and consolidation.

The foregoing presented a lot of cognitive neuroscience in a relatively short presentation. It is not imperative that the reader master this content to comprehend what follows. It was presented to provide a thorough explanation and justification for some of the hypotheses to follow. For those whose principal interest is imparting knowledge through teaching, the following are the main ideas that are important to remember regarding the cognitive neuroscience of memory.

At the neuron-to-neuron connection level, the strength of a memory is contingent upon the following principles:

1. Strength of neuron activation

2. Frequency of neuron activation

3. Number of connections neurons have to other neurons

At this juncture, we can already draw some implications that these principles have for teaching. Principle number 2 implies that the more times a person experiences something, the more likely they are to remember it and the more likely it will become an item of knowledge. During the era when behaviorism dominated the field of psychology, researchers often employed what they called a *learning curve*. The learning curve was a plot of the strength of a memory versus the number of exposures someone had to the item. Reflecting principle 2, several exposures were required, the number being contingent upon the person and the item to be remembered, before a memory was consolidated and the item remembered for some specified duration.

Principle 2 can also be characterized as the "use it or lose it" principle. From a teaching perspective, principle 2 suggests that the concepts, principles, and procedures that are foundational and vital to subsequent learning should be covered more extensively, revisited frequently, and used often by students. They must "use it or they will lose it." This idea becomes an important consideration in planning and designing curricula. What are the big ideas, answers to essential questions, and enduring understandings that require emphasis? These will be the items the educator needs to spend the most time on, give the students the most experience with, and revisit with the greatest frequency.

The operations of the medial temporal lobe structures also demonstrate the importance of the preceding practices. As described, the hippocampus does not contain memories. What it contains is, in effect, reinstatement codes that allow the hippocampus to re-create the original experience in the brain areas that processed the original experience. As discussed, if the hippocampus reactivates these memories multiple times, the memories will consolidate in the cortex and become long-term memories independent of the hippocampus. In addition, new experience does not immediately override past experience; it is interleaved and gradually added to it. In this way prior knowledge is foundational, and new information is added to or built on this foundation of prior understandings.

Principle 3 states that memory strength increases with the number of connections a neuron has to other neurons. This also has direct teaching implications. It implies that the more connections and relationships a teacher helps students make between the items of content, the more likely the items will become long-term memories and an item of knowledge. Experiencing items in multiple contexts and in forms that engage multiple sensory modalities will increase retention and learning. Both approaches significantly increase the number of connections item representations will have in the cerebral cortex. Principle 3 is why adding pictures, graphs, videos, models, and other learning representations to lecture presentations increases retention. Increasing connections between the items of learning also increases the number of potential perceptual cues that can trigger the recall of memories.

Principle 1, the strength of activation, can be effected through the affective aspects of teaching and learning. As discussed, neurons are separated by a gap called a synapse and require a neurotransmitter for connection. The human memory system operates primarily using glutamate and GABA neurotransmitters. However, memory neuron dendrites have receptor sites for what are called *modulatory neurotransmitters*, like the neurotransmitters associated with the feelings and emotions system. These neurotransmitters are released in the fluid surrounding memory neurons in response to certain feeling and emotion conditions and can play a role in activating neurons and impacting the strength of neuron activation. At the behavioral level, this means that students who are excited and enthusiastic about a learning experience will have the benefit of modulatory neurotransmitters that can enhance neuron activation and hence memory formation.

The involvement and actions of prefrontal and frontal cortex processing areas in creating memories suggests a fourth memory principle. These areas are activated when memory formation involves active constructions like ordering items in time, connecting items to contexts, and creating semantically coherent relationships between items (thinking about them). All these activities involve working memory, which is a temporary storage area that the brain uses to facilitate processing in the prefrontal and frontal cortex. Working memory also connects the prefrontal/frontal cortex to long-term memory areas and procedural memory.

Information is temporarily held in working memory by reciprocal activation between the connected areas. For example, working memory will activate an item in long-term memory. Long-term memory will, through feedback connections, in turn activate working memory. These activations go back and forth, keeping the information active in working memory so that it can be processed by the prefrontal and frontal cortex. This action also increases the activation times of memory neurons and increases the likelihood that potentiation will occur and long-term memories will be formed. Principle 4 is expressed as follows: activation of a mutually reinforcing network that achieves equilibrium (coherence between representations) will enhance memory formation.

As nonlinearly connected elements with feedback loops, the prefrontal/frontal, working memory, and long-term memory systems are equilibrium-seeking systems that will attempt to create coherence among the items represented. This will be more thoroughly discussed in the next chapter.

Principle 4 strongly implies that learning and memory are enhanced when students are consciously engaged in finding patterns of relationship and connection among the semantic features of the items presented in a learning experience. Becoming involved in creating meaning and understanding by finding the pattern of organization and order within content will greatly enhance memory formation and retention.

Cognitive Psychology of Memory

Given this discussion of the biology of memory and knowledge accumulation, we should expect to find that the four principles manifest in behavioral studies of memory from cognitive psychology. And indeed, we do.

Cognitive psychologists have tested which is more likely to result in a long-term memory: trying to memorize through repeated exposure or focusing on how items are related to one another and to other things. The research results show that creating relationships is more likely to produce durable long-term memories (Reisberg 2010). We remember best what we think about. This result is an exemplification of principle 4. It also implies that principle 4 is more powerful in creating memories than principle 2 is. In biological terms, Wagner, Koustal, and Schachter (1998) state that the greater the activation of the left prefrontal cortex and left hippocampus during verbal learning, the greater the retention.

Cognitive psychologist Daniel Reisberg (2010, 160–61) states that "we remember best what we organize best" and "plainly, the better your understanding, the better (and longer lasting) your memory will be." He cites research results that justify these conclusions. Discovering the order within content or imposing an order will enhance learning and memory. Understanding means creating semantically coherent relationships among the items of content. This requires involvement of the prefrontal/frontal cortex regions and working memory, which, as discussed, increases the likelihood that a memory will be formed.

Reisberg also discusses the related idea of the impact of context on memory. For example, he cites research by Bransford and Johnson (1972) where a passage was given to research participants that described a process in a completely abstract fashion; the description given could have been applicable to several different processes. Some of the participants received the passage with a title, "Doing the Laundry," while others received the passage without a title. Participants who received the titled passage easily understood the passage and were able to remember it after a delay. Those who received an untitled passage were not able to understand the passage and did poorly on a memory test.

This experiment demonstrates several different effects on memory. It demonstrates the impact of understanding on memory formation and retention and the impact of organizing content within a context. Reisberg states that it also demonstrates the importance of tying new material to a framework of prior knowledge. Because the participants had prior knowledge of doing laundry, the abstract descriptions and the passage made sense and were understood.

To this I would add that it also demonstrates the difficulty in learning and creating memories (knowledge) of content that are purely abstract and devoid of specific concrete referents. Studies have been conducted that compare completely abstract courses on critical thinking with courses where critical thinking was taught within the context of a specific subject area. Teaching the subject in context was found to be more effective from both a retention and a subsequent application perspective. This illustrates the importance of connecting abstract ideas to concrete referents using examples, metaphors, and analogies familiar to students.

The context of "Doing the Laundry" supplied a summarizing or generalizing concept under which subordinate details, concepts, and other content could be organized and given structure. The key was the fact that students had prior knowledge of the context and its contents. A teaching strategy that is sometimes employed is to begin lecture presentations with advanced organizers that show the organizational structure of the content the teacher is going to present. If the elements of the organizer are abstract, they may not have a lot of meaning to the students until they see the details or specifics, and they themselves abstract the specific back to the general. It is typically easier for students to abstract from the specific to the general (induct) than it is for them to understand how the specific is part of the general (analyze).

Context also plays a role in a memory phenomenon that cognitive psychologists refer to as *encoding specificity*. This term refers to the fact that what is in memory is the stimulus as understood and the context in which the stimulus was experienced. Memories that are created when the hippocampus is engaged are not simply item memories;

they are item-plus-context memories that include peripheral items associated with the principal target of encoding. The context encoded also includes what one thinks and understands about a stimulus.

An example from an experiment by Barclay et al. (1974) is discussed by Reisberg (2010). In the experiment, participants were given different sentences like "The man lifted the piano" or "The man tuned the piano." The first sentence caused the participant to think of the piano as something heavy, while the second caused the participant to think of the piano as a musical instrument. After a delay, the individuals who were given the hint "something heavy" could easily recall the word "piano" if they experienced the sentence "The man lifted the piano," but the hint "something that produces a sound" was much less effective at eliciting the response "piano" for those same individuals. Conversely, the individuals who experienced the sentence "The man tuned the piano" easily recalled the word "piano" when the hint was "something that produces a sound." The hint "something heavy" was much less effective at eliciting the response "piano" from those individuals. Other researchers, such as Tulving (1983), have produced the same results with similar experiments.

These experiments illustrate the difficulty learners have in using or applying knowledge outside the context in which it was learned. Research (Woolfolk 2007) indicates that students have little ability to transfer knowledge between domains. The problem lies with the fact that there are no cues in the context and associated elements of the new context or domain that connect or relate to the item of knowledge. It is the effect shown in the experiment described above. As there is no connection in the brain between the items that constitute the context in which something is learned and the new context or domain, it is not viewed or understood as knowledge that would be applicable. Chapter 4 addresses this issue and proposes a process for making knowledge more transferable.

With time, there is a tendency toward abstraction in memory. As numerous related events are experienced, details begin to fade away. Details are abstracted, and the abstraction becomes the primary and strongest representation. For example, after experiencing thousands upon thousands of fire events, what remains in memory is what was common or similar across the different events. What was specific to each event is lost. This results because of the nature of the brain's architecture, as previously discussed. The architecture is productive and uses the same neurons and assemblies of neurons to represent those semantic features that are similar across events. In accordance with principle 2, these are the neurons and neuron assemblies that get activated frequently and, therefore, have the strongest connections and form the most enduring memories.

This process also leads to what psychologists refer to as the formation of schemas and scripts in memory that represent the pattern of what is typical and normal in a situation. "Normal and typical" are the abstracted elements that were similar across multiple instantiations of the situation in the past. The development of schemas and scripts can both help and hurt learning and understanding. They help learning and understanding by doing the following:

- Allowing a student to further understanding by matching a current circumstance to previously learned patterns of relationship
- Telling the student what is typical or normal in a situation
- Allowing students to make inferences and predictions
- Helping fill in the gaps and facilitate understanding with only partial input
- Aiding in recalling complex events

As will be explained in the next two chapters, humans attempt to create coherence between new experiences and things learned from past experiences. In the effort to provide a framework for understanding new information, people invoke their inventory of existing schemas. This can result in the following problems when encountering new information and circumstances that are incongruent with existing schemas:

- Omitting details that don't fit in existing schemas and, therefore, make little sense to individuals
- Changing unfamiliar things to familiar things
- Supplementing what is actually there to make things seem more logical
- Thinking that material is closer to their existing schema than it is

These findings are confirmed by numerous researchers. For example, Brewer and Treyens (1981) asked research subjects to wait in the researcher's office before an experiment began. The subjects were then taken into another room and asked what they saw in the researcher's office. The subjects responded with items that are normally and typically found in the office of a researcher. For example, one-third of the subjects reported seeing a bookshelf with books when, in fact, there was no bookshelf or books.

Another important finding from cognitive psychology is that depth of processing makes a difference in memory formation and retention (Hyde and Jenkins 1969; Parkin 1984). Attention to meaning (logical relationships) results in better recall than does attention to surface characteristics. Attention to meaning involves thinking about and creating relationships between the items of content. The ability to recall depends on the existence of a rich set of connections between the items to be remembered and connections to things already known. The greater the number of connections, the greater the number of paths leading to items in memory and the greater the likelihood that a given cue will activate the memory. Connections serve as retrieval paths. The results of these experiments are a reflection of principles 3 and 4. The greater the number of connections, the stronger the memory. And engaging in thought processes that involve creating meaning (logical connection / semantic coherence) and finding patterns of organization in content produce more enduring memories.

The same two principles are manifested in findings regarding the influence of the level of elaboration in a learning experience. Craik and Tulving (1975), for example, conducted a study in which participants were given a word and then a sentence with a blank space for a word left out of the sentence. They were then asked to decide whether the word given fits into the sentence as the missing word. Some of the sentences given were simple, while others were complex and much more elaborate. After a delay, participants were asked to list all the words they remembered. The participants had much better recall of the words that fit into the more elaborate and complex sentences. The participants had to think more about the elaborate sentences, and there were more connections that could be established between words in the sentences and items already in memory. The experiment demonstrated the impact of both principle 3 and principle 4.

A simple mnemonic can be used to help remember the four principles:

SORT

    S - Strengthen the memory by creating motivation and enthusiasm for what is to be learned.

    O - Return to important items to be learned and remembered often.

    R - Create many relationships between the items of content and between content items and things previously known. Experiencing content in multiple contexts and modalities (with different senses) helps.

    T - Involve students in thought about content that involves making logical connections and finding patterns of organization and structure.

Nonlinear Systems and the Nature of Perception

Nonlinear Systems Theory

Basic Nonlinear System Properties

Many of the human brain's unique capabilities, such as perception, language, logic, and reason, are a result of the fact that connectivity between neurons in the brain implements a complex nonlinear system. To understand how the brain creates these capabilities requires a qualitative understanding of the basics of nonlinear systems theory.

Robert M. May, theoretical physicist turned mathematical biologist who is most famous for demonstrating many of the characteristics of nonlinear systems using the logistic equation, was an apostle for the teaching of nonlinear systems theory to all students. In a 1976 paper in *Nature*, May contended that the world would be a better place if all students were given a calculator and asked to explore the behavior of the logistic difference equation (Gleick 1987). The logistic difference equation is a simple nonlinear difference equation that describes the growth of a population or species in an environment that has a limited carrying capacity. On the face of it, May provides a simple solution for making the world a better place. What May is concerned about is that a standard education creates the paradigm and framing context that things in the world proceed linearly. As May states, a knowledge of nonlinear behavior would "counter the distorted sense of the world's possibilities that comes from a standard scientific explanation" (Gleick 1987, 80). It would also create a better understanding of human relational systems, such as education, business, politics, markets, economics, and communications, and all other systems where the relationship between the elements is nonlinear.

Mathematics itself is linear, excepting specifically the mathematics of nonlinear systems, developed, for the most part, since the 1970s. May argued, "The mathematical intuition so developed ill-equipped the student to confront the bizarre behavior exhibited by the simplest of discrete nonlinear systems" (Gleick 1987, 80). The scientific world applauded May's mathematical and biological contributions but never followed his advice for making the world a better place. While I would concur with May's thesis, the difficulty lies with the fact that a first course in quantitative nonlinear systems theory requires background knowledge of advanced calculus, differential equations, and linear algebra. This significantly reduces the potential audience for this topic. Understanding nonlinear systems qualitatively, however, does not require this background.

Systems theory, in general, originated with the work of biologists in the 1920s. During this time, physiologist Walter Cannon articulated the principle of homeostasis for living organisms. Homeostasis is the self-regulating process by which biological systems maintain internal stability while adjusting to the circumstances of an external environment. An example would be the human body's internal responses and actions to maintain a constant internal temperature in the face of changing outside temperatures. The development of systems thinking as a major scientific movement is attributed to Ludwig von Bertalanffy. Bertalanffy was the first to articulate that systemic concepts and principles can be applied to many different fields of study. He states, "The parallelism of general conceptions or even special laws in different fields is a consequence of the fact that these are concerned with 'systems' and that certain general principles apply to systems irrespective of their nature" (Capra 1996, 49). This happy circumstance allows us to develop the qualitative concepts of nonlinear systems using nonlinear systems that everyone is familiar with, like human relational systems. The results we obtain are qualitatively applicable to all nonlinear systems. The billions of neurons in the human brain often have connections to as many as ten thousand other neurons. A significant percentage of these connections are reciprocal feedback connections that make the system nonlinear. There is no science or mathematics that describes a system as complex as the brain. However, much can be learned about the brain's general operation and nonlinear behavior by examining the behavior of simpler, more tractable nonlinear systems for which science and mathematics does exist. This approach is analogous to the approach taken in macroeconomics. While it is impossible to model the economic behavior of billions of people on the planet, the simplified models employed in macroeconomics reveal a lot about the qualitative behavior of economic systems.

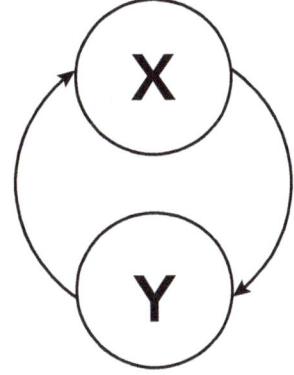

Figure 2.1
Simple two-element system

The first characteristic to understand about a nonlinear system is that the state of the elements is codependent. A change in any element brings about a change in all the other connected elements. If we were to express or model a nonlinear system mathematically, we cannot express it as a function. There are no independent elements or variables in a nonlinear system. To illustrate, let's consider a simple nonlinear system consisting of two elements, X and Y, shown in figure 2.1.

A change in the state of element X brings about a change in the state of element Y. Because of the feedback connection between X and Y, the change in Y brings about a subsequent change in X. The subsequent change in X then brings about another change in Y, and so forth. There is a constant back-and-forth, give-and-take, until the system reaches some state of equilibrium, and the back-and-forth exchanges cease. In simpler nonlinear systems, the following different forms of equilibrium can occur:

Stable equilibrium—Subsequent changes near this state bring the system back to the state of equilibrium.

Unstable equilibrium—Subsequent changes near this state take the system away from the state and toward another equilibrium state.

Periodic equilibrium—A repeating series of states that are stable. Here the dimension of time is used to achieve stability.

Mixed stability (saddle point)—There is only one small path or set of states near this state that is stable and brings the system back to this state. All others are unstable and move the system away from this state.

We can illustrate these different forms of equilibrium with examples. Suppose that the two elements X and Y are two people involved in a conversation. We will call the people Larry and Jane. Larry wishes to successfully communicate his thoughts to Jane. Larry expresses his thoughts verbally to Jane. If the words that Larry uses are simple and if Jane's interpretation of the words have the same reference and meaning as Larry's, then the process is linear and Jane can simply respond with "Yes, I understand." Real-world conversations are rarely that simple. More typically, Jane will respond back to Larry in a way that causes him to think that Jane has not completely understood, or even has misunderstood, what he was trying to say. In response to Jane's feedback and reaction to his statements, Larry could respond with additional statements that add to, elaborate, or further justify his original statements. He might also alter or change them if Jane objected to his original statements. Larry transmits his response to Jane, who, in return, responds back to Larry. This back-and-forth, give-and-take continues until some form of equilibrium is reached. The equilibrium could be **stable**, where both parties are "on the same page" and statements from each mutually reinforce the same meaning or understanding. The equilibrium could also be **unstable**, wherein both parties agree to disagree or Jane ends the discourse by telling Larry that she has no idea what he is talking about.

Nonlinear systems can also exhibit **periodic stability**. In our example, this might occur as follows. Let's say that Larry and Jane are husband and wife, and the discussion is about where to go for vacation. In these types of conversations, Larry always insists on going to the mountains and Jane always insists on going to the beach. They resolve the impasse by going to the beach one year and going to the mountains on alternate years. In this form of stability, equilibrium is reached by using the dimension of time to balance the system.

One additional form of equilibrium is **mixed stability**. Mathematicians call this type of stability a saddle point. An analogy is made to a saddle. A marble placed on the saddle has only one stable location and only one narrow path to that location: along the centerline of the U shape of the saddle. All other locations are unstable, and the marble will roll off the saddle. In our example, this stability would be a very narrow path of discourse that leads to concurrence or understanding. All other positions or statements lead to an instability. For example, let us say that Larry and Jane disagree on every subject except their favorite restaurant. All other conversations lead to disagreement and instability.

This simple example demonstrates several important attributes and characteristics of nonlinear systems. Because of the codependent nature of the relationship between system elements, nonlinear systems have the following attributes and characteristics:

- Nonlinear systems are dynamic and change in time.
- Nonlinear systems are equilibrium seeking.
- The elements in a nonlinear system either are at an equilibrium point or are transitioning toward some form of equilibrium.

These attributes and characteristics are seminal to understanding the operation of human systems such as memory, perception, and human logic and reason. I am going to postulate that given the nonlinear connection configuration of the brain's neurons, a major process that enables these functionalities is the drive to achieve equilibrium among the brain's neuronal representations.

After studying numerous nonlinear systems, I postulate that there are five fundamental impacts that determine the states of a nonlinear system. System states are determined by the collective influence and ultimate equilibration of the following impacts:

1. Attributes and characteristics of the elements of the system
2. Terms of relationship between system elements
3. Driving forces on the system
4. Environment in which the system exists
5. History of the system

To understand system behavior, all five of these impacts must be considered simultaneously. These are the qualitative impacts that determine the behavior of a nonlinear system. If the system is modeled mathematically (quantitatively), these impacts translate into the following impacts:

1. Attributes/characteristics — range of possible values of system variables
2. Relationship — mathematical operators (+, −, x, ÷, differential, integral, etc.)
3. Driving force — coefficients, parameters, active equation terms
4. Environment — boundary conditions
5. History — initial conditions

These system impacts can be illustrated by continuing with the Larry and Jane communications example. Let's say that Larry is thirty years old, and Jane is five. Larry's conceptual inventory and vocabulary, which are part of his attributes and characteristics, are considerably larger than Jane's. For Larry to successfully communicate with Jane, and for them to reach equilibrium with respect to understanding, Larry must stay within the conceptual content of Jane's words and relate those words in ways that are familiar to Jane.

What Larry says and how he says it will be different contingent upon the relationship that Larry has with Jane. Whether Jane is the governor, his boss, his wife, a coworker, his friend, or his daughter (different terms of relationship) will impact the nature of what and how Larry communicates.

For human relational systems, the driving forces are often feelings and emotions. Let's say that Larry is a car salesman who needs to make one more sale to meet his monthly quota, and Jane is his customer. Larry is highly motivated, and his communication will be emotionally charged. Larry might use exaggeration and hyperbole to convince Jane that she cannot leave without the car and needs to buy it today.

The nature of the environment will also have an impact on the nature of communication between Larry and Jane. If Larry and Jane are alone and having a private conversation, it is more likely that the discourse will be direct and unequivocal than if the discussion was held in a staff meeting with Larry and Jane's supervisor and coworkers present. In this environment, they may be reluctant to express exactly how they feel.

The history of communication between Larry and Jane also has an impact. Have their prior discussions been meaningful and productive or have they been argumentative and inconclusive? This will impact how the statements of each party are received, interpreted, and understood. In summary, the nature of communication between Larry and Jane and the type of equilibrium that is reached will be impacted by all five of these factors.

Similarly, if we were to ask whether a teacher will be successful with a lesson, we need to consider all five impacts in this highly nonlinear process. The attributes of the teacher that are impactful are the teacher's command of the topic, her ability to construct an effective lesson, and her knowledge of effective instructional-delivery methods. The attributes of the students that are important are their prior knowledge and skill and their intellectual capabilities, given the nature of the lesson. Terms of relationship include whether the students are engaged and successfully undertaking the knowledge-construction process that the lesson calls for. Is the teacher successfully relating and communicating to the students? Driving forces would include the motivation and interest level of both teacher and students. Are the students interested and motivated to learn? Is the teacher caring and supportive or indifferent and just going through the motions? The environment in which this process is occurring is also highly impactful. Do the students come from a problematic environment such that they arrive at school with emotional issues and health issues and are inadequately nourished? Needless to say, such conditions will affect how they interact with the teacher and the instructional process. The history of the educational and social experiences of the students and teacher will also have a bearing. All five of these impacts will influence whether the lesson is successful in achieving the goals that the teacher has for the lesson.

This example provides some insight into the difficulty of providing every child with successful learning experiences. It also explains the difficulty of achieving success with the current reform efforts utilized in public education. The main education reform that has been implemented in the United States is the development of state educational standards and accountability tests. Educational leaders and teachers are held accountable for the performance of their students on these tests. In the state of Texas, contingent upon these test results, schools are given grades ranging from A to F. Those schools with a poor grade face potential punitive actions from the state. Educational policy, in general, reflects Robert May's concern regarding linear thinking. Teacher- and administrator-quality policies, for example, address only the attributes and characteristics of teachers and administrators. It does not address the attributes and characteristics of students; terms of relationship between teachers and students and between the students and the learning experiences; motivations and other driving forces; the environment that the students must contend with and its associated impacts; and the students' instructional and social histories. Successful education reform would have to address both academic and social issues. There are no silver bullets in education reform. It is not a linear process.

Bifurcations in Nonlinear Systems

An attribute that is unique to nonlinear systems is the ability to adapt to changes in one of the five impacts discussed previously. This adaptation takes the form of changes in stability. States that were formally stable can become unstable and new stabilities emerge. The technical term for adaptations that result in changes in the stability of different states is bifurcation. Bifurcation can be qualitatively illustrated with the following example. Suppose Larry and Jane are a married couple and that living together in their home is a stable state for both of them. Suppose also that Larry has an elderly mother who can no longer live independently. Larry cannot afford to place his mother in an extended-care facility, so he must move his mother into the house that he shares with Jane. His mother and Jane despise each other. His mother did not want Larry to marry Jane and has been rude and critical toward her for the entire duration of their marriage. When Larry moves his mother into the house, what was a stable state for Larry and Jane becomes unstable. Jane leaves and moves in with her parents. This represents a stable state for Jane. The system is still intact because they remain married; however, the system has experienced a bifurcation. The state of being at the house is stable for Larry and his mother, while the state of being at her parents' house is stable for Jane. They remain separated, and Jane comes to the house only for special occasions or if there is a dire need. The interaction with Larry's mother when she is there creates instability, and Jane soon returns to the stable state that exists in her parents' house.

With apologies to the nonmathematically minded, I must use some mathematics to facilitate an understanding of human perception. Let's consider the simple one-dimensional nonlinear equation:

$\dot{x} = kx - x^3$ (equation 1)

This equation states that the rate of change of the state of some element x with time, $\dot{x}$, is equal to some constant k multiplied by the current state of x, minus the cube of the current state of x. If the x-cubed term was not present, the equation would be linear and the trajectory of the system would be either exponential growth or decay. The rate of growth/decay would depend on the value of k. For example, a large negative k would be rapid decay, while a large positive k would be rapid growth.

To find equilibrium states for this nonlinear equation, we set $\dot{x}$ equal to 0, which is the state of no change with time, and solve for x algebraically as shown here:

$kx - x^3 = 0$ (equation 2)

$x(k - x^2) = 0$ (equation 3)

$x = 0$ and $(k - x^2) = 0$ satisfy the equation or

$x = 0$ and $x^2 = k; x = \pm\sqrt{k}$

We can see that there are equilibrium states at $x = 0$, $x = \sqrt{k}$, and $x = -\sqrt{k}$. If we are modeling a real physical system and k is negative, then the equilibrium points at $\pm\sqrt{k}$ do not physically exist because we would be taking the square root of a negative number, which is an imaginary number. So, for $-k$ and $k = 0$, there is only one equilibrium state at $x = 0$. If k is positive, the equilibrium states are $x = \pm\sqrt{k}$. X cannot be both 0 and $\pm\sqrt{k}$, so the equilibrium state at $x = 0$ must disappear. For $+k$, the state of the system at $x = 0$ is an unstable equilibrium state. The system, therefore, undergoes a bifurcation as k moves from positive to negative. If k is the rate of growth per unit time, we can consider it as a driving force for change. As can be seen, the increase in driving force was the impact factor that made the state $x = 0$ change from stable to unstable and led to the bifurcation (adaptation) in the nonlinear system described by equation 1.

To increase understanding, we can give equation 1 a physical interpretation. Let's say that equation 1 mathematically models, in very simplified fashion, the rate of change in the budworm population of a forest. If the forest is dying, the unit growth rate of the budworms (k) will become negative because of a declining food supply, and the population of budworms will eventually go to zero ($x = 0$). If the forest is healthy and growing, the unit growth rate (k) will be positive, and the budworm population will increase exponentially. As the population grows, birds flying above the trees will start to notice them and begin to feast on them. The impact of the birds on the population is modeled with the minus x^3 term. The equilibrium state, for a positive unit growth rate, is at $\sqrt{k}$. This is the point at which the budworm growth balances the number of budworms eaten by the birds. This would represent the stable equilibrium state and the ecological niche the budworms can occupy.

Mathematicians and scientists who mathematically model nonlinear systems sometimes employ the useful metaphor that the values of the variables at different states represent forces that move the system in different directions or to different states. The action of the system elements is viewed like the impacts of a force field, such as an electric or gravitational field. The changes of state with time are then viewed as a trajectory under the influence of a force field, like an electron in an electric field, for example, or water molecules moving in a stream under the influence of gravity. When viewed in this context, the mathematical integration of the expression of the rate of change of the elements with time metaphorically becomes the potential energy associated with different states of the elements. For example, we can integrate equation 1 to get a depiction of the potential energy associated with states of the system. The result of the mathematical integration is the following equation:

$$PE = -\frac{kx^2}{2} + \frac{x^4}{4}$$

Sketches of this equation for different values of the growth-rate coefficient k are shown in figure 2.2.

We can learn a lot about the qualitative behavior of our simple system by examining the sketches. The solid circles can be thought of as marbles moving along the curves of the sketches under the influence of gravity. The height of the curve can be thought of as the magnitude of the potential energy of the marble. We can see from figure 2.2 the results we obtained in the prior discussion. As k goes from negative to positive, there is a bifurcation. For k less than or equal to 0, the marble will finally come to rest at the origin, or $x = 0$. As the growth rate goes from negative to positive, the driving force of the growth rate causes the system to bifurcate, the origin, or $x = 0$, becomes unstable, and two new equilibrium states emerge at $x = \sqrt{k}$ and $x = -\sqrt{k}$. The marble shown on the left side of the rightmost sketch will eventually end up at $x = -\sqrt{k}$; the marble on the right of this sketch is shown at the stable state of $x = \sqrt{k}$; the marble in the middle is at the unstable state $x = 0$. Any slight force on the marble or change in the state of the marble at this unstable point will move the marble to either the left stable state or the right stable state, depending on its direction.

Understanding system behavior around an instability is crucial to understanding nonlinear systems. As in the preceding example, any small change from the unstable equilibrium at $x = 0$ will move the system to one of the two stable states that the system has after the bifurcation. The condition of the system at this state can be said to be sensitively dependent at the instability. The existence of instabilities makes prediction of

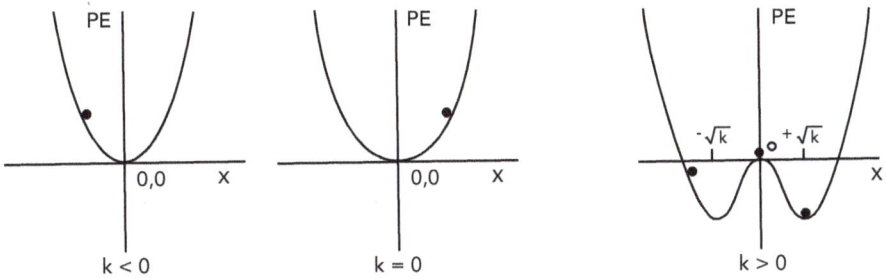

Figure 2.2 Sketches of potential energy metaphor

the behavior of nonlinear systems difficult. In popular literature, colloquialisms such as "tipping point" and "the straw that broke the camel's back" have emerged. What these colloquialisms coincidentally express is the behavior of a nonlinear system at an instability. A very small change, perhaps even imperceptible, brings about a significant alteration of the state of the system. All of us have had the experience of thinking we are doing the same thing and getting a different outcome each time. If this is your experience, you are dealing with a system at an instability. Another common experience is getting what seems to be an overly emotional response from someone who has had a bad day. That person is in an emotionally unstable state and, congratulations, you are the person who put the last straw on the camel's back.

Conversely, we have all had the experience of doing different things and always getting the same result. If this is your experience, you are dealing with a system that is in a state of strong stable equilibrium. Your efforts were not sufficient to move the system to your desired state because of the strong forces maintaining the status quo. The rightmost sketch in figure 2.2 gives a qualitative indication of the energy required to move the system to a different state. This is depicted by the size of the hump between the left stable state and the right stable state.

Meteorologists and nonlinear systems pioneer Ed Lorenz coined the phrase "butterfly effect" (Gleick 1987). The statement was that if there was a single unstable weather system between South America and France, then a butterfly flapping its wings in South America could affect the weather in France. All of these colloquialisms describe the same effect: the behavior of nonlinear systems at an instability. A small change brings about a large effect. If the small change is imperceptible, many people will interpret the change as random. This sentiment is captured in the following quote from French mathematician Poincaré: "A very small cause, which escapes us, determines a very considerable effect that we cannot fail to see, and then we say that this effect was due to chance" (Poincaré [1912] 1987, 4).

The potential-energy metaphor provides us with a useful qualitative device for understanding the nature of human perception.

Self-Organization in Nonlinear Systems

Another attribute unique to nonlinear systems is the ability to self-organize under certain conditions. The common conception of the nature of change in the universe is that the universe becomes increasingly less organized and more disorderly with time. This is the concept of entropy. Beginning in the nineteenth century, engineers and scientists noted that no process involving energy conversion, like an engine, was 100 percent efficient, and many such processes were not reversible. For example, coal burned to drive a steam engine cannot be unburned to get the coal back in its original form. The experienced loss of energy associated with energy-conversion processes was quantified and given the name entropy.

Scientist Ludwig Boltzmann showed that entropy was a measure of the state of order or disorder of the molecules constituting a system. The loss of energy from entropy is attributable to this reduction in order or increase in disorder of the molecules of a system. Haken (1981) provides the example of an automobile traveling down a road. This automobile has kinetic energy, or the energy of motion. The automobile also has only one degree of freedom, that being the direction in which it is traveling. Let's say that the driver puts on the brakes. There is friction between the tire and the road, which causes the tire, the brakes, the air inside and outside the tire, and, to a degree, the road to heat up. Heat is the kinetic energy of motion of the molecules that compose a substance. The molecules, particularly those in the air, have many degrees of freedom, meaning they can move in many directions. During the braking process, the kinetic energy of the car, with one degree of freedom, has been converted into the kinetic energy of molecules with many degrees of freedom. There is a loss of energy in this process because of entropy, and the process is irreversible. It is not possible to recover the energy dissipated by the tire into the atmosphere and put it back into the tire.

If you have a young child at home, you have experienced entropy. There are many places (degrees of freedom) in the child's room where they can place their personal items like toys, clothes, and books. Left to their own devices, in time, children's items will go from an orderly organization in their closet, toy chest, and desk to every conceivable surface where an item can be placed. Children will have increased the disorder and entropy of their room. This process is reversible, but it requires an external organizing force, like a parent, to direct and get the process of organization underway. This corresponds to the intuitive idea of order and organization, that it requires an external organizing force and effort. The way of nature is toward disorder. However, nonlinear systems can organize themselves (self-organize) without the imposition of any directive organizing force. The second law of thermodynamics, which describes entropy, is not repealed in self-organizing nonlinear systems. To self-organize, the nonlinear system must be open. The addition of energy to an open nonlinear system compensates for any entropic energy losses that may occur.

The concept of self-organization in scientific discourse was first introduced in 1947 by Ross Ashby, who articulated it in the context of systems theory. It has been studied and documented by others since, including by Heinz von Foerster, Ilya Prigogine, Hermann Haken, Humberto Maturana, and Francisco Varela.

The qualitative ideas involved in self-organization can be illustrated with straightforward examples. A group of people walking across a crowded intersection exemplifies the basic process. The first two requirements for self-organization to occur are that the system be nonlinear and far from stable equilibrium. Let's say that we have an intersection in New York City that pedestrians are crossing. If only a few people are crossing the intersection, the process is linear, and each person's movement is independent of everyone else's. If we knew how fast a person was walking and the distance of their path across the intersection, we could use a linear equation to calculate the time required for each person to cross the intersection. Now let's say that it is 5:15 p.m. and the intersection is packed with people trying to cross. The system of people crossing the intersection has now become nonlinear because the ability of any one person to cross is contingent upon the movement of all the other people in the intersection. The people in the intersection now have a codependent relationship to one another.

Prigogine (1997) states that self-organizing systems must have a dissipative structure. What he means by this is that the degrees of freedom or possible change must decrease with time. In our example, when the intersection was uncrowded, a person could choose any path they wanted to cross the intersection. As the number of people in the intersection increases, the degrees of freedom, or the number of paths that can be taken, decreases. Ultimately, as the intersection becomes completely packed with people, the degrees of freedom go to zero and the movement of people stops altogether. This is another characteristic of self-organization—it typically occurs at or near an unstable equilibrium state.

Everyone wants to get across the intersection before the light changes, so the system has a lot of driving force. When the system grinds to a halt, people try to make small changes in their path to make progress. The system undertakes small *perturbations* to attempt to move the system forward and continue progress. This is a trial-and-error process. The next requirement for self-organization is that one of the small changes or perturbations makes progress and begins to relieve the impasse. Let's say, in our example, that someone finds a gap that creates progress by moving up and to the right.

What happens next is that someone else in the crowd will move behind the person who made progress, then another person will move behind the second person, and soon others will follow suit because progress is being made. What began as a group of people acting independently became a group of people acting together to form a straight-line structure that restores progress and relieves the impasse. The system self-organized into this structural configuration. If you looked at the intersection, you would see a series of conga lines that allow people to successfully cross the intersection. PBS's program *NOVA* had an episode on this process called "Emergence," which can be seen on YouTube.

This illustrates an additional requirement for self-organization. A constructive change (perturbation) that locally relieves the instability must be able to be communicated to the different elements of the system. The change must also meet the requirements of the five factors that impact the state of the system, like attributes and characteristics of the system elements, driving forces, and so on. In our example, everyone can move and shift in different directions (attributes) and everyone is driven by the desire to get across the intersection. To satisfy the impact factors, the change must be *communicative and resonant* with system factors. In summary, self-organization can occur if the following requirements are met:

1. The system is nonlinear.
2. The system is far from stable equilibrium.
3. The system has a dissipative structure.
4. The system is at or near an instability (unstable equilibrium).
5. The system can undertake perturbations (local changes) that restore a measure of progress.

6. The successful perturbation can be communicated to system elements.

7. The perturbations and changes are resonant and meet the requirements of system elements and the factors that influence those elements.

An example of requirement 7 would be a speaker who is trying to cause an audience to self-organize into a mob that takes action. For this to occur, the speaker's message must "resonate" with the audience.

We can look at an additional self-organizing system to see another important aspect of self-organization. A liquid between two plates that is heated from below will self-organize into convection roles, as illustrated in figure 2.3.

As the liquid is heated from below, the liquid near the heat source becomes lighter than the liquid above. This is because heat increases the energy of the liquid molecules, causing them to get farther apart and make a unit volume of the liquid lighter in weight. As the lower liquid gets lighter, the force of gravity will cause this liquid to move upward and the cooler liquid above to move downward. This movement is opposed by the intermolecular forces between the liquid molecules. This opposing force is characterized by a macro property called *viscosity*. The higher the viscosity, the more resistance there is to movement or flow.

When the hotter liquid moves up, it is no longer being heated and is being cooled by contact with the cooler liquid as it rises. When it reaches the top, it is cooler than the liquid below it and begins to fall because of gravity. This is the process that creates the rolls.

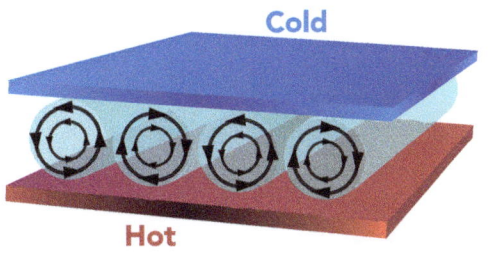

Figure 2.3 Convection rolls in a liquid heated from below

J. A. Kelso (1995) states that movement of the liquid begins when the Rayleigh number exceeds 1, indicating that the driving force of gravity is exceeding the ability of the liquid to remain motionless. The Rayleigh number is the ratio of the driving force, gravity in this case, to the force that holds the system together (viscosity). He notes that convection roles represent a dynamic structure that accommodates the driving force and at the same time meets the needs of the retentive force to keep the system together. This specific geometry, the convection role, maximizes the cooling of the heated liquid at the bottom of the system, thus allowing the system to stay together and not turn into a gas.

This is an important observation. Self-organization represents a situation where competing forces are close to balanced. Competing forces are accommodated and end up working together to maintain the integrity of the system. Note that this is yet another equilibration process undertaken by nonlinear systems. I have used this idea in my leadership courses. When there is conflict between employees with different needs, a solution is to create a relational structure that accommodates the different needs and gets the competitors to work together to accomplish higher-level goals that both value and will benefit from. Note that this is different from compromise. In a compromise, everyone gets half a loaf and neither party is completely satisfied. If in the future, one of the parties gets a power advantage, they will work to get the full loaf and impose their will on the other party.

One tactic used by school principals to resolve teacher conflicts is to remind them that they are there for the students, not to satisfy their personal needs. They can pursue their differing approaches, but they must do so with the idea in mind that whatever they do must be in the best interest of students. Here, the principal is counting on the fact that this higher-level value is held by both parties and can be used to both "accommodate" their individualities and get these opposing forces to work together to achieve a common goal that both parties value and agree to. The principal is trying to metaphorically create a "convection role" that allows the system to progress and stay together.

It is my hypothesis that self-organization to achieve equilibrium between the brain's representations is a ubiquitous process that occurs when the brain's representations of, for example, rules that relate and organize the regularities of experience fail to address, explain, or provide guidance for a response to a new circumstance not previously experienced. This is the process that Jean Piaget referred to as accommodation: the cognitive process of altering cognitive structures (schemas) and understandings so that new information can be incorporated when existing knowledge falls short and needs to be changed to deal with the new circumstance.

Chaos

A nonlinear system does not necessarily self-organize. The conditions discussed earlier must be met for self-organization to occur. If driving forces are strong, the system can go from instability directly into chaos. As long as the system stays together, the behavior of the system exhibits a deterministic character. This deterministic character is the subject of what is called chaos theory. The states of the system never repeat, and adjacent trajectories diverge rapidly from each other, but the terms of relationship between the elements and the element characteristics and attributes work to confine the trajectories and create patterns. The action of relationships and attributes to confine the trajectories and create patterns is called *control by strange attractors*. Chaos in social relationships is a state of violence and ultimately revolt or war. Mental chaos is severe cognitive dissonance and other psychological maladies. A state of chaos is not something you ever want a classroom to reach. As such, for our purposes, we need not go into further detail regarding chaos in nonlinear systems.

Perception

Perception is the remarkable ability we share with other animals to recognize objects and actions in our external environment. Perception is enabled first by the action of our senses. The information from our senses is integrated by the brain to provide the mental images of objects and actions that we experience. Senses respond to changes/differences in certain physical properties of objects and actions in our external environment. Our ears respond to the amplitude, frequency, and timing of air vibrations produced by objects and actions. Our ears are capable of sensing air vibrations from twenty to around twenty thousand cycles per second. Sound waves (air vibrations) make the eardrum vibrate, which in turn produces waves in the inner ear fluid. These waves vibrate hair cells in the cochlea of the inner ear. Hair cells are the primary auditory receptors. Their vibrations generate action potentials, or electrical signals, that convert the mechanical information entering the ear into a neural signal that the brain can process.

Hair cells along the surface of the cochlea are tuned to respond to different frequencies of vibration. Cells at the base of the cochlea are activated by high-frequency sounds, while cells at the apex of the cochlea are activated by low-frequency sounds. Hair cells in between respond to mid-frequency sounds. Through this scheme, our sense of hearing breaks down the complex frequency content of sounds into parts or components. This separation of frequency components is maintained as the neuron activations move from the hair cells through several subcortical areas and ultimately to the primary auditory cortex located in the superior temporal lobe of the brain. Neurons throughout this auditory pathway are tuned to respond to specific frequencies. This produces a tonotopic mapping of the frequency content of sounds. In the cortex, information is integrated and combined to produce, ultimately, the sounds that we experience, which have the full frequency content of the original air vibrations. The scheme of breaking up sensed stimulus into components or parts and then recombining them in the cortex occurs in every single sensory modality.

Why is this the scheme for sensory processing? Why not process and transmit the original combined information? One benefit of the scheme is saving memory space. To facilitate perception or re-recognition of prior experiences, the brain creates memories of those past experiences. If each of these past experiences was processed and stored in their original form, we would need memory space for each sound experience. There are virtually an infinite number of different sounds produced in the world. Recall from chapter 1 that memories are reactivations of the brain areas that originally responded to and represented the original experience. By breaking the stimulus down into components, the brain can use those frequency components that are common to different sounds and add only those frequency components that differ to both create and activate memories of different sounds. This is considerably more efficient than recording each individual sound in its entirety.

The brain implements what is called a productive system. An example of a *productive system* is language. In language, twenty-six letters can be variously combined to produce the approximately two hundred thousand words of a typical language. These words, in turn, can be variously combined to produce an unlimited number of ideas. Think of the amount of memory space we would need if each idea we had was made up of different words and each word was made up of different unique letters. The process of reading would be quite cumbersome indeed. LEGO bricks are another example of a productive system. Using a few basic shape elements, a lot of different figures can be produced with LEGO bricks.

We can perceive that the same note is being played on a trumpet or a piano. We can also perceive the difference in the sound of the two musical instruments. In representing each, the brain uses the same base frequency information in its representation and adds only the frequency content that is different between the two produced sounds. Again, this is a much more efficient scheme for both creating and activating memories, as well as for facilitating perception.

An additional benefit of this processing scheme is that it enables and facilitates abstraction and inductive generalization of experience. Because the brain is using many of the same components in representing different objects and actions with similarities, it automatically records in memory what those different objects and actions have in common—in other words, the semantic features they share. This enables the mental creation of classes and categories based on similar semantic features. For example, the sounds from musical instruments share many of the same frequency components. Human voices share frequency components that differ from those of musical instruments. The brain's processing scheme enables thoughts like "I hear music" or "I hear people talking." These thoughts are enabled because of the shared semantic features, in this case, frequency components, between these different collections of items.

Another important feature of sensory-information processing is the organization of sensory information with respect to space and time. This is required to reconnect the separately sensed components of the semantic features of objects and actions into the coherent, composite images we experience. It is also necessary to connect and relate information from different sensory modalities to the same object or action. In the case of sound, we have two ears at different physical locations. Because they are at different locations, the sounds (air vibrations) they experience will vary in time of arrival and intensity (amplitude). Information regarding time of arrival and intensity is sent to space-specific neurons in auditory-processing areas that are activated only when sound comes from certain locations (Gazzaniga, Ivry, and Mangun 2009). These neurons are tuned to different combinations of intensity and time of arrival. Each sensory modality uses time and space information to determine both what and where the sensory information came from.

The senses of smell and taste respond to the chemical content of gases that enter the nostrils and the chemical composition of things we put in our mouth. In each sensory modality, a physical property is converted into a neural activation that is processed by different brain areas and then sent to the cerebral cortex.

In taste, the same breakdown and separation scheme seen in hearing is employed. There are five basic "tastes" detected by around ten thousand taste buds in the mouth: salty, sour, bitter, sweet, and umami. Umami is what you taste when you eat protein-rich foods, like hamburgers. Each basic taste category has a different method of transducing chemical information into neural activations. For example, in detecting salty taste, sodium ions in dissolved salt enter an ion channel in a taste bud sensitive to salt. The sodium ion depolarizes and thus activates the cell. Each of the ten thousand taste buds is sensitive to only one of the five basic tastes. The complex range of tastes we experience results from the combination and integration of activations from the different taste bud cells. This occurs in the primary gustatory cortex (insula) and the orbital frontal cortex (Bear, Connors, and Paradiso 2007).

The orbital frontal cortex is also a principal processing area for feelings and emotion. This association undoubtedly accounts for the fact that our response to smells and tastes is often emotional. Emotional expressions like "that stinks" or "it doesn't pass the smell test" attest to the connection. A bad taste is often referred to as "disgusting." The primary gustatory cortex is located in the insula and operculum. The emotional reaction of disgust is also generated in the insula. The connection between smell, taste, and emotion makes sense. Emotion is a primary driver and motivator of behavior. In connecting the two, the brain is motivating what to eat and what not to eat. This is also reflected in the nature of the five particular tastes detected. Umami reveals that a protein-rich food has been eaten; a sweet taste indicates a carbohydrate has been consumed; a salty taste indicates that electrolytes important for body function have been ingested. These are all ingredients necessary for the body to maintain its functionality and health. A bitter taste discourages consumption. Many toxic plants taste bitter.

The reader may have had the experience of receiving an injection in their arm and experiencing a taste in their mouth. This occurs because the sensory-processing system is nonlinear and there are recurrent feedback connections. When the brain detects the chemical in the blood, it activates and sends an activation signal back to the taste buds. Not all injections are tasted, because they are composed of chemicals that are not detected by the taste buds.

The somatosensory system, or sense of touch, includes different types of receptors under the skin that respond to pressure, temperature, and pain information. There are also specialized nerve cells in the musculoskeletal junctions that send the brain information about the state of muscles and limbs. Information from the somatosensory receptors is sent to Broadman cerebral cortex areas 1, 2, and 3 via the spinal cord (Gazzaniga, Ivry, and Mangun 2009).

Our visual system detects the properties of light reflected off objects. Like the other sensory systems, it is a productive, hierarchical system that breaks down the semantic features of objects contained in reflected light and recombines them in the later stages of cerebral-cortex processing to produce the final visual images we experience. It is instructive to examine how the brain detects and processes shape information. The shape-processing system, like all other sensory modalities, breaks shape information into parts or components. Researchers David Hubel and Torsten Wiesel received the Nobel Prize in 1981 for their discovery of the mechanisms by which this system operates. Shape-processing cells in the primary visual cortex are connected in a way that makes them sensitive to and activated by edges. These cells also have a receptive field, meaning they respond to input that originates from a specific location in the field of vision of the eye. Shape-detecting cells in the primary visual cortex are activated by ganglion cells in the retina of the eye that respond directly to impinging light. When a shape-processing cell receives input and is activated by a ganglion cell, it will inhibit the activation of adjacent cells. The response of all the cells receiving ganglion input is muted by this inhibition. When the edge of an object is outside the receptive field of a ganglion and is receiving less light reflection, the ganglion cell will not activate. The connected cell in the cortex will not activate and will, therefore, also not inhibit its

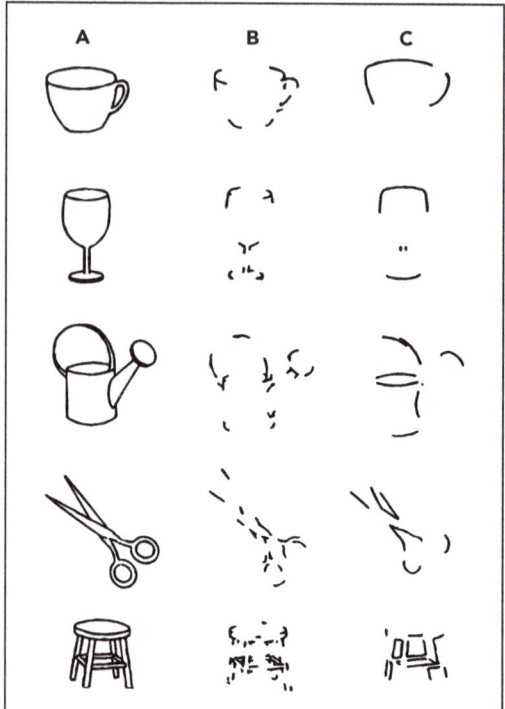

Figure 2.4
Combining shape elements to create a composite representation

neighbors. Its immediate neighbor that is still receiving ganglion input and is no longer being inhibited from the side will activate strongly. This action makes these processing cells edge detectors. Hubel and Wiesel determined that there are thirty-some shape elements, or edge types, that are detected, like different straight-line segments at different angles in the visual field. As processing moves up the hierarchy of the shape-processing area of the visual cortex, these elements are combined to produce the shapes we experience in visual images. Also, as activations proceed up the shape-processing hierarchy, information from areas that process for properties like color, luminance, and motion is incorporated to refine shape representations.

Figure 2.4 is a schematic that illustrates how shape elements could be combined to create a final representation of an object.

Figure 2.5 illustrates the idea that neural activations higher in the hierarchy of the neuron-connection configuration result from or are composed of collections of activations from neurons lower in the hierarchy.

As schematically illustrated in figure 2.5, final representations, such as those in images, are composites of lower-level representations. The illustration also shows how a neuron or collection of neurons can be part of several different composite representations.

As discussed before, the productive, hierarchical nature of neuron-connection configurations facilitates abstraction of the features of objects and actions that share similarities. The breakdown of sensed semantic features into elements, or components, and the use of the same elements when representing different objects and actions that share similar features records those similarities when memories of those items/actions are created. The faculty of abstraction and the process of inductive generalization of objects/actions that share semantic features is thus hardwired in the brain.

The next schematic, figure 2.6, shows in simplified fashion how seeing the written word "fire" might be processed by the brain.

The process begins with recognition of shape elements. These shape elements are combined into representations of letters, which are then combined into letter combinations. These letter combinations are then combined into words. In the final step, at the word level, words are combined to create an idea or concept.

The representation hierarchy is nonlinear, meaning there are feedback connections to the lower level from each level of the hierarchy. This wiring scheme enables and facilitates the human capacity for prediction, or determining what comes next, using representations stored in memory. When a representation is activated, it will activate all of the representations it is connected to and, therefore, associated with.

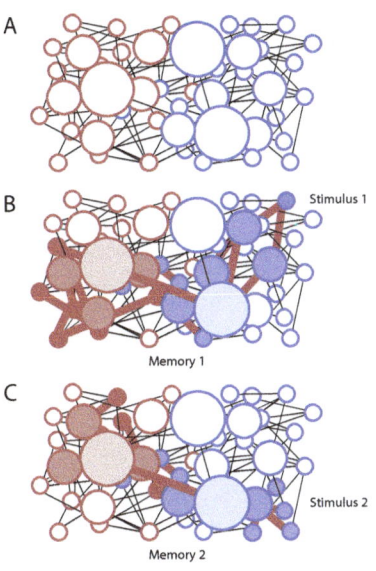

Figure 2.5 Model of the hierarchical and productive structure of memory circuits

For example, at the word level, reading the word "fire" activates associated words like "flame" and "heat." When you are reading about a fire event, your brain anticipates seeing these words and preliminarily activates and primes the words for subsequent full activation when you have the experience of reading the words. This speeds the reading process and makes it more fluid. The activation process also extends down the hierarchy, priming letters and even shape elements. In general, nonlinear connection facilitates speed, fluidity, and the capacity for prediction in mental processing. If the title of your book is *A Firefighter's Diary*, and you see the letters *f i r*, your brain is looking for and anticipating the letter e. If the title of the book is *Tree Species in British Columbia*, it is not.

Perception, or recognizing something in a mental-image representation as a such and such can be thought of as re-recognition of something priorly experienced and recorded in memory. As such, it constitutes a "judgment" that something is a such and such, the neural definition of "such and such" being the associated and related semantic features of some object/action.

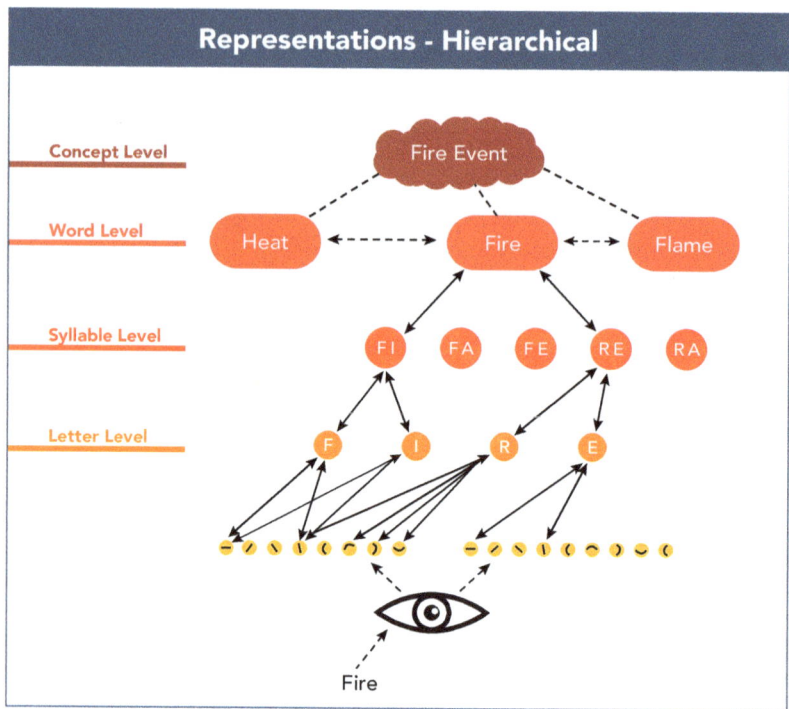

Figure 2.6 Hierarchical and productive mental processing of a written word

The re-recognition process is enabled by the connection of neural representations of the current experience and the memory of prior experiences of similar objects and actions. Again, perception, as I'm defining it here, is a conscious judgment regarding the content of a sensorially derived mental image. The image of the current experience is automatic and uninvolved with conscious processing. A visual image, for example, contains size, shape, color, and other information pertaining to objects. A person's mind consciously decides based on this content what the objects in the image are.

Researchers Wong and Wang (2006) simulated the process of perception with a neural network with feedback loops, where various decision choices or judgments were represented by distinct groups of neurons in the model. In their mathematical model of this network, *basins of attraction* emerged around stable equilibrium points corresponding to perceptual decisions. The term basin of attraction means those states around a stable equilibrium state that will lead back to the stable equilibrium state. Referring back to the sketches shown when discussing bifurcation, the basin of attraction of the stable equilibrium states $x = \sqrt{k}$ and $x = -\sqrt{k}$ are those values of x that will result in the state (the marble) moving back to these stable equilibrium states. The basins of attraction in Wong and Wang's model were separated by saddle regions, or saddle equilibrium points. There were also unstable equilibrium states that developed. Figure 2.7 illustrates Wong and Wang's results schematically for the case where two items of information, or

Figure 2.7 Semantic model of perceptual judgment

two semantic features, form the basis for making a perceptual decision. One can think of the ball resting on an unstable equilibrium point in the schematic (ball on the peak) as being in a state of ambiguity until receiving sufficient energy (accumulated information) to move it into the basin of attraction, and ultimately the stable equilibrium state representing a specific decision.

To illustrate the process of perception using the schematic model in figure 2.7, let's say that we see an object moving in the sky toward us. We don't yet have enough information, in terms of semantic features in our mental image, to decide what it is. This would be the situation of the ball in the figure 2.7 at the peak representing an unstable equilibrium state. Our perceptual decision is going to be based on two semantic features: (1) what type of noise we hear and (2) whether the object has wings that move. We are trying to determine whether the object is a bird, a plane, or Superman. Let's say that as it approaches, we see that the object has wings. The object is, therefore, not Superman. As the object gets closer, we see that the wings move, and we can hear no noise. We now have sufficient information to perceive the object and make the judgment that it is a bird. In figure 2.7, the ball now moves into the basin of attraction for this decision and ends up at the stable equilibrium representing the decision that the object is a bird. This is represented by the marble in the right side of the figure now resting at the decision point.

In actual human perception, considerably more information is utilized and equilibrium structures are undoubtedly more complex. Figure 2.7, however, is a good qualitative illustration of the basic nature of the perception process.

Dehaene (2007) discusses how Turing's optimal algorithm for sequential statistical inference successfully describes perceptual-based human decisions. This algorithm, originally developed by Turing to break Germany's Enigma code during World War II, quantifies the weight of an item of information in favor of a particular hypothesis as the logarithm of the ratio of the contingent probability of the hypothesis given the item of information to the contingent probability of the hypothesis not given the item of information. The weights of all the supplied items of information are added to determine the total weight of information in favor of a specific hypothesis. When a certain threshold is reached, a decision in favor of the hypothesis can be made. This illustrates how human decision-making based on associative memories seems to exhibit a statistical character. This will be further discussed in chapter 4.

The discussion of perceptual decisions also illustrates why the human mind can deal with ambiguous input. Human perceptual judgments can be characterized as the consideration of the weight of the evidence for a given hypothesis. Even when such evidence is not completely clear or complete, if it is sufficient to "move the ball" into the basin of attraction of a particular decision, the decision will be made. How much input it takes can vary by individual and circumstance. Given the nonlinear construction of the perceptual system, a task such as recognizing a distorted face is much easier for a human than it is for digital facial recognition software, which struggles with ambiguous input.

Theory of Knowledge

Philosophic Background

There has undoubtedly been speculation concerning the nature of knowledge since Homo sapiens evolved the capacity for speech and symbolic representation some 150,000 to 200,000 years ago, a time estimate derived from archaeological, paleontological, genetic, and linguistic evidence. The formal examination of the nature of knowledge has been for the most part the province of philosophers until the twentieth-century emergence of the sciences of psychology, cognitive psychology, and cognitive neuroscience. Any derivation of a theory of knowledge and learning intended to guide effective teaching practices, therefore, naturally begins with an examination of the progress made by centuries of philosophic inquiry.

Using the language of philosophy, the first question asked is metaphysical: What is knowledge? A metaphysical inquiry seeks the ultimate reality of a thing like knowledge. Using only the tools of logic and reason, metaphysics seeks to uncover the essence of something—the properties that determine the thing and without which it would cease to be the thing. The idea that every object of consideration has an essence that determines the kind of thing it is and that is the causal source of its behavior has been central to Western philosophy and science from, at least, the time of the ancient Greeks up until the present time. Other first postulates that have guided inquiry in the Western world are that objective, universal, timeless knowledge and truths, external to the individual and independent of point of view or perspective, do in fact exist and can be discovered using logic and reason operating on the content of experience. These are first postulates deemed by their adherents to be obvious and not in need of proof, much like Euclid's postulates that prelude the development of geometry. As they are unproven first postulates, they have, of course, been challenged by some philosophers. Beginning with existentialism and continuing to postmodernism, the contention of philosophers from these schools of thought is that all knowledge is subjective, exists in the mind of the knower only, is contingent upon point of view or perspective, and is determined by situations and circumstances. Knowledge then, is the creation of the individual rather than the discovery of an external reality. This great dialectic will be further examined later in this chapter.

Ancient Greek Philosophy

One of the terms of the democracy of ancient Greece was that political offices, assemblies, and courts were to be composed of average citizens. No professional training or education was provided to prospective officeholders. There were no specially trained lawyers or representatives. A citizen might be a sheepherder one day and a judge the next. Under these circumstances, the success of an individual was greatly contingent upon their power of persuasion and oratorical skill. This gave rise to a class of wandering for-profit educators called Sophists. Sophists taught things relevant to human activities: rhetoric, or the art of winning arguments for or against any proposition, and practical vocational facts and procedures.

Sophists had a very humanistic and pragmatic orientation. They believed that there was no reality gap between the way the world appears to common sense and the way the world actually is. Given this perspective, there was no need for philosophical inquiry to discover the "order" or "meaning" of the world as something separate or different from the world rendered by perception and commonsense judgment. This sentiment is captured in the statement of Protagoras, the most famous of the Sophists, that man is the measure of all things that are and are not. Such a conclusion is based on the subjective character of perception and judgment. One person might find a room cold while the other finds it hot. Each judgment is equally justified. When men differ, such as in how hot or cold a room is, there is no objective truth by virtue of one being right and the other being wrong. To declare one right and the other wrong would require some absolute definition and set of criteria regarding cold and hot that is independent of the perception and judgment of individuals. Since this is not possible and such knowledge would not be accessible to humans even if it existed, humans must, of necessity, rely on their individual perception and judgment to know. All knowledge is, therefore, subjective and a contingent construction of the individual. It is in this sense that man is the measure of all things. Since certain knowledge is impossible, we should remain agnostic with respect to absolute truth. If there is absolute truth, free from point of view or personal interest, we have no way of ascertaining it. One opinion can be better than another, if the argument for it is stronger, but it cannot be truer. Disbelief in objective truth makes the majority, for all practical purposes, the arbiters of what is true. Truths then are truths with a small t, not a capital T.

As one can note, the contentions of the Sophists are essentially the same as those of today's postmodernist philosophers. At first blush, these ideas seem rather liberating and empowering. Postmodern philosophers, such as Michel Foucault (1972), have contended that throughout history those who claim to be in possession of absolute knowledge and truth (truth with a capital T) have used this contention as a basis and justification for subjugating and controlling other people and exercising hegemony over them.

Individuals whose viewpoints and beliefs differed from the mainstream or from those in authority were marginalized or, in Foucault's words, "othered." As might be expected, the postmodern viewpoint has appeal to those who advocate for social justice and a voice for those populations and viewpoints that have been historically marginalized.

The viewpoints of the Sophists and postmodernists, while liberating, create practical problems. For one, if everyone has their own personally created knowledge and inventory of ideas regarding what is true, and if everyone's individually created knowledge and truth are equally legitimate, and if those ideas differ among individuals, how do we reach agreement as a collective or society on matters of importance to the aggregate? We end up with a situation, such as currently exists the US Congress, where individuals cannot agree on the nature of the problem, much less work collectively toward a solution. Communication in general becomes difficult if we have materially different ideas about what is what. If my buzzard is your turkey, I may be hesitant to accept your invitation for Thanksgiving dinner. As philosopher Bertrand Russell (1945) asks, What do we tell the man who thinks he is a poached egg? Do we tell him that the majority disagrees with him or that the government thinks he is wrong? Since we cannot in philosophic discourse a priori assume the existence of either a government or majority rule, we have a real problem here. As intuition may be telling you, the answer here may have something to do with pragmatism. We will defer further discussion on pragmatism until later in the chapter.

The concerns expressed earlier were shared by the philosopher Plato, who lived during the time of the Sophists. Plato worried about a lapse into complete moral and intellectual anarchy. For example, the Sophists point of view is fundamentally amoral. It deals with pragmatic outcomes for individuals rather than appealing to universal ideals, principles, or virtues. Plato's philosophy was the antithesis of Sophist philosophy. Plato sought a path to absolute, timeless, and universal knowledge and truth. For Plato, it is the eidos, the Idea or Form, of something that is universal, immutable, and timeless. He states that the world we come to know through perception, the world as revealed by the senses, is imperfect and constantly changing. A flower or painting may be beautiful today, but in time it decays, becomes damaged, and ceases to be beautiful. The Idea of beauty, however, existed before the perception of the flower or painting and exists after the flower or painting ceases to be beautiful. Similarly, particular individuals, such as John, Lucy, and Ben, last for some finite time, but the Idea of humankind lasts forever. I can bring a triangle into existence by drawing it with my pencil and then eliminate it with an eraser, but the Idea of the triangle existed before I drew it and persists after I erase it. It is the Idea and not the particular that has the property of timelessness and changeless.

Plato's general theory of knowledge is as follows. He divides thought into the world of the senses and the world of the intellect. The senses provide raw data, but it is the intellect that sees and understands what the data have in common. Knowledge is derived through the intellect. The world of sense is the world of perception of the imperfect particulars of experience. The world of the intellect he divides into the world of reason and the world of understanding. The world of understanding begins with hypotheses drawn from a generalization of experience. It then proceeds by using logic to make inferences as to what follows from these generalizations. He places mathematics and science into this world. For example, Euclidean geometry begins with initial definitions and unproven postulates and then proceeds to logically derive what follows from these definitions and postulates. Plato states that this type of knowledge is hypothetical—a derivation from hypotheses. Clearly, such knowledge is contingent upon the veracity of the initial hypotheses that are unproven and typically some generalization of experience. Plato discounts inductive generalization of empirical experience as a source of absolute knowledge. In his dialogues, Plato repeatedly demonstrates the inadequacy of the inductive generalizations of experience made by the participants. His path to absolute immutable knowledge is through the world of reason and the process of the dialectic. In the dialectic process, Plato invites participants in the conversation to create a definition, or the Idea, of something, like justice or knowledge, through an inductive generalization of their experience. He then, through the character Socrates, introduces a circumstance that demonstrates the inadequacy of the Idea and often suggests that the antithesis or opposite of the original idea is required to accommodate the new circumstance. For example, in the beginning of the *Republic* dialogue, Plato invites an elderly man to generalize his life experience and provide a definition of justice. The definition he supplies is that justice is telling the truth and giving others what is owed to them. Plato, through the character Socrates, then introduces the circumstance of a man who deposits his sword and other arms with another for safekeeping. When he returns to collect the arms, he is clearly no longer sane and in control of his faculties. If the arms were to be returned to him, in his current state of mind, he would likely injure either himself or someone else. Would it be just to tell him the truth and return what is owed to him? The original definition, or Idea, fails and the antithesis, lying and withholding what is owed to him, appears to be the more appropriate response. The participants in the dialogue then revise their original Idea of justice to "doing good to friends and doing evil to enemies." The new Idea is more abstract and at a higher logical level. It preserves the original Idea of justice, which was an appropriate response to a sane individual, and it also accommodates the circumstance of an insane individual. Both the original thesis and the antithesis are examples of doing good contingent upon the mental state of the individual. Plato then demonstrates the inadequacy of this new definition by logically arguing that doing evil cannot be a component of the Idea of justice. In general, the dialectic process continues until participants are satisfied that the final Idea is universal and timeless and an expression of absolute knowledge and truth. The final Idea must be sufficiently comprehensive, must capture the essence of the Idea, like justice, and must express what all instances and examples of the Idea have in common. Having achieved this character through the dialectic process, inferences made through logic from the final Idea represent true categorical knowledge, not merely hypothetical knowledge. It was stated that the dialectic leads to an Idea at a higher logical level. A definition of logical level is in order. If an Idea is composed of a relationship between elements, the Idea is at a higher logical level than the elements of which it is composed. For example, the Idea of a plant is at a higher logical level than the Idea of a flower, a tree, and grass. The Idea of an animal is at a higher logical level than the Idea of a tiger, a lion, and a zebra.

So, what was Plato's contribution to our understanding of the nature of knowledge? Plato's work was the first philosophic examination of the nature of a concept. The modern word or expression for Plato's eidos, or Ideas/Forms, is *concept*. Plato's concept was composed of the common attributes, characteristics, and relationships found among and between a group of things perceived to be similar in nature. Today, we would refer to such a grouping as a *category* or a class.

Neuroscience provides the understanding that knowledge expressed as words that refer to classes and categories is enabled by our brain's capacity to inductively generalize worldly experience. Plato takes induction for granted and does not examine it philosophically. In fact, he is derisive of generalization as a source of true knowledge. Plato characterizes knowledge derived from a generalization of experience as hypothetical knowledge or opinion. He demonstrates the inadequacy of human generalization of experience time and time again in his dialogues. To give an example that demonstrates Plato's thesis, if we were to separately ask individuals in a group for a definition or their Idea of love, we would likely get a different definition or Idea from each individual. Each definition would be an inductive generalization of the specific experience of that individual. Remember that Plato seeks knowledge that is absolute, timeless, and universal—Ideas that express truth with a capital T. This type of knowledge must capture the essence of the Idea: those attributes, characteristics, and relationships that comprehensively and unambiguously define something, separate from other things and without which it would cease to be the thing. Importantly, the Idea must capture the essence of **all** instances of the thing.

As discussed, Plato's path to this type of absolute knowledge is the dialectic. It begins with the imperfect generalization of experience. An instance or circumstance is then introduced that is not accounted for or accommodated by the original Idea. The circumstance demonstrates the inadequacy of the original Idea and the failure to capture all instances of the Idea. A new, more general Idea that accommodates for the idiosyncrasies of the problematic instance or circumstance is then developed.

It is important to note that the tool Plato uses to reveal the inadequacy of the original Idea and to assist in formulating the new Idea is logic. Logic renders what necessarily follows from an Idea or proposition. As Plato appropriately observes, knowledge derived from inductive generalization is contingent knowledge. A statement of how the world happens to be for the individual making the generalization. Such generalization has caveats—it comes with the implicit qualifiers: until the current time and as far as I know. As Plato demonstrates, a new and different circumstance could require a change or modification to the original generalization. A resident of Greece at the time of Plato could make the inductive generalization that all swans are white. This generalization would have the implicit qualifier "as far as I know, and until the current time, given my experience." Were that Greek to go to Australia, they would have to alter their original generalization after seeing a black swan.

Plato sets the future of philosophy on specific paths. The first is the quest for absolute knowledge and truth with a capital T. The second is a strong preference for logic and deduction as the path to such knowledge. We can see this influence in the philosophy of Leibniz, who attempted to derive the nature of the universe as the logical consequences of two basic principles: the principle of contradiction and the principle of sufficient reason. Leibniz believed that both principles were intuitively obvious and not in need of proof. The principle of contradiction is that something cannot both be the case and not be the case. Logically, it cannot both be *p* and not be *p*. The principle of sufficient reason is the idea that everything must have a reason, cause, or ground. It is evident in the philosophy of Spinoza, who first argued for the veracity of his initial definitions and axioms and then proceeded to logically deduct his worldview. It is also found in the analytic philosophy of Bertrand Russell. Russell attempted to find atomic concepts—fundamental and having no parts or relationships to other concepts—and to build a system of knowledge using logic. British philosopher David Hume used his skepticism of knowledge derived from inductive generalization to conclude that science as necessary truth could not exist. Science deals with causal relationships. Hume concludes that the fact that some effect B is caused by action A is nothing more than the observation and inductive generalization that B seems to always follow A in time. It cannot be deductively proven through logic that B is the logically necessary consequence of A. Hume, like Plato before him, concludes that science is simply hypothetical knowledge or opinion.

The conclusion that the universe is logical has been the predicate of many philosophers. This predicate, however, has a very untenable consequence. Since logic produces what necessarily follows, a logical universe is a predestined universe. That means, for example, that the assassination of Julius Caesar was logically necessary and something that was contained in the Idea of Caesar.

Despite the philosophic skepticism of the nature of inductive generalization, it is clear that it is an important, if not requisite, method by which knowledge is constructed. Every deductive argument must proceed from initial definitions, premises, or postulates. The validity of the deductive argument is contingent upon the veracity of these initial factors. How does one arrive at these initial factors if not through inductive generalization of worldly experience? While, for example, Leibniz's two principles seem to be intuitively obvious, it is because we, like Leibniz, live in a universe where things exist uniquely, and effects are caused. It is our experience of the world that gives this this intuitive sense. If we understand the caveats that come with inductive generalization and the contingency of such knowing, there is no reason to discount the results of this knowledge-construction process. We must, however, understand that a circumstance may arise that violates the idea or rule derived through inductive generalization. Such a violation or inadequacy is then dealt with through a form of dialectic process.

I hypothesize that Plato's dialectic process is, in the abstract, a principal method by which humans construct knowledge when their inventory of existing knowledge fails to provide them with a rule that facilitates accomplishing a goal or solving a problem. The thesis is that when a circumstance is encountered that is not addressed by, accounted for, or explained by an individual's preexisting inventory of knowledge, a process ensues subconsciously that, in the abstract, is the dialectic process described by Plato, and subsequently by the philosopher Hegel. I hypothesize that the neurological process that enables and facilitates the behavioral dialectic process is self-organization within the nonlinear system of neural representations of the semantic features of experience in the brain. In the next chapter, I will argue that many advancements in fields like science demonstrate, in the abstract, the dialectic process.

Historian Will Durant credits Plato with defining the purpose and goal of education in general. Durant ([1926] 1961, 27) states,

> Therefore, the essence of a higher education is the search for Ideas: for generalizations, laws of sequence, and ideals of development; behind things we must discover their relation and meaning, their mode and law of operation, the function and ideal they serve or adumbrate; we must classify and coordinate our sense experience in terms of law and purpose; only for lack of this does the mind of the imbecile differ from the mind of Caesar.

Durant generalizes Plato's ideas to the notion of rules as currently defined in the field of cognitive science. Rules are the concepts, theories, principles, and generalizations that the intellect constructs to organize, structure, and give meaning to the manifold of human experience. They symbolically represent the way the world/universe is in the mind of the individual that constructs them. Rules are what enable the higher-order thinking processes unique to humans: verbal communication, rule-based decision-making and problem-solving, planning, strategizing, design, and creation. Without rules, the conscious, purposeful undertaking of these activities is not possible. While the notion of Idea as concept is explicit within the works of Plato, the more general notion of Ideas as rules is certainly implicit within Plato's works and would support Durant's contention.

Durant and his wife, Ariel, spent their lives researching and documenting the history of Western civilization. They published an eleven-volume *History of Civilization* between 1935 and 1975, of which one volume won the Pulitzer Prize, and were widely recognized for their achievements. Durant was once asked: If all the books in the world were destroyed and only one could be spared with which to rebuild Western civilization, which book should that be? Durant responded that it should be Plato's *Republic*. Such was his regard for Plato's work.

At a minimum, we can credit the following to be Plato's contribution to our understanding of the nature of knowledge:

- Identifying that the concept, and perhaps the rule, is the form and structure that conscious human knowledge takes

- Delineating that similarity and invariance across a collection of things is the fundamental construct that underpins concepts/rules

- Identifying inductive generalization and deductive process (logic) as mechanisms for the construction of knowledge and demonstrating at least a portion of the relationship between these processes

- Discerning that knowledge is constructed by the intellect from the manifold of information contained in perception

- Developing the dialectic as a knowledge-construction process

To give his Ideas the character of absoluteness, universality, and timelessness, Plato had to solve several problems. The solution to timelessness was straightforward, as previously shown. For example, humans perish, but the Idea of humankind is eternal. Plato's path to absoluteness was the dialectic process. The dialectic is a process of discovery. For something to be discovered, it must exist. To resolve this dilemma, Plato postulated that his Ideas had a separate and independent existence from the particulars that they generalize and characterize. He postulates that Ideas are immaterial and have a separate and independent existence in and of themselves. Even if there was no justice in the world, the Idea of justice would exist. So where do these immaterial Ideas exist? Plato's answer is that they reside with God, who is pure Form, or Idea.

Another issue with Plato's Ideas is how material objects, separate and distinct from Ideas, possess the features of or could be affected by immaterial Ideas. Plato's answer is that material objects have features in common because they resemble the Ideas. They are imperfect copies that partake of the Idea. Owing to this imperfection, there can be many of them. There are, for example, many beautiful things that imperfectly resemble and partake of the Idea of beauty.

Aristotle, Plato's most famous student, regarded his teacher's theory of Ideas as mystical and scholarly nonsense. Another problem with knowledge being exclusively contained in the form of Ideas is the nature of notions that express Ideas that are, for example, primarily relational in nature. For example, what is the Idea of small? Something is small only with respect to something that is large. How could one through dialectic process arrive at the ideal notion of "smallness"? Aristotle states that Plato's Ideas are simply universals. Universals are words like animal, tree, or rock that may be predicated of many things that share commonalities. They are subjective notions, not objective entities. A universal does not exist by itself; it exists in particular things. For example, blueness exists because there are blue things. Humankind does not exist; Jane, Trevon, and Javier exist.

Aristotle's solution to the problematic aspects of Plato's Ideas was to make them material, place them within objects, and give them causal powers. For Aristotle, this solves the problem of how material objects can be influenced by and come to resemble Ideas: by making them a material aspect of the objects that determines what they are and that controls what they do.

Aristotle contended that all material objects have two aspects: Matter and Form. Matter is what the object is made of, and Form is what makes the object what it is. For example, if we have a statue of Socrates, Matter would be the marble the statue is made of, and Form would be the shape of the statue giving it its likeness to Socrates. To quote Aristotle directly,

> We are in the habit of recognizing, as one determinate kind of what is, substance, and that in several senses, (a) in the sense of matter or that which in itself is not a "this," and (b) in the sense of form or essence, which is that precisely in virtue of which a thing is called a "this," and thirdly (c) in the sense of that which is compounded of both (a) and (b). (Pojman and Vaughn 2011, 229)

We can see that Aristotle has not abandoned Plato's notion of Ideas, he has made them material and placed them inside of objects. Aristotle contends that his Forms are what give objects their essence: those attributes and characteristics and the relationships between them that define a category of objects and without which an object would cease to be a member of the category. Aristotle's Forms not only impart essence but also determine and control all the actions and changes in state that are associated with the object. Aristotle's answer to why horses gallop would be that it is in their nature to do so, a nature brought about by their Form.

Aristotle studied and made careful observations and descriptions of plants and animals. He observed what appeared to be a force within living things that directed their growth and development as well as their activities, such as reproduction, self-nutrition, and movement. He overgeneralizes these observations and contends that all objects have such a force within them that determines what they are and what they do. A metaphor for the modern reader of Aristotle's Forms is DNA, if we added the proviso that DNA controlled every aspect of what an organism is as well as controlled and determined every action the organism undertakes.

Aristotle calls the Form of living things the *soul*. The soul is what brings life. A dead body and a live body both have the same matter; it is the soul that brings life. He gives the soul different aspects. To humans, he gives an additional and unique aspect he terms the rational soul, which is the faculty of reason and reflection. To this aspect he accords an additional faculty called the mind. The mind is the source of our knowledge of the world. How does the mind acquire this knowledge? He maintains that perception is a matter of the soul literally taking on the Forms of the objects of the world. Aristotle believes that the senses transfer the actual properties of objects to the soul. In the act of thinking, the soul takes on the nature of what it is thinking about. As Aristotle states,

> The thinking part of the soul must therefore be, while impassable, capable of receiving the Form of an object; that is, must be potentially identical in character with the object without being the object. (Pojman and Vaughn 2011, 235)

Learning and the accumulation of knowledge then, in accordance with this thesis, is a matter of experiencing a world that impresses itself on our intellect or mind—entities capable of taking on the essence, or Form, of things in the world. Aristotle is often credited with being the "father of science." Consistent with his theory of knowledge, Aristotle's science consisted of making careful observations and recordings of the nature of things in the world. His science is descriptive knowledge of the way things are observed to be. Through careful observation and recording, classes and categories of objects could be constructed, which captured the essence of objects, as well as taxonomies that related the classes and categories. So detailed and meticulous were the descriptions developed by Aristotle and his students that some of them were utilized up until the nineteenth century. Based on his theory of knowledge, the actions associated with objects and the changes in the state of objects that were observed and documented were ascribed to the object's Form. For example, in Aristotle's cosmology, the Earth is heavy because its proper place is at the center of the universe, a place it will move toward because it is in its nature, or Form, to do so. Causality then is reduced to the influence of the object's Form. This premise, however, creates an intellectual hole large enough to drive a Mack truck through. It precludes the possibility that something is the way it is or that a change has occurred because of the interaction or relationship between separate and distinct things. For example, it would not admit of the modern explanation that the element hydrogen, separate and distinct from the element oxygen, could combine with oxygen to produce water (H_2O), a substance distinct and separate from either hydrogen or oxygen, with its own attributes and characteristics different from the elements of which it is composed.

Aristotle is also the father of logic, the first to develop a formal system of reasoning. The system that he developed, and that subsequent philosophers added to and further embellished, is independent of the semantic content of the items put into relationship. The truth of an inference or conclusion arrived at through formal logic is contingent upon only conformance to the requirements of the syntactic structure of the argument. For example,

If all As are Bs, and

If all Bs are Cs,

then it is logically necessary that all As are Cs.

In this example, it is the syntactic structure of the argument that renders the logical necessity of the conclusion. What A, B, and C are, or the semantic features of A, B, and C, is irrelevant to the validity of the argument.

Aristotle's fundamental structure for the form of an argument that rendered logically necessary conclusions was the syllogism. A syllogism is structured as follows:

1. It begins with a premise or proposition that is a statement about some essence (attribute or characteristic) belonging to a class or category. For example, "Man is a rational animal."

2. It has a second proposition or premise that assigns a particular to the class referred to in the first premise or proposition. For example, "Socrates is a man."

3. It then deducts a conclusion regarding the particular. For example, "Socrates is a rational animal."

4. The order of the first and second proposition can be changed. For example, the argument could be:

Socrates is a man.

Men are rational animals.

Socrates is a rational animal.

Aristotle developed numerous forms of the syllogism that included qualifiers and negations. He believed that, in total, his syllogisms constituted the whole of logic and defined the manner in which reasoning could render necessary knowledge and truth. If, in fact, the entirety of knowledge consisted of the descriptive knowledge of Forms, his belief would have been justified. If the only path to knowledge was careful observation and description of items in the world and the creation of classes, categories, and dichotomies, then reasoning is predicated on these classes and categories, and the syllogism becomes the only required mechanism for such reasoning. Today, we understand that the creation of classes and categories is only one form of constructing knowledge. Aristotle supposes that thought begins with a premise or proposition and then seeks conclusions. Modern science, for example, begins with hypotheses (conclusions) and then seeks justifying premises—premises arrived at by the observation of outcomes under the controlled conditions of an experiment.

To formally define the nature of propositions or premises in his syllogistic argument structure, Aristotle notes that every such premise or proposition consists of a subject and something that is predicated of the subject. For example, in the premise "Socrates is a man," Socrates is the subject and being a man is what is predicated of Socrates. Aristotle states that words like "Socrates" and "man" fall below the level of something that could be true or false. Truth or falsity is contingent upon the proposed relationship between these words. Man, and Socrates, cannot be true or false. That Socrates is a man can be true or false. This is a very important concept. Subsequent philosophers like Locke, Hume, and Kant arrived at similar conclusions. For example, Hume asserts that reason is the discovery of truth or falsehood in the agreement or disagreement of ideas. As philosophy progressed, there was eventually little disagreement among philosophers that determining the validity of a premise was a matter of ascertaining whether the proposed relationship between the items related and connected in the statement was coherent with the knowledge of the individual items put into relationship. Given our knowledge of man and Socrates, it is likely that the statement "Socrates is a man" is a true statement. Given our knowledge of spoons and watermelons, it is unlikely that the statement "The spoon ate the watermelon" is true.

Aristotle also noted that a premise, or proposition, expresses a state of being. He defined ten categories of being. (See table 3.1.)

Aristotle's categories of being can also be interpreted as being human judgments concerning the state of being of something. His designation of categories of being were impactful on subsequent philosophers, such as Immanuel Kant. Kant stated that human knowledge is not simply a record of the contents of perception, it involves judgment regarding the nature of the content of the perception. In his philosophy, he begins with Aristotle's categories and derives his own. Any theory of human knowledge must address the nature of the relationship between items that are components or elements of that knowledge. Determining the nature of a relationship is an act of judgment. The kinds of relationships that humans can know and utilize in making these judgments is obviously a critical component of any theory of knowledge and learning. Aristotle's categories of being provides a beginning for this type of understanding and is a contribution to comprehending the nature of human knowledge. He was criticized by

Table 3.1

	CATEGORY OF BEING	EXAMPLE
1.	Substance	plant, tiger
2.	Quantity	three inches long
3.	Quality	blue, rough
4.	A relative	double, nephew
5.	Where	downtown, south of Athens
6.	When	yesterday, today
7.	Being in a position	standing, sitting
8.	Having	has a sword
9.	Acting on	cutting, separating
10.	Being an effect	being cut, being separated

subsequent philosophers for not having philosophically derived or justified these specific categories.

Amazingly, Aristotle's philosophic positions and explanations were not seriously challenged until the end of the sixteenth century. They held sway for almost two thousand years. Aristotle was the predominant influence on thought and intellectual enterprise on the European continent throughout the Middle Ages (Morton 2005). There were several reasons for this. One was the lack of competing philosophic systems of comparable depth and power to those of Plato and Aristotle. But perhaps the most important reason was the compatibility of Aristotle's philosophy with Christian doctrine. Beginning around AD 500, with the collapse of the Roman Empire, Christian (Catholic) faith became the dominant force in the evolution of social and political systems on the European continent. Those places where Aristotle's philosophy might have deviated from church doctrine were reinterpreted and brought into conformance by Catholic philosophers and theologians like Saint Augustine, in the fourth century, and St. Thomas Aquinas, in the thirteenth century. What prevailed in the Middle Ages, as Peter Morton (2005) states, was "an extensive science and philosophy based equally on common sense, Aristotelian principles, and Christian faith."

Modern Philosophy

The beginning of the end of Aristotle's intellectual reign over Western thought was the publication in 1543 of Copernicus's discovery that the Earth was in motion around the sun. In Aristotle's system, the Earth was at the center of the universe, with the moon, sun, planets, and stars revolving around it in circular orbits.

Aristotle's system of ascribing causality to the Form of objects was undermined by the Galileo's experiments in the sixteenth century. Galileo performed experiments and detailed studies of the motion of falling bodies, rolling balls, and pendulums. He demonstrated that these motions were the result of the interaction of the object with the force of gravity. The idea that phenomena in the universe were the result of the interaction of separate and distinct things began to replace Aristotle's notion that observed phenomena were strictly the consequence of the nature, or Form, of objects. Aristotle's system was entirely qualitative. Galileo, and then Isaac Newton, demonstrated that phenomena could be described and understood quantitatively. By performing experiments, measuring quantities, and relating them mathematically, the regularities manifest in the phenomena of the universe could be revealed and understood. Newton's development of three laws and a simple equation that accurately described the motion of objects had a profound impact on thinkers of his era. While the evolution of the modern paradigm, that the world and universe could be understood by applying logic, reason, and/or mathematics to careful observation and measurement of phenomena, can be attributed to the confluence of the work of several important thinkers, philosophers, scientists, and mathematicians, it is the work of Newton that provided the strongest justification for this viewpoint. As discussed previously, Aristotle is often called the "father of science." If we think in terms of modern science and how it is conducted, the title perhaps more appropriately belongs to Copernicus or Galileo.

By the end of the sixteenth century, the vacuous and circular nature of Aristotle's explanations was widely recognized. As Morton states,

> Critics of the Aristotelian method illustrated this point with the following rhetorical example. Followers of the Aristotelian method might explain how a sleeping powder achieves its result by claiming that it possesses "dormitive" qualities: that which is potentially asleep becomes actually asleep in the presence of these qualities. This claim is obviously true, but it doesn't help us understand how sleeping powders work. (Morton 2005, 44)

As we can see, Aristotle's system is missing two critical components of knowledge: an understanding of how and why the phenomena we experience occur.

Beginning with Galileo and continuing with René Descartes, Aristotle's theory of perception was undermined. Recall that Aristotle's thesis is that the soul literally takes on the Forms of objects in the world. The senses transfer the actual properties of objects to the soul. Both Galileo and Descartes conclude that the sensation, and subsequent perception, of the size, shape, solidity, and motion of objects is, in fact, an actual rendering of the physical properties of objects. However, both Galileo and Descartes contend that the sensations of touch, taste, smell, and sound do not render qualities that exist in the object being sensed and perceived.

Galileo uses the analogy of tickling. If we lightly run a feather or hand over our body, we will have the sensation of being tickled. He says that everyone understands that the sensation belongs to us and does not belong to the hand or the feather. If we run the feather or hand over a statute, no one believes that the motion produces the same tickling. Tickling, therefore, is not a property of the hand or feather, it is something that exists in the consciousness of the individual.

Both Descartes and Galileo understood sound to be the effect of the vibration of air particles causing the eardrum to vibrate. Descartes points out that if the ear produced a sensation that resembled the cause of the sensation, the sensation would be of the motion of air and not a sound. In summary, both Descartes and Galileo conclude that the sensations of touch, taste, smell, and sound are not, as Aristotle postulated, creations in the mind of the actual properties of objects but things that exist only in the consciousness of the individual experiencing the sensation (Morton 2005).

Descartes illustrates the interpretive nature of perception of sensory input with an example of a soldier who believes he is wounded in battle only to later realize that the sensation was brought about by a buckle under his armor. If the sense of touch produced a sensation identical to the cause of the sensation, there would be no such confusion.

Descartes ([1641] 1952) illustrates his interpretation of the relationship between the senses and perception through the example of perceiving a piece of wax. Descartes's wax is beeswax. He states that being fresh from the hive, it has the sweetness of the honey that it contains and the odor of the flowers from which it was derived. His vision renders it size, shape, and color. It is hard and cold to the touch, and when he taps it, it makes a distinctive sound. "All of the things which are requisite to cause us to distinctively recognize a body, are met within it" (80).

He then brings the wax to a fire, and it melts into a blob of liquid. All of its formerly sensible qualities, its smell, taste, and so forth, are now gone. It did not disappear; it is still the wax, albeit now a liquid blob with none of its formerly sensible qualities. It is nevertheless still the same object. To recognize that it is the same object cannot be rendered by the senses since its sensible qualities disappeared. He argues that it cannot be his imagination that tells him it is still the same object because the number of possible changes the wax could undertake would be infinite and hence unimaginable. This leaves only one alternative: knowledge of objects can only be through the intellect. The intellect, he states, is the faculty of judgment. He doesn't originally perceive the wax from sensory input, he judges and infers that it is wax from the input supplied by his senses. Descartes concludes that our ideas of the world do not come directly from the senses. We require our intellect to organize our myriad sensations into a coherent, structured depiction of the world (Morton 2005).

Descartes's conclusion does, however, create a philosophical problem. It implies the existence of innate, a priori ideas (knowledge) in the mind—ideas not derived from experience. If sensation provides merely the data on which the mind renders a judgment that results in the perception of something as a such and such, where does the idea or knowledge of a such and such come from? This difficulty led British philosopher John Locke to reject the notion of innate ideas and to develop a philosophic system known as empiricism, which postulates that all knowledge of the world must be derived from sensory experience.

I believe that the enduring portion of Descartes's argument is that conscious perception is a judgment. Descartes ([1641] 1952) also describes a situation where he peers out of his window and sees hats and coats. He judges that he must be seeing men. He points out that it could, in fact, be hats and coats on automatic machines instead. It was solely through the faculty of judgment that he thought that what he saw was men.

This idea is important to the field of education. Teachers implicitly presume that students will perceive what they want them to perceive in educational representations like pictures, diagrams, models, and graphs. However concepts may originate, which will be examined subsequently, they do affect and control what is consciously perceived. This means that what someone is perceiving is determined by their prior knowledge and experience. In the next chapter, I present an example where a teacher wishes students to perceive that the molecules of a gas in a heated balloon are moving faster than the molecules in a balloon that has not been heated. The diagram illustrates this using a vector representation for velocity. The arrows drawn from the molecules in the heated balloon are longer than the arrows drawn from molecules in the unheated balloon. If students do not have the concept of a vector representation in their inventory of knowledge, they will not perceive what the teacher wishes them to perceive nor make the subsequent desired judgment that the molecules in the heated balloon are moving faster.

Philosopher Hilary Putnam (1975), in analyzing the philosophic notion of intentionality—the idea that conscious thoughts are always about something (have a subject)—comes to an analogous conclusion. Putnam asks the reader to consider an ant moving through sand, who creates a pattern in the sand that is a likeness of Winston Churchill. The ant did not intend to create an image of Churchill nor does the ant have prior knowledge of Churchill to guide the creation of such an image. The image is perceived to be that of Winston Churchill only to humans who have prior experience and knowledge of Winston Churchill and his appearance. Similarly, Putnam asks the reader to consider a tribe of people who live in a desert and who have never seen a tree. A picture of a tree flies out of the cargo hold of an airplane flying over the tribe. The mental image of the picture formed by a member of the tribe who finds it and the mental image formed by a person with prior knowledge of trees is the same. However, the image is meaningless to the tribespeople, whereas to the person with experience and prior knowledge of trees, the image represents a tree. Putnam concludes that mental images and representations do not intrinsically refer to anything. If there is a relationship of reference, it is because of a prior interaction between the mental image, or representation, and something in the world—a relationship of cause and effect.

From Putnam's work, for the current purpose of analyzing the nature of perception, we can also conclude that perceiving something as a such and such requires prior experience and knowledge of the such and such. We can additionally stretch Putnam's conclusion to imply that this conceptual knowledge must be a construction from prior experience.

Experience as the basis of knowledge was the central premise of Locke's philosophy. Locke argues against the existence of innate ideas by pointing out that if there were innate ideas, then everyone would be in possession of them. However, people think differently, and some would not assent to the ideas Descartes proposes to be innate. In addition, people have no intuitive awareness of the principles that rationalists such as Descartes and Leibniz claim to be innate until they are taught those principles (Scott-Kakures et al. 1993). Locke ([1689] 1959) begins with the assertion that the mind is a blank slate, or tabula rasa. The worldly empirical experience of the individual is written on this blank slate. It is empirical experience that is the source of our ideas, and we can think only in terms of those ideas. Locke's use of the term *idea* conforms to the modern concept of perception or percept, rather than to the modern sense of idea as a synonym for concept. Locke states that there are two sources for ideas: sensations, which are the source of our ideas concerning the external world, and reflection, which gives us ideas of the operation of our minds on sense ideas.

Locke subdivides ideas into simple ideas and complex ideas. Locke's simple ideas are the sensorially derived attributes and characteristics of objects. He further subdivides simple ideas into qualities of objects derived directly from sense perception—like size, shape, solidity, and motion—and secondary qualities, like taste, odor, sound, and temperature. Consistent with the conclusions of Galileo and Descartes, Locke asserts that the primary qualities resemble and are the real properties of objects, while the secondary qualities exist only in our consciousness. Our perception of objects is of a collection of attributes and characteristics of the specific entity. Locke calls these collective perceptions complex ideas. To Locke, *complex ideas* are simply a combination of simple ideas. For example, our complex idea of a swan is something with white color, long neck, orange beak, black legs, a certain size and shape, webfeet, the specific noise it makes, and the power of swimming (Scott-Kakures et al. 1993).

How do objects create the sensations that we experience and that form the basis of our ideas of the world? In keeping with the scientific viewpoint of his time, Locke attributes causality in the material world to mechanical interaction. He adopts the viewpoint of the time that objects consist of tiny particles called *corpuscles*. Corpuscles have only primary qualities and affect each other and other objects by mechanical means alone (through motion/impulse). Our sensations are explained as the actions of the corpuscles of an object on our sense organs. Primary qualities are the direct action of the corpuscles, while secondary qualities reflect the particular configuration and collective interaction of corpuscles acting on our sense organs. For example, the sense of the red color of an apple is the result of the particular way the corpuscles of the apple are interacting and affecting the eyes. Obviously, today we have a better scientific understanding of sensation. Locke's theory was consistent with the science of his time. It was not philosophically derived; it was scientifically borrowed.

Why do we have an idea (perception) of objects rather than a random assortment of sensations? To answer this question, Locke invokes the concept of substance, a concept originated by Aristotle. Substance is the substratum wherein the properties of objects subsist and from which they result. For example, an apple is not just roundness and redness but a substance in which roundness and redness subsist. Under this model, a substance composed of corpuscles gives rise to sensations through their interaction with sense organs.

Locke attributes the formation of concepts from ideas (perceptions) to a faculty of the mind that operates on ideas. It is the faculty of abstraction, or determining what is common to ideas of particulars. The mind has the capacity to collect ideas or real existences into categories that share similar patterns of qualities. He states that this gives rise to words. Words can either express the abstraction of simple ideas, like white or solid, or they can represent the abstraction of complex ideas, like swan or dog.

He uses his theory of words to assail metaphysics. Locke states that what metaphysicians present as knowledge is simply something verbal. All existing things are particulars, but we can frame general ideas through abstraction that are applicable to many particulars and to these ideas associate names. Their generality is attributable to the fact that they are applicable to many particulars. However, as concepts in our mind, they are just as particular as anything else that exists; they are words. He also assails the metaphysical idea of essence as being something with a distinct existence and with causal powers—the power to make things what they are. He states that distinct categories are not a fact of nature but a consequence of the nature of language. There are different things in nature, but the differences proceed by continuous gradations, and the boundaries of the categories by which humankind sorts objects are the creation and invention of mankind (Russell 1945). This idea was expressed in the twentieth century by Gregory Bateson ([1979] 2002, 35), who asserted that "the division of the perceived universe into parts and holes is convenient and may be necessary, but no necessity dictates how it shall be done." Einstein ([1949] 1979) expressed the same idea when he asserted that all concepts are freely chosen posits.

To explain our knowledge of causality, Locke uses the concept of power. He states that power is the ability to bring about change in the state of objects. We understand power by observing effects and forming an idea of some change in the state of objects. Changes brought about by physical objects, which he calls *passive power*, he attributes to the transfer of motion from one object to another. This is consistent with the science of his time. Another form of power, which he terms *active power*, is the power of the mind, through the will and intellect, to change the state of objects. An example of this power would be the thought that causes you to raise your hand to reach for an object.

Locke must also account for knowledge gained through reason. For Locke, the mind has no object of consideration but its own ideas—it is only conversant about ideas. Knowledge obtained through reason is then the agreement or disagreement of ideas. We can expand on Locke's conclusion by noting that since abstract ideas (concepts), represented by words, are formed through the abstraction of simple and complex ideas, knowledge obtained through reason is additionally the agreement or disagreement of concepts or abstract ideas.

Locke's empirical philosophy was revolutionary in its time. Prior philosophies were rationalist in nature. For example, consider Leibniz's assertion that true knowledge was the logically necessary consequences of two intuitively known principles and Descartes's postulation of innate concepts placed in the mind by God. As for enduring contributions to the theory of knowledge, I believe we can credit Locke with the following:

- Positing idea of perception as a foundational source of knowledge about the world
- Articulating the relationship between the abstraction of perceptions and words
- Suggesting that the nature of knowledge has something to do with the nature of language
- Developing the idea that reason was the agreement or disagreement of ideas and, by extension, the agreement or disagreement of concepts

Eighteenth-century British philosopher David Hume inherited the empirical philosophy of Locke and took it to its logical limits. In keeping with his predecessor, he asserts that all knowledge is derived from experience. He categorizes the elements, or atoms, of knowing into impressions, simple ideas, complex ideas, and general ideas (Russell 1945).

Impressions are images of the world that are impressed on the mind by sensory input. Thoughts such as "the object is cold," "the object is blue," or "the object makes a noise," or any reported immediate sensory experience are the impression that the object makes on the individual. Simple ideas are remembrances, or what today we would call memories, of the impressions created by direct experience. Hume states that these remembrances are less vivid than the original impressions. In keeping with the premise of empiricism, Hume asserts that all simple ideas must be derived from impressions. The same can be said of his next category, complex ideas. Complex ideas are combinations of simple ideas. Hume points out that complex ideas need not resemble the objects that gave rise to simple ideas. For example, the idea of a unicorn is the combination of the idea of a horse and a horn. The unicorn does not exist, but the idea of the unicorn can be analyzed into simpler ideas (horn/horse) that, in fact, do exist and have been experienced.

Hume gives words a limited role. For Hume, words are merely signs or designators for the idea the word is associated with. The meaning of the word is the content of the associated idea. Hume's last category is general ideas. These are said to represent the collection of particulars (ideas) annexed to a word. General ideas make us recall other particulars that are similar in nature. Hume's definition here is consistent with the practice of most philosophers, beginning with Aristotle, to avoid Plato's idea of a concept as something that has a separate existence by relegating a concept to a word that has universal applicability to a group of particulars sharing similar attributes.

Having defined the elements of knowing, Hume addresses the operations of the mind on those elements. He asserts that the mind creates relationships between ideas and defines seven types of relationship:

1. Identity

2. Space and time

3. Causation

4. Resemblance (similarity)

5. Contrariety (difference)

6. Degrees in quality

7. Proportion in quantity or number

Hume's relationships among ideas have the same sense as Aristotle's categories. Both can be understood as judgments the mind makes with regard to the content of ideas, a construct the philosopher Kant also used in his theory of knowledge.

Hume defines resemblance as the process whereby a current impression reminds someone of previously experienced impressions/ideas because it is similar in content; it resembles the prior experience. Causation is the process, or, as Hume subsequently contends, the habit of mind of noting the relationship that some event of experience B seems to always follow a preceding event A. For example, when someone stands near a fire, they get warm, or if a billiard ball strikes another billiard ball, the struck ball will move. In both cases, the mind makes the judgment that the first event "caused" the second event.

Hume recognizes two types of reasoning. The first he defines as the *relation of ideas*. Ideas are related in a proposition whose truth can be ascertained by inspecting the ideas involved in the relationship. He maintains that the truth or falsity of such propositions can be determined a priori, or before experience. This would, for example be a proposition like "a square has four sides" or "3 + 5 = 8." The truth of the proposition is determined by inspecting the meaning or content of the ideas associated with the terms. The modern interpretation of this type of reasoning is deductive reasoning using formal logic. This type of reasoning does not produce new knowledge of the world; it produces what necessarily follows from the ideas or premises put into relationship.

Hume's second category of reasoning is determining *matters of fact*. The truth of matters of fact is determined by inspecting the world to see if it is the case. The proposition, for example, that "the box is heavy" can be determined by lifting it. The truth of the proposition or proposed relationship is determined a posteriori, after the experience. The truth cannot be determined by simply inspecting the meaning or content of the ideas associated with the terms (box/heavy). Such knowing does not involve the idea of contradiction. It could be the case that the box was not heavy. This is not a contradiction but a different "matter of fact."

Hume stays true to his theory of knowledge and subsequently deducts conclusions that are both counterintuitive and problematic for other philosophers, such as Immanuel Kant. Consistent with Hume's theory, causal knowledge must be a matter of fact; it can never be a priori necessary truth discovered through reasoning alone. Science, for example, involves conducting experiments to provide evidence for a hypothesis. How many experiments are necessary and sufficient? It is possible that the next experiment could produce a different outcome. Science and necessary causality rely on the assumption that the future will resemble the past. What in experience justifies this assumption? Hume states that there is nothing in empirical experience to justify this assumption; the course of nature could change. What is in experience is the matter of fact that some event B always seems to follow some event A. Causality then is simply the habit of mind or the custom of associating two events that follow each other in time. Science as necessary causal knowledge is, therefore, not possible.

Prior philosophers, such as Locke, associated causality with the concept of power. Recall that Locke postulated two forms of power: the passive power of objects to transfer motion to other objects, and the active power of the mind to generate thoughts and move parts of the body. Hume discounts the idea of power in the same way he discounted causal necessity; it is not to be found in the impressions formed by experience. He uses the billiard ball example. He states that if we look for an impression of power in the motion of a billiard ball, we will not find it; we will only find the impression of motion. Additionally, we find nothing in our impression of the motion that tells us that when the billiard ball impacts another billiard ball, it will cause it to move. What is in our impressions is that one event simply follows another; we do not have an impression of necessary connection, only the experience of the conjunction of the events. It is possible to conceive that something else could occur.

As for Locke's concept of active power, Hume states that since we have no impression of how the mind produces the movement of the body or generates thoughts, we must dismiss the idea of active power. Similarly, he dismisses the idea of substance. We have no impression of substance, only an impression of the qualities of objects produced by the senses.

Note that when Hume defines his category of reasoning called *relation of ideas* as he does, it yields the logically necessary conclusion that we cannot justifiably have concepts of substance or power or the concept that a certain effect is the necessary consequence of a certain cause. These are very counterintuitive conclusions because humans do, in fact, have and use these concepts. For example, a Little League baseball player, with no knowledge of philosophy or physics, believes that the ball being thrown at him and the bat he is holding are substances. His senses inform him that the ball is white, solid, and round and moving toward him, but he understands that these are attributes and characteristics of the substance that inhere in the ball. To him, the ball is not just a collection of sensible qualities, it is some substance that has these qualities. The baseball player also believes he knows that swinging the bat will give it the "power" to propel the ball forward when it impacts the ball. Given his experience, you'll never convince him that the bat didn't "cause" the ball to propel forward and that the ball propelling forward was not a necessary consequence of the action he undertook.

Hume's philosophic system has the general problem of accounting for concepts that humans have that are not directly obtainable from the content of impressions or simple ideas that are the memories of those impressions. Empiricism, in general, has the problem that it assumes that mental representations (for example, impressions) derive from sensations that have causes, and that these representations resemble their causes. We experience sensations but not their causes. Our experience would be the same if sensations arose spontaneously without cause. The foundational principle on which empiricism is based must be assumed, therefore, independent of experience; it is not contained within the content of mental representations (impressions/ideas) (Russell 1945).

Kant stated that Hume's philosophy woke him from his dogmatic slumber. He found his attack on rationalism persuasive and liberating but was disturbed by its consequences (Scott-Kakures et al. 1993). In one work, Hume eliminates the possibility of religion, science, and metaphysics based on reason (Russell 1945). The problems Kant saw with the empirical philosophy of Locke and Hume led him to the conclusion that there must be some innate concepts known a priori, before experience, that are apodeictic—necessarily true independent of sense experience. He undertook what was, in effect, a reconciliation of rationalism and empiricism. To do so, he had to demonstrate the possibility and necessity of innate knowledge of this character.

Modern scholars have placed rationalism into three categories based on the thesis on which specific forms of rationalism rest (*Stanford Encyclopedia of Philosophy* 2021). The first is the intuition/deduction thesis: some propositions are known by intuition and others are knowable by being deduced from intuition. Leibniz belongs to this school of thought. He asserted that we know by intuition the principle of contradiction, something cannot both be *p* and not be *p*, and the principle of sufficient reason, everything has a cause. From these two intuitive propositions, true and necessary knowledge about the world can be obtained deductively using formal logic. Leibniz contended that the senses give us knowledge of particular or individual truths, or states of affairs, but they do not give us the whole of it or general truths that have the character of necessary truth because what has happened before will not necessarily happen again.

The second category of rationalism is the innate knowledge thesis: we have knowledge of some truths by our nature. Descartes falls into this school of thought. As discussed previously, his theory of the nature of perception moves him in this direction. Descartes hypothesizes three types of ideas: (1) adventitious ideas derived from sensation, like the sensation of heat; (2) invented ideas that are created from other ideas, like the idea of a unicorn; (3) and innate ideas like God, extension, and substance. Descartes states that God places innate ideas in our mind at birth (*Stanford Encyclopedia of Philosophy* 2021).

The intuition/deduction thesis has the problem of accounting for what intuition is and how we can be certain that it provides justified true belief. The innate knowledge thesis has the problem of accounting for the source of innate knowledge and, as pointed out by Locke, it has the problem that not everyone is in possession of the knowledge contended to be innate. For example, children do not accept that the same thing cannot both be and not be (*Stanford Encyclopedia of Philosophy* 2021).

Kant had a formidable task to reconcile empiricism and rationalism given the philosophical problems of each system. His conclusion was that certain knowledge must exist prior to experience in order for there to be the possibility of perception and knowledge derived through reason. As such, his philosophy falls into the third category of rationalism, the innate concept thesis: some concepts we employ are part of our rational nature.

Kant's ([1781] 1990) theory of knowledge is developed in his *Critique of Pure Reason*, published in 1781, a book considered to be one of the greatest works of philosophy ever published. He received very little response to his book and was highly disappointed. The problem was that his contemporaries simply did not comprehend it. His arguments are exceedingly complex and lengthy, and he uses unconventional word meanings. For example, he calls the section of the book that begins his derivation of the necessary conditions for the possibility of intuitions the "Transcendental Esthetic." By transcendental, he means transcending in the sense of both beyond and before. The meaning of esthetic, as used in this title, is "sense or feeling," which is an ancient etymological meaning (Durant [1926] 1961). A more comprehensible title for this section would have been "Before Sense." Because of the lack of response to his work, Kant ([1783] 1950) wrote the *Prolegomena to Any Future Metaphysics* in 1783. The *Prolegomena* is a summary of the main arguments of the *Critique*, with examples, which Kant felt would be more comprehensible to his contemporaries. The summaries of Kant's theory that I will present primarily come from the *Prolegomena* and from Scott-Kakures et al.'s (1993) interpretation of the *Prolegomena*.

Part of Kant's goal with the *Critique* was to refute the results of Hume's work that he found problematic. To facilitate the ability to compare his work with that of Hume's, he defined and distinguished two types of judgments. The first he termed *analytic*. An analytic judgment expresses nothing in the predicate that is not already contained in the subject. An example of this type of judgment would be the statement "The bachelor will not have a wife at the party." The truth of this statement is guaranteed by the meaning and content of the concept "bachelor." This type of judgment, therefore, produces necessary conclusions, the type rendered by formal logic. Kant's analytic judgments correspond to Hume's "relation of ideas."

Kant called his second type of judgment *synthetic judgments*. A synthetic judgment is amplicative; more information is contained in the predicate than is contained in the subject. An example of this type of judgment is the statement "The box is heavy." The truth of this statement is contingent upon how the world, in this case the box, happens to be. We would have to have the experience of lifting the box to know if it's true. This type of judgment corresponds to Hume's matters of fact. It is knowledge gained through experience of the world, or a posteriori (after experience) knowledge. Analytic truths, in contrast, can be known a priori (before experience). We don't have to go to the party to know that the bachelor will not have a wife with him. Note that denying the truth of an analytic judgment involves a contradiction, while denying a synthetic judgment does not. The bachelor having a wife at the party would contradict the concept of a bachelor. The box could be heavy or not. We won't know until we lift it. To deny that it is heavy before we lift it does not involve a contradiction. It is in this sense that an analytic judgment is universally necessary, whereas a synthetic judgment is not—things could be otherwise.

Using Kant's definitions, Hume's general principles can be summarized as follows (Scott-Kakures et al. 1993):

1. Only analytic truths are capable of being established before experience (a priori).

2. No necessary and universal truth can be established by experience (a posteriori).

Kant agrees with principle 2, the contingent nature of experiential learning. He, therefore, does not dispute Hume's contention that concepts like causality and substance cannot be directly derived from the contents of experience. Humans do, in fact, have these concepts, so they must be innate and a priori. In addition, these concepts are synthetic. The judgment of causality is that every effect has a cause, and the judgment of substance is that the attributes and characteristics we sense come from some source we can call a substance. Since these two concepts are innate and not contingent upon experience, and they express synthetic judgments, they constitute synthetic a priori judgments. Kant, therefore, disagrees with principle 1. His task is to prove the existence of synthetic a priori judgments such as those in the preceding examples. He goes a step further and presents arguments that synthetic a priori judgments are not only possible but also necessary for there to be the possibility of intuitions, perceptions, and reason.

Kant's general argumentative process is referred to today as *Kantian logic*. He asked the question: What must be the case for the result or outcome to be such as it is? This is the kind of logic a detective would utilize to solve a crime. The detective looks at the evidence and then constructs a theory as to what had to transpire to produce the evidence that he or she has. Similarly, a scientist whose experiment fails to justify his beginning hypothesis asks, in Kantian fashion, What theory or principle would explain the outcomes the experiment produced? The philosopher Charles Sanders Peirce would later define this type of reasoning method as abduction. Kant asked the questions: What must be the case for there to be the possibility of intuition, perception, and reasoning, and what must inhere for them to be such as they are?

Before continuing this discussion, a clarification of terminology is in order. What is initially presented to the mind that becomes a perception or a conclusion upon the application of a judgment is termed an *intuition* by Kant. This corresponds to Hume's impression. The modern term for this from neuroscience is mental *image* or *representation*. You can experience what is being referred to by these terms if you eliminate all your conscious thoughts by silencing your inner speech and then looking around the room you are in. What you are experiencing is Kant's intuition or Hume's impression. If you reactivate your conscious thought, you might make a "judgment" regarding the contents of your intuition, like "I see a cup on a table." In the language of neuroscience, the image (intuition) is subconscious, and the recognition of specific objects is a conscious judgment of the contents of the image (intuition) that is called a *perception*.

To demonstrate the existence of synthetic a priori judgments, Kant uses the example of mathematics. Everyone in Kant's time would agree that mathematics consists of analytic truths that are not contingent upon experience. There is no possibility, for example, that you will ever have an experience that contradicts the fact that $7 + 5 = 12$. Kant invites the reader, in the *Prolegomena*, to examine the addition of $7 + 5$ in the manner that Hume describes as the *relation of ideas*, which renders, in Kant's vocabulary, analytic, universally necessary truths. He states that no matter how long you inspect the intuitions of 5 and 7, you will not find anything that tells you that their sum will equal 12. In other words, you cannot discover 12 just by thinking about the numbers 5 and 7. To arrive at this conclusion, you must go beyond the concepts of 5 and 7 and use empirical intuitions like fingers, stones, or the beads of an abacus. You count 5 of those objects and then continue counting 7 more to arrive at the conclusion that $7 + 5 = 12$. Analysis of the concepts does not suffice, there must be an appeal to intuition derived from experience. In similar fashion, Kant asks the reader to perform the same exercise with a triangle. It is a priori necessarily true that the sum of the enclosed angles of a triangle is 180°. He states that no matter how long you think about the intuition (image) of the triangle, all you will discern is that it consists of three straight lines and three angles. There is nothing in the intuition or image of a triangle that tells you that the sum of its interior angles equals 180°.

Kant then asks how knowledge derived from experiential intuitions, like counting to conclude that $7 + 5 = 12$, can be knowledge that is necessary and universally a priori? He concludes that the only possible way is that what is derived from the empirical intuition be confined to features of the intuition given to us a priori. In other words, for judgment to be a priori, the concepts applied to the intuitions must be given to us before experience; they must be innate.

The appeal to experiential intuition, such as that in the arithmetic example, was not concerned with the contents or semantic features of the specific intuition, only with the "form" of the intuition to preserve universal necessary status. The conclusion that 7 + 5 = 12 did not depend on whether someone used fingers, stones, or beads to count. They were using the semantic-free formal features of these different entities. It was not an appeal to anything specific to fingers, stones, and beads; it was an appeal to what was common to, invariant in, and part of all three—their form or formal features.

Kant concludes that another condition that is required to preserve the necessary and universal character of this knowledge derived from these experiential intuitions is that these formal features themselves be necessary and universal. This is only possible if they are a requirement for the possibility of intuitions themselves—conditions imposed on all intuitions. Kant states that these forms anticipate experience and anything that is intuited will conform to the conditions imposed by the forms. Conformance to the forms is a necessary condition for all possible intuitions.

What are these necessary and universal forms of intuition? Kant says that if we stripped from intuitions of objects and phenomena everything belonging to sensations, what remains is space and time. Therefore, to be intuited as an external thing, something must be intuited as situated in space and time.

Locke and Hume are silent with respect to the question of how the manifold of our sensory input gets organized to produce the unified intuitions that we experience. Kant's answer to "what must be the case" for all our sensory data to congeal into the organized unities we experience in intuition is that they be organized with respect to space and time. These forms are the concepts necessary for this organization. They are innate and prior to experience and are required for the possibility of intuitions being such as they are. Without them, we would experience only a jumble of disorganized sensations.

Kant states that math reflects the formal features of space and time. The formal features of the mathematics of numbers are codified in the progression of time. For example, the number line 1 . . . 2 . . . 3 conforms to the form of time. In similar fashion, the formal features of space are codified in geometry. We can, therefore, be sure that experience will never give us counterexamples to the arithmetic and geometric judgments we establish a priori. It is in this sense that mathematics is a priori. With the foregoing argument, Kant appears to have refuted Hume's first principle.

Kant states that his conclusion comes with a big caveat. He states that nothing can be known independent of its being a possible object of intuition; we cannot know objects as they are in themselves. We can only know them as they appear to us in intuitions. This implies that knowledge is subjective and contingent upon the nature of the knower. This conclusion was to have a profound impact on subsequent philosophy coming from the continent of Europe and was to move philosophy in a completely different direction after Kant. More on that later.

Let us examine the idea of "thing in itself" in more detail. In Kant's time, he could examine the world only at a human scale. Today we have the technical capacity to examine the world and its contents at different scales. Let's consider a flower. We get an intuition and subsequent perception of the flower at a human scale. Now let's get into a hot-air balloon. At some height, the flower becomes a small dot of color. At a greater height, it disappears as a separate entity and simply blends into the landscape. Now let's examine it at increasingly smaller scales. The petal of the flower becomes a collection of cells, then a collection of molecules, and then a collection of atoms with electrons, protons, and neutrons. Which of these is the thing in itself? It appears that the answer is contingent upon the scale at which we examine and experience the flower.

Contemporary philosopher Daniel Dennett (2013) states that every organism has a set of things in the world that are important to it. Those things that matter constitute the ontology of things that exist for the organism and those things that the organism needs to discern and anticipate if the organism is to survive and carry out its functions. He invokes the German word *Umwelt*, which is the world around the organism that it must keep track of to do its job. The organism's *Umwelt* is its manifest image, or the world as it seems to the organism given its sensory and perceptual capability. Does an ant need to know the difference between a stationary automobile and an office building? No, those things are both simply obstructions in the path of the ant. A human, however, needs to know the difference. Each organism evolved capabilities shaped by the contingencies of its environmental circumstances—capabilities required to survive and "do its job."

It is apparent then that the "thing itself" is contingent upon what organism is experiencing the thing and at what scale the thing is being experienced. If we could sense and perceive at the scale of atoms, we would experience a different thing than what we experience at the human scale. If we had the sensory and perceptual apparatus of lizards, we would also experience a different thing. It is apparent that the "thing in itself" as some universal, independent, separate existence independent of the sensing and perceiving entity does not exist in the physical world. It is a unicorn, a conception without a real physical instantiation. The sense that Kant implies for "the thing in itself" is, therefore, an apparition we need not concern ourselves with.

For Kant, the concepts of space and time organize the myriad manifold of sensory information into intuitions. The next question is how the myriad manifold of intuitions gets organized into the thoughts, ideas, and concepts we experience in our minds. He notes that intuitions immediately come under some form of judgment in our minds. For example, the judgment that something in our intuition is a such and such. Kant says that a judgment like "something is a chair" requires two conditions to be met. First, that something (chair) must be presented to the senses and result in an intuition organized with respect to space and time. Second, the mind must apply a judgment to the content of the intuition; in this case, the judgment that the content is a substance that falls under the category/class of "chair." The concept of "chair" being the collection of objects with similar attributes and characteristics that are referred to with the word *chair*.

As Scott-Kakures et al. (1993, 267) interpret Kant, to experience a chair is not to just passively register the shape, color, and so forth in an intuition, rather it is to judge the chair "to be an enduring physical object (substance) in space and time with certain determinate characteristics, standing in various determinate objective relations to other objects."

To claim knowledge about a particular (object/action), we need to form a judgment concerning the particular. Kant calls this faculty the *faculty of understanding*. Kant's answer to the question of how the myriad manifold of intuitional content morphs into the organized thoughts, ideas, and concepts we experience is that we have innate, a priori concepts (judgments) like substance and causality that facilitate and enable the organization. The statement "every effect has a cause" is not an analytic judgment. It contains something in the predicate beyond what is in the subject.

Kant also concludes that for something to be an object of judgment, it must conform to the "form" of the judgment. He asks us to consider the possibility of experiencing something uncaused and having no causal effect on anything else. It cannot be solid and take up space, because that would produce the effect of preventing other objects from taking up the space that it occupies. It wouldn't be capable of causal interaction with our senses, so it would be invisible. How then could it be something we experience and then claim knowledge of? His answer is that first it must conform to the forms required to be an object of intuition (space and time), and then it must conform to the formal organizing concepts that Kant calls the categories of judgment. Satisfying these conditions is a necessary condition for an experienced phenomenon to be a possible object of judgment.

The next obvious questions are, What are these formal categories of judgment and where do they come from? Kant agrees with Hume that categories of judgment cannot come from experience-derived intuitions. These are simply spatiotemporally organized associative groupings of sensory information. Categories of judgment must, therefore, be innate because they are necessary for the possibility of any kind of judgment.

Since categories of judgment are not derived from experience, they, like the pure forms of intuition, must not be contingent upon the specific content or semantic features of experience. In Kant's terminology, they must be "pure forms of judgment" that can accommodate all possible semantic features of the objects of experience. Satisfaction of all the criteria and requirements Kant imposes on the pure categories of judgment leads him to the conclusion that they must be the judgments facilitated by the forms of formal logic. Formal logic is independent of the content and semantic features of the items put into relationship. The truth of a conclusion is guaranteed by the syntax of the logic, not by the semantic content of things put into relationship. If one thing is indeed contingent upon another—if P, then Q—it does not matter whether "if P, then Q" is "If it is raining, then the streets will be wet" or "If it has wings, then it can fly."

It is the independence from semantic content and the necessity of the truth obtained from formal logic that has made it the preference and focus of thinkers from Aristotle to Leibniz to Kant to Piaget and to others, continuing into the twenty-first century. These features have caused these thinkers to hypothesize that the mind embeds, and thinking reflects, the principles and structures of formal logic. The results of modern cognitive science, however, indicate precisely the opposite. They indicate that thought is influenced by the content, the meaning, or, in other words, the semantics of the material being contemplated (Reisberg 2010). Obviously, this science was not available to Kant. His hypothesis allowed him to produce a coherent theory and body of philosophy that was self-consistent.

Kant's pure forms of logical judgment are shown in the table 3.2.

Table 3.2

CATEGORY	JUDGMENTS		
Quantity	Universal	Particular	Singular
Quality	Affirmative	Negative	Infinite
Relation	Categorical	Hypothetical	Disjunctive
Modality	Problematical	Assertoric	Apodictic

Examples:

- Quantity universal judgment: all As are Bs
- Quantity particular judgment: some As are B
- Quantity singular judgment: this A is a B
- Relation categorical judgment: Cs are Ds
- Relation hypothetical judgment: if P, then Q
- Relation disjunctive judgment: As are either Bs or Cs

- Quality affirmative judgment: As are Bs
- Quality negative judgment: no As are Bs
- Quality infinite judgment: As are non-Bs
- Modality problematic judgment: possibly, As are Bs
- Modality assertoric judgment: actually, As are Bs
- Modality apodictic judgment: necessarily, As are Bs

From these logical judgments, Kant derives his categories of judgment, shown in table 3.3.

Table 3.3

CATEGORY	JUDGMENTS		
Quantity	Unity	Plurality	Totality
Quality	Reality	Negation	Limitation
Relation	Substance	Causality	Community
Modality	Possibility	Existence	Necessity

From the logical judgment of **relation**, Kant straightforwardly derives that categorical judgments are judgments of **substance**: something in which the contents of intuition inhere and subsist. **Hypothetical judgments** are interpreted to be judgments of **cause and effect**. And **disjunctive judgments** he calls judgments of **community**, or how a collection of objects might relate to one another. For example, they might relate in the sense that something, call it C, can affect either A or B. Isaac Newton's judgment that for every action there is an equal and opposite reaction would be a judgment that fits into this category.

Categories of **modality** are sometimes confused for dispositional attitudes toward beliefs, as in, you feel that something is possibly the case, probably the case, or definitely the case. They are actually logical constructs, as in, there is a **possible** world in which something could be true or the case, something is true and is the case in the **world we live in**, or something is true and is the case in all possible worlds we can conceive of; it is **necessarily** true (*Stanford Encyclopedia of Philosophy* 2022).

Judgments of **quantity** that express **unity** are judgments that something is the case or true for a singular particular. This type of judgment expresses the **unity** of the particular with something, for example, "This item is a ball." The judgment of quantity expressing **plurality** would be the judgment that something is the case for a group of items, as in, "Some of these items are balls." The category of quantity expressing **totality** is the judgment that something is the case for all members of a group, as in, "All of these items are balls." Note that these judgments presuppose that one has delimited the group of things judged.

Judgments of **quality** are judgments of presence, absence, or contingent presence. A judgment of **reality** would be an affirmative judgment that something is present in an intuition; it is a judgment of identification. A judgment of quality-**negation** is a judgment that something is absent. A judgment of quality-**limitation** is a judgment expressing qualification, like A is present until B and absent after B. Note that these categories are not completely independent of one another and that some presuppose others.

Now let us apply Kant's categories of judgment to an intuition that contains a chair. The judgment of quantity-unity would render that the chair is a singular item: **this** item. The judgment of quality-reality would render the judgment that the chair is in the intuition: **this** item **is**. The judgment of relation-substance would render that the chair is a substance: **this** item **is a substance**. The judgment of modality-existence would render that the chair exists in the world that we live in: **this** item **is a substance** that **exists**. So far, we have a singular item in an intuition that is a substance that exists in the world. We do not have the judgment that it is a chair. To judge something in intuition to be a chair requires the capacity to organize the contents of intuitions into classes and categories of substances that share similar semantic features or specific sensorially derived attributes, characteristics, and relationships among those attributes and characteristics. It requires a semantic-feature processor, a capacity that Locke calls the *faculty of abstraction*. Kant is silent regarding this faculty. He must be for his philosophic system to remain coherent and logically consistent. Recall that his concepts of space and time, a priori and necessary for the possibility of intuition, are pure "forms" independent of the semantic content of experience. His categories of judgment, a priori and necessary for the possibility of judgment and reason, are the "forms" of formal logic independent of the semantic content of experience. To postulate a mechanism contingent upon the specific content of experience (semantic features) would undermine the premises of his arguments and render his philosophic system incoherent. This presents us with a problem that we will have to solve by other means.

Epistemologists often apply two criteria when evaluating the truth of theories: coherence and correspondence. *Coherence* is the requirement that the system of beliefs be such that they do not produce any contradictions; the system of beliefs must be consistent within itself; some beliefs cannot contradict others. The system of formal logic, for example, is coherent. Noddings (2012) points out that historians have revised many historical "facts" because they contradicted a body of accepted and firmly established beliefs. The "fact" was incoherent with and contradicted other more firmly established "facts." The revision of the incoherent "fact" was necessary to produce a coherent rendering of history.

As Noddings also points out, coherence alone cannot be the sole criteria for rendering a body of knowledge or a set of beliefs that are true. The body of knowledge must also *correspond* with "states of affairs," or the facts rendered by experience of the world. Einstein ([1949] 1979) states that while concepts are freely chosen, posits and theories are human constructs, their validity (truth) is dependent on how they conform to experimental outcomes: states of affairs—experiential configurations of objects and events. He expresses the general thesis of modern science with this statement. In the field of physics, Einstein's general theory of relativity is a coherent theory that corresponds with experimental outcomes when applied to large objects like planets. Quantum mechanics is a coherent theory that corresponds with experimental outcomes when applied to very small objects like electrons. The problem for physics is that general relativity and quantum mechanics are incoherent with each other. Modern theoretical physicists, therefore, have embarked on a journey to find a "theory of everything" that combines these two theories into a single coherent theory of the physics of the universe.

The task of this chapter is to find a theory of knowledge that is both coherent within itself and correspondent with states of affairs, like the experimental results of cognitive science. Writing in 1945, philosopher Bertrand Russell (1945) states that no philosopher in history has ever produced a philosophic system that is both completely coherent and correspondent. He also states that philosophy never resolves anything definitively, rather it renders what could not possibly be the case. In keeping with Russell's thesis, we will have to look elsewhere—at results from cognitive science and nonlinear systems theory and work backward in Kantian fashion to derive a theory of knowledge that is both coherent and correspondent. In addition to what Russell states, philosophy frames the conversation and identifies the concepts (variables) and relationships germane to an intellectual quest or inquiry. I believe that philosophy has provided us with a good context in which to evaluate results from cognitive science and nonlinear systems theory.

With Kant, we have brought our philosophic discussion of the nature of knowledge to the beginning of the nineteenth century. His work was profound in its time. Nineteenth-century philosophers could neither improve on Kant's work nor competently dispute it. Instead, they moved in a different direction. Philosophers on the continent of Europe felt that Kant had indisputably proved that knowledge was contingent upon the nature of the knower. They interpreted this to mean that all knowledge was subjective. In so doing, they dismissed Kant's contentions regarding the possibility of objective knowledge that everyone would assent to beyond knowledge of physical facts or states of affairs.

Nineteenth-century German philosopher Arthur Schopenhauer ([1819] 1958) did not dispute Kant's contentions regarding knowledge obtained through logic and reason. He contracted Kant's categories into knowledge obtained through the application of the principle of contradiction (knowledge of substances) and knowledge obtained through the application of the principle of sufficient reason (knowledge of causality and changes in the state of objects). Schopenhauer's philosophy made such knowledge subservient to the will (feelings/emotions). He states that we do not do things because they are logical or conformable to reason; we do things because we want to do them and then invent or rationalize reasons for our behavior. The will, for Schopenhauer, is the strong blind man who carries on his shoulders the weaker man (logic/reason) who can see. The purpose of knowledge is to supply information necessary to achieve our desires and actualize our will.

The philosopher Friedrich Nietzsche carried these themes forward. He used the subjective nature of knowing, and the consequence that all knowledge is, therefore, relative and can never be considered to be true in the absolute, to advocate for Supermen who would reject all conventional knowledge claims and moral and ethical principles derived through reason and establish their own—ones that would allow them to fully actualize their will and desires without limit. The will he asserted to be the will to power.

Sigmund Freud took the work of Schopenhauer and Nietzsche to its logical limit with his pseudoscientific psychology. He postulated that sexual desire was the primal drive behind all human behavior. I use the term *pseudoscientific* because modern scholars have discovered that many of Freud's patients were fictitious. He invented them to support his theories. Subsequent research, unsurprisingly, has failed to confirm most of Freud's contentions.

Nineteenth-century philosopher Søren Kierkegaard moved in a different direction altogether (Sontag 1988). He asserts that existence is simply there; it cannot be explained or expressed objectively with logic and reason. It is simply subjectively known. Existence, however, is more than just there; it must be lived out through actions directed by subjective thought. For Kierkegaard, objective truths are limited to statements concerning states of affairs in the external world, like "The apple is red." The most important truths for Kierkegaard are what he calls *subjective truths*. Subjective truths are contingent upon our values and their foundations. He states that pagans and Christians see a different world. He adds that truth also depends on our attitude, commitment, and sincerity. A pagan praying to an idol with passion manifests more subjective truth than a Christian praying with a false spirit. Correctness of values is less important than commitment to them.

Kierkegaard elaborates his view of the contingent nature of knowing with assertions such as the following:

- Values determine facts.
- The individual sees the world they "will" to see.
- The individual is the creator of his or her own world.
- Ideas can be created from a variety of points of view.

- No single view can be taken as correct.
- The world is the subjective construction of the individual.

Those familiar with the current political discourse in the United States might wonder if the participants were devotees of Kierkegaard's philosophy. Of course, unless someone studied philosophy in college, it is unlikely that they would have much knowledge of his work. Ironically, the current political debates in the United States reflect his views.

In a paper discussing the political debate on American gun control policy, Braman and Kahan (2006) state that their research indicates that statistics and academic research do not influence or compel people's views on gun control policy. People's views are based on their sociocultural values and worldview. Based on their values and worldview, people will accept certain statistical arguments and research results and reject others. What people believe to be true and what they accept as knowledge are determined by their cultural identity. This is precisely Kierkegaard's viewpoint: values determine facts and individuals see the world they want to see. One can see the same dynamic in the debate over inoculations for the virus that causes COVID-19, where some people completely dismiss the legitimacy of rigorous, vetted science because it disagrees with or presents difficulties for their preexisting views based on their political values.

Dismissing the possibility of objective knowledge is both problematic and dangerous. The moon is not made of cheese and no cow ever jumped over it. The current trend to reject all facts, knowledge, and truth that don't cohere with a group's sociocultural values prevents effective communication and collaboration on issues that are important to the welfare of all groups collectively. There can be no political or policy progress on climate change, for example, if science is dismissed as "just another opinion," and people can't even agree that climate change is occurring.

Kierkegaard's philosophy is not a philosophic inquiry into the nature of knowledge, it is his prescription for how humans should conduct themselves to create a life with meaning and consequence. He begins with two premises, which he does not provide justification for: (1) all knowledge is subjective and (2) knowledge is not what matters; it is action directed by subjective thought. His philosophic derivations are coherent with these initial premises and demonstrate the necessary consequences of those premises: knowledge is the creation of the individual in accordance with their values; knowledge is equivalent among individuals, and no single point of view is more correct than another.

Kierkegaard's philosophy reprises the philosophy of the Sophists. He also reprises Plato's concerns that such a philosophy ultimately leads to intellectual and moral chaos. When someone submits to surgery, they believe that the physician is in possession of objective knowledge that will allow them to cure their objective malady. If the doctor informed them that their knowledge was subjectively arrived at in accordance with their personal values, it is unlikely that they would submit to surgery. When you drive your car over the Golden Gate Bridge, you assume that the bridge was built in accordance with objectively derived engineering principles and that it won't collapse and plunge your objective car into the objective bay.

The other difficulty with Kierkegaard's position relates to the nature of values. As Hume first suggested, and as the research of psychologists like Jeffrey Haidt (2013) and neurologists like Antonio Damasio (1994, 2010) support, our values and motivations are principally derived from our feelings and emotions. Logic and reason can alter or change our values, but the evolutionarily stronger human feeling- and emotional-processing system often prevails. Many people equate their values with self—they are their values. Suppose that you and I are individuals who hold this viewpoint. Suppose also that our values are different and diametrically opposed. Since we equate values with self, then the adoption by society at large of the other person's values poses an existential threat to me, or at least a significant diminution of my condition. You and I, then, will begin to see each other as threats and enemies. Taken to the limit, this can lead to conflict and ultimately revolution or war. Plato's fear of social anarchy is then actualized.

Finally, Kierkegaard's views justify the position that some inane contention that someone reads on the internet, which is coherent with their values, has the same legitimacy as the contentions of vetted, peer-reviewed science and academic research. When the work of scientists and scholars who have dedicated their lives to the pursuit of knowledge in a specific field, and whose peer-reviewed work is done in accordance with the highest standards of scientific and academic inquiry, is regarded as simply another opinion and accorded the same truth value as any other contention to be found in the media or on the internet, then we have started down the slippery slope of a erasing several hundred years of intellectual progress as a civilization and have embarked on a path that leads back to the Middle Ages.

Kierkegaard's influence was enormous on subsequent philosophy from the continent of Europe. Existential philosophers like Jean-Paul Sartre, Paul Tillich, and Martin Buber carried forward his themes. The following are the common tenants of existential philosophy:

- There is no preexisting order or meaning in the universe.
- Any meaning in life must be personally created.
- Humans have complete freedom to define themselves and create meaning.
- We find meaning through human action and interaction; existence precedes essence.
- Meaning creation requires rejection of externally imposed frameworks for understanding—rejection of fixed categories and operations.

Existentialism rejects the modern paradigm, including the preferential status of scientific knowledge, metaphysics, the quantitative research paradigm, systems, the idea of humans as elements of an orderly system, and the idea of human nature. In keeping with these tenants, we are what we make of ourselves instead. Existentialism was the antecedent of postmodern philosophy. This philosophic viewpoint will be discussed later in the chapter.

Kierkegaard's philosophy was also influential on the philosophic approach referred to as phenomenology. Edmund Husserl (1859–1938) was its first practitioner. He sought the "original intuition" of things from the immediate data of consciousness and before using prior knowledge and prejudices. His views were important to the formulation of the modern-day qualitative research paradigm.

Kierkegaard's influence can also be found in the approach to understanding called *critical theory*. Critical theory asserts that philosophy must be engaged with the great struggles and social movements of its time. Practitioners of this approach included Karl Marx, Jürgen Habermas, and Michel Foucault. Kant likened himself to Copernicus and his influence. Given the preceding discussion, it appears that Pandora might have been a better metaphor.

Philosophy in Great Britain during the nineteenth and twentieth century took a different direction altogether. It was a direction influenced by advances in the field of formal logic after Kant. The approach taken is exemplified by the analytic philosophy of Bertrand Russell (1872–1969). Analysis, in general, involves breaking something down into its constituent elements, or parts, figuring out what each part means, determining the relationship among the parts, and determining how they contribute to the whole. Russell (1919) argues that reality can be analyzed—broken into irreducible elements and relationships. He asserts that many of our concepts are ill-defined and contain a great number of underlying assumptions. Instead of deducting from these diffuse and ambiguous concepts and creating higher levels of abstraction, he advocates that we should ascertain what more fundamental elements, or atoms, of understanding can be found to be our starting point with which we can build our understandings. Russell asks us to go back to the logical foundations of things we take for granted. He asserts that all thought proceeds from initial premises and definitions. His goal is to reduce these to the smallest and most fundamental set of premises and definitions—atomic elements of understanding. Once we have these, more complex concepts can be deduced using the structures of formal logic. Russell's approach is analogous to that of Leibniz. Instead of deducting from two basic principles, Russell's "foundations" are the clarified, irreducible atomic elements of the different concepts we employ.

Russell's most momentous demonstration of his approach is the Herculean derivation of the entirety of mathematics from the atomic concept of natural numbers. He and his collaborator, Alfred North Whitehead, had the thesis that all mathematical propositions can be deduced from the properties of natural numbers using the ideas and propositions of formal logic.

Russell and Whitehead define their atomic elements for mathematics to be natural numbers. They note that a number like 3 is not identical with a trio like Jones, Smith, and Roberts. The number 3 is something all trios have in common and is what distinguishes all trios from other collections like duos and quartets. The number 3 is then an abstract concept that expresses the similarity that is characteristic of a collection, and a number is, therefore, one of the bundles into which similarity collects a class (Russell 1919). From this definition, Russell and Whitehead proceed to derive the entire edifice of mathematics. So voluminous was their work that they had to hire a moving van to transport their manuscript to the publisher.

Their derivation, however, has an element that some, myself included, find problematic. Whenever they can no longer proceed with their logical derivations, they define a new element that allows them to continue to make progress. For example, to solve the problem of the square root of a negative number, they define the entity "i," which when multiplied by itself equals -1. The original problem was that any number multiplied by itself is a positive number. Without this new entity, the square root of -4 does not have meaning. With this new entity, the square root is $2i$, which when multiplied by itself equals -4. With this new definition, Russell and Whitehead can proceed with their logical derivations until the next problem arises and some new element must be defined.

It seems to me that introducing new elements as required to make progress violates their hypothesis that all mathematical propositions can be deduced from the properties of natural numbers using the ideas and propositions of formal logic. As Kant concluded when he stated that he could not see that $5 + 7 = 12$ by just thinking about the concepts of 5 and 7, I cannot see the concept of the imaginary number "i" in the concept of natural numbers or as the logically necessary consequence of the properties of natural numbers.

Another thing that dooms the enterprise of analytic philosophy is that anything that consists of elements in nonlinear relationship cannot be analyzed or reduced via the methods of analysis. What something nonlinearly constituted is and what it does are the consequence of the back-and-forth, codependent interaction of the elements. This interaction produces phenomena that cannot be reduced to and understood by a consideration of the elements and their relationship. The phenomena that emerge are a consequence of the codependent interaction as the entity moves toward some state of equilibrium. As discussed in chapter 2, the influences of the nature of the elements and their relationship, the environment the elements find themselves in, the driving forces they are subject to, and the history they have experienced must all be considered together in understanding the constitution and behavior of a nonlinearly connected entity. These factors combine to produce emergent phenomena that cannot be reduced or predicted from an analytic consideration of parts and relationships. It is the whole that is understood. There is a limit to reductionism.

As this discussion demonstrates, most philosophy subsequent to Kant did not attempt to directly derive a comprehensive theory of knowledge. The direction that Schopenhauer and his successors took emphasizes the will or the feeling and emotion aspect of human beings. Logic and reason were considered to be tools that could be used to actualize the will. The direction taken by Kierkegaard and his intellectual descendants presumed that all knowledge was subjective. Individuals were postulated to create personal meaning from perception, intuition, and reflection ex post facto experience—experience before essence. This philosophy never addresses how this might occur. By what mechanism are these meanings created? The philosophic specializations of epistemology and philosophy of mind also emerged subsequent to Kant, but these paths of inquiry typically dealt with individual specialized issues, such as the mind-brain relationship, intentionality, and the nature of consciousness. Ideas from these specializations are referenced and used in various sections of this book. In summary, the trend post-Kant was toward other aspects of the human experience or toward investigation of special issues rather than toward the production of a complete philosophic system defining the nature of knowledge.

At this juncture, we can examine what philosophic inquiry has revealed about the nature of knowledge. Chapters 1 and 2 discuss mathematical and scientific results from the fields of cognitive science and nonlinear systems theory. The results from these disciplines must be brought into correspondence and coherence with results from philosophic inquiry to produce a credible theory of knowledge. To begin, we know that our senses provide semantic information about the nature of the world outside of us that is organized by our brain into the coherent mental events we experience as images—Locke's ideas, Hume's impressions, and Kant's intuitions. Kant's philosophy tells us that for the organization of sensations to be such as we experience them, they must be organized with respect to space and time. Let's call Kant's conclusion supposition number 1. This is the first supposition that we will need to bring into correspondence and coherence with the contents of chapters 1 and 2.

Beginning with Galileo, philosophers agreed that obtaining knowledge from images, evaluating the content of images, requires a judgment regarding the content. Cognitive science refers to this process as *perception*, for example, the perception that a mental image contains a chair. Kant's philosophy clarifies for us the nature of judgments. What he calls a *judgment of perception* is a subjective judgment of the semantic content of an image (intuition). Such a judgment might be "The sun is shining, and the rock is getting warm." The second form of judgment that Kant recognizes he terms a *judgment of experience*. This would be a judgment like "The sun is causing the rock to warm." Note that the second form of judgment asserts something beyond what is in the semantic content of the image or intuition. The image contains only a shining sun and a rock warming. The second judgment imputes a causal relationship between these two pieces of information. It is a product of the mind of the individual and not merely a report of the content of the image. Note also that what the philosophers are calling **a judgment is the mind creating a relationship between the contents of the image**. This idea will become critically important in creating correspondence and coherence between philosophy and the contents of chapters 1 and 2. Let's call Kant's differentiation of the two types of judgments that the mind makes regarding the content of images supposition 2.

Kant asserts that for the mind to undertake a judgment like the sun caused the rock to warm requires that certain concepts like causality be innate. The required innate concepts are his categories of judgment. Hume attributes the idea of causality to a "habit of mind" of noting that some event B, like the rock warming, seems to always follow some event A, like the sun shining. Locke ascribes causal judgments to the development of the concept of power, which is the observation of the ability to bring about a change in the state of objects and produce effects. For Locke, the idea of causality is hence learned or abstracted from experience. So, which is it, an innate concept, a habit of mind, or an inductively learned concept? Note that "habit of mind" implies an innate mechanism or functionality in the brain. When an infant first kicks a rattle in her crib, does she already have the idea of causality in her mind? Does she abstract all her kicking, pushing, and throwing outcomes into the concepts of power and causality, or does her brain have a mechanism or "habit of mind" that she will come to intuit and refer to as "cause" when she learns language? Let's call this question 1. It is something any theory of knowledge will have to answer.

Another "judgment of experience" is the identification of something in an image or intuition as a such and such, like the object is a chair. Kant postulates that this requires the innate concept of substance: something in which attributes and characteristics (semantic features) inhere. For Hume, this capacity is an operation of the mind that implements the relationship of identity—identifies something. Hume's system also requires the capacity to form general ideas, a collection of particulars with similar semantic features that are annexed to words. Locke asserts that we have the concept of substance—a substratum wherein the properties of objects subsist. He does not address where this concept would come from. He cannot do so because his general thesis is that all concepts come from the faculty of abstraction applied to the contents of ideas, his word for sensory images. This represents an incoherence in Locke's philosophy because, as Hume points out, images consist of the sensorially derived attributes and characteristics of substances, not of the underlying substance that gives rise to those attributes and characteristics. This led Hume to conclude that the concept of substance cannot come from experience.

Every philosophic system we have examined, save Kant's, either implicitly or explicitly requires the faculty of abstraction. Plato implies the faculty of abstraction when he states that knowledge begins with the inductive generalization of experience. Aristotle's system implicitly implies this faculty when he states that knowledge involves the careful observation and recording of experience to determine the Form of things and the subsequent creation of dichotomies of categories and classes of like kinds that share a Form. Descartes's system presumes the existence of concepts of classes and categories of like kinds placed in the mind by God. Locke explicitly states the necessity for a faculty of abstraction, and Hume implicitly includes it when he describes the ability of the mind to form general ideas. As discussed, Kant's system must for reasons of coherence exclude such a capacity since his system is based on formal logic and is, therefore, independent of the semantic content of experience. However, as previously shown, the judgment that something is a such and such requires a semantic feature definition of a such and such.

We can appreciate the necessity of the faculty of abstraction by considering the following simple thought experiment. Imagine we live in a world where everything is unique and different. The thing that I reside in and all of its contents, along with what is outside of my residence, are completely different from the thing you reside in and what is inside and outside of your residence. In such a world, we would require a different word for each and everything we experienced. If I spoke to you about something in my life, you would have to have had an experience of the same thing and you would need to know what word I had associated with the experience. In short, communication would be impossible. Any information I gave you through communication would also be of no use to you since everything in my "world" is different from everything in your "world." In Kantian fashion, we must conclude that for there to be the possibility of communication and associated activities like describing, discussing, explaining, and teaching, we must live in a world that can be organized into like kinds or categories and classes consisting of particulars that share attributes, characteristics, and relationships. We can also conclude that for these activities to be possible, the mind must have the capacity to create categories and classes. In other words, the faculty of abstraction is a priori and necessary for there to be the possibility of communication and its associated activities.

Imagine now that we live in a world that is randomly and constantly changing. What is an apple today may be a mouse tomorrow. In such a world there would be no purpose or use for knowledge and memory because what is the case or true today would be completely and unpredictably different tomorrow. One could not plan a shopping trip to Dallas because the road to Dallas might randomly turn into a valley of boiling lava. Once again, in Kantian fashion, for there to be the possibility of knowledge and a purpose for memory, we must live in a world where objects are permanent, at least for some duration, and in which many patterns of change in the state of objects with time occur in a repeated, orderly, and relatively invariant fashion. For there to be the possibility of higher-order thinking processes such as decision-making, problem-solving, planning, strategizing, and designing requires such a world and the capacity to sort these permanent objects and other phenomena into like kinds based on similar semantic features and the capacity to recognize the repeated, orderly, and invariant changes in the state of objects and phenomena with time. In summary, knowledge, language, higher-order thinking, and a purpose for memory require, a priori, the faculty of abstraction and the mental process of induction—detecting, sorting, and recording the invariant patterns manifest in experience and present in mental images. Let us call this supposition 3.

To provide further analysis of supposition 3, let us consider the Analogies in Kant's *Critique of Pure Reason*. In the First Analogy, Kant begins with the assertion that we do not directly perceive time. What we perceive is a succession in time of representations of phenomena. The perception of time requires a substratum, or some fixed frame of reference. It is the idea of the permanent that makes possible the representation of a change from one state to another. Kant hypothesizes that this invariant frame of reference is object permanence. Object permanence is the necessary condition under which phenomena such as objects are determinable in experience, as well as a change in the state of objects. It is because we understand objects as invariant semantic features connected through invariant relationships that persist through time that the perception of time and changes with time are enabled. Kant's argument is coherent with the previously described nature of neuronal representation of the objects of experience.

Kant begins the Second Analogy in the same manner as the first: with the assertions that we do not directly perceive time and that what we perceive is the successive representation of objects and events enabled by the senses. He then asks how we can come to know that a successive change in representations that we experience corresponds to an objective change in the real world external to us. He presents the example of the apprehension of a house that stands before him. This apprehension would consist of a series of successive representations. It might begin at the roof and end at the foundation, or vice versa. He might apprehend it from right to left or from left to right. There is no determined order that necessitates a particular beginning and ending point in the series of representations constituting his apprehension and perception of the house. Conversely, if he apprehends a ship floating down the stream of a river, his perception of its place lower down the river follows upon his perception of it higher up the course of the river, and it is impossible that in his apprehension this be reversed. Every apprehension of an event is a perception that follows upon another perception. In the apprehension of an event in which change occurs, versus the apprehension of a permanent object, the succession of perception is necessary. This distinguishes the subjective sequence of the apprehension of the former (house) from the objective sequence of the latter (ship). Kant ([1781] 1990, 130–31) concludes the following:

> The latter must consist in the order of the manifold in a phenomenon, according to which the apprehension of one thing (that which happens) follows that of another thing (that which precedes), in conformity with a rule. In conformity with this rule then, it is necessary that in that which antecedes an event there be found the condition of a rule according to which this event follows always and necessarily.
>
> It is by means of perception and comparison of similar consequences following upon certain antecedent phenomena, that the understanding is led to the discovery of a rule, by which certain events always follow certain phenomena. The general rule which we are furnished with is "everything that happens has a cause."

I believe that Kant's analogies can be interpreted to define two large categories of human knowing. He makes a compelling case for the necessity of object permanence as a basis for knowing. To be known, an object must persist in time, at least for some duration. Object permanence is also required to determine that a change in the state of other objects has occurred. He also states that we know that an objective change has occurred in the world because the change perceived seems to follow a rule. That means the change is orderly, repeatable, and has the attribute of invariance. He states that when we experience similar sequences of one thing following another necessarily (in accordance with a rule), we are led to the general rule that everything has a cause, the concept of causality. This seems to imply that the concept of causality is an inductively learned generalization of experience. Oops! That would be incoherent with his premise that this concept is innate and a priori. To give Kant the benefit of the doubt, we could presume that what he intended to imply was that we "discover" the innate concept of causality. The quote from Kant supports Locke's contention that the concept of causality is inductively learned through experience. This is the most probable answer to question 1 posed earlier.

The first large category of knowing that Kant's analogies define is knowledge of permanent objects and phenomena with attributes and characteristics rendered by the senses that are organized with respect to space and time. Given the foregoing discussion regarding the faculty of abstraction as applied to objects, the structure of such knowledge would be classes and categories of objects and phenomena that share similar attributes, characteristics, and relationships among those attributes and characteristics. The second large category of knowing is changes in the state of objects and phenomena that seem to proceed according to a rule. The structure of this type of knowledge would be the nature of the change and the relationship, such as causality, that brings about or accounts for the change.

A clarification of the preceding is required. The proposed two large categories of knowing are knowledge that is incarnated in the form that cognitive science calls *rules*: ideas, concepts, theories, principles, and generalizations that symbolically represent the way the world/universe is in the mind of the individual. It is not intended to categorize all human knowing. Humans know a great number of things associatively through their worldly experience that may not be codified into rules. These two categories are types of knowledge that are grist for the mill of logic and reason. They are the type of knowledge that is required for higher-level thinking activities like verbal communication and is rule-based: problem-solving, decision-making, strategizing, planning, and design. Let's call the supposition that these two categories of knowing are the structure of knowledge that constitutes the basis for logic and reason supposition 4. Another point of clarification: by other phenomena, I am referring to things like the force of gravity and electromagnetic attraction and repulsion—phenomena experienced but not incarnated as objects.

The final item that we need to consider is the operation of our minds on the contents of our thought, in other words, the nature of logic and reason. Plato states that we generalize experience to arrive at rules. We then make deductions as to what follows from these rules. Recall that Plato characterizes this knowledge as hypothetical and incomplete. To gain true knowledge, he advocates undertaking the dialectic process demonstrated in his dialogues. Induction and deduction are hence implicit in his notions of mental processing of information obtained from experience. Aristotle asserts that our minds can take on the Form of the items of our experience. We receive knowledge of the Forms through reflection on our experience of them. Knowledge of objects and actions is knowledge of the Forms—descriptive knowledge of what something is and what it does. Forms can then be sorted into classes, and categories and dichotomies are created. Reasoning is predicated on these classes and categories using the mechanism of the syllogism, a form of deduction. Locke states that the mind has no object of consideration but its own ideas. Knowledge obtained through reason is then the agreement or disagreement of ideas. Hume recognizes two types of reasoning. He defines the first as the relation of ideas. Ideas are related in a proposition whose truth can be ascertained by inspecting the ideas involved in the relationship. He asserts that the truth or falsity of such propositions can be determined a priori by inspecting the meaning or content of the ideas put into relationship in the proposition. His second category of reasoning is determining matters of fact. The truth of matters of fact is determined by inspecting the world to see if they are the case. What he means by the "relation of ideas" is that a proposition like "A horse and carriage transports passengers to a locale" can be assessed as true by inspecting the meanings of the words (ideas) put into relationship. A horse and carriage are certainly capable of transporting people from one location to another. The statement is true, a priori, by virtue of the meanings of the words. A statement like "The horse-drawn black carriage transported Lady McDonald to the castle" is a "matter of fact" whose truth would need to be verified by someone who experienced the event. Note that "relation of ideas" does not require the structures and propositions of formal logic. It is, in lieu, the determination of coherence between the ideas (concepts) put into relationship. It involves answering the question, Given the meanings of the words, is the proposed relationship between them coherent with those meanings? Because Kant's judgments are the structures of formal logic, it follows that logic and reason for Kant proceed according to the rules of formal logic.

As the prior discussion illustrates, the type of thinking we experience requires the "faculty of abstraction" and the capacity for inductive generalization using those a bstractions. The discussion immediately preceding gives us a question we need to answer: Do logic and reason proceed according to the rules of formal logic as Aristotle, Kant, and others have suggested, or according to the "relation of ideas" process hypothesized by Locke and Hume?

It is well documented that individuals who are not both trained and practiced in the use of formal logic perform very poorly when given tests of logic. Psychologists, who perform such tests, typically employing categorical syllogisms, routinely report participant error rates as high as seventy to ninety percent (Johnson-Laird 1983; Gilhooley 1988; Rips 1990). Research subjects affirm consequents, deny antecedents, and invariably struggle with modus tollens (Braine and O'Brien 1991; Evans, Newstead, and Byrne 1993). Every individual, however, has a well-developed sense of what seems logical or illogical to them. What forms the basis for such beliefs and from what does the human sense of what is, or is not, logical arise?

The psychological testing itself provides a clue. When research participants are given the rule "If A is true, then B is true," then are given the fact that "B is true" and are then asked what follows, they will almost always erroneously respond that "A is true." However, when participants are given a rule like "If it is raining, then the streets will be wet," then are given the fact that "the streets are wet" and are asked what follows, most participants will correctly answer that nothing necessarily follows. Their extensive empirical experience with wet streets and rain events allows them to reason that wet streets do not necessarily imply a rain event. An errant sprinkler system adjacent to a street or a leaking tanker truck would suffice to wet the streets. Both the preceding rules have precisely the same syntax, or logical structure. The basis on which research participants reason does not appear to be reference to logical structure or syntax; it appears to be reference to the semantic content of their prior empirical experience. In general, the weight of research evidence is highly problematic for any claim that formal logic reflects the way that people think. As Reisberg (2010, 448) states, "Instead, the evidence is driving us toward the view that thought is influenced by the content, the meaning, and the pragmatics of the material we are contemplating."

Another example of human logic processing is illustrated by what is called Wason's four-card selection task, illustrated in figure 3.1. This test has been performed thousands of times by cognitive scientists.

The participant's task is to examine the logical statement and to tell the researcher which cards must be turned over to determine whether the cards comply with the stated rule or logical statement. Each card has a letter on one side and a number on the reverse side. In Wason's (1968) research, 96 percent of participants gave wrong answers. Other researchers have used variations of this problem and found better performance (Reisberg 2010). For example, Griggs and Cox (1982) used the variation shown in figure 3.2.

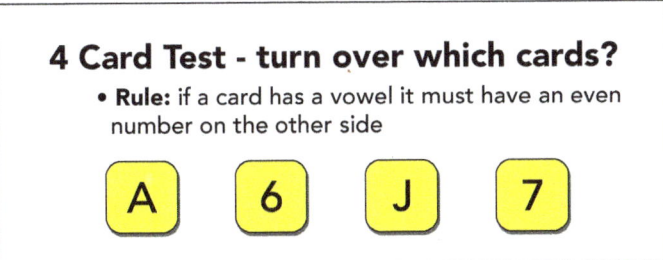

Figure 3.1 Wason's four-card test

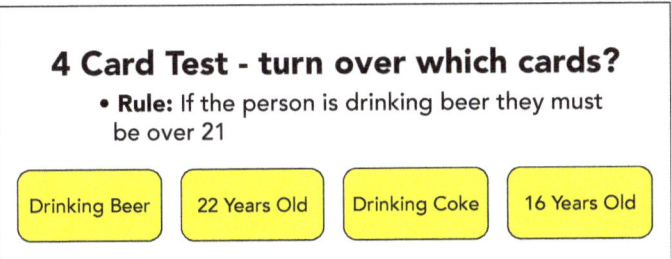

Figure 3.2 Variant of the four-card test

In this version of the test, 73 percent of participants answered correctly, picking the card labeled "Drinking Beer," and the card labeled "16 years old." These two tests have precisely the same logical form or syntax. The correct answers in the first test are also the first and last card: "A" and "7." The difference between the two tests relates to the content, or semantic features, associated with the symbols. In the first test, the symbols are pure abstractions without specific referents. There are no semantic features to relate to determine coherence with the requirements specified by the rule. Conversely, in the second test, the words or symbols have referents with numerous relational connections, formed through experience, between the semantic features of the items represented by the words and associated with the symbols. In the second version of the test, the problem is solved by reference to the relationships among the semantic features of the elements involved without reference to formal inferential structures or their syntax.

Precisely the same pattern emerges in a phenomenon known as *belief bias*: if an argument's conclusion is believed to be true based on the totality of one's knowledge, an individual is likely to judge that a conclusion follows logically from premises, irrespective of the logical form (syntax) or formal logical validity of the argument. Additionally, if the conclusion is something people believe to be false, they are likely to reject the conclusion as invalid, again, with indifference to the formal logical validity of the argument (Reisberg 2010; Evans and Feeney 2004).

The hypothesis suggested by the preceding examples is that human logical judgment is the process of creating coherence among the semantic features of the mental representations of the objects, actions, and events under consideration. These representations are an expression of the regularities of experience: invariant semantic features connected through invariant relationships, as recorded by the Hebbian process in the nonlinear, hierarchical, feature-based architecture of the brain and connected and organized through the action of the medial temporal lobe, frontal lobe, and subcortical structures that constitute the memory system. It appears then that the "relation of ideas" concept of logic is more coherent and correspondent with results from cognitive science, those "ideas" being representations of the abstracted, inducted, and organized semantic features of experience codified through representations like language.

Another requirement of any theory of knowledge is that it is coherent and correspondent with the idea of an organism that evolved to its current form. The basic idea of evolution is that with time, species experience genetic mutations that produce some diversity of attributes and characteristics in the species. When a change in environment occurs and environmental stressors emerge, it is those members of the species whose attributes and characteristics are most adaptive to the change that survive and are "naturally selected." As biological anthropologist Terrence Deacon (1997, 38) states,

> A full evolutionary account cannot stop with a formal description of what is missing or a scenario of how selection might have favored the evolution of innate grammatical knowledge. It must also provide a functional account of why its particular organization was favored, how incremental and partial versions were also functional, and how structures present in nonhuman brains were modified to provide this ability.

Deacon's adaptation that explains the nature of language is the evolution of vocalizations or words as symbolic representations that not only refer to things in the world but also connect other words to form logically closed (semantically coherent) groups that together coherently express an idea. This dual ability to relate to things in the world and to relate to other words (vocalizations) allows words to take on their symbolic character. Animals, like vervet monkeys, make different vocalizations that alert other monkeys to various types of dangers (Deacon 1997). The ability that monkeys do not have, nor do any other animals, is the capacity to connect and relate a sequence of vocalizations together to express an idea. Meaning as a consequence of the coherence of word-to-word relationship is essentially the "relation of ideas" expressed by Locke and Hume. Note that the relation of ideas involves coherence among the semantic features of the words put into relationship and is independent of syntax or formal logical structure. The evolution of connectivity between vocal representations that refer to objects and actions in the world seems to be a simpler and more plausible evolutionary step than the evolution of semantic-free syntactic structures like grammar and formal logic.

Supposition 1, derived from Kant's philosophy, is that sensory information must be organized with respect to the concepts of space and time to produce the organized intuitions and subsequent perceptions that we experience. To facilitate perception, the brain must indeed organize such information so that we can determine not only "what" items are in our images (intuitions) but "where" they are located. Each sensory modality handles this processing in a different manner. For example, we have two ears at two different physical locations on our body that receive sounds from some physically located source. These sounds vary in intensity and time of arrival because of the difference in the location of each ear. Information regarding time of arrival and intensity variation is sent to space-specific neurons in the auditory-processing area that are activated only when sound comes from a certain location.

The neural representation of space is more direct in vision processing. Sensory detectors in the retina create a topographic map that is maintained throughout the visual-processing system. Shape is a crucial element in perceiving "what" an item in an image is. The part of the visual cortex that processes shapes utilizes information from areas that process attributes like color, luminance, and motion. Spatial and temporal information must, therefore, be maintained in each processing area to produce the coherently organized shapes we experience in visual images.

Our memory of past events, called *episodic memories*, is enabled by the structures of the medial temporal lobe. Information from the sensory association areas of the neocortex related to "what" an item of experience is enters the entorhinal cortex via the perirhinal cortex. Information from the polymodal sensory-association and parietal lobe areas about "where" items are located and what they are associated with enters the entorhinal cortex via the parahippocampus. These streams of information remain segregated in the entorhinal cortex but are combined in the hippocampus. The hippocampus relates the two types of information to produce coherent memories of what, where, and when things transpired. From this discussion, we can see that Kant's thesis was generally correct. However, what is innate is not the concepts or forms of space and time but the brain structures evolved to process and record information that is manifested in spatial and temporal dimensions.

Supposition 2 relates to the two categories of judgment postulated by Kant. The clearest delineation from neuroscience of distinctions in types of human judgment comes from Gazzaniga's (2011) work with split-brain patients. These are patients whose corpus collosum, the connection between the left and the right sides of the brain, has been severed. Although both hemispheres can undertake rudimentary language and image processing, it is clear that the left hemisphere is specialized for language, while the right hemisphere is specialized for detailed perceptual image processing.

Gazzaniga describes an experiment where the word *pan* was flashed to the right hemisphere of a split-brain patient. The patient could point to a picture of a pan with their left hand in response. If the word "water" was flashed to the right hemisphere, the patient's left hand could point to a picture of water. However, if the words were flashed together, the patient could not put them together into the concept of water in a pan and pointed to the empty pan picture instead. In contrast, when the same sequence was shown to the left brain, it quickly solved the problem. In another experiment, a match and then a woodpile were shown to the right hemisphere of a split-brain patient. The patient was then asked to pick out one of six pictures reflecting a causal relationship; the right brain could not pick out a picture of a burning woodpile. Again, the left brain easily handled this task. Gazzaniga summarizes that the right hemisphere is poor at making inferences. It leads a literal life. The right hemisphere is specialized for literal perceptual processing of sensory input and representations that consist of mappings or association of perceptual information (images). It is superior at focusing attention on perceptual details and perceptual grouping, apprehending complex perceptual patterns, and making perceptual distinctions and judgments. **It cannot make judgments, however, beyond the information present in the perception.** It relies on the left-brain language areas for this task. Note that this is consistent with a hypothesis that conscious relational judgments are enabled through words that represent and articulate relational connections.

Gazzaniga characterizes the left-brain language area and the associated left prefrontal cortex symbolic-reasoning areas as the "interpreter." These left-brain areas interpret observations and perceptual information derived from right-brain processing in a context consistent with what it knows (contents of long-term memory). Gazzaniga states that the interpreter (left-brain areas) is driven to make sense of or to create a coherent story out of experience. It gets the gist from input, tries to find a pattern, and puts it together in a way that makes sense. Importantly, Gazzaniga summarizes that separate processing systems in the brain do not operate under a centralized authority. The brain is a complex, self-organizing system: many different subsystems working together that produce emergent properties that are greater than the sum of their parts. For example, the sense that a certain event has transpired is emergent from the interaction and equilibration of our perceptually based image-representation system, symbolically based interpretational system, and our feeling/emotional-processing system. We may see a photo of two friends: one dressed in a tuxedo and the other in a flowing white dress with a veil and feel a sense of happiness that the two friends have become united in matrimony. Our image-based system sees and represents two familiar faces in specific dress. Our symbolic system recognizes the dress as iconic and symbolic of a wedding, and our emotions/feeling system produces a state of happiness in response to the recognition that this event has occurred. In this scenario, the perceptual image system renders only two familiar faces in specific dress. The "experience" invoked by the photo is emergent from the interaction of the various brain systems processing and responding to the input. Note that Gazzaniga's characterization is congruent with the hypothesis that meaning creation and inference are primarily a semantic coherence process. Gazzaniga's research also corresponds with Kant's two forms of judgment: judgment pertaining to the specific content of images and judgment regarding the nature of relationships among the contents of images. The next chapter discusses in detail the two systems of reasoning that are implied by Kant's two forms of judgment and the types of knowledge supplied by each system.

Next, let us examine evidence from neuroscience concerning the faculty of abstraction. Neurons from the sensory interface to the sensory association areas of the brain, where representations are fully processed into the images we experience, are organized, and are connected in a productive hierarchical configuration. Neurons higher in the hierarchy are connected to collections of neurons lower in the hierarchy. Lower-level neural assemblies representing elements of the semantic features of objects and phenomena sensed are variously combined to produce, ultimately, the fully processed images we experience. For example, thirty some shape elements are combined in various ways to produce the numerous complex shapes we experience. As the system is productive, the same sets of neural circuits are activated when semantic features are shared by different objects that are experienced. The same sets are part of the composite representation when semantic features of different objects share similarities. This results in a natural mechanism for abstracting similar features (attributes/characteristics) of objects and phenomena.

For example, let's say that a child is outside viewing a robin, and her mother says, "Look at that bird." The next day, the child sees a crow, and her mother again says, "Look at that bird." Say that the family goes to the zoo the following weekend and they view an eagle in a cage; the child hears her mother say, "Now that is a big bird." While the different birds have variations, they share semantic features like a similar general shape, feathers, wings, a beak, and talons. The birds also have the ability to fly. In each of the bird experiences, the child's brain is using the same neural assemblies to represent those semantic features that the birds have in common. The meaning of the word *bird* in the child's mind becomes all the features that the birds in the experiences have in common. Since the same neural circuits are repeatedly activated, the semantic features the birds have in common will become more strongly connected than the semantic differences between the birds, like size and color. What the experiences had in common will constitute what gets activated when the child subsequently hears or uses the word *bird*. The brain naturally implements the process of abstraction and inductive generalization of experience. The hardware of the brain, therefore, naturally implements the "faculty of abstraction" and the capacity for inductive generalization.

Let us now examine where we stand with regard to our suppositions and questions. The configuration of neural circuits and the processes they support are correspondent and coherent with the supposition that sensory information is organized with respect to space and time. The configuration and operation of these neural circuits also implement the "faculty of abstraction" and inductive generalization of experience. Kant's two forms of judgment are correspondent and coherent with results from neuroscience. It is also highly probable that the concept of causality is inductively learned. Neuroscience also supports the view that the process of "logic and reason" is the process of determining coherence between the semantic features of mental representations (images) put into relationship. This corresponds to the "relation of ideas" hypothesis expressed by Locke and Hume. Empirical research in neuroscience does not support the contention that "logic and reason" proceed according to the ideas and propositions of formal logic. We now require a theory of language that is correspondent and coherent with the preceding hypotheses.

Theory of Language

The hypothesis that human judgment primarily consists of establishing relationships of semantic coherence requires a compatible theory of language. Terrence Deacon's (1997) theory based on the semiotic philosophy of Charles Sanders Peirce is such a theory.

Deacon's completely articulated theory is extensive and complex. What follows is a broad outline of it, as it relates to the development of a theory of knowledge.

Peirce determined three categories of referential connection between a sign token, like a word, and something in the world, like an object. He termed these categories *icons*, *indexes*, and *symbols*. He inferred a hierarchical relationship among these categories (Deledalle 2000).

Deacon (1997) interprets *iconicity* as the base on which all forms of representation are built. What, for example, makes a caricature sketch of an individual iconic is that part of the interpretive recognition process that is the same for the sketch and the face it portrays. The interpretive process that generates iconic references is fundamentally perception (Deacon 1997). Recognition of iconicity is enabled by the Hebbian process of recruitment and fractionation. With repeated encounters with given objects, events, and phenomena, the invariant features associated with them grow into a highly and strongly interconnected representational network, which facilitates subsequent perception, or re-representation. These features become iconic of the objects, events, and phenomena. For example, if we experience multiple events involving a fire, the characteristic shape, color, and motion of flames, heat, light, smoke, odors, and combustion of objects by the fire will all be sensorily derived and defined features common to each fire event. When numerous fire events are experienced, these features, invariant across the events, will neurally potentiate and consolidate in memory and become iconic of fires.

Since the features of these representations, or icons, are related by physical contiguity or temporal continuity, they serve to *index* one another because their neural representations are connected. In other words, one seems to "point to" or refer to the other. Deacon (1997) suggests that day-to-day associative learning is the basis for all indexical interpretations. For example, the thought that "where there is smoke, there is fire" is an indexical relationship among icons learned through association. Indexes are at a higher level hierarchically than are icons. Prior iconic relationships are necessary for indexical reference, but prior indexical relationships are not necessary for iconic reference. When words become associated with objects, events, and phenomena, they take on indexical capabilities. For this indexical relationship to hold, there must be a correlation in time and place between the word and its object.

Many twentieth-century philosophers of language distinguished two aspects of word meaning: an ability to refer to something in the world (reference) and the idea one has in mind when hearing or using the word (sense). Association of words with the items of experience imparts the first attribute but not the second. Words as indexes are not yet symbols. Words also represent other words and enter into specific relationships to the other words of a language. It is word-to-word relationship that creates the *symbolic* nature of words as well as the sense of words. As Deacon (83) states, "Symbolic reference derives from the combinatorial possibilities and impossibilities, and we, therefore, depend on combinations to discover it (during learning) and to make use of it (during communication)." Words describe the relational structure between icons. Words relating to other words form a system of relationships that **allows words to be about indexical relationships** and not simply indexes. It is this dual reference that allows words to both "point to" objects (reference) and "point to" other words (sense).

Word relationships form logically closed groups. Because of logical relationships between words there emerges relationships of inclusion and exclusion, or a grammar. Certain combinations are permissible, while others are not. **Since words are indexed hierarchically to icons that represent the semantic features of experience, the basis for logical judgment or the judgment that sentences are logically closed is of necessity a judgment as to coherence among the semantic features (icons) indexed to the respective words that have been put into relationship.** For example, the sentence "Sarah flew a plane to New Orleans" is logically closed because the semantic content (iconic elements) indexed to each of the words related in the sentence facilitates a coherent relationship between these words at the word-to-word level. There is also a coherent relationship at the icon-to-icon representation level. We understand that Sarah, a human being, has attributes (icons) that make her capable of boarding a plane that in turn has attributes (icons) that make it capable of transporting her to the specified city. Conversely, the sentence "To New Orleans, Sarah a plane spoke" is illogical and impermissible. The semantic content of the word *spoke* does not permit a coherent or logically closed relationship between the words of the sentence. The implication here is that the grammatical structures that researchers find in language are epiphenomena of a sematic feature processor.

Shown in figure 3.3 is a schematic illustration of Deacon's model of language. I have included the references to Kant's representations that persist in time, or objects, indexed by nouns and invariant action sequence representations in time, often indexed by verbs.

Note that coherence is both hierarchical between levels (symbol to index to icon) and heterarchical at the same level (between words and between icons). The isomorphic relationship describing the instantiation at the neuron level is a state of equilibrium in the activated neural networks representing the items. Note that this conclusion is coherent with the requirements imposed by the nonlinear connectivity of the brain's representational circuits. In the schematic in figure 3.3, the symbolic representation (word) "fire" is indexed to the iconic semantic features of odor, smoke, heat, and light. These icons

Figure 3.3 Deacon's model of language

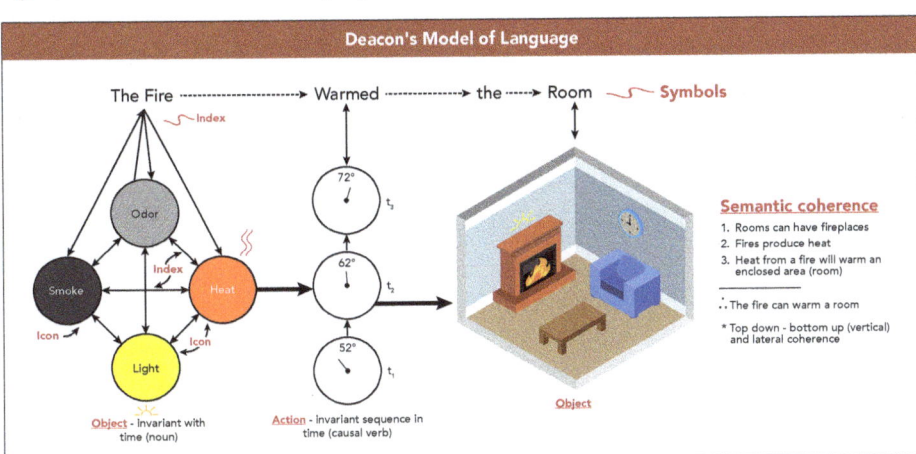

are also indexed to one another. Rather than list the iconic features associated with the symbol "room," I have depicted an image of a room. The iconic semantic features shown are furniture, a thermometer, and a fireplace. The proposed relationship between the symbols "fire" and "room" is the word (symbol) "warmed." This is an action that connotes a change in the state of the room. It is schematically illustrated by a thermometer depicting an increase in temperature with time. The schematic is consistent with my thesis that the two broad categories of knowledge are objects/phenomena and actions, which are changes in the state of objects/phenomena. The logical closure or sense that a coherent relationship between the two objects exists, as proposed in the sentence, results if there is a connection between the icons (semantic features). In the sentence in figure 3.3, fireplaces can be an iconic feature of rooms, fire in the fireplace can produce the iconic feature heat, and heat can increase the temperature in an enclosed room. It is the case, then, that the iconic semantic features indexed to the words have a connection or relationship at both the icon and the word level; therefore, coherence and "logical closure" is attained.

As the preceding illustrates, language facilitates and enables the "relation of ideas." The human sense of logical or illogical is determined by whether the semantic features (icons) associated (indexed) with the words support the relationship proposed between the words. "I ate a pie" is assessed as plausible and logical, while "I ate the Empire State Building" is judged as illogical and impossible. The semantic features (icons) associated with I, a human being, and Empire State Building do not support the proposed relationship "ate." At the level of neuron representations, there is no connection between eating and office building representations.

As Gazzaniga states, the language areas of the brain will attempt to try to make sense of the input it receives. For example, the sentence "I ate the Empire State Building" would perhaps be interpreted to mean I ate a cake decorated and shaped to resemble the Empire State Building. At the neuron level, the process that is occurring is the attempt to reach a state of equilibrium between the nonlinearly connected neural representations of the semantic features (icons) associated (indexed) to the words put into relationship. The conclusion then is that human logic and reason is the process, facilitated by symbolic representations, of achieving semantic coherence (logical closure) between the semantic features (icons) indexed to or associated with the symbols. The homomorphic neuronal process is the attainment of equilibrium between the brain's representation of the items put into relationship.

Humans have developed two principal symbolic systems: language and mathematics. Deacon's big insight is that to be a symbol, something not only must refer to something in the world but also must refer to and be relatable in a coherent (logically closed) fashion to other symbols. The relationship between the symbols must express a comprehensible idea. Are emojis symbols? No, they are icons that refer to specific emotions. A language of emotions using emojis could conceivably be constructed. The requirement would be the ability to put together a string of emojis that uniquely express and define an emotional state or idea not contained in the individual emojis themselves. Computer languages and formal logic qualify as symbolic systems. These systems are specialized to specific applications and are not typically or ubiquitously used in K–16 education like language and mathematics are.

Words are defined by Russian psychologist Lev Vygotsky ([1934] 1986) as the abstracted characteristics of the objects, phenomena, actions, and events of experience logically connected. By logical connection, he means that the connection constitutes a judgment as to the nature of the relationship between the attributes/characteristics. His thesis is coherent with the theory of language, discussed previously. Also, given the previous discussion, we can concur with Vygotsky's thesis that thought is not merely expressed in words, as eighteenth- and nineteenth-century philosophers presumed, it comes into existence through them. Words or symbols, as defined by Deacon, are also the enablers of higher-level cognitive processes such as communication and rule-based decision-making, problem-solving, strategizing, planning, and design (creation).

These ideas can be further elaborated by considering Peirce's triadic theory of knowledge (Hoopes 1991; Deledalle 2000). Peirce asks us to conceive of **one**: complete, undifferentiated, infinite totality. What can be said about one? Nothing; it is both total being and nonbeing. Everything, however, has a limit and can be differentiated from unity (one) with respect to a change in attributes or characteristics. This brings about the idea of **two**, or secondness. To express something intelligible, we also require the idea of **three**, or thirdness, which is a relationship that mediates between one and two. Peirce (Hoopes 1991, 192–93) provides an example in the following quote:

> The fact that A presents B with a gift C, is a triple relation, and as such cannot be resolved into any combination of dual relations. Indeed, the very idea of a combination involves that of thirdness, for combination is something which is what is owing to the parts which it brings into mutual relationship. But we may waive that consideration and still we cannot build up to the fact that A presents C to B by any aggregate of dual relations between A, B, and C.

From this, we can conclude the following:

- All finite things can be differentiated with respect to a change in attribute or characteristic.

- Creating meaning requires creating a relationship—relationship is the basis of meaning.

- The aim of inquiry (learning) is to find patterns of relationship in worldly experience.

The conclusion is coherent with both the knowledge of mental processing obtained from neuroscience and Deacon's theory of language. Also, considering the foregoing discussions, it also provides an abstract definition of teaching. Teaching is helping students create patterns of relationship that give meaning to the content of their experience. In a formal setting like a class, that experience comes through learning representations like readings, lectures, examples, videos, charts, matrices, models, demonstrations, and simulations. Teaching is helping students connect the dots of experience by building relationships.

A question that needs to be answered is where knowledge of words that express ideas that seem to be purely abstract, without direct referents to worldly experience, comes from. Steven Pinker (2007) does an elegant job of demonstrating that even our most abstract words and concepts have their roots in physical experience. For example, he shows how the abstract political statements in the Declaration of Independence metaphorically relate back to physical experience. The mechanism for giving these words their meaning is the human capacity for creating metaphors. This process will be explained more fully in the next chapter. A simple example will suffice for the time being. Let's say that I make the statement "Although I was resistant at first, the lecturer's arguments compelled me to rethink my position." Embedded in the statement is the physical idea of a force moving an object that has inertia. I was not going to move from my position until the force of the arguments was sufficient to move me. As will be discussed in the next chapter, it is the connection to physical roots that makes learning through language less difficult than learning through purely abstract systems, like algebra.

Since learning through the creation of relationships between symbolic representations is the postulated general mechanism for rule-based knowledge construction, let us now look at different aspects of language to evaluate whether supposition 4, the postulation that there are two basic units of knowing—objects/phenomena and actions (changes in objects/phenomena)—is supported.

Kolln and Gray (2017) state that 95 percent of all sentences are in one of seven forms, shown in table 3.4. The other 5 percent of sentences consist of phrases like "Ouch!" and "Why not?"

The first two sentence types express the state of being of some object or phenomenon. The relationship is expressed with verbs like *is* and *was*. Sentence types 4 to 7 express an action or change in the state of objects/phenomena that are the subject of the sentence or the object of the action. Sentence type 3 uses a linking verb to express either a state of being of an object or an action undertaken by an object. Sentence types, therefore, appear to support the notion that objects/phenomena and actions are the fundamental units of knowing. Next, let's examine the parts of speech from which all statements or word relationships are constructed (see table 3.5).

Nouns express objects/phenomena. Verbs express the state of being of objects or actions that change the state of objects. Adjectives express the attributes and characteristics of objects/phenomena. Adverbs express the attribute/characteristics of actions and can express the attributes and characteristics of adjectives and other adverbs. Pronouns express objects/phenomena. Determiners, prepositions, and conjunctions express relationships.

I believe the breakdown of types of sentences and the nature parts of speech supports the premise that the two fundamental units of rule knowledge are objects and actions. It is important to note that references going forward in this book to attributes, characteristics, and relationships refer to both concrete and abstract semantic features and relationships and specify specific state of being or changes in state of being. For example, "The box is in the car" expresses a state of being of the box and the attribute of location. The statement "The phrase is ambiguous" expresses a state of being of the phrase and the abstract attribute of ambiguity.

One additional item is required to complete the task of creating correspondence and coherence between this proposed theory of rule-based knowledge and neuroscience.

Table 3.4

1. Subject	Form of be	Adverbial	
The dog	is	in the yard.	
2. Subject	**Form of be**	**Subject complement**	
The sky	is	blue. [adjective that describes subject]	
My father	is	a soldier. [noun phrase that renames subject]	
3. Subject	**Linking verb**	**Subject complement**	
My brother	looks	tired. [adjective that describes subject]	
My sister	became	a nurse. [noun phrase that renames subject]	
4. Subject	**Intransitive verb**		
The man	cried.		
5. Subject	**Transitive verb**	**Direct object**	
The bat	hit	the ball.	
6. Subject	**Transitive verb**	**Indirect object**	**Direct object**
The teacher	gave	Juan	the pencil.
7. Subject	**Transitive verb**	**Direct object**	**Object complement**
The coach	called	the effort	outstanding. [adjective]
The teacher	considers	the students	scholars. [noun phrase]

We need a physical mechanism for deduction. The work of Johnson-Laird, Byrne, and Schaeken (1992) and Johnson-Laird and Goodwin (2005) and Johnson-Laird (1983) defines such a mechanism.

Their generalized model of the deductive process is as follows:

1. Constructing a representation of the premises of the problem.
2. Invoking the representation of the applicable rule.
3. Formulating a semantically coherent conclusion from the representations.
4. Checking for alternative conclusions.
5. Considering the collusion to be correct, if no alternative conclusions are found.

Table 3.5

Part of Speech	Function/idea	Examples	Question answered
Noun	person, place, thing, or concept	cup, dog, Paris, computer	who or what
Verb	expresses action or state of being	is, was, hit, run, sing	did what, is what
Adjective	describes nouns	blue, smooth	which one, what kind
Adverb	describes verbs, adjectives, other adverbs	quickly, slowly	when, where, why, how, in what manner, to what degree, under what conditions
Determiner	limits or determines nouns	a, the, 2, 12	how many, which, how much
Pronoun	replaces a noun	I, she, he	who or what
Preposition	relates a noun to other words	to, at, with	where, when, why, how
Conjunction	connects words, phrases, and clauses	and, or, when	what else, under what
Interjection	exclamation	oh! hi! well	emotional expression

Johnson-Laird, Byrne, and Schaeken (1992) present the following simple example that captures the essence of the process.

Problem: If there is a circle, what follows?

Rule: If there is a circle, there is a triangle.

Rule representation:

Given/model: There is a circle.

Conclusion/deduction: There is a triangle.

The conclusion or deduction that there is a triangle follows as semantically coherent with the rule through the comparison of the representation of the rule and the representation of the circumstance to which the rule is applied.

In experiments that test participant performance on tests of abstract logic, when given a rule like "If there is a circle, then there is a triangle" and the information that there is a triangle, most participants will incorrectly state that there is a circle. The Johnson-Laird model supports this incorrect conclusion. To answer correctly would require a representation wherein there was a triangle and not a circle. As Johnson-Laird, Byrne, and Schaeken state, the problem arises because a direct comparison of semantic features yielding the correct solution requires that the collection of representations exhaustively represents the possible states of the elements involved in the relationship. This is the reason why participants in tests of abstract logic struggle with purely abstract logic but can easily process an inferential relationship like "If it is raining, then the streets will be wet." In this case, they can access a wealth of episodic and semantic representations that would inform them that streets can be wet without rain. The contrast between participant performance on tests of purely abstract logic versus logic involved with propositions that have numerous semantic features supports Johnson-Laird, Byrne, and Schaeken's theory.

Theory of Knowledge

The philosophic questions concerning knowledge are the metaphysical question "What is knowledge?" and the epistemological question "What can humans know and how do they go about knowing it?" Human knowledge that takes the form of rules and is symbolic in nature, per Deacon's definition, is knowledge of objects/phenomena and actions (changes in the state of objects) and the relationship between them. As discussed previously, rules are the concepts, principles, theories, and generalizations that represent the brain's organization of experience. Rules enable higher-level human cognitive activities like communication and rule-based decision-making, problem-solving, planning, strategizing, and design (creation). Human rule-based knowledge also includes the procedures for applying rules to accomplish goals. The basic units of knowing are defined as follows:

objects/phenomena: Abstracted, similar, and invariant attributes and characteristics of a group of entities and the relationship among those attributes and characteristics.

actions: Abstracted, similar, and invariant changes in the state of objects/phenomena with time and the relationship that connects or accounts for those changes.

procedures: An invariant sequence of actions, coherent with and the necessary consequences of a rule, that lead from the current state to a desired state.

This discussion also suggests a definition for meaning/understanding and teaching:

meaning/understanding: Creating a relationship that achieves semantic coherence (logical closure) between the items put into relationship.

teaching: Helping students create relationships that create meaning and provide understanding of the content of their experience; helping students connect the dots of experience.

Note that events are not listed as a fundamental unit of knowing. I define events as abstracted combinations of objects involved in actions. Events are things like concerts, parades, and conventions where items involved in actions are similar and invariant across multiple instantiations and, therefore, can be abstracted and indexed to a symbol.

The operation of the mind on the symbolically indexed items of knowing—in other words, human logic and reason—is postulated to be as follows:

logic/reason: The process of creating relationships between the brain's representations of the items (objects/phenomena, actions) put into relationship that achieves coherence (logical closure) between the semantic features of those items put into relationship.

This process is primarily conducted through the symbolic systems of language and mathematics. At the level of neurons, the hypothesis is that the human memory and logic/reasoning system is a semantic-feature process that, because of the brain's nonlinear connectivity, attempts to achieve equilibrium between the representations put into relationship by thought.

The types of relationships supported by the human mind and its symbolic system are postulated to be those listed in table 3.6. These can also be thought of as judgments in the context of Kant and other philosophers' definition of judgments. Table 3.6 lists the questions the relationships or judgments answer, the relationship type, and a description of the nature of the relationship. The relationships proposed are analogous to Aristotle's categories, Hume's operations of the mind, and Kant's categories of judgment, except they are, consistent with the preceding theory of knowledge, relationships between the semantic features of objects/phenomena and actions. Since it is postulated that thought comes into existence through language and other symbolic representations, the relationships listed are those manifest in language and mathematics.

As Kant's postulated two types of judgments and Gazzaniga's work with split-brain patients indicate, symbolically indexed knowledge, as defined previously, does not include all human knowing. Initial knowing, supported by the brain's capacity for association and image creation, leads to the development of iconic representations of the regularities in experience. The form of such knowledge is images produced by the human perceptual system. As Gazzaniga states, the predominantly right-brain processing of images involves attention to perceptual detail, perceptual grouping and apprehending perceptual patterns, and making perceptual distinctions and judgments, like "The sun is shining and the rock is warming." Importantly, these types of judgments do not go beyond the information contained in the image.

Table 3.6

Question answered	Relationship type	Description
1. What?	State of being—existential	(a) Relationships between attributes and characteristics of objects
		(b) Relationships of parts to wholes
		(c) Relationships of item to contexts
2. When?	Temporal	Relating points in time
3. Where?	Spatial	Relating positions in space
4. Why?	Causal	Relating causes to effects
5. How?	Action nature	Relationships of manner, extent, and degree
6. How much?	Quantitative	Relationships of amount and size
7. Necessary?	Logical	Relationships created through logical connectives: and, or, not, if/then
8. Why care?	Feeling/emotion	(a) Relationships of value—important/unimportant
		(b) Relationships of valence—positive/negative, good/bad

The next chapter discusses the work of two researchers who have defined two systems of reasoning that cohere with the preceding distinction. Stephen Sloman (1996) describes a system in which reasoning is derived from perceptually learned associations and a symbolic system in which reasoning occurs through the use of rules. He notes that human cognitive hardware associatively encodes and processes regularities in experience. In so doing, it detects and records similarities, regularities, and covariations. It enables a form of statistically based reasoning. If there is a sufficient degree of similarity between a current perception and an associative representation in memory, the brain will reason through association. For example, the system would support the inference that if there is smoke, then there is a fire.

Daniel Kahneman (2011) also delineated two systems of human reasoning. He characterizes his System 1 as the innate abilities we share with other animals. These include the ability to perceive the world around us, recognize objects and actions, and undertake behaviors adaptable to our environment. Kahneman's System 1 is automatic and largely subconscious in its knowledge acquisition and, therefore, requires no conscious effort to accumulate. I hypothesize that Sloman's system of associative reasoning, Kahneman's

System 1, Gazzaniga's right-brain processing, and Kant's first type of reasoning are one and the same: a system of knowing facilitated by the brain's capacity for association and for recording similarities and regularities in memory and generating perceptual images. In the remainder of this book, I will refer to this functionality as the *associative learning system*.

Because the vast majority of formal conscious learning, like school learning, occurs through the brain's symbolic representational system, it is the focus of this book. A significant amount of learning in pre-K to second grade does, however, of necessity, come through the associative learning system. For example, arithmetic facts are learned associatively. As Kant demonstrates, we cannot employ reason or the relationship of ideas to learn that 7 + 5 = 12. We must count and then memorize that fact. Arithmetic facts are learned by repeated exposure and memorization in the associative learning system. The same is true for things like learning the shapes of letters and numerals, letter-sound relationships, and other topics in early education.

Developmental psychologists of the twentieth century like Jean Piaget and Lev Vygotsky were the first to reveal that children's thinking and reasoning differs from that of adults. Their work was instrumental in moving educators toward instruction that was "developmentally appropriate." Piaget showed that young children, in what he called the *preoperations stage*, reasoned largely through the use of perceptual images and associations. The child at this stage also focuses on only one aspect of an image. An example is provided by Piaget's experiment where a researcher forms two lines with the same number of objects in each line and has a child count the objects and agree that they are the same. The researcher then spreads the objects in one of the lines farther apart and asks the child which line has the greater number of objects. The preoperational child will answer that the expanded line has a greater number of objects. This results because the child's thought is image based, focused on one dimension (length), and the child associates, based on past experience, that greater length means more.

From this stage, children progress to what Piaget referred to as the *concrete operations stage*, where they can reason symbolically if the symbols refer to concrete physical objects. In Piaget's final stage, young people can reason with symbols (words) that are purely abstract, without direct physical referents. These would be words like *equality* and *conservation* that are applicable to numerous different physical instantiations. Note that these words are at a higher logical level and consist of abstractions of classes with concrete referents. They are classes of classes.

Vygotsky examined children's word meanings and arrived at analogous progressions in children's thinking and word usage. For example, at one stage, children use the same word for different objects if those objects have a single physical feature in common. This again reflects the image-based, one-dimensional nature of their thought. In Vygotsky's final stage, word meanings are the abstracted attributes and characteristics of objects and actions connected through a relationship that expresses a judgment as to the nature of the relationship. Consistent with the foregoing, this would indicate the development of the capacity to reason through symbolic representations.

Piaget ([1970] 2006) experimented with children's concepts of movement and speed. Judging the relative speed of two different moving objects, like cars, requires simultaneously considering the distance traveled and the time required to travel the distance. For example, to compare the relative speed of two cars traveling over two different courses requires that an individual keep four items in working memory simultaneously to arrive at a conclusion. A preoperational child will always say that the car that arrives first is the fastest regardless of the path taken. According to Piaget, it isn't until the final stage of development that young people have a fully formed concept of speed.

My hypothesis regarding Piaget's and Vygotsky's observed developmental progression is that they reflect the development with time of increases in working-memory capacity and the development of a higher level of symbolic representation, or the capacity to abstract concrete classes into fully abstract classes of classes and to even higher logical levels. There has yet to emerge, from modern research, a consensus opinion or set of systemic conclusions regarding the developmental progression of children's thinking. I believe more research is required to assist teachers in making developmentally appropriate decisions regarding curriculum and content. Most of these decisions are made empirically based on experience of what children at each grade level seem to be capable of comprehending. Many teachers rely on the historical traditions of what is taught at each grade level, the level of content implicit in the learning representations—for example, the books and other materials that they are supplied with—and their own personal experience to make decisions as to what is developmentally appropriate.

The next chapter is my attempt to answer the second part of the epistemological question concerning knowledge: How do humans acquire knowledge and learn? As the reader might suspect from the foregoing, two of my main methods of knowledge construction are (1) abstraction and inductive generalization and (2) deduction, or the relation of ideas. Induction has a forward path that corresponds with the concept of synthesis and a backward path that corresponds with the concept of analysis. Deduction has a forward path that corresponds with the concept of logic, or achieving semantic coherence (logical closure) between representations, and a backward path that corresponds with the concept of abduction, or Kantian logic. To these two methods of knowledge construction, I have added three others. One is reflective abstraction, which is, in essence, inductive generalization of actions and procedures, which intend to accomplish goals, into rules. The forward path is trial and error and the backward path is reflective abstraction of actions that produce outcomes into rules. The second addition is dialectic process, which is a process for developing new rules when one's existing inventory of rules fail. There is only one path proposed for this knowledge-construction process. The final knowledge-construction process proposed is application. Two aspects of application are elaborated: (1) direct application of rules to accomplish goals and (2) contextual teaching and learning.

At this point, a word of caution is perhaps in order. The preceding derivation of a theory of knowledge is my own. It does not reflect a consensus of opinion of scholars and researchers in the field. In fact, some would not give up on the idea that mental processing reflects some innate syntactical-processing mechanism like an innate formal logic or grammar. What I have attempted to do is to develop a theory of knowledge that is coherent and correspondent with results from cognitive science, philosophy, language, systems theory, and educational research.

A Note on Postmodern Philosophy

Postmodern philosophers dismiss the possibility and validity of any theory of knowledge such as the one I have just presented. Their viewpoint is summarized by the following quote from educational philosopher Nel Noddings (2012, 121):

> Postmodernism suggested that we cannot study "knowledge in general" in any meaningful way. Knowledge is so thoroughly contaminated with social and political power that we simply must concentrate on the sociology of knowledge. From this perspective, it is chasing a will-o'-the-wisp to seek foundations for knowledge, and even accounts of where knowledge came from or where it leads are incomplete if the ideological context is not described. Knowledge is established by power, not by justification in the neutral sense that Socrates envisioned.

Postmodern philosopher Michel Foucault (1972) contends that is not possible to think of knowledge without considering the relationship between knowledge and the desire for power and control. Foucault asserts that all historical systems of knowledge express a truth-power relationship. Based on his analysis of history, during past epochs, certain groups used claims to knowledge and truth to legitimize power relationships over other groups. Each epoch produced an episteme, or set of underlying assumptions, that governed the intellectual outlook, the emergence of ideologies, the formation of institutions, and the practices by which people controlled, regulated, governed, and defined one another. Those in possession of what they contended was objective/universal truth presumed the right to hold and use power over others (Gutek 2009). For example, during the Middle Ages in Europe, church-approved doctrine constituted the episteme that controlled every aspect of life. Since there are, according to Foucault, many claims to truth rather than one universal, timeless, and objective set of truths, he advised that all texts be examined in terms of who is exerting power and why. Foucault's claim is in essence that the historical impetus for knowledge creation was the desire for power and control. This goal influenced the context used for the creation of specific claims to knowledge, or epistemes.

While Foucault is correct that individuals and institutions have in different eras misused claims to knowledge and truth to further their ambitions and self-interests and to marginalize those who disagreed, this is a claim about the social and political use of knowledge, not a demonstration of the nature of knowledge itself. This history of use does not invalidate or preclude the possibility of epistemology or epistemological analysis, nor does it preclude a scientific investigation of the nature of knowledge such as that undertaken by cognitive science. What might have been Newton's power motives in formulating his laws of physics, or as Noddings (2012, 121) asks, "How is social power involved in claiming that 2 + 3 = 5, or that Mumbai received 37 inches of rain on one day in 2005, or that human beings cannot leap over tall buildings in a single bound?"

Postmodern philosophers such as Jacques Derrida and Richard Rorty take the position that we have only our language ability to make meaning and create understanding.

Worldly phenomena acquire their meaning through language. In their view, thought is not possible without language. This position coincides with that of Vygotsky ([1934] 1986), who asserted that thought is not merely expressed in words, it comes into existence through them. Through the mechanism of inner speech, thought finds its reality and form in words.

Derrida (1976) stated that language imposes a structure on the world by categorizing and subdividing it. Without language, these subdivisions would not exist. As Gregory Bateson ([1979] 2002, 35) states, "The division of the perceived universe into parts and wholes is convenient and may be necessary, but no necessity dictates how it shall be done."

Derrida connects the existentialist position that individuals construct knowledge from perceptions, intuitions, and reflections that result consequent to experience to the assertion that we have only language to create meaning and understanding to conclude that all knowledge is necessarily subjective, personally and socially constructed, and subject to change with time. We cannot step outside of language to acquire word meanings, nor do we have access to objective criteria outside ourselves with which to establish such meanings.

Rorty ([1989] 2006, 5) summarizes this position as follows:

To say that the world is out there, that it is not our creation, is to say with common sense, that most things in space and time are the effects of causes which do not include human mental states. To say that truth is not out there is simply to say that where there are no sentences there is no truth, that sentences are elements of human languages, and that human languages are human creations. Truth cannot be out there—cannot exist independently of the human mind—because sentences cannot be out there. The world is out there, but descriptions of the world are not. Only descriptions of the world can be true or false.

Derrida coined the neologism *différance* to summarize the nature of language. This word combines *difference* and *defer*. Generally, it intends to convey that words are different from what they represent or refer to and that words defer to other words or acquire their meaning through other words such that their meaning is forever deferred and cannot be given definitively.

Taken to its logical limit, the postmodern position rejects the modern paradigm. There cannot be objective truths that express the universal timeless realities of the universe—realities that are "discovered" through the application of logic and reason to empirical experience. This position rejects the privileged status of science as a method for obtaining unbiased objective truth and reduces it to one of many ways of creating understanding. The exercise of pure logic and reason or metaphysical speculation is similarly rejected as a path to objective universal truth since it is language based and dependent. In the limit, the postmodern position reduces philosophy to literature.

Since language conveys only personally and socially constructed meaning, and language use and derived meaning is contingent upon how a group decides to use words, the resulting text or discourse is meaningful only in terms of the cultural system that it is part of. There is no one true "knowledge" but a variety, each of which is meaningful to the person or group that constructs it. In the absence of external criteria, no claim to knowledge is superior to others, or equivalently, there is no preferred context for creating meaning—all contexts are created equal.

While the preceding appears well reasoned, democratic, and liberating, it is problematic from a variety of perspectives. The most obvious problem is the complete relativism that the postmodern position implies and creates. While it supports giving a voice to groups that have been historically marginalized and whose claims to knowledge have been dismissed, it must also admit claims to knowledge and understanding emanating from groups that postmodernists would adamantly oppose, like neo-Nazis.

The postmodern position begins with the existential position that individuals create personal meaning from perception, intuition, and reflection ex post facto experience. It never addresses the question of how this comes about. By rejecting the possibility of epistemology and cognitive science as legitimate theories of knowledge, it does not have a way of answering this question. One of the best responses to postmodernism comes from George Lakoff and Mark Johnson. Lakeoff and Johnson (1980, 194) point out that what the postmodern position misses is that "our understanding, even our most imaginative understandings, is given in terms of a conceptual system that is grounded in our successful functioning in our physical and cultural environments." Meaning is never disembodied but is derivative from our physical and cultural experience. Knowing is grounded in the neural mechanisms that record the invariant patterns in our world as rendered by the senses. Knowing is relationally based or interactional and, as such, embodied.

Regarding Bertrand Russell's query about what we tell the man who believes he is a poached egg, we don't tell him anything. In the manner of pragmatic philosophy, we ask him, "How is that belief working out for you? As a poached egg, do you have a satisfactory social life? What kind of work can a poached egg do to support themselves, make a living to provide for food, shelter, and clothing?" This is Lakoff and Johnson's point.

I would, therefore, conclude that postmodernism is a social philosophy rather than an evaluation of the nature of epistemology. As Noddings (2012, 116) states, "Although those who reject universal truths should be credited with positive social/ethical motives, rejection of the traditional notion of truth may be too heavy a price to pay."

Construction of Knowledge

Associative Learning

This book is primarily concerned with learning that is conscious and intentional. For example, the type of learning that occurs in formal settings like schools. It is also principally focused on learning that is facilitated by the uniquely human capacity for symbolic representation and the creation of symbol-to-symbol relationships. Formal learning utilizes two symbolic systems: language and mathematics. Conscious learning involves the creation of **rules** that symbolically represent the way the world/universe is in the mind of the individual. In keeping with the idea of rules used in cognitive science, I define rules as ideas, concepts, theories, principles, and generalizations. Formal learning also involves the procedures and actions necessary to use rules to accomplish goals. In summary, this book is primarily concerned with rule-based learning and actions.

Rules are the enablers of what is called *higher-order thinking*. In the field of education, definitions of higher-order thinking abound. For purposes in this book, I will define it as rule-based communication, decision-making, problem-solving, planning, strategizing, and design/creation.

Many of these activities are possible without symbolic representation and rules. Animals like wolves make decisions, solve problems, communicate, and undertake other actions that serve their needs. They accomplish this through their associative learning capacity. For example, if you are trying to teach your dog to respond to the command "sit," you move the dog into a sitting position and emphatically say the word "sit." As you repeat the sequence over and over, your dog will ultimately associate the sound of the word with the action. If you then tell your dog, "I wish you would respond to my commands more quickly," he will not understand because he, unlike you, does not have the capacity to form an idea from symbol-to-symbol (word-to-word) relationships. If, however, you only reward the dog with the treat when the dog responds quickly, there is some possibility that the dog will eventually associate the reward with a rapid response.

During the first half of the twentieth century, most psychologists and educators believed that all human learning was associative. There were notable exceptions, such as

Russian psychologist Lev Vygotsky and French psychologist Jean Piaget. It was a time when behaviorism was the dominant force in American psychology and education. From Ivan Pavlov, whose dog associated the ringing of a bell with the reception of a treat and began to salivate whenever he heard a bell (classical conditioning), to John Watson and B. F. Skinner, who theorized that all human behavior, including learning, could be controlled by administering either a reward or a punishment in response to a demonstrated behavior (operant conditioning), behaviorism greatly influenced educational practices. During this era, teachers received training in academic content and in eliciting behaviors in students that were thought to be conducive to learning. It was a time when successful learning was rewarded with extrinsic rewards like gold stars, awards, and praise, while poor performance was condemned and otherwise dealt with. To share an anecdote, a friend of mine attended a stern British boarding school in the 1950s and early 1960s. He reported that one of his math teachers required that all homework be done in ink. If a mistake was made while solving a problem, the student was to put a line through the error and continue. The teacher could then see how many mistakes were made by the student. If too many mistakes were in evidence, the student was asked to extend their arm in class to receive a smack on the back of the hand with a ruler. My friend reports that to this day, some sixty years later, he is still filled with anxiety and trepidation whenever he does math, but that he rarely, if ever, makes a mistake. He also believes this experience had an impact on his decision not to become an accountant or an engineer.

Beginning in the late 1950s and early 1960s, there was a growing realization by psychologists that a great deal of human behavior could not be explained by behaviorist theory. It was not the stimulus itself that determined behavior, rather it was how people understood or interpreted the stimulus. The work of the Vygotsky and Piaget became more influential, and the field of cognitive science began to emerge. Linguist Noam Chomsky was particularly influential in demonstrating the limitations of many of Skinner's theories. The focus of research began to shift to how the brain implements the phenomena we experience as the mind. From both a psychological perspective (cognitive psychology) and a biological perspective (cognitive neuroscience), researchers began to study areas like perception, attention, memory, language, and reasoning. Advances in technology like computerized axial tomography (CT), positron emission tomography (PET), and functional magnetic resonance imaging (fMRI) allowed scientists to see which parts of the brain were involved in implementing phenomena of the mind, like the formation of memories and the comprehension of speech. Coupled with advances in molecular biology, new technology allowed neuroscientists to fashion theories and create models of cognitive processes. From the 1960s to the present there has been a veritable explosion of information about the mind and the brain and their relationship to learning.

Another change that occurred with the decline of behaviorism was the emergence, in the field of education, of attention to pedagogy—the idea that how students experience and engage with content makes a difference. If you ask the average person what teaching is, they will typically respond that it is telling someone what you know and/or showing them what you can do. If you subsequently ask them to tell you the difference between the "good" and the "bad" teachers they experienced, they will respond with anecdotes such as "The good teachers explained things in a way I could understand" or "The good teachers understood why I was struggling and could help me overcome my difficulties." These are certainly attributes associated with good teaching. If we collected all the anecdotal statements from people about "good" teachers and analyzed them, we could abstract the idea that "good" teachers were the ones who employed effective pedagogical practices. How students experience and engage with content, with the aid of the teacher, makes all the difference in the world. Pedagogy matters! The design and delivery of instruction is a critical factor in whether instruction is effective or not. The interaction between student and teacher is a dynamic, nonlinear process that can result in student learning, or it can fail to bring about learning.

The remainder of this book deals with the following:

- The way humans construct and use their knowledge of rules
- The derivation of a set of first principles that define the requirements for successful knowledge construction, which can be utilized to
  » design effective learning experiences
  » diagnose the reasons for learning failures
  » design effective curriculum and instructional delivery methods
    audit existing curriculum and instructional practices

Before delving into the details of rule-based learning, it is important to further elaborate on associative learning, since our associatively learned knowledge is grist for the mill of rule-based learning.

As discussed previously, the architecture of the brain and the cellular process of memory creation in neural networks is such that the brain automatically, without conscious effort and engagement, captures the invariant and recurring patterns manifest in our experience. These patterns are of two general types: (1) the semantic features and the relationship between them of objects that persistent in time and are frequently experienced and (2) the recurring changes in the state of those objects with time—changes that appear to follow a rule. I define semantic features as the attributes and characteristics of objects and the changes in the state of objects that are sensed and can be perceived. It consists of all the features that define state of being.

As also previously discussed, the productive nature of the neuronal architecture of the perceptual system, wherein networks that represent elements of semantic features are variously combined to produce the composite images we perceive, naturally results in abstraction of perceived semantic features into classes and categories of objects and actions. Associative learning is a capability we share with animals. Even if animals do not have words for rocks, plants, and predators, they have a sense that they are part of a class or category of objects that share semantic features in common. This sense allows them to undertake appropriate behavioral responses to classes or categories of objects. They have a sense of what constitutes a potential food source and what constitutes a potential threat (like a predator) and can execute an appropriate behavioral response when encountering something that associatively seems to be in such a class or category.

In addition to associative learning, humans, with our ability to represent things symbolically, have the capacity to learn by constructing and using rules. The duality of knowledge systems is well documented in the literature. For example, in a 1996 paper, Stephen Sloman summarized the research to that time on human reasoning and made an empirical case for two systems of thinking: one in which inferences are drawn from a network of learned associations and another that uses symbols in a rule-governed way to reach conclusions. His paper sought to reconcile the two schools of thought on human reasoning that had emerged: one that postulated an associative system that encodes and processes statistical regularities in the environment and another that postulated symbols processed according to a set of rules that are productive and systematic. The rules and symbols are productive in the sense that they can encode an unlimited number of referent properties and can be composed with one another to generate an unlimited set of propositions. They are systematic in that the ability to encode certain facts implies the ability to encode others. Another attribute of the rule-based system is that it requires conscious effort and the construction of a chain of reasoning.

The associative system, in encoding and processing the statistical regularities of an individual's environment and experience, records frequencies and correlations among the features of the world. Constructs such as variability and covariation are implicit in associative memory representations. As Sloman states, associative thought uses similarity, contiguity, and temporal relations to draw inferences and make predictions that approximate those of a statistician. The statistician's work is rule-based; however, the operation of the brain's associative network does not require rules. If there is a sufficient degree of similarity between a current stimulus and an associatively generated representation in memory, the brain will reason through the association. For example, past experience will facilitate the inference that if something has wings, it can probably fly. This is an association created by encoding past experience.

It is important to emphasize that although the operation of the brain's associative system of reasoning can and has been successfully modeled with statistical techniques such as the use of Bayesian networks, there are no sets of statistical rules in the brain by which it is computing conclusions. Statistical calculations and models are not homomorphic with brain processes. It is the nonlinear and hierarchical connectivity of the brain that facilitates associative reasoning. Once equilibrium is reached between the perceptual networks representing the stimulus and the networks representing the memories of sufficiently similar past experiences, the full range of associated semantic features and their relationship to one another in memory are activated. This association of past to present enables inferences such as "if there is smoke, then there is fire" and "if it has wings, then it can fly." The fact that association can be modeled as the contingent probability of A given B is handy for modeling purposes, but what this probability models is the strength of the neuronal connections between representations of A and B. For example, in the case of smoke and fire, the connection strength is exceedingly high.

Another notable delineation of two systems of thinking comes from the work of Daniel Kahneman. Kahneman (2011) refers to his two systems of thinking as System

1 and System 2. He states that System 1 includes many of the innate abilities we share with other animals. We are born with the ability to perceive the world around us, recognize objects and actions, and undertake behaviors adaptable to the contingencies of our environment. Other mental activities that are part of System 1 are things we have learned and that have become fast and automatic through prolonged practice. System 1 has learned many things through the association of ideas: things like trees can have apples and thunderstorms produce lightning. Through repeated practice, System 1 has automated skills like reading and appropriately responding to social situations.

Another attribute of System 1 is that it operates automatically and quickly, with little or no conscious effort. If you want to wash your hands, System 1 knows that a sink is a source of water, soap is a cleaning agent, and that a certain level of pressure from your hands will move the levers or fixtures that allow the water to flow from the faucet. You do this without conscious thought and could conduct a conversation with someone, using System 2, while doing it. System 1 is what allows us to address the typical requirements of our everyday lives quickly, efficiently, and smoothly.

We address the demands of our lives with System 1 until we run into difficulty and events occur that violate the model of the world maintained by System 1. System 2 then takes over and undertakes a more detailed analysis in a conscious, effortful, intentional, and orderly manner. Perceptual attention to the details of the problem is allocated and long-term memories of relevant rules are activated to create a coherent "story" that makes sense of the event and enables a rule-based plan of action to be created that resolves the difficulty. System 2 is much slower and expends a lot more energy than System 1. If all our actions and responses required System 2 processing, life would be very tedious, effortful, and much less efficient.

The brain will often shift things learned through System 2 into System 1. For example, what is called "expert performance" demonstrates many of the characteristics of System 1. During my career as an engineer, I had encountered certain classes of problems so often I could automatically invoke the appropriate equations and create the required graphs with little or no conscious effort. I could think about what was for dinner and what mood my wife would be in when I got home while doing it. This anecdote demonstrates an important attribute of System 1. System 1–driven actions are directly cued by the perception of circumstances without conscious thought. Mental processing goes from perception directly to actions coherent with the contents of perception. The rules that describe and delineate "the way the world is" are implicit and subconscious within System 1.

Understanding System 1 associative learning is valuable because the contents of this system are grist for the mill of System 2. System 1 supplies descriptions, impressions, intuitions, intentions, and feelings to System 2. When operated on by System 2, these become our conscious beliefs about how the world is and our conscious voluntary actions guided by those beliefs.

Of necessity, some teaching and learning in formal settings, like schools, is associative and involves System 1. A considerable portion of pre-K to second-grade learning is associative. For example, the Common Core objectives for kindergarten include recognizing letter-sound relationships and grade-appropriate sight words, identifying shapes, and recognizing and printing numerals. These learning goals are of necessity accomplished by repeated exposure and practice until associations are formed in the student's long-term memory. The progress of this associative learning process could be measured using the old "learning curve" by plotting the number of exposures to the material versus the accuracy and speed of recall of the material. The learning curve reflects the molecular and cellular process of repeatedly activating the neuronal circuits representing, for example, the visual grapheme of letters and the auditory phoneme of their sounds. The more the two are contemporaneously activated, the stronger the connection will be between them and the more likely a long-term memory will result. Neurons that fire together wire together.

Significant associative learning also occurs in later grades. For example, Newton's laws are simply given to students as principles that describe the relationships between force, mass, and motion. Students are asked to accept and remember (memorize) the laws. In fact, Newton's laws are derivable from a principle known as Hamilton's principle. Hamilton's principle states that the path an object will take is the path that minimizes the sum of the difference between the object's potential and kinetic energy along the path. The universe is parsimonious. We know this law empirically as: objects take the path of least resistance, or perhaps intellectually as Occam's razor—the simplest explanation is usually the most correct. The reason Newton's laws are not derived for the student from Hamilton's principle is that following and understanding the derivation would require a knowledge of advanced calculus, specifically, the calculus of variations. This knowledge would not be in the inventory of a high school or freshman college student.

To cite another example, students who take high school biology are required to "learn" the Krebs cycle, a process that takes place in the mitochondria of a cell wherein energy originally from ingested food is converted into ATP (adenosine triphosphate), an organic molecule that the cell can use to power its operations. Before entering the Krebs cycle, glucose (from food) is converted through glycolysis into two molecules of pyruvate. Pyruvate then interacts with coenzyme A and through a chemical reaction in which enzyme action strips one carbon atom from pyruvate and attaches it to oxygen, two molecules are chemically reduced to form NADH, and acetyl-COA is produced. The Krebs cycle then begins with two molecules of acetyl-COA transferring their two carbon acetyl groups to four-carbon oxaloacetate to form citrate, the first product of the Krebs cycle.

The preceding description was taken from a biology textbook. When a ninth-grade student reads or hears this description, they experience it as: some complicated chemicals react with others to produce yet another complicated chemical by some mysterious process that is beyond my comprehension. To "learn" the Krebs cycle, the student has no option other than a brute memorization of the description; a memorization achieved by repeatedly reading the description and perhaps trying to form a mental image in memory of the graphic that usually accompanies the description. The vocabulary is foreign to the student, as are the chemical processes, such as chemical reduction.

Unless the student pursues a degree in biology, this will be the only time in their lives that they will ever encounter the Krebs cycle. The likelihood that it will be retained in long-term memory is exceedingly low. The law of memory at work here can be colloquially stated as the "use it or lose it" principle. The memory networks of the brain have no criteria or mechanism to determine if something is important to retain. Degree of importance is implicit in the cellular and molecular memory mechanism. If something is represented, and the representational circuits are activated again and again, then that something is likely to be retained in memory. The implicit logic that results is: if something is encountered and represented over and over, it must be important. Recall that the length and strength of memories at the neuron level are determined by the following:

- Strength of activation
- Duration and frequency of activation
- Number of connections to other neurons and neural networks
- Achievement of equilibrium between neural networks such that they mutually and reciprocally activate each other

The Krebs cycle example can be generalized to any academic content where the learner is unfamiliar with the elements and relationships in a description or cannot comprehend and follow the inductive or deductive arguments of a teacher or textbook author. To "learn" the material and regurgitate it on a test, the student must simply memorize the material. Regrettably, a significant amount of school learning occurs by this process. For example, many students get through high school math simply by memorizing the algorithms and procedures for getting answers to math problems. They never develop a conceptual understanding of math; in lieu, they learn the game of math. High school students quickly learn that it isn't necessary to follow a teacher's or textbook author's derivation or logical justification of theorems. The teacher or author will eventually get around to illustrating the procedures and algorithms for getting answers to problems. Given the nature of most mathematical assessments, this is all students will need to know to get through the course.

Simply learning mathematical algorithms and procedures during high school is probably acceptable for those who go on to college and prepare for science, technology, engineering, and mathematical professions (STEM). First, these individuals need to know the algorithms and procedures since they are fundamental to the more complex mathematical operations that their college math courses will require. Second, they will eventually develop a conceptual understanding from their subsequent math courses and the science courses that require the application of mathematical understandings. Unfortunately, not having a conceptual understanding is problematic for those students who do not go on to study for STEM professions. Ostensibly, the reason for teaching abstract math to everyone is to prepare people to solve practical problems in their lives that involve quantities. A conceptual understanding of mathematics is required to apply math outside the very specific context in which it is learned. In one's daily life, there's no tutor around to create a diagram, supply the givens, and suggest the algorithm to you to obtain an answer to a quantitative problem. In my graduate classes, I conduct an informal survey. I ask everyone who is not a STEM professional to raise their hand if they have ever formulated an algebraic or other abstract mathematical equation to solve a problem in their life since leaving college. After surveying thousands of students, I have yet to have anyone raise their hand.

Despite my lengthy diatribe concerning the teaching of the Krebs cycle, I must concede that there are some topics in K–16 education that simply must be taught through association. They are things like the shapes of letters and numerals, letter-sound relationships, word pronunciations, or some scientific principles that have explanations that are beyond the reach of students. Memorization through repetitive association is the principle learning process. This process can sometimes be aided using mnemonic strategies. Mnemonic strategies work because of the neuronal memory principle cited previously: the strength of a neuron's or a neural network's memory of past activation is enhanced and increased as the number of connections to other neurons and neural networks are increased. Mnemonics create a structure in memory to which new items to be memorized can be associated and connected, thereby facilitating recall. One example, called a peg-word system, is to memorize the following rhyme:

One is a bun	Six is sticks
Two is a shoe	Seven is heaven
Three is a tree	Eight is a gate
Four is a door	Nine is a line
Five is a hive	Ten is a hen

Memorization of the rhyme itself is facilitated by the fact that the words rhyme and, therefore, share phonetic representations in memory and the fact that the count sequence from 1 to 10 is already in long-term memory. The basic process is to visualize, in the mind's eye, the item in the rhyme and the thing to be remembered. For example, if you wanted to memorize a grocery list consisting of ten items, you might visualize a loaf of bread being next to a package of buns on a grocery shelf, then visualize a shoe squishing a grape on the grocery store floor, then visualize a tree full of apples, and so forth.

Another mnemonic device that is often taught to students is memorization of the name ROY G. BIV, which turns the seven colors of the rainbow into a single unit to be memorized. The first letter of the colors Red, Orange, Yellow, Green, Blue, Indigo, and Violet becomes a name. A similar mnemonic involves memorization of the name H. He. Libebcnof and the phrase "Nena my gal sips chlorine." This mnemonic renders the first seventeen elements of the periodic table.

1	2	3	4	5	6	7	8	9	10	11	12	13	14	15	16	17
H	He	Li	Be	B	C	N	O	F	Ne	Na	Mg	Al	Si	P	S	Cl

Such methods rely on a single connection and a connection that is artificial and not semantic in nature. Memory research from the field of cognitive psychology is clear that we remember best what we understand best. Understanding involves finding the pattern of organization and discovering the pattern of connection among the semantic features of objects, actions, and events. Deeper and more elaborated processing that focuses on the meaning and the order within experience produces the most durable and long-lasting memories. Linking to prior understanding to increase the number of connections between neural representations enhances both memory consolidation and subsequent retrieval (Reisberg 2010; Bransford 1979; Craik and Tulving 1975; Conway, Cohen, and Stanhope 1992).

Recall that my hypothesized neural definition of "understanding" is the achievement of equilibrium among the neuronal circuits representing the semantic features of the objects, actions, and events of experience. In summary, repeated "learning with understanding" experiences wherein rules (concepts) are constructed in a variety of contexts using multiple modalities result in the most durable and useful knowledge. This type of learning optimizes the neural requirements for memory formation: strong, frequent, and prolonged activation of representational neural networks, many connections within and between representations, and achievement of equilibrium among the networks representing the semantic features of objects, actions, and events. The foregoing can be summarized with the following principles of learning:

Principle 1: New knowledge is constructed by individuals, from their experience, and is built on the foundation of prior understanding.

Principle 2: Individuals remember and recall best what they understand best. Understanding involves finding a coherent pattern of connection and relationship between the semantic features of objects, actions, and events.

Principle 3: Learning and recall are enhanced by experiences that maximize the number of connections and the strength of the connections between the brain's representations of the semantic features of objects, actions, and events by

» Linking new content to prior understandings

» Experiencing content in multiple modalities and in multiple contexts

» Experiencing deeper, more elaborated processing of content that focuses on meaning and understanding—finding the pattern of organization and order within content

» Experiencing repeated exposure to content

The next section begins the discussion of consciously created knowledge using the human capacity for symbolic representation. This is the knowledge developed within Kahneman's System 2, or what Sloman refers to as the rule-based system of reasoning.

Consciously Constructed Knowledge

Human Executive Function

Conscious thought is intentional, meaning it has a subject; it is about something. Very often, there is also some mental goal regarding the subject of the thought. In other words, conscious thought is typically goal directed. Once a goal for thought is established, the mind goes through a series of steps that are collectively referred to, in cognitive science, as human executive function. Goal representation occurs in the frontal pole of the prefrontal cortex of the brain (Broadman areas 9/10). This area remains active throughout the thought activity and acts to integrate the contents of the mental activity into a general framework consistent with the goal of the thought activity (Gazzaniga, Ivry, and Mangun 2009). The representation of goal would contain the features that define the successful attainment of goals.

The representation of goal activates a dynamic filtering process in the prefrontal cortex that does the following:

- Focuses attention and perception on the goal-relevant and salient elements of the environment of the individual

- Activates the goal-relevant and salient portions of long-term memory

The amount of sensory information available in a human's environment, at any given time, is enormous. For purposes of conscious thought, it is only necessary, and it is highly efficient, to focus attention on, perceive, and bring into consciousness only those items relevant to the subject/goal of thought. For example, if a picture or graph relevant to the goals of a lesson is presented to students, the student's frontal eye fields (Broadman area 8), which are proximal to the goal representation area, will direct the fovea of the eye toward the center of attention (picture/graph) and inhibit response to unattended information from the periphery of the eye. The prefrontal cortex modulates the salience of perceptual signals by inhibiting unattended information (Shimamura 2000). Similarly, if a student is taking a chemistry test and answering a question pertaining to water, the prefrontal cortex will activate the relevant contents of long-term memory, such as the chemical formula for water and its physical and chemical properties while inhibiting the student's memory of drinking a glass of water or splashing in the water at the beach. The activity of the prefrontal cortex as a dynamic filter to help retrieve and select information relevant to task requirements has been extensively studied by researchers such as Thompson-Schill et al. (1997) and Thompson-Schill, D-Esposito, and Kan (1999), who report that the greater the filtering demand of a task, the greater the activation of the left inferior gyrus of the prefrontal cortex (Broadman areas 44/45). In their experiments, Thompson-Schill and her associates documented the interaction between this area of the brain and the left temporal cortex, which is hypothesized as the long-term store of semantic information, when task demands required dynamic filtering of semantic information.

The next step in executive function protocol and process is the connection of goal-relevant perceptual information and goal-relevant long-term memory content through the working-memory system of the prefrontal cortex. The working-memory system is the primary area for interaction among representations of goals, relevant perceptions, pertinent long-term memories, and action plans relevant to goals. A couple of metaphors are useful for understanding how the working-memory system operates. The working memory-system operates like a switchboard that allows multiple parties to be connected and to communicate with one another. Working memory integrates the activity of different brain systems like perception, long-term memory, goal representation, and the procedure/action control areas. The working-memory system has reciprocal connections to the various areas of the brain that contain (represent) the information required to achieve a goal. These reciprocal connections allow working memory to activate the information areas that, in turn, reciprocally activate neurons in working memory. This back-and-forth activation allows information to remain active while it is being processed. The working-memory system is, therefore, not only a connecting hub but also a temporary storage area where information from other brain areas can be actively processed and utilized. It, therefore, can be thought of as a spreadsheet or workbench where items like data, tools, and parts are brought together to be combined or processed to produce some final product.

To illustrate the operation of working memory, we can think of the process of solving a mathematical problem. The goal is, of course, to obtain a solution to the described problem. First, executive function activates the perceptual system to obtain the problem specifications and the givens from the problem description. Next, long-term memory is accessed for an appropriate equation that relates the knowns (givens) to the unknown, which is the desired solution to the problem. The next step in the executive function process is the activation in procedural memory of the sequence of steps or algorithm needed to process the equation and obtain an answer. This can be, for example, the steps involved in manipulating an algebraic equation to obtain a solution. The working-memory system serves to connect the information from perception to the equation in long-term memory and to the algebraic manipulation procedure. It not only acts as a temporary store of information but also keeps all these representations active through the process of reciprocal activation of the neural networks representing the required information for problem solution.

The original concept of working memory emerged from the behavioral work of psychologist George Miller. Miller (1956) gave research participants strings of letters, numbers, or words and tested how many they could remember and for how long. Miller's conclusion was that human beings can remember from five to nine items for a period of about twenty seconds. Miller referred to his conclusion as the magic number seven. In Miller's model, working memory is viewed as a limited resource with a finite number of slots available for temporary storage. His model was later refined by Baddeley and Hitch (1974), but the magic number seven has withstood the test of time. The test is quite simple to implement and has been performed innumerable times. In fact, if you take a course in psychology, you will likely be given the opportunity to take the test. It should be noted that the preceding describes only the temporary storage aspect of the working-memory system. The previous, more fully elaborated description is derived from cognitive neuroscience.

Cognitive psychologists also described a working-memory process that they referred to as *chunking*. Chunking is the combination of different items in working memory into fewer items or, perhaps, a single item. For example, if you are given the words guitar, violin, tuba, coronet, drums, viola, and saxophone, working memory could "chunk" them into one idea: musical instruments. The idea of chunking is useful in understanding how working memory functions in the parsing of written and spoken language. Let's say you hear or read the sentence "My younger sister, after a long absence due to a prolonged bout with illness, has returned to her place of employment." This sentence has twenty-one words, or three times the size of working memory. It is not possible to load all these words into working memory and retain them while you make sense of and gain an understanding of the sentence. My hypothesis of how this process works is that sentence fragments or parts are held in working memory until they can be combined (chunked) into or made suggestive of a single concept that is then activated in long-term memory. Once this long-term memory is activated, the spaces in short-term memory are then available for a new set of words to process in working memory. In the preceding sentence example, the idea of a younger sister is activated in long-term memory, then the words "after a long absence" can be chunked or result in the activation of the idea of "gone" in long-term memory. Next, "due to a prolonged bout with illness" can be chunked into, or can result in, the activation of the idea of "sick" in long-term memory. Finally, "has returned to her place of employment" is chunked into and activates the idea of back to work. The longer sentence is chunked into "younger sister gone sick back to work"—seven ideas all activated in long-term memory. Chunking, in my view, is retention in working memory until a corresponding and summarizing idea in long-term memory can be activated. This then frees up the seven spaces to process the next sequence of words. In the preceding example, the seven summarizing ideas are not necessarily the new contents of working memory but are the activated long-term memories connected through the working-memory system.

The nature of the working-memory system can provide an explanation for why long-term retention rates from lectures alone are so low. Measured long-term retention rates after thirty-minute lectures often range as low as 5 to 10 percent, if the information presented is new to the learner (Masters 2013). My hypothesis to explain this result is that the process occurs too fast for the working-memory system to parse the words, connect to previously learned items in long-term memory, and create a relationship between those items that facilitates and enables understanding. Too much information is presented too quickly. The newer the information, the more difficult it is for working memory to connect to prior understandings in long-term memory. In the absence of such a connection, the entire contents of the communiqué must be retained in working memory and processed until a new long-term memory can be consolidated. This can easily exceed both the time and capacity constraints of the working-memory system and result in failure. I think everyone has had the experience of hearing something in a lecture that they did not fully comprehend, taking the time to try and make sense of it, and realizing that they didn't even hear the next few sentences the lecturer said.

The section on language discussed the concept of logical closure. This is the idea that to be understood, the words in a sentence must have a relationship that creates coherence between the semantic features of the items the words relate to and symbolize. Logical closure can be reached when parsing a sentence like "The man ate the pie" since the semantic features of the words in the sentence connect coherently. It cannot be achieved for the sentence "The pie ate the man." The key to an effective lecture is to allow logical closure to occur for one idea before moving on to the next idea. If a lecture requires learners to hold ten items in working memory for an extended length of time before the lecturer connects them into a coherent summarizing idea, it is not likely that the summarizing idea will be understood and learned. Consideration of the nature of language and the operation of the working-memory system suggests the following formula for more effective lectures:

1. Use vocabulary and rules that are familiar to learners and are part of their prior understandings.

2. Overtly connect new ideas/rules to prior knowledge and understandings.

3. Proceed one big idea at a time and allow students to reach logical closure on this idea before moving on to the next.

4. Facilitate logical closure by

    » Allowing time for questions and discussion

    » Engaging students in active knowledge construction with an inductive or deductive learning activity, or informal assessment, or other activity that requires students to actively engage with the content and organize it mentally to achieve logical closure and understanding

5. Never require the retention of more than three new ideas/rules in working memory before combining them in the lecture presentation.

6. Engage multiple modalities whenever possible by using learning representations like pictures, graphs, samples, or models.

The magic number seven for the capacity of working memory was derived by asking study participants to passively remember a list of items. No other demands were placed on working memory. Many practitioners feel that in an active learning environment, with many items moving in and out of working memory, limiting the items to be temporarily retained to three or four is safer and more likely to produce a positive outcome.

Learning activities like reading and listening to lectures are considered by many to be passive rather than active learning. Knowledge, however, is not an objective entity. If I am in possession of it, I cannot simply give it to you. Consciously developed knowledge must be constructed by the learner. A very common form of teaching that occurs in colleges, universities, and in some high schools has the following pattern. First, the student is asked to read a segment of the textbook or papers provided by the teacher before the next day's lecture. The teacher then presents content to the student in a lecture format.

The class session typically allows time for asking questions or for an in-class discussion of the material presented. After a few iterations of the reading/lecture cycle, the student is usually asked to write a paper or to produce some other work that demonstrates their understanding of the readings and lectures.

Educational psychologist David Ausubel (1963, 1977) was one of the first researchers to understand and articulate the idea that reading and listening to presentations, regarded by most educators as passive learning, were, in fact, active forms of learning that required students to actively create cognitive structures from the content of the material presented. Ausubel was influential in bringing the ideas of schema theory to classrooms (Eggen and Kauchak 2006). The term *schema* originated with Jean Piaget (1952, 7), who theorized that the building blocks of knowledge and intelligence were schema structures that consisted of "a cohesive, repeatable action sequence possessing component actions that are tightly connected and governed by a core meaning." These action sequences manifest themselves in the brain in terms of concepts, theories, habits, strategies, motor schemes, plans, and expectations (Flavell 1963). Piaget (1985) theorized that knowledge emerges from reflection on and abstraction of physical and mental actions. With time, the direct connection of schemas to actions was lost. Most educators and psychologist today interpret schema to mean a cognitive framework that reflects a mental organization of experience. Schemas are viewed as the concepts, theories, principles, and generalizations that organize knowledge and guide actions. This idea of schema conforms to the idea of "rules" as defined in cognitive science. It is this latter sense of schema that Ausubel uses.

In Piaget's model of cognitive development, a new experience is either assimilated into a person's existing schema structures or must be accommodated for by the restructuring of the person's existing schemas. Assimilation is the direct incorporation of new information into a person's existing cognitive structures. If the new information has idiosyncrasies that do not allow it to be directly assimilated, then existing cognitive structures must be changed or altered to "accommodate" the new information (Flavell 1963).

Ausubel (1963, 1977) contended that students' existing cognitive structures (schemas) were the determining factor in whether new material was meaningful to students and whether new knowledge was acquired. To facilitate learning and the assimilation of new knowledge, Ausubel advocated the use of advanced organizers. Advanced organizers express the structure and organization of the material to be presented to students. They are the conceptual big ideas that will serve as anchors for new information and umbrellas under which the details of the presentation can be placed. The goal of the advance organizer is to give students a framework to help them integrate and interrelate the material in the presentation. Figure 4.1 illustrates the structure of an advance organizer that might be used for a presentation on vertebrates (Eggen and Kauchak 2006).

Step one in Ausubel's recommended instructional process is the presentation of the advance organizer. The teacher explains the overarching big ideas to students in language that the student comprehends. Ausubel explains that assimilation of the new material requires using cognitive structures already in the student's mental inventory. He also advocates the use of examples and analogies to help students comprehend the big ideas. The thesis guiding this first step is, for example, that students must understand

Figure 4.1 Advanced organizers

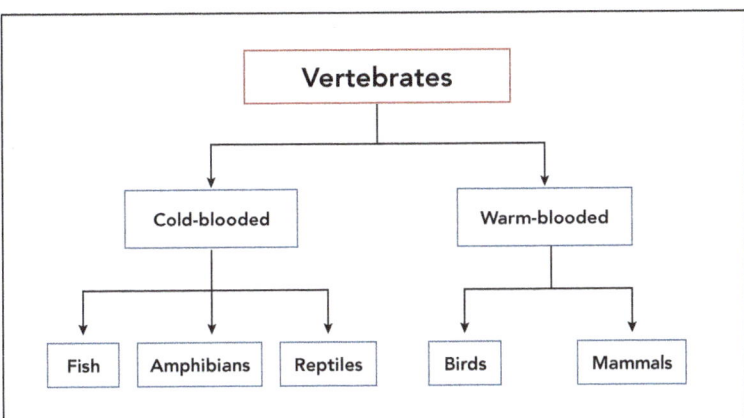

the idea of culture before a teacher provides specific, detailed information regarding a specific cultural group.

Step two is the presentation of the material that fleshes out the big ideas. Ausubel (1963, 1968) refers to this step as progressive differentiation: presenting general ideas first, then presenting material with increasing detail and specificity.

The third step of the process Ausubel (1963, 1968) calls *integrative reconciliation*. This is the process of relating new ideas to each other and integrating new ideas with prior understandings. Ausubel hopes to engage students in meta-behaviors and meta-cognitions during this step that cause them to reflect on content, note similarities, think about linkages, and reconcile discrepancies with prior understandings (Joyce, Weil, and Calhoun 2009).

Both Joyce, Weil, and Calhoun (2009) and Eggen and Kauchak (2006) present instructional models based on Ausubel's work. Step three includes activities such as questioning students, asking students to generate examples of the new ideas from their experience, asking students to summarize or express the essence of the material using their own words, and examining the material from an alternative point of view. In addition, steps such as voting, choral response to questions, and an activity called *think-pair-share* are also included. Think-pair-share is a process in which a student thinks about the answer to a question, pairs up with another classmate to discuss their answer, and then reports out the consensus answer of the pair. Eggen and Kauchak also discuss breaking the big-idea inventory into segments, each of which is covered by a presentation and integration cycle.

The success of Ausubel's approach is contingent upon several factors. The first is how well students understand the graphic organizer. As a graduate student, I had a professor who was fond of advanced organizers. I did not find his presentation of the big ideas in the advance organizer particularly useful or meaningful. It wasn't until I experienced the details of the presentation and then abstracted those details back to the big ideas that they made sense. Part of the problem was his use of technical jargon that was unfamiliar to students and the fact that he did not provide examples. A similar dynamic occurs when classroom teachers begin a lesson by giving students the dictionary definition of new vocabulary that will be used in their presentation. The students will not understand the new vocabulary until they see how the word is used in the presentation in context with other words that they know. Expressing a similar idea, Russian psychologist Lev Vygotsky (1968), in his book *Thought and Language*, cites famous Russian author Leo Tolstoy. Tolstoy, who began his career as a language teacher, stated that having students learn dictionary definitions of words was pointless. It was not until the student heard the word used several times in context with other words that they understood, and subsequently used the word themselves, that they fully comprehended its meaning. "But to give the pupil new concepts deliberately . . . is, I am convinced, as impossible and futile as teaching a child to walk by the laws of equilibrium" (Tolstoy 1903, 143).

The preceding illustrates two "musts" when utilizing advanced organizers. First, it is imperative to use words familiar to students. Second, using examples or analogies that students can relate to is critical. Third, it is also necessary for the teacher to either overtly abstract and relate the details of the presentation to the main ideas or to guide and scaffold the students in the abstracting and relating process.

The most important stage of the process is stage three, or Eggen and Kauchak's stages three to five, which actively engage students in constructing knowledge. One of the requirements for success here is engaging all students in the process. I have had the experience, as have all teachers, in which questions are always answered by the three or so students who fully understood the presentation before the questions were asked. The rest of the class remains silent or views their cell phones/laptops. Asking students to write down the answers to questions or to write down examples of the presented new ideas from their personal experience, to be turned in at the end of the class, is helpful. Breakout groups or think-pair-share exercises are also helpful to ensure engagement by all students. The idea is to design knowledge-construction activities that require participation by *all* students.

A second principle for increasing success is to design the knowledge-construction activity such that it directly invokes the desired meta-behavior or meta-cognition. For example, the teacher could directly ask students to compare and contrast specific items in the presentation to discern similarities or directly ask students to create relationships that connect the details of the presentation. Questions can be posed that either suggest or directly ask for some specific knowledge-construction behavior.

Shown in figure 4.2 is an advance organizer, or concept map, for lessons on the early history of Rome and the beginnings of the Roman Empire.

This is the knowledge structure, or schema, that a teacher would want students to construct from readings, presentations, and other activities. The big ideas are underlined and the relationships between them are colored blue on the chart. To help students connect the details that support and flesh out the big ideas, a form like the one following for students to fill out can be provided. The form is shown already filled out.

Figure 4.2 Concept map for lessons on the early history of Rome

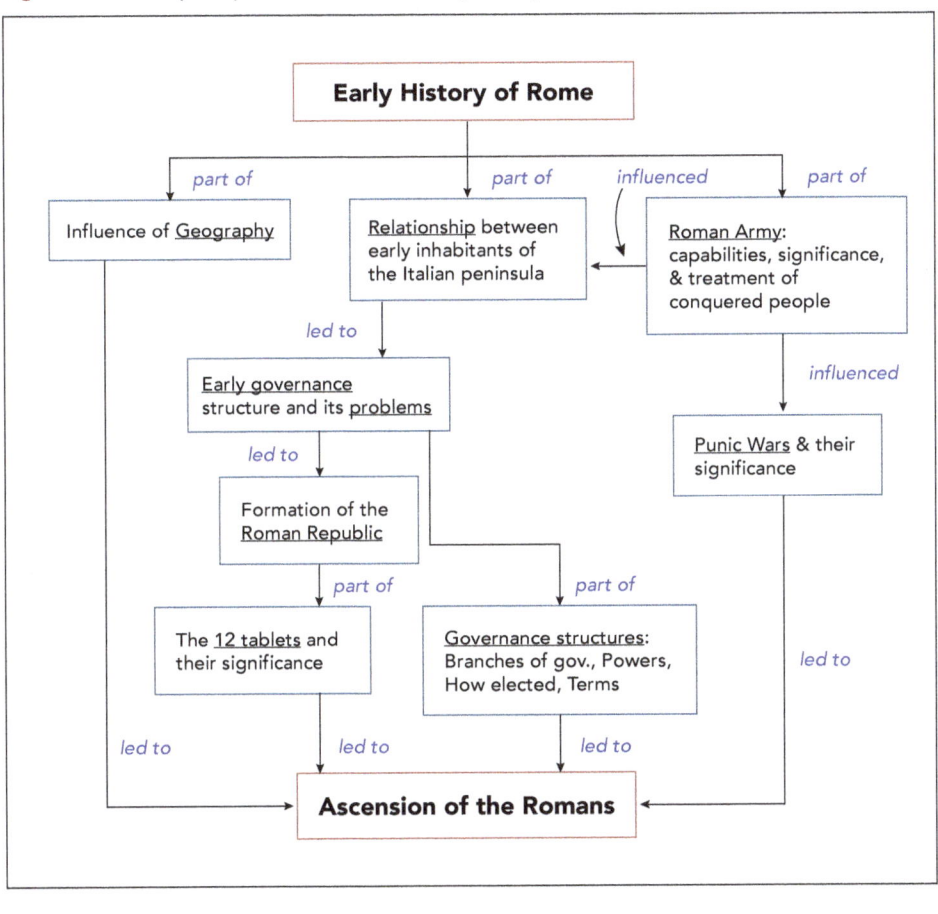

Power Notes (Big Ideas): Geography and Inhabitant Relationships

1. Rome's geographical location was strategic because it:
   a. had fertile soil and a water source_____
   b. was close enough to the ocean for trade but far enough away to avoid attack
   c. was central to the rest of the Italian peninsula (Alps and southern tip)_____
2. The early inhabitants of the Italian peninsula were:
   a. Greeks in the south, Latins in the middle, and Etruscans in the north_____
3. The Latins (early Romans) learned much from their neighbors:
   a. Etruscans: writing, art, architecture_____
   b. Greeks: trade, commerce, governance_____

Note that the form consists of statements and requires students to provide the details that support the statement. An organizing form can also be provided that requires the student to answer essential questions that develop the big ideas. The following form illustrates this approach.

Essential Questions: Roman Army

How was the Roman army organized?

_____
_____
_____

What were its capabilities?

_____
_____
_____

How did Roman treatment of conquered people benefit its goals?

_____
_____
_____

How were the Punic Wars significant to Rome?

_____
_____
_____

Returning to human executive function, the next step in the executive process is the activation of a sequence of actions in procedural memory that is coherent with (1) the activated and connected goal, (2) perceptual representations, and (3) long-term memory representations. The action sequence is the collection of steps intended to accomplish the goal. If a procedure exists in memory for going from the current state A to the desired or goal state B, it will simply be activated. Note that this assumes that there is a previously developed connection between the specific goal, perceptual and long-term memory rule representations activated, and the action sequence. If no such connected procedure or set of actions exist in memory, it must be developed from information in the goal and perceptual and long-term memory rule representations. A candidate for the location of physical procedural memories is the supplementary motor area (Broadman area 6) of the frontal cortex. This area has extensive connections to the prefrontal cortex and temporal lobe memory areas. It responds when sequences of previously learned action procedures are internally activated by goal and motivational states (Gazzaniga, Ivry, and Mangun 2009).

Recall that Piaget's thesis for the creation of knowledge was the individual's reflection on and abstraction of their actions and the consequences they produce. Piaget believed that this process resulted in the creation of abstract rules in long-term memory. This is what Piaget (1952) means when he states that a schema is a tightly connected action sequence that is governed by a core meaning. The conceptual rule codifies and symbolizes an action sequence. The thesis of this book is different and proposes a language rather than action-based predicate for the formation of rules. What I believe Piaget does correctly describe is how connections are made between representations of rules and representations of action sequences. Instead of being *the* way rules are derived, in my model of learning, reflective abstraction is *one* of the ways in which rules can be derived.

If I sort a collection of names by first listing all of those that begin with the letter A, then list those that begin with the letter B, and then with the letter C, and so forth, I can codify and symbolize this set of actions with the concept (rule) *alphabetize*. If, at some future time, the concept (rule) alphabetize is activated in long-term memory, its representation is connected to and can activate the action sequence previously described. It is in this way that rules can activate action sequences.

Let us take the example of determining the slope of a line. Determining the slope is our goal. A straight line is a functional relationship between some variable *y*, the dependent variable, and another variable *x*, the independent variable. The relationship for a straight line is one of proportionality. The slope of the line is a constant for all points along the line. For other functions, it varies for each *x* value and corresponding *y* value. The concept of the slope of a function (for two variables) is that it is the change in the dependent variable divided by the change in the independent variable: $\frac{\Delta y}{\Delta x}$. If perception tells me that I have a graph of the line, the rule for slope should activate the following process in procedural memory:

1. Find a point on the line.

2. Read and record its *x* and *y* values.

3. Find a point to the right of the first point picked.

4. Read and record its *x* and *y* values.

5. Subtract the *y* value of the second point picked (on the right) from the *y* value of the first point picked.

6. Subtract the *x* value of the second point picked (on the right) from the *x* value of the first point picked.

7. Divide the result from step 5 by the result from step 6 (difference in *y* values divided by difference in *x* values); this is the slope.

If a beginning algebra student only knows the abstract idea of slope, will this activate the action sequence described? It will activate the sequence only if it already exists in procedural memory. This means that it would have to have been previously performed and a connection would have to have been made to the abstraction that codifies and symbolizes the sequence. A connection in the brain must be made between the action sequence representation and the abstract representation of the rule. To ensure that the action sequence and the rule are connected, both should be taught and directly connected by the teacher. To state this behaviorally, the student should **know what the rule tells them to do**. The student should know the actions that are codified by, conform to, and are coherent with the rule. This must be learned; it does not happen automatically.

Failing to directly teach the application of rules is like asking someone to play a piece of classical music on a piano after having finished an academic class on music theory. In time, through a trial-and-error process, the student may be able to play the piece. However, the process is greatly quickened and made more efficient if a teacher demonstrates the direct connection between the theory and the execution of a song on the piano. In training programs for extremely high-stakes occupations like police officer, physician, and airline pilot, care is taken to carefully connect theory and practice over an extended period. I personally have had very little luck simply teaching theory and then expecting students to correctly and efficiently apply the theory when completing their assignments. This, however, is common practice in the field of education. I believe that one of the big weaknesses in K–16 education is that we do not sufficiently teach students how to use and apply the large inventory of rules we teach. A great deal of school learning, therefore, becomes inert and unusable to solve problems and achieve goals in the student's life after they finish their formal education.

Following activation or development of an action sequence, the next step in the human executive function process is to implement the mental and/or physical actions derived from the prior step and to monitor progress by comparing outcomes with goals. Several areas of the brain, principally the anterior cingulate cortex, are tasked with detecting conflicts and deviations between goals and perceived outcomes. When such a conflict or deviation is detected, compensatory actions are activated and implemented. These can include the following:

- Increasing attention and focus on perceptual input (is there something the individual didn't "see" that's relevant?)
- Searching long-term memory for additional rules that might be applicable
- Possibly altering goal criteria and specifications

If all these actions fail to close the gap between goal and outcome, there is the possibility that new rules could be evolved through a nonlinear self-organizing process among the brain's neural representational circuits. I will defer my hypothesis regarding how this process occurs until a later section of the book, since it is one of my hypothesized methods of how humans construct knowledge.

In summary, human executive function protocol consists of the following steps:

1. Set intention and goal.
2. Focus attention on the goal-relevant perceptual features of the environment.
3. Activate the goal-relevant contents of long-term memory (rules).
4. Combine the preceding to formulate a plan of action.
5. Carry out the plan.
6. Monitor outcomes and affecting compensations as required.

Those who have been involved in a strategic planning process for an institution should recognize the preceding steps. These steps also describe, in abstract, the job definition of a chief executive officer. Whether you are a school principal or president of General Motors, the preceding outline describes the nature of your job. Finally, the executive function process is nothing less than the fundamental human problem-solving process. No matter what problem you solve, the preceding steps describe the process you use: the human executive function process built into the brain.

For example, suppose I gave you the job of CEO of General Motors. I might then suggest that you undertake the following steps:

1. Set goals.
   As head of a publicly held company, you would want to increase shareholder value by increasing sales, enhancing your margin through cost reduction, and reducing your cost of capital by shoring up your balance sheet.
2. Perceive your current state.
   What do the current financials look like? What are the current capabilities of your factories and other capital assets? What knowledge and skills do your employees possess? What threats to your business do you face? Where are your opportunities in the current environment?
3. Invoke the available knowledge to guide and inform the creation of strategic plans and actions.
   » Personal knowledge and expertise
   » Employee knowledge and expertise
   » Knowledge and expertise of outside consultants
4. Create plans of action.
5. Implement plans.
6. Set up control, assessment, and feedback systems that will inform you of progress and the required compensations needed to achieve your goals.

If you followed this outline and had capable and friendly vice presidents reporting to you, it might be a couple of years before the rest of the employees figured out that you don't know much about the car business. To them, you would seem to be doing all the things expected of a CEO. Obviously, your ability to carry out these steps effectively and successfully would be greatly enhanced if you had prior knowledge and experience in the automotive industry.

Human Executive Function and Teacher Scaffolding

Scaffolding is the active back-and-forth assistance that teachers provide students during the learning process. It includes asking questions to focus and direct student activities, providing feedback and revision, supplying additional information, and providing encouragement to students (Woolfolk 2007). It is my hypothesis that teacher scaffolding is, in fact, augmentation of a student's executive function.

Vygotsky (1986) theorized that most student learning occurred in what he called the *zone of proximal development*. This is the phase of learning where students can solve problems and accomplish tasks only when supplied with teacher scaffolding. The assistance of the teacher is required for successful completion of tasks. Vygotsky visualized three phases in the learning process:

1. Teacher presentation and/or demonstration of content.

2. Student application of the presented content, with teacher observation and scaffolding.

3. Student independent performance and demonstration of mastery of the content

His view conforms with the modern instructional model called *direct instruction*. This model is often characterized in the field of education by the words "I do, we do, you do." In step one, the teacher delivers the content of the lesson and models the appropriate way to use the new concepts or to perform the new procedure being taught. In step two, the student is required to use the concept or to perform the procedure. During step two, the teacher walks around the classroom and provides scaffolding assistance to all those who require it. In step three, the student applies the concept or procedure independently. Step three is typically a homework assignment or the production of some work product. Direct instruction has the same structure as the age-old apprenticeship model of teaching. However, instead of years to learn a craft under the tutelage of a master, the student has a much more limited time to learn and master a new concept or skill.

It has been estimated that on any given day in the United States, over 93 percent of the students in K–12 are receiving instruction via the direct instruction model. One reason for this is that direct instruction conforms to the intuitive notion of what teaching is: telling people what you know or showing them what you can do. The direct instruction model couples this with the process of helping students use what you told them about or showed them to do. Research seems to support Vygotsky's contention that a great deal of the actual learning occurs in step two and is contingent upon the effectiveness of teacher scaffolding (Eggen and Kauchak 2006). Eggen and Kauchak (2006, 294) state that the zone of proximal development is "instructional pay dirt."

The first step of human executive function protocol is the definition of intention and goal. The instructor sets the goals of the learning experience. Professionally trained teachers are taught to begin lessons with a clear and comprehensible explanation of the goals of the lesson. Many teachers use a strategy that goes by the acronym KWL. The K stands for activating student's prior knowledge by asking the question: What do we know about the topic or subject? The W stands for asking the question: What do we want to know about the topic? And the L stands for the question: What have we learned about the topic? This is a summarization step at the end of the lesson. In actual practice, the W is what the teacher wants the students to know about the topic. Rare is the student who wants to know how to factor a polynomial or how to rhyme sentences in iambic pentameter.

Human goal-setting is strongly influenced by feelings and emotion. The feeling- and emotion-processing areas of the brain, like the orbital prefrontal cortex, medial prefrontal cortex, amygdala, and insula, can be thought of as an additional sensory and perceptual system. This system provides two crucial pieces of information: whether something in the environment is important to the individual and whether it is good or bad for the individual. In neuroscience, this is expressed as *valence* (good or bad, ±) and *value* (important or unimportant). Humans will have goals and motivations that draw them toward things that are good and valuable and away from things that are bad or unimportant. Modern researchers like Antonio Damasio (1994, 2003, 2010), Joseph LeDoux (1996, 2002), Joshua Greene et al. (Greene et al. 2001, 2004), and Jonathan Haidt (2013) have insightfully documented the crucial role of the human feeling and emotional system in setting goals, directing actions, and making judgments and decisions.

The British philosopher David Hume ([1739] 1982) was the first to assert that feelings and emotions played the predominant role in determining human actions. The philosophical expression for the influence of feeling and emotion on actions is the *will*. This position was taken to its logical limit by the philosopher Arthur Schopenhauer ([1918] 1958), who asserted that reason was the slave of the will. Schopenhauer stated that we don't want something because we have reasons for it, we find reasons for it because we want it. He used the metaphor that the will is a strong blind man who carries on his shoulders the lame man (intellect/reason) who can see. This thesis was carried forward by the philosopher Friedrich Nietzsche and subsequently by Sigmund Freud, who was known to be strongly influenced by both Schopenhauer and Nietzsche. Freud theorized that human goals and intentions were derived from subconscious sexual desires (the id) that had to be tempered by reason (the ego) for humans to undertake socially appropriate behavior congruent with the demands of their environment.

Considering the body of literature on feeling and emotion versus logic and reason as the determiners of human behavior, a plausible hypothesis is that human goals are a negotiated settlement or attempt to reach equilibrium between the brain areas processing feeling/emotion information and those processing logic and reason (semantic) information. In cases where equilibrium cannot be reached, the evolutionarily stronger feeling/emotion system prevails (Damasio 1994; Haidt 2010). Although science has not provided a final answer to this dialectic, we can still conclude that feeling and emotion play a very significant role in providing motivation, setting goals, and maintaining vigilance in the pursuit of goals.

Understanding the significant role that feelings and emotions play in learning, modern educators have paid increasing attention to the affective dimensions of learning. Research in the 1990s (Brophy 1998; Noddings 1992) began to shift educators away from reliance on extrinsic rewards (grades, gold stars, individual honors) and toward developing intrinsic motivation in students. Literature became available that delineated methods for motivating students, and many school districts began providing in-service training to teachers on the affective dimensions of learning. Motivational literature emphasized the necessity for giving clear and understandable explanations of the goals of the lesson to students. In addition, an explanation of the compelling reasons for the learning goals and activities was recommended. Why is it important and worth learning? How is it relevant to the student in the real world that the student lives in?

To be intrinsically motivating, a lesson must be seen as valuable from the student's point of view. This means that they must know enough about the topic to care and find value in pursuing it. Introductory activities such as considering case studies, vignettes, paradoxes/incongruities, and mysteries can be helpful in creating motivation for the lesson. Immersing students in questions, problems, challenges, and activities they find motivating, meaningful, fascinating, and energizing can connect to their natural curiosity and encourage active engagement (Eggen and Kauchak 2006; Wiggins and McTighe 2005). Knowledge is an active construction by the learner, so active engagement is mandatory. As with any leadership situation, success is contingent upon the degree to which the students' goals align with those of the teacher.

A teacher plays an executive function–scaffolding role not only in helping students to form goals but also in maintaining the goals throughout the learning experience. The extent to which this is necessary is contingent upon the age of the student. For example, doctoral students, who are thirty-three years old on average and highly motivated, require no assistance in forming and maintaining goals. Students in the early grades, however, require considerable assistance. When immersed in the alligators of performing tasks, the students easily forget that the goal is to drain the swamp.

The importance of maintaining goals is that they are what fixes attention toward relevant perceptions and the salient contents of long-term memory. Losing sight of goals will impede perception of goal-relevant information and the relevant contents of long-term memory. In the early years, a teacher must also encourage students to stick to it and not give up on their goals when they encounter difficulty. Many people will say that what made the difference for them was a teacher who believed in them and always offered aid and encouragement. No one ever said that it was the expert design of the sixth-grade curriculum that made the critical difference in their education.

The second way that teachers' scaffolding can augment executive function is in focusing perceptual attention. As discussed previously, perception is interpretation and judgment of information coming from the sensory systems. As such, perception is contingent upon the prior experience of the individual. For example, people learn the shape, color, texture, and taste of a banana. It is through experience of the semantic features that they "learn" what a banana is and can perceive something as a banana when receiving certain stimuli from the sensory system.

Suppose that I took a class to an art museum with the goal of teaching different classifications of art. I might give the students the task of telling me what the difference was between the pieces of art I identified as Impressionist and the other paintings. The task I have given them is determining the attributes and characteristics that constitute the category of art designated as Impressionist and that differentiate this category from other genres of art. Seminal to this task is the ability to perceive and discern those attributes and characteristics. The results of this exercise will likely be quite mixed and contingent upon the student's prior knowledge of art and artistic techniques.

If, however, I scaffold their perception by telling them what to look for, I will get better and more consistent results. I might ask them to try to see the type of brushstrokes used by the artist. Do they appear to be long and flowing or do they consist of dots, short strokes, or splotches of paint? I might then ask them to examine how the painter creates shapes. Are there abrupt lines that separate objects in the painting, like one might see in a drawing, or does the painter creates shapes simply by using different colors? Does the use of color in this manner give the painting a more airy or fuzzy feeling rather than the feeling they get when looking at a photograph? If I augment perception in this manner, I am much more likely to achieve my goal of teaching students the differences among various genres of art. In the preceding example, the specific characteristics I called students' attention to—short strokes or dots and color changes to create shape—are two of the defining characteristics of Impressionism.

One of the benefits of scaffolding perception is that it helps to equalize learning outcomes and consistency among learners who have widely varying background experiences and prior knowledge. Note that in doing so I am not violating the philosopher John Dewey's (1933) admonition not to give students answers but to assist them in finding their own answers. I am simply facilitating the ability to formulate answers and increasing the probability that the answers I get will conform to the learning objectives of my lesson.

When I first began teaching university classes, I found that I could predict a student's final grade from the grade I gave them on their first assignment. An A on the first assignment was almost always predictive of a final grade of A. If I assume that performance on the final exam was indicative of how much students learned in my class, it was clear that the A students learned a lot more than the C students. This concerned me. Were my lessons not sufficient to get all students to my desired level of content mastery? I could console myself only with the thought that all students knew more than they did on the first day of class. The reasons for the disparity in performance included level of effort expended, differences in basic cognitive skill and ability, and, most importantly, differences in prior knowledge and experience. I was able to increase the number of students who achieved mastery by altering my curriculum, changing my instructional delivery methods, and, importantly, scaffolding individual students. However, it is impossible to completely overcome the disparity in prior knowledge and experience in one course conducted over one semester.

The next executive function that teachers can augment through scaffolding is the recall of relevant information from long-term memory. The teacher can remind students what prior knowledge is needed to complete a step in a learning activity and assist them in applying it. In the same fashion that perception cues associative memories, teachers can use cues, clues, questions, and prompts to activate task-relevant long-term memories. The process involves the teacher recognizing what the student requires from long-term memory to complete the task they seem to be stuck on and using questions or other cues to draw the required information from long-term memory. This process is contingent upon whether the cue or question contains information that activates an element of the student's representation of the required rule in long-term memory. It is the same process that occurs in the parlor game charades, where a person receives clues from somebody and must guess the person, place, or thing. For example, let's say that such a parlor game proceeds as follows.

Clue	Response
Scientist	I don't know
Nobel prize	I don't know
Wild hair	I don't know
Relativity	Einstein

In the preceding example, if the first clue was relativity, most people would have immediately responded with Einstein. The association between Einstein and relativity is obviously extremely strong. The first two clues could be any number of people and are not terribly helpful in activating a memory of a specific person in long-term memory. Many people would have guessed the answer after the third clue because of the numerous depictions in the media of Einstein and his iconic hairstyle.

Questioning can also be used as a learning tool. A good example of the technique comes from Plato, the master questioner. In the dialogue with Meno, Plato, through the character Socrates, asserts that the human soul is immortal. Socrates theorizes that humans die, go to heaven, and are subsequently reborn. Since the soul is immortal, this happens an innumerable number of times. While in heaven, the soul has knowledge of everything. When the person is reborn, they remember nothing and must accumulate knowledge anew. However, the knowledge they accumulate is simply the discovery of knowledge already in their possession. Knowledge is simply the recollection of things known from prior lives.

To prove his theory, Socrates asks Meno to pick one of his servant boys and tells Meno that despite the boy not having had any formal education, he will prove that the boy knows how to construct a square twice the size (area) of an original square. His contention is that the knowledge is already in the mind of the boy, and the boy simply needs to draw it out by answering questions.

Socrates begins by drawing a square and getting the servant boy to agree to the following facts about the square through the following questions:

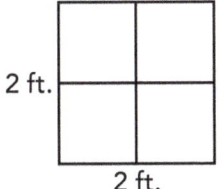

Figure 4.3 2 x 2 square

Socrates's questions	Boy's responses
Are the sides of the square equal?	Yes
Are the middle lines equal?	Yes
Is the size not 4, or 2 times 2?	Yes

Socrates then asks the boy what the length of the sides must be to double the size of the square. The boy responds that it should be 4, or double the original side length. Socrates then draws a square with side length 4 and continues his questioning.

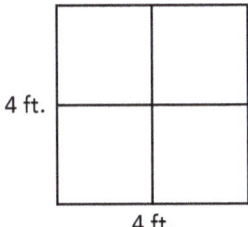

Figure 4.4 4 x 4 square

Socrates's questions	Boy's responses
Is your new square not 16 or 4 times larger than the original?	Yes
So on how long a line should a square of size 8 be based?	No answer
Should it be longer than 2 but less than 4?	Yes

Notice that the last question asked the boy to confirm Socrates's logical evaluation of the required line length. A question that would have evoked the boy's logic would have been: If 4 is too large and 2 is the original length, what would the length of the side have to be to double the size of the square?

The boy now offers the guess that the correct line length must be 3. Socrates then goes on to demonstrate that this leads to a square of size 9 and is not the correct answer. He then asks the boy once again what size line is required and the boy admits that he is stumped, "by Zeus."

Socrates then goes back to the drawing of size 16 and draws diagonals across each of the four squares that are of original size 4 (see figure 4.5) and asks the following questions:

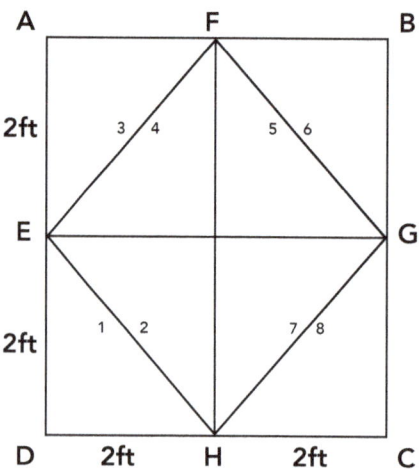

Figure 4.5
4 x 4 square with diagonals

Socrates's questions	Boy's responses
Do these lines divide each of the smaller squares of original size 4, which comprise the larger square, in half ?	Yes
How many of these halves are in the square of original size 4?	2
How many are in the square formed by the diagonal lines?	4
What is the relationship of the size of the square formed by the diagonal lines and the original square?	It is double?

The crucial step in getting the answer was drawing the diagonal. The idea of the diagonal came from Socrates and not from the servant boy through questioning. Therefore, Socrates has not proven his original premise. He has, however, demonstrated how learning can be achieved through questioning. He introduces a new element, the diagonal, and guides the boy through the process of using the new element, along with the boy's existing knowledge, to solve the problem and create new knowledge. The generalized process of teaching through questioning is to (1) use questions to activate required prior knowledge, (2) introduce a new element or idea, and (3) get the student to create a relationship between existing knowledge and the new idea or element through questioning. Socrates did the third step by asking the boy to add the halves in both the original square and the square formed by the diagonal and then to relate the two. Through this relationship new knowledge was created.

A teacher can also scaffold a student's working-memory system. Recall that the working-memory system allows task-relevant information from perception and long-term memory to be sustained and remain activated so that it can be processed and manipulated. With its extensive connection to many brain areas, the working-memory system provides a critical link that enables integration of distinct sources of information from different areas of the brain and hence facilitates the formation of new long-term memories. Additional areas of the prefrontal cortex interact with the working-memory system to manipulate items in working memory. For example, Brodmann areas 9 and 46 are involved in temporal ordering of information. People with lesions in these areas, for example, can remember the ingredients in a recipe but cannot organize food preparation actions in a proper time sequence (Jasper 1995). The working-memory system in conjunction with other prefrontal cortex areas enable the construction of source memories. Source memory is the memory of not only an item but also where, how, and when the item was experienced. Source memory also includes the context in which the item was experienced or what was associated with the item when it was experienced. Gazzaniga, Ivry, and Mangun (2009) has hypothesized that the prefrontal cortex and working-memory system act to sustain representations long enough for links to be formed in long-term memory and, therefore, memories to be consolidated.

A teacher observing a student performing a learning task can refresh the contents of a student's working memory. Recall that items in working memory remain for an average of approximately twenty seconds. The teacher does this by reminding the student of the perceptually derived information or item from long-term memory they require to perform the learning task. In other words, what they need to be thinking about. What the student is trying to load into working memory is in the teacher's long-term memory. A teacher can extend the student's working memory by providing them information from their long-term memory store. The teacher provides the fact, concept, or other item that the student requires or is having difficulty with.

Teachers can also control both the contents and operation of a student's working-memory system. Plato, through Socrates, demonstrates this in the example previously discussed. Socrates asked the boy to count the number of halves in the original square and in the square made up of the diagonals of the original square. In doing so, he is loading the perception of those two numbers into the boy's working memory. He then asked the boy what the relationship was between those numbers. This request controls how the perceptual information is to be manipulated within the working-memory system. We can see from this how a teacher can scaffold and direct both the contents of working memory and how those contents are operated on and used.

Teachers can also augment and scaffold the next step of the executive function process: the combination of information from goal, perceptual representations, and long-term memory representations to formulate a mental or physical procedure, or sequence of actions, to achieve the goals of the learning task. If a representation of the procedure to achieve the goal is already in the student's procedural memory, the teacher can help activate it. If no such procedure exists, it must be developed from the contents of the goal, perceptual representations, and long-term memory representations. A teacher can assist and scaffold this construction process. As previously discussed, it is important that the student understand what set of actions is implicit in the rules in their long-term memory. Behaviorally, what does the rule tell them to do? What actions are coherent with the rule? This is a crucial part of the learning process since it enables students to apply rules to accomplish goals.

Using the previously discussed process of learning the concept of the slope of the straight line as an example, the teacher could scaffold development of the process for calculating the slope as follows. She could begin by pointing out that the slope is the change in the dependent variable y divided by the change in the independent variable x. She could then point out that to perform this calculation, the student needs x and y values at two different points along the line. The teacher could then ask the student, "Where can we find those values"? This directs the student to the graph and cues the first step in calculating the slope. If necessary, the teacher could continue this type of process, supplying an item of information and then asking a question that suggests a specific procedure or process. Scaffolding the development of procedures from rules facilitates both the construction of procedures and the connection between procedures and rules.

The final step of the executive function process that can be scaffolded by teachers is the monitoring of progress toward goals and the implementation of compensations when a divergence exists between student outcomes and learning goals. Scaffolding here consists of observing students and providing feedback. Good feedback must be quick and specifically relevant and such that the student knows exactly what to do to respond appropriately and coherently to the feedback. The feedback should suggest to the student a specific action or response. To say that an answer is wrong and that the student should keep on trying is not providing good feedback. The student should be informed as to what is lacking or where a mistake might have been made. Teacher feedback augments the executive process by directing students to reexamine the task instructions and goals, reexamine (re-perceive) the information provided in the learning representations (for example, graphs, pictures, other exhibits), or search again in long-term memory for the rule relevant to the learning task.

A teaching strategy in which feedback is the primary learning methodology is the use of portfolios. In a portfolio strategy, students produce work products, receive feedback from the teacher, and resubmit the work product after incorporating the teacher's feedback. The same general rules for good feedback apply to this process. The effectiveness of the process is contingent upon the quality of the teacher's feedback. As discussed earlier, the feedback should specify what is lacking or incorrect with respect to a rubric or some other specification of adequacy and completeness. It should also suggest what else might be considered or looked at (scaffolding perception) and what other concept and ideas (rules) should be considered and incorporated. To be effective, there should be at least two cycles of submission and feedback. During my graduate studies, I had a teacher who was an absolute master of the portfolio strategy. A glutton for punishment, she allowed unlimited resubmittals of work products and provided exceptional feedback each time the work product was submitted. There was absolutely no excuse not to make an A in her class.

Students can themselves monitor the progress of their executive function activities. This is commonly referred to as *metacognition*. The most important aspect of metacognition is understanding what you don't know and where the shortfalls are that are keeping you from achieving your goals. This identifies where you need help. Students should be encouraged to engage in metacognition and not be hesitant to ask questions and seek help. The learning environment should, therefore, be supportive and welcoming to those who seek assistance. Many successful people in life have good metacognitive skills. They have a realistic sense of what they lack to achieve their personal goals and are not hesitant to seek help in getting what they need to be successful. Many students are hesitant to ask questions in class because they fear judgment by either the teacher or their peers. This means that teachers should provide multiple avenues for students to get assistance, some of which are not public.

Scaffolding is a critical component of effective teaching practice. I believe it currently receives insufficient attention and elaboration in teacher preparation programs. There is insufficient understanding of how critical scaffolding is to the success of several models of teaching. Knowing where scaffolding will be required is also a critical part of the design of lesson plans and curriculum. When I served as a member of the school board of the Fort Worth Independent School District, I made it a practice to visit the classrooms of teachers who received awards for teaching excellence or were designated as master teachers. They shared various things in common, but the one attribute they all shared was excellent scaffolding skills. As reflective practitioners, they learned where students typically encountered difficulties and had developed effective strategies to help students overcome those difficulties.

The promise of cybernetic, computer-driven education or software that delivers instruction will not be fulfilled until artificial intelligence advances to the point where it can accurately diagnose learning difficulties and provide specific and accurate executive function scaffolding. Until that time, live person-to-person instruction will continue to be more effective.

Throughout history it was the intuitive sense of teaching that prevailed: telling learners what you knew and showing them what you could do. As mentioned previously, this was often coupled with scaffolded application by students of the new ideas and procedures in an apprenticeship type of structure. In the mid-1960s, the direct instruction model was developed by Bereiter and Engelmann (1966). Their model was rooted in the behaviorist theory of the 1950s and 1960s. It was based on behavioral principles such as overt responding, frequent and specific feedback, and contingency management (Magliaro, Lockee, and Burton 2005). During the 1970s and 1980s, modifications arising from what was called *teacher effectiveness research* were made to the direct instruction model (Brophy and Good 1986; Rosenshine 1971). Additional modifications reflecting the influence of cognitive psychology were also recommended during the 1980s (Gagne 1985; Hunter 1982). The work of Madeline Hunter was particularly influential during this period. My tenure as a school board member overlapped this time. Whenever I called the principal of one of the high schools in the district I represented and asked how things were going, she would invariably respond with "Fine, we're here just paddlin' with Madeline."

Modern, up-to-date incarnations of the direct instruction model can be found in *Models of Teaching* (Joyce, Weil, and Calhoun 2009) and *Strategies and Models for Teachers* (Eggen and Kauchak 2006). Modern versions still include the basic structural elements articulated by Bereiter and Engelmann (1966): (1) review, (2) presentation, (3) guided practice, (4) corrections and feedback, (5) independent practice, and (6) review and summarization. As previously discussed, research indicates that most of the learning occurs during steps 3 and 4. These are the steps that involve teacher scaffolding of student learning. The ideas previously presented on scaffolding can be used to strengthen these steps.

The direct instruction model of learning is still by far the most used model in K–12 education. There are multiple reasons for this. First, the model generally conforms to most people's intuitive view of what teaching is. Second, it is a model that is easily taught to and understood by prospective teachers in training. Third, it is easy to implement. Someone with mastery of the content of a lesson can readily develop a lecture presentation or demonstration of a procedure. Lessons based on alternative teaching methods, such as inductive learning, require considerably more time and creativity to develop. Fourth, the teacher has complete control of the learning process. And last, but not least, direct instruction allows the teacher to cover a large amount of content in a short period of time.

In 1972, the publication of the first edition of *Models of Teaching* by Joyce, Weil, and Calhoun brought the work of researchers pursuing alternative models of teaching to a wide audience. The idea of varying teaching procedures for different teaching objectives was both new and controversial at the time (Eggen and Kauchak 2006). Joyce, Weil, and Calhoun's book included teacher-friendly interpretations of the work of researchers like Hilda Taba (1966) on inductive learning and David Ausubel (1977) on the development of schemas, as well as models derived from the authors' own research. While the use of alternative models and methods for different learning goals is now widely accepted, *Models of Teaching* began a dialectic in education that continues to this day and includes the following:

- Student-centered versus teacher-centered instruction
- Active versus passive learning
- Constructivist learning versus directed learning

The section on scaffolding of executive function can be summarized with the following learning principles:

Principle 4: Learning is enhanced when instructors augment through scaffolding the human executive processes that learners engage in when processing content.

Principle 5: Instructors should be careful not to overload working memory. Learners should be allowed to reach logical closure on a presented concept before proceeding to the next concept.

My goal in this book is to derive and delineate all of the ways that the human brain constructs knowledge and the process by which such construction takes place. My theory of knowledge and learning is derived from results in cognitive science, nonlinear systems theory, linguistics, philosophy, and educational research. I have attempted to create a coherent theory from these sources that corresponds to research results and empirical experience. Since I have attempted to be comprehensive and include all human knowledge-construction processes, the teaching models found in the literature fall into one of the categories that I have delineated. In subsequent sections of the book, I will also discuss knowledge-construction processes not currently found in the literature. Since my categorizations are driven by brain processes, my categorizations of instructional models will differ somewhat from those found in literature. Shown in table 4.1 and figure 4.6 is my delineation of the processes the brain utilizes to construct knowledge of rules. There are five fundamental processes defined for the construction of rules. Four of these have a forward as well as a backward path to rule construction.

Table 4.1

Knowledge construction process	Forward path	Backward path
1. Induction	Synthesis	Analysis
2. Deduction	Logic	Abduction/Kantian logic
3. Reflective abstraction	Trial and error	Reflective abstraction
4. Application	Procedural learning	Contextual learning
5. Dialectic	Dialectic process	Dialectic process

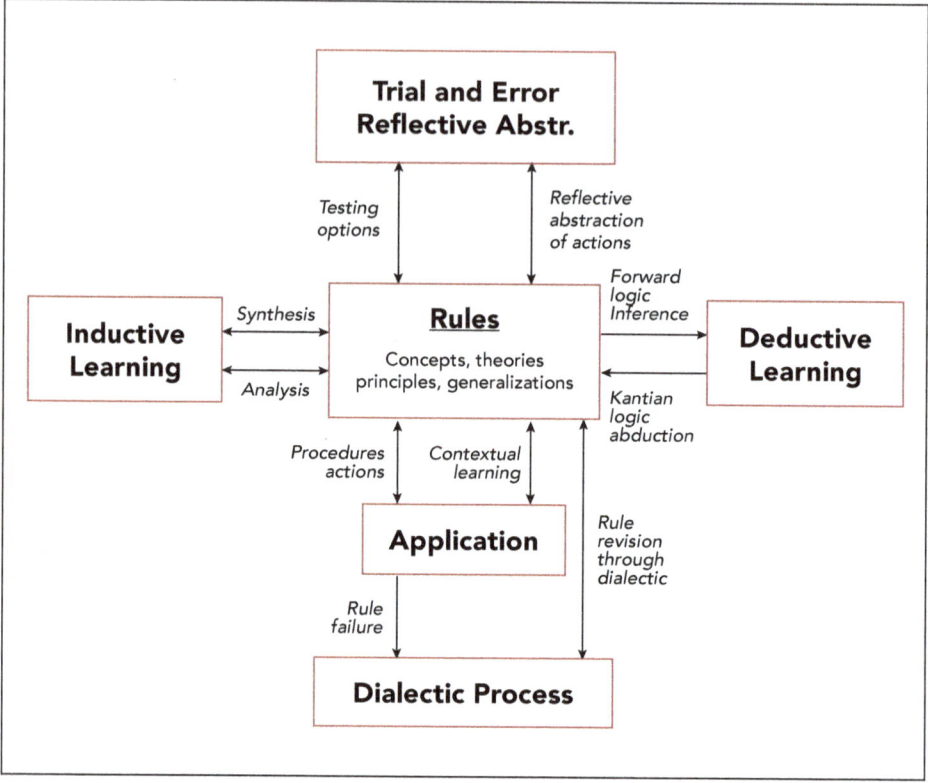

Figure 4.6
Schematic of knowledge-construction processes

Inductive Learning

Conscious inductive learning is the creation of knowledge through the detection and recognition of patterns of similarity among the objects and actions that one encounters in one's experience of the world. In the case of objects, the process involves recognizing and abstracting the similar attributes and characteristics (semantic features) of a group of examples and the relationship that exists between those attributes and characteristics. In the case of actions, the process involves recognizing and abstracting the invariant changes in objects with time and the consistent relationship that connects or accounts for those changes.

Induction is, hence, the process of ordering experience by organizing it into rules that reflect judgments as to the patterns of consistency in one's experience. The result of the process is the creation of classes and categories. These classes and categories are rules that reflect an individual's organization and ordering of the world. As discussed previously, object and action categories are represented and codified through symbols such as words. Unlike associatively created classes and categories, consciously created rules require conscious judgment as to the nature of the relationship between the semantic features of objects and actions. This is a judgment that goes beyond the information present in the perception of the object or action. For example, let's say that we perceive a group of three marbles and three rocks. The content of the perception is simply rocks and marbles and their semantic features. The idea that there are three of each is a human judgment. The idea that these objects can be counted and represented by a number is a human construct. The fact that there is an equal number of rocks and marbles is also a human judgment. Neither the idea of a count nor the idea of equality is contained in the perception. Both are human judgments of the information present in the perception. The judgments of number and equality are judgments as to the nature of the relationship between the objects.

Inductively created rules facilitate all forms of deductive reasoning: conditional, propositional, and categorical. To illustrate a simple example of categorical reasoning, we can examine the following statements:

Socrates is a Greek.

Greeks are mortal.

Therefore, Socrates is mortal.

These statements place Socrates in a class or category and state that, as a member of the class or category, he shares the attributes and characteristics of the class or category. In this case, mortality. Categories help humans reason about, organize, and keep track of the world. For example, if I can place someone in the category of conservative Republican or liberal Democrat, I can reliably predict how they will stand on a variety of social, economic, and political issues. If I decided to run for political office, I could utilize this knowledge to help design my campaign.

As discussed previously, to facilitate perception, the brain naturally inducts an individual's experience. One of the differences between natural induction and conscious inductive learning is time. In a formal learning situation, we are trying to do in one hour what the brain does naturally over a protracted period. Illustrated in figure 4.7 are schematic diagrams of the structure of rules for objects and actions. Filled-in examples are also shown.

We can examine an example inductive learning lesson and observe the knowledge-construction process. Let's say that my goal is to teach three of the nine possible quadrilateral shapes: rectangle, parallelogram, and trapezoid. The goal of the lesson is for the students to know what attributes/characteristics something referred to as, for example, a rectangle has that distinguishes it from other shapes and what relationship those attributes and characteristics have to each other. After stating the goals of the lesson and employing some other introductory activity to generate interest, I could pass out a set of nine shapes large enough for students to measure the lengths of the line segments and the interior angles.

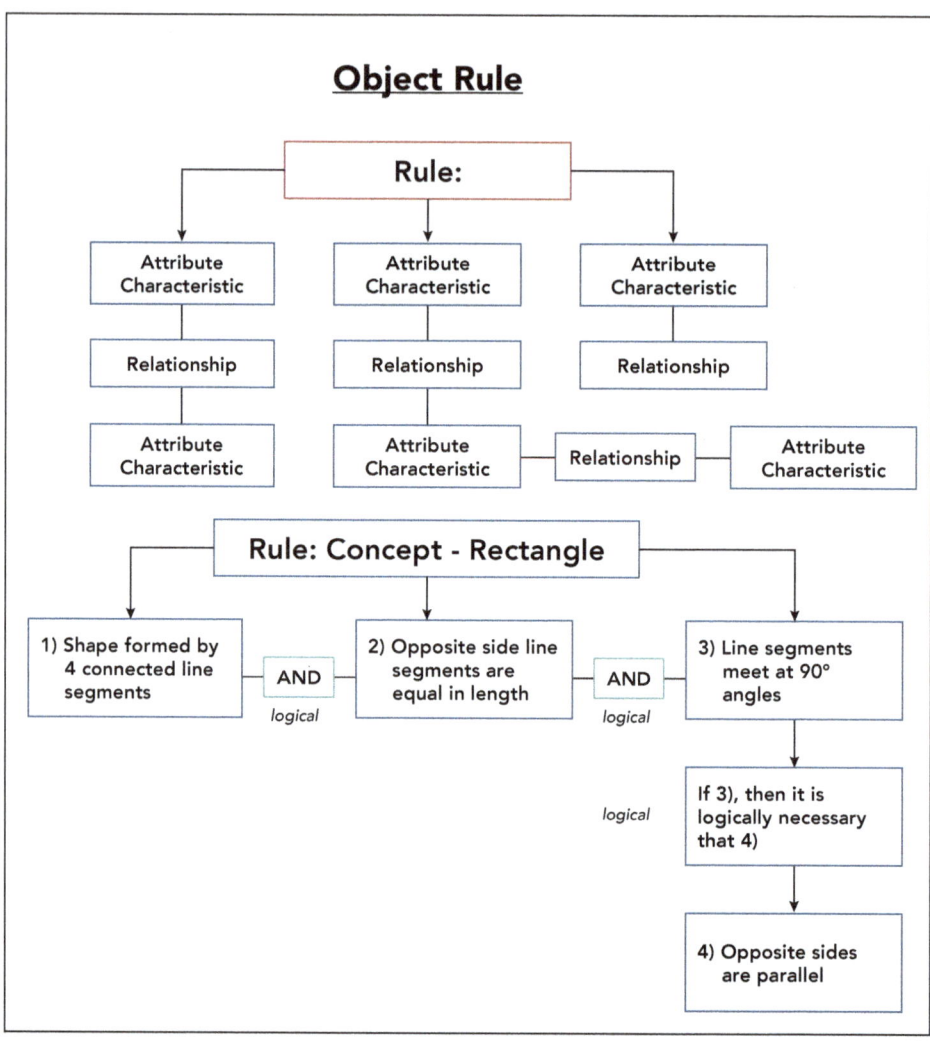

Figure 4.7a
Schematic of the rule structure for objects/phenomena

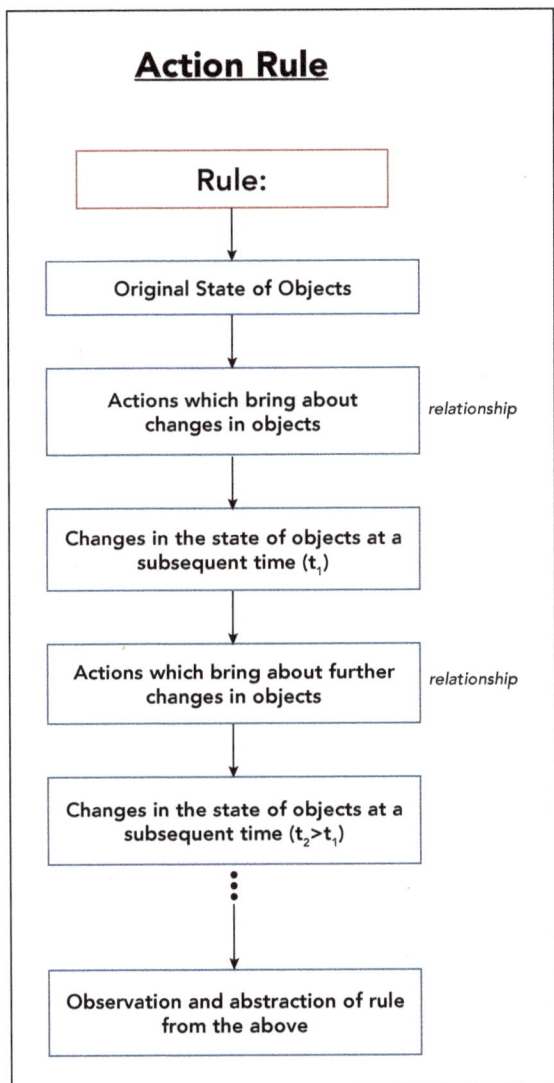

Figure 4.7b
Schematic of the rule structure for action rules

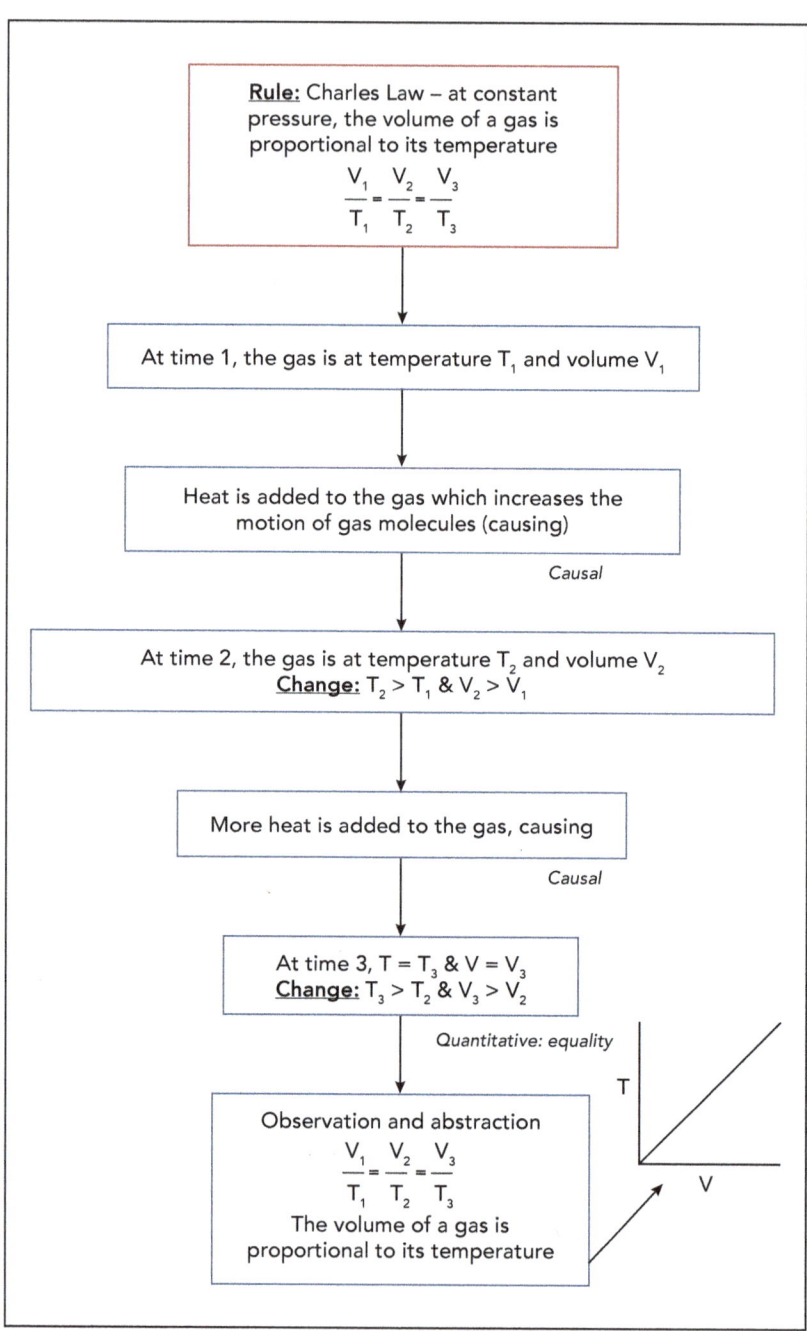

Figure 4.7c
Schematic structure for Charles's Law

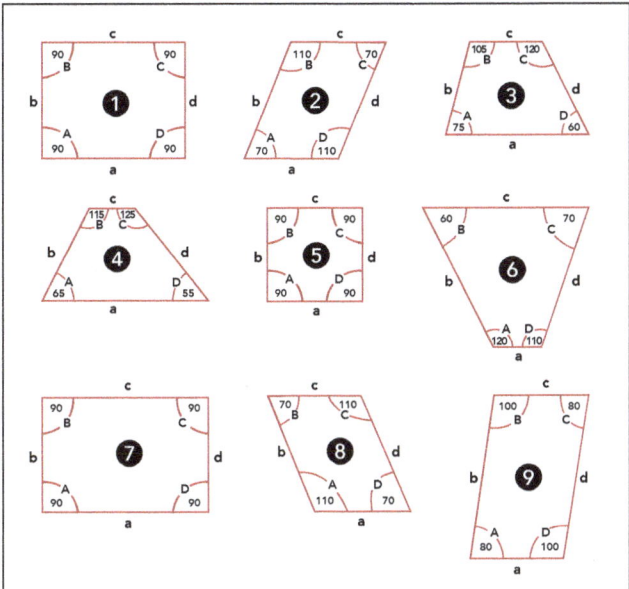

Figure 4.8
Geometric shapes

I would then pair off students and conduct a simple cooperative learning exercise. I would ask each pair to compare and contrast the shapes and to try to sort them into like kinds. I would also ask them to determine what features they used to sort the objects. After completing the sorting, I would call on each pair to show their groupings and to present their hypothesis as to why the shapes were placed in the groups they created. A cooperative learning activity offers several benefits. First, you know that each student is engaged. Second, prior knowledge can be activated through the demands of the task. And third, students speak the same language. Sometimes a student who understands an idea and explains it to another student in language familiar to that student can be more effective than a teacher explaining the idea using the teacher's vocabulary. One disadvantage is that it is difficult for the process to result in a final concept that is as complete and correct as the teacher wishes. At this stage of the lesson, I am fine with that because my goal with the exercise is engagement and activation of prior knowledge.

The next stage of the lesson is to ask the student pairs to measure the lengths of the line segments and the interior angles of the shapes with a ruler and compass (figure 4.8) and to fill out the information in table 4.2.

Table 4.2 contains a lot of data. To prevent overloading working memory, I would provide the following sorting guidelines. I would ask the students to first sort the figures according to the number of side pairs that are parallel. The groupings would be two parallel side pairs or one. This will separate the rectangles and parallelograms from the trapezoids. Next, I would ask the students to look at the angle measures in the group with two pairs of parallel sides and see how many of the four angles are equal, to split

Table 4.2

Figure	side lengths				angle measure				which sides are parallel		which sides are equal
	a	**b**	**c**	**d**	**A**	**B**	**C**	**D**	**a-c**	**b-d**	
1	6	5	6	5	90	90	90	90	Yes	Yes	a = c, b = d
2	4	6.4	3	4.6	70	110	70	110	Yes	Yes	a = c, b = d
3	6	4.1	3	5	75	105	120	60	Yes	No	none
4	7	4.5	2	5	65	115	125	55	Yes	No	none
5	4	4	4	4	90	90	90	90	Yes	Yes	all sides
6	2	6.7	7	6.3	120	60	70	110	Yes	No	none
7	7	5	7	5	90	90	90	90	Yes	Yes	a = c, b = d
8	2	5.4	4	5.4	110	70	110	70	Yes	Yes	a = c, b = d
9	4	7.1	4	7.1	80	100	80	100	Yes	Yes	a = c, b = d

Checking for parellel:

sides a-c: if angles A + B = C + D = 180

sides b-d: if angles A + D = B + C = 180

this grouping into two classes. This will separate the parallelograms from the rectangles. In these two separated groups, I will ask them to note which angles are equal and which pairs of sides are equal. This will call their attention to two of the defining characteristics of rectangles and parallelograms. This is highly directive and is being done to manage the demands on working memory and to guide the students toward the important defining characteristics of the category and the relationship between the characteristics. The choice as to how directive to make the lesson, in general, is based on the age of the students and the teacher's appraisal of the strength of the students' prior knowledge and their capabilities relevant to the task.

The final step of the lesson is to have each group report their final groupings and their hypothesis as to the attributes, characteristics, and relationships that define the group. At this stage, I would interact verbally to summarize and reinforce each concept so that it is clear to students what makes a rectangle a rectangle, a trapezoid a trapezoid, and so forth.

The knowledge construction occurs first in the compare, contrast, and sorting activity. The defining characteristics of the shape are the line segment lengths and angle measures. The shapes are ultimately defined by the relationship between those characteristics. Knowledge is also constructed by asking students to form a hypothesis that expresses that relationship. An inductive lesson, as described, offers several advantages over direct instruction:

- Students are engaged.
- Students are directly constructing knowledge, rather than receiving it from the teacher.
- The learning progress of each student can be monitored.
- The method closely aligns with the brain's natural inductive learning process.
- The level of engagement and amount of time students work with the content facilitates consolidation into long-term memory and retention.

The disadvantages when compared with direct instruction are the amount of time inductive lessons take up and the requirement for more creativity and effort on the part of the teacher to create the lesson. The idea of a rectangle, quadrilateral, and trapezoid can be directly taught in under ten minutes. In fact, if I were a middle school math teacher, I would teach the first three quadrilateral shapes as illustrated and the remaining six, like kite and rhombus, using direct instruction. Given my content-coverage requirements, I simply would not have the time to cover all quadrilaterals in the fashion shown earlier. However, after the first lesson, students should have a firm grasp that the distinctions between shape types are based on line segment length and angle relationships. With this foundation, it is likely that directly teaching the remaining shapes would work well. In general, content-coverage requirements are the enemy of deep engagement with content. The decisions regarding deep engagement should be based on the importance of the rule and how foundational it is to the development of subsequently taught rules.

One incarnation of inductive learning found in the literature is a model referred to as *concept attainment* (Joyce, Weil, and Calhoun 2009; Eggen and Kauchak 2006). In this model, examples of the target concept, as well as nonexamples, are shown to students. For instance, using the example discussed in the previous section on scaffolding, students might be shown examples of Impressionist paintings as well as nonexamples, like Renaissance-era paintings and various forms of modern art. The students would then be asked to compare the examples and to contrast them with the nonexamples to determine what similar attributes/characteristics and relationships characterize the examples and differentiate them from the nonexamples. The students are then asked to form and present a hypothesis of the target concept.

In the next step, students are presented with more examples and nonexamples and asked to test their hypothesis on the new data. The idea here is to refine and improve their original hypothesis by testing whether their hypothesis accurately describes the new examples and clearly differentiates them from the nonexamples. This process can be repeated several times. The teacher comments and scaffolds the discussion of the student-proposed hypothesis at the end of each repeated cycle to help guide the students toward the target concept structure.

To illustrate the basic idea, let's say the teacher is trying to teach the concept of a noun. The concept the teacher is developing is that a noun is a word that designates a person, place, or thing. The following are the examples and nonexamples that could be presented to students:

Examples	Nonexamples
fish	after
cloud	into
tree	became
lake	went
New York	is

If students are struggling, the teacher could provide the clue, "Think about what the word describes or represents." One of the challenges that students face in inductive learning is knowing what attributes, characteristics, and relationships to look for. This requires the teacher to be prepared to scaffold student perceptions. After students develop their hypothesis of the target concept, another set of examples and nonexamples would be presented to allow students to test whether their hypothesis accurately characterizes the examples and differentiates them from the nonexamples.

A teacher could simply tell students that a noun is a word that represents a person, place, or thing. The advantage of developing this concept inductively is that it offers extended and elaborated engagement with the idea and engages the student in thought about the concept. This makes it more likely that the concept will be consolidated into long-term memory and be more readily recalled. Typically, inductive learning would be employed to teach concepts that have more dimensions than the preceding example to justify the expenditure of time required.

Another example of inductive learning found in the literature is simply called the *inductive model*. The description and illustration of this model to follow is a composite and modification of the various incarnations of the model found in the literature. The specific topic used to illustrate the model is the same as that used in an example of the model found in *Models of Teaching* (Joyce, Weil, and Calhoun 2009). The steps involved in implementing the composite model are as follows:

1. Set the goal for the activity.
   Example: The goal of the example lesson is to develop an understanding of the classification of nations as "first world" and "third world."

2. Collect and enumerate data.
   Example: The students are instructed to research and gather statistical data, such as educational attainment levels, per capita income, gross domestic product (GDP) per capita, and tax revenue per capita, for a group of nations.

3. Compare and contrast attributes and characteristics in the data set and create like-kind categories.
   Example: Some nations have low educational-attainment rates, low per capita income, low GDP per capita, and low tax revenue per capita, while other nations rank much higher in terms of these statistics.

4. Create relationships between the abstracted attributes/characteristics of a created category that reflect judgment regarding the nature of the relationship.
   Example: There is a positive correlation between educational attainment, per capita income levels, and per capita GDP. At this juncture, the graphic organizer in figure 4.9 can be presented to students to help them think through and understand how the gathered statistics (attributes and characteristics) relate to one another.

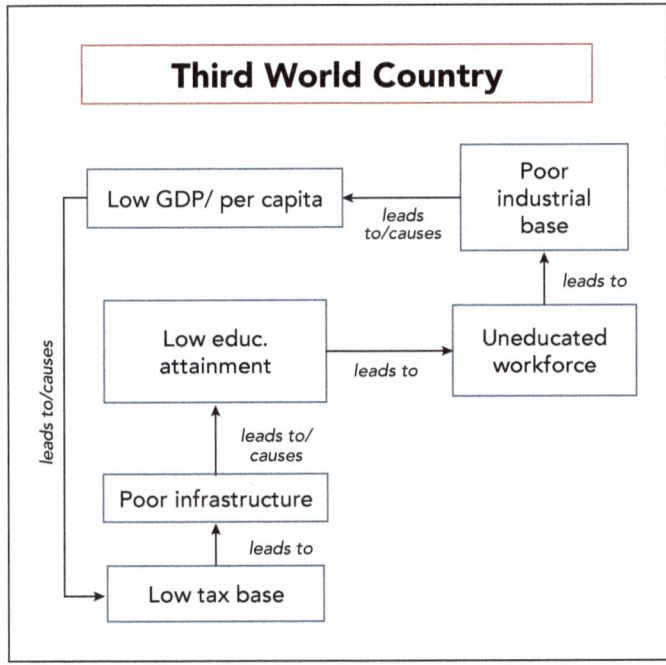

Figure 4.9
Relationships between the common attributes of third world countries

The teacher could then present and discuss with students the vicious cycle that third world countries find themselves in. A low tax base and low tax revenue per capita mean that there is insufficient money for infrastructure like schools. The lack of funds to provide adequate schooling results in low educational attainment levels. Low educational attainment levels result in an insufficient number of trained professionals to support high-revenue-generating businesses that require employees like engineers and accountants. This in turn results in a poor industrial base, low income per capita, and low GDP per capita, which, in turn, results in low tax revenue. This completes the vicious cycle that prevents third world nations from progressing. A discussion such as this helps students deepen their understanding of the relationships among the attributes and characteristics of third world countries.

5. Develop labels and symbolic-level representation—relate the new category to concepts previously learned.
   Example: Nations that rank low on the statistics gathered are called *third world nations*, while those that rank high are referred to as *first world nations*. To strengthen their command of the new concept and to help connect to prior understandings, the teacher could pose the following problem to students: It appears that adequate tax revenue is a key to third world nations making progress and getting out of their rut. Zambia, a third world nation, is rich in natural resources, including important mineable minerals. What actions or policies would you recommend that the government of Zambia undertake to increase its tax revenues and begin to develop infrastructure, such as adequate schools?

The preceding example reveals several ingredients necessary for this inductive learning lesson to be successful. First, students need to understand the relevant attributes and characteristics to create the categories. For example, students need to know what GDP is and what is meant by educational attainment level. They also need to understand the relationships between attributes and characteristics—for example, between educational attainment and the level of training employees in high-revenue-generating industries, the key to higher incomes and GDP, require. The level of scaffolding and support supplied by the teacher will depend on the age of the student and their prior knowledge.

Another example of inductive learning found in the literature is called *discovery learning*, or *guided discovery*. This model is very useful for helping students "discover" patterns in things that exhibit invariant changes with time. As such, it is a useful approach for teaching science principles. The model follows a process similar to that the preceding lesson. The difference is the pattern is manifest in terms of consistent changes in the state of objects and invariant relationships that connect or explain the changes. The following example, from *Strategies and Models of Teaching* (Eggen and Kauchak 2006), is designed to allow students to "discover" the consistent or invariant change in the state of a gas that is heated at constant pressure. The attributes of the gas that are being considered are temperature and volume. The relationship between these two attributes, known as Charles's Law, is what is to be "discovered."

The lesson begins with the teacher filling three balloons with an equal amount of air and making sure the students note that the balloons are all the same size and, therefore, contain an equal amount of air. The teacher then puts one balloon in a beaker of boiling water, another balloon in a beaker of water at room temperature, and the third balloon in a beaker of ice. Two of the balloons change size as shown in figure 4.10.

The teacher then pairs up students, displays the drawing and graph shown in figure 4.11, and asks the students to compare the drawing to the balloons and to compare both to the graph. She then asks the student pairs to make as many conclusions as they can and to be prepared to supply evidence in support of their conclusions.

Construction of Knowledge **147**

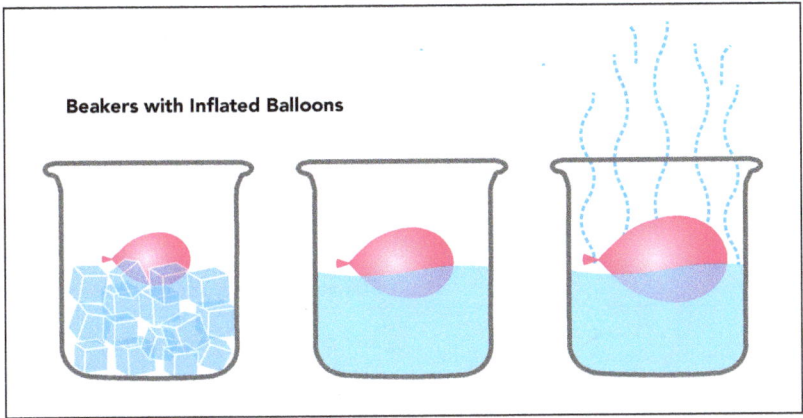

Figure 4.10
Balloons in different temperature environments

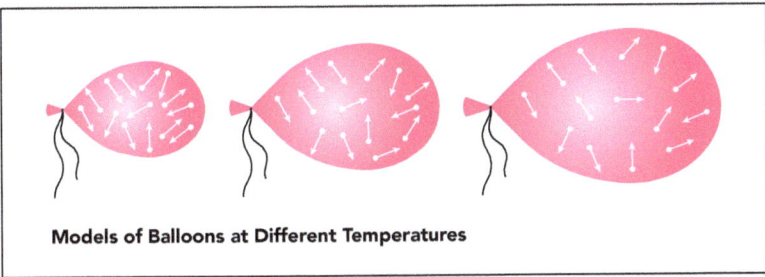

Figure 4.11
Schematic of the state of molecules in balloons at different temperatures

Figure 4.12
Graph of the quantitative relationship between balloon volume and temperature

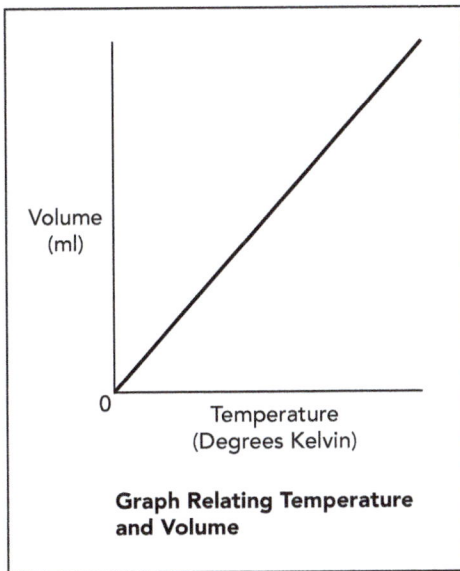

Next, the teacher engages the class in discussion. She asks the students for their conclusions. One pair responds that the masses in each balloon are the same because the number of molecules (dots) in each balloon are the same. The teacher then calls attention to the graph and asks for a conclusion derived from the graph. Another student pair responds that the graph shows that volume is proportional to temperature. The following is a summary of student conclusions and supporting evidence derived from the discussion.

Conclusions	Supporting evidence
1. The mass of air in the balloons is equal.	The number of dots in the three drawings is equal.
2. The molecular movement increases in the heated balloon.	Arrows in the third balloon are longest.
3. The volume of the heated balloon increases and the volume of the cooled balloon decreases.	Visual observation.
4. Temperature and volume are directly proportional.	The graph shows that they are proportional.

The teacher then asks the class: If we know that volume and temperature are proportional, what do we know about their ratios? A student replies that they are equal, and the teacher then writes down the formula $\frac{V_1}{T_1} = \frac{V_2}{T_2}$ and states that this formula is called Charles's Law. The class concludes with an in-class problem that requires students to use the formula.

Note the generalized or abstract pattern of the lesson. Instead of comparing attributes and characteristics of a group of samples as was done in the prior lesson that developed an object concept, the students are asked to discern the pattern of change in the attributes and characteristics of an object resulting from some action. The teacher wants the students to discern the pattern that adding or withdrawing heat from the gas in the balloon, and thereby increasing or decreasing the temperature of the gas, increases or decreases the volume of the gas in the balloon. The graph reveals the precise nature of the relationship that connects or expresses the change in attributes and characteristics of the object. In this case, the relationship is one of proportionality. The relationship is also one of causality. Raising the temperature of the gas increases its volume. In summary, induction of an action or event concept involves discerning the pattern of change in objects and the relationship that connects or explains the change.

We can look at this lesson from a requirement for success perspective. One of the conclusions that the class stated was that molecular movement increased in the heated balloon. The evidence cited was that the arrows in the third balloon where the longest. This perception requires the observer to know the basic idea of a vector representation.

A property like velocity has both a magnitude and a direction and can be represented by an arrow (vector) that shows the direction of the velocity and whose length is proportional to the magnitude of the velocity. There is a good possibility that if the teacher wants students to perceive what is cited previously, she will have to scaffold the perception by calling students' attention to the arrow length and reminding them that the arrows represent the direction and the proportional magnitude of the velocity of the molecules.

The lesson also does not address the direct causal relationship between temperature and volume. The reason the balloon expands is that the addition of heat energy increases the velocity and kinetic energy of the molecules. The faster-moving molecules impact the surface of the balloon with greater force and, therefore, push the surface out more than do the slower-moving molecules at the lower temperature. This could be directly presented by the teacher and illustrated with an analogy as follows. Let's say that we take a large unfilled balloon, stretch it over a frame, and attach it to the frame. We are now going to throw two baseballs at the balloon fastened to the frame. One baseball will be thrown by a toddler and another by a professional baseball pitcher who can throw 100 mph fastballs. The teacher could then ask the students which throw they think will push the surface of the balloon farther from the frame edges. This clearly illustrates the causal process that is occurring.

The observation that the graph shows that volume and temperature are directly proportional requires knowledge of the algebra of straight lines. For these two variables to be directly proportional, the line must pass through the origin of the graph, the point where $v = t = 0$. I think it would have been safer for the teacher to have passed out a graph with numbers that students could read and asked them to divide the values for volume by the values for temperature for several points along the line. Doing this, they will readily see that $\frac{V_1}{T_1} = \frac{V_2}{T_2}$.

My goal with the prior discussion was not to sharpshoot Eggen and Kauchak's lesson. It is a good example of discovery learning. That's why I discussed it. I am also not trying to re-present examples of existing models of learning. Several books, like Eggen and Kauchak's, do an excellent job of presenting various models of teaching. My goal in this book is to demonstrate how different existing models of teaching relate to and are coherent with the theory of knowledge and learning I have developed. In so doing, I hope to provide a stronger theoretical basis for such models. Finally, I am developing principles that I hope will maximize the number of students who achieve success when experiencing various models of teaching. Eggen and Kauchak's lesson will work for many students. The preceding amendments are intended to increase the number of students who achieve the learning goals of the lesson. It is in this spirit that the suggestions are made.

Consideration of the preceding model yields the following principles of learning for induction:

Principle 6: To successfully induct an object rule, the learner must "see" and comprehend the attributes and characteristics of a collection of objects that are similar and invariant across the collection and that distinguish the collection from other objects. They must also "see" and comprehend the nature of the relationship that connects those attributes and characteristics.

Principle 7: To successfully induct an action rule, the learner must "see" and comprehend the invariant changes in object attributes and characteristics brought about by actions and the invariant relationship that connects or brings about the changes.

For example, to induct the concept of a third world country, the learner must comprehend the meaning of attributes like gross domestic product and tax base and "see" that the magnitude of these attributes is much lower in one group of nations than in another group. They must also "see" and comprehend relationships between attributes such as a low gross domestic product producing a low tax base. In the Charles's Law example, the learner must "see" or discover the nature of the change between the attributes of temperature and volume when heat is added to the gas. They must also "see" and comprehend that the action of adding heat and increasing the kinetic energy of the molecules of the gas connects and brings about changes.

Metaphors, Analogies, and Other Literary Devices

When reading a dense, abstract philosophical argument by an author, like Immanuel Kant, I often find myself desperately wanting the author to present an analogy or example. By abstracting the features and relationships of the more concrete analogy or example, I can then reread and better comprehend the abstract argument. Metaphors, analogies, and other literary devices are great teaching tools that enhance comprehension, understanding, and learning. They belong in the category of inductive learning because they involve the abstraction and comparison of features and relationships between different entities.

George Lakoff and his associates have extensively and comprehensively analyzed the use of conceptual metaphors in language. A strong metaphor embedded in ordinary language, cited by Lakoff and Johnson (1980), is "argument is war." When we say someone *demolished our argument* or *attacked our points* or that *our positions were indefensible*, we express the abstract features and relationships of an argument in terms of the abstracted features and relationships of the concrete concept of war. The word *demolished* expresses the idea that something that was is no longer because of some action. In a war, it is perhaps a building exploded by a bomb. In an argument, it is the successful refutation of one person's arguments by another. In both cases, something that was is no longer because of an action.

Steven Pinker (2007) discusses how the abstract words and concepts that are used to communicate ideas in areas like politics and human relationships and in virtually any arena in which discourse is fundamentally abstract have concrete roots. He cites examples such as "events as objects, states of objects as locations, knowing as having, communication as sending, helping as giving, time as space, and causation as force" (Pinker 2007, 237). He illustrates his point using the Declaration of Independence as an example. The Declaration of Independence begins with the sentence "When in the course of human events it becomes necessary for one people to dissolve the political bands that have connected them." Pinker shows that "the course of human events" uses the metaphor that a sequence of events is motion along a pathway. "Dissolve the political bands that have connected them" uses the metaphor that political alliances are bonds. It can also be noted that the words "dissolve" and "bands" have direct physical meanings but are used abstractly in the sentence.

Pinker then states what is the basic principle of using metaphors as a learning tool. He says that children may not understand political alliances or intellectual argumentation, but they certainly comprehend rubber bands and fights. Conceptual metaphors provide a way for people to learn about new abstract ideas. "They would notice, or have pointed out to them, a parallel between a physical realm they already understand and a conceptual realm they don't yet understand" (Pinker 2007, 241). This is the fundamental principle of learning through metaphor and analogy.

The use of metaphors and analogies in teaching is limited only by the creativity and insight of the teacher. It is a powerful strategy that needs to be more frequently utilized. One example used in physics instruction is the use of water flow, a concept familiar to students, as a metaphor/analogy for the flow of electricity. The metaphors are "voltage is pressure," "current is water flow," "resistance is a constriction in a pipe," "power is the quantity of flow during a given time," and "a ground is a reservoir attached to a pipe." Another metaphor used in biology is "a cell is a factory." The instructions for building parts are in the central office, the nucleus. These instructions are read by a messenger, RNA, and communicated to a machine and operator, the ribosome, which builds the parts. Similarly, other organelles in the cell carry out other "factory functions," like gathering and processing raw materials to be used in manufacturing parts.

The key to successfully use a metaphor/analogy is also contained in Pinker's statement that the parallels can be pointed out to the learners. It is my experience that the abstraction of the concrete examples often requires scaffolding for students to comprehend the parallels.

The same neural architecture that enables language to create classes of classes facilitates the creation of metaphors. Words like *animal* are the abstracted features and relationships of subclasses like elephants, bears, tigers, and so forth. They are what the subclasses have in common. In this case the connection is direct. In the case of metaphor/analogy, the connection is made through the comprehension that the attributes/characteristics (features) and relationships of two different classes/categories abstract to the same higher-level concept. For example, in the "argument is war" metaphor, the ideas that someone "demolished one's arguments" and that a "building was demolished" are both abstracted to the idea that something that was is no longer because of an action.

Gick and Holyoak (1980) present an example of analogical problem-solving. Research participants were given the following problem: Direct application of radiation of sufficient strength to kill a tumor will also destroy any intervening tissue. Is there a way to kill a tumor with radiation while sparing the intervening tissue? Gick and Holyoak gave some research participants the following story as a hint. An army wishes to attack a castle. All the bridges that lead to the castle are wired such that the weight of an army passing over them will cause them to explode. The leader of the army wisely divides the troops into smaller groups that can travel over the various bridges leading to the castle and arrive at the castle simultaneously, in force, without setting off the explosives. With this hint, 75 percent of research participants were able to solve the tumor problem. For participants not given the hint, only 10 percent were able to solve the problem. We can clearly see the benefit of the analogy, but we can also ask why 25 percent were unable to use the analogy. The foregoing discussion provides the clue. To apply the analogy, participants need to abstract the attributes/characteristics and relationships of the analogy to the more general and higher-level idea that force can be spatially divided but directed to a central point such that the impact of the divided forces is separate along the paths that the force acts but additive at the central point. Of all participants, 25 percent did not make this abstraction.

High school geometry is taught by taking students through a series of proofs that proceed according to the rules of formal logic. It has always been the ardent hope of educators that in doing so, students will learn the rules and methods of logic and be able to apply them to other domains, such as the creation of arguments or computer programming. In other words, the hope is that students will transfer their knowledge outside the domain and context in which it was learned. This has been studied extensively, and there is no evidence that such transfer occurs (Woolfolk 2007). The problem is the same one encountered in the tumor problem. Consideration of the foregoing leads to the following rule for transferring knowledge outside the context or domain in which it was learned.

Principle 8: Rules developed in one context or domain can be transferred to another if:

1. They are abstracted to more general, higher-level rules.

2. The new domain or context is understood as a circumstance to which the more general, higher-level rules are applicable.

For the rules of formal logic to transfer beyond geometry, they must be understood as a coherent system in and of themselves at the more general and more abstract level. Also, a new application, such as computer programming, must be seen as a domain in which these rules are applicable—elements and relationships are seen as conforming to the rule structure of the higher-level abstract system. To use an analogy, the idea of a bomb demolishing a building must be abstracted to "something that was is no longer because of an action" to apply the idea to argumentation and to state that "someone demolished another's argument."

To teach formal logic inductively would require that the exemplars of mathematical proofs, philosophical argument, and computer programming, for example, be abstracted to the more general level of formal logic. This would be a formidable task indeed. The other option, which is the method currently used, is to teach formal logic deductively as an abstract system in and of itself. The important point here is for educators not to presume that what is taught is easily or automatically transferable beyond the context in which it is learned. I find this assumption to be made often. The human memory system is a relational system. The neuronal principle that undergirds the preceding rule of transfer, as well as many of the other rules of learning cited in this book, is that a connection must be made between representations of knowledge consolidated in memory. To use the word *demolished* in both war and argumentation there must be a connection between the contexts, or domains. The connection for metaphors and analogies, such as war and argumentation, occurs at the higher, more abstract level.

Many literary devices, in addition to metaphor and analogy, can be used to enhance learning. Even a device such as hyperbole can be used to make a point emphatically. The use of personification is also a common strategy. As Kahneman (2011) points out, the human mind has a special aptitude for the interpretation of stories that involve active agents that have personalities, habits, and abilities. Therefore, personification can be a powerful analogical learning device. There is a reason why ancient civilizations passed their knowledge to younger generations in the form of stories and allegories. They were more likely to be remembered. I have had several former students tell me that they have forgotten many of the theories that I taught them, but they remembered every one of my anecdotal stories that exemplified the theories. Some academics oppose the use of personification because they fear that students will attribute agency and intelligence to inanimate objects and actions. I believe the reticence to use personification can be mitigated if the students realize that the explanation is metaphorical and not literal. If an author states that the arms of the wind held the kite in the air, I believe students get the idea, without thinking that the air has arms that it is consciously extending.

One of the big advantages that learning through the symbolic system of language has over the symbolic system of mathematics are the concrete roots discussed previously. Most words, even the most abstract words, have some basis in concrete experience that can be a source of understanding. Mathematics, beginning with algebra, however, involves relationships among purely abstract entities. What does a variable like x symbolize? It symbolizes all conceivable quantities. It is a pure abstraction.

If I were to make the statement to a class of ninth-grade students that Henry, a fellow student, was absent because he was ill with the flu, they would understand my message immediately. They clearly understand the semantic features of the words "ill" and "flu" and that those features can prevent one from carrying out life's routine activities. If I next asked them to tell me what "$x^2 + y^2 = 25$" was, they would reply that it was a mathematical formula. It is highly unlikely that they would respond that it is a circle with radius 5. The students speak the English language, they are not yet very conversant in the language of mathematics. To understand that the equation is a circle, the students must comprehend and relate a series of abstract entities. The first is the idea of a Cartesian coordinate system with two orthogonal axes that allow one to represent two different quantities or variables independently. If we plot a point on this coordinate system, draw a line from the point to the origin, and then draw a projection down to the x axis, we create a right triangle. The sides of the triangle are the x and y values of the point. The length of the hypotenuse of the triangle, which is the distance (d) of the point from the origin, is given by the Pythagorean theorem as $\sqrt{x^2 + y^2} = \sqrt{d^2}$. If we square both sides, we get $x^2 + y^2 = d^2$. From this we can see that the original equation describes a set of points that are a distance of 5 from the origin. The definition of a circle is the set of all points equidistant from some reference point. Mathematics, as shown earlier, involves relationships among and between purely abstract entities. There are no direct concrete referents to use to help make sense of the relationships. This is the reason why mathematics is more difficult for students than language-based learning.

The difficulty in understanding that the foregoing equation represents a circle results from the fact that sense-making and comprehension are developed through a coherence relationship between purely abstract attributes and characteristics. The referents of the symbols are not concrete objects or abstractions drawn from concrete objects. In addition, the relationships in mathematics must be constructed in accordance with the rules of formal logic. Henry's dilemma and the consequences of it are easily understood because they are coherent with the semantic features of the words "illness" and "flu." That the foregoing equation represents a circle is understood as the logically necessary relationship that exists among a set of points in a plane that are equidistant from some reference point. For this specific equation, the reference point is the origin.

The human-understanding and sense-making process is the same for mathematics as it is for any other type of knowledge. It involves creating coherent relationships between the attributes, characteristics, or changes in objects. The difference in mathematics is that the attributes, characteristics, and changes are abstract entities without direct physical referents. With sufficient time, use, and practice, mathematical entities become increasingly familiar as constructs with comprehensible abstract attributes and characteristics. A sense of how these constructs can be related to each other and what relationships are permissible and impermissible also develops.

STEM professionals know the abstract attributes and characteristics of mathematical constructs, such as polynomials and functions like e^{-at}, sin at, and ln at. They know what the graph of these constructs looks like, how to perform mathematical operations using them, and what phenomena in the real world they can describe. For example, if the rate of change of a quantity is proportional to the amount of the quantity at any given time, the change of that quantity with time can be described by an exponential function ($q = q_0 e^{at}$). The exponential function describes, for example, the growth of a population with time or the growth of money in a savings account that compounds continuously at some interest rate. If the acceleration or the rate of change of the rate of change of a quantity is negatively proportional to the quantity at any given time, the change of that quantity with time can be described by either a sine or cosine function ($q = q_0 \cos at$). If q_0 is the starting angle, this equation describes, for example, the motion of a pendulum with time. How do STEM professionals know these things? They have considerable experience working with and relating these mathematical constructs and have developed a knowledge of their abstract attributes and characteristics as well as the kind of mathematical relationships that can be constructed given these attributes and characteristics.

The United States has always lamented the fact that too few of its citizens develop sufficient mathematical and scientific knowledge to become STEM professionals. There always seems to be an insufficient number of engineers, for example, to meet the demand for these professionals. From the preceding, it is clear that one of the keys to increasing the number of students who become STEM professionals is to keep them in the game long enough to gain facility in operating in a world composed of abstractions. Regrettably, many students decide very early in their education that "they are not good at math or mathematics is something they will never fully comprehend." These students get through their mathematical education by memorizing procedural algorithms rather than by developing a conceptual understanding of mathematics.

Using Jean Piaget's stages of cognitive development as a framework, some researchers have reported that on average, 50 percent of high school and college students operate at the concrete-operations stage of development and that many never reach the formal-operations stage (Cohen and Smith-Gold 1978; Pascarella and Terenzina 1991; Ewing, Foster, and Whittington 2011; Woolfolk 2007). It is the formal-operations stage of cognitive development, the ability to reason with purely abstract entities, that enables the type of mental processing required for a conceptual understanding of mathematics. Taken at face value, this research is problematic indeed for mathematics education. I prefer to remain more optimistic and suggest the following to increase the number of students who succeed in developing a conceptual understanding of mathematics and progress to careers in STEM:

1. **Increase the connection between mathematics and the concrete physical quantities that mathematics represents.**

    The utility of mathematics is in solving practical problems in the real world. I believe at least one-third of mathematical instructional time should involve mathematical modeling of physical phenomena. Students should learn how to express quantitative relationships in the real world in terms of mathematical expressions. End-of-chapter word problems, common in current textbooks, require students to translate verbal descriptions into equations. While this is helpful, it is not what I am advocating. I am advocating the direct teaching of interpreting a physical situation in terms of mathematical relationships. I have supervised more than a few engineers who could readily perform the procedures required to solve a differential equation but who struggled greatly to write a differential equation describing a physical process. I have long been an advocate for increased emphasis on mathematical modeling. Modeling can help to create the kind of link that words in language have to the physical roots from which they originated.

    I understand that many mathematical operations do not have physical expressions or analogs, for example, factoring polynomials. However, whenever possible, mathematical instruction should be supplemented with physical and geometrical thinking and connections.

2. **Whenever possible, state relationships in qualitative terms before expressing them quantitatively.**

    Albert Einstein, in his autobiography, states that one of the things that helped him to better understand physics was learning its principles qualitatively before he learned them quantitatively. When Einstein was young, his parents gave him a book that expressed scientific relationships qualitatively. It had very few equations. He states that learning science first in terms of ordinary language greatly facilitated his subsequent understanding when the principles were presented to him quantitatively (Einstein [1949] 1979). To illustrate by example, Einstein first understood the principle behind general relativity qualitatively before he expressed it quantitatively. He performed a thought experiment about the forces someone in a falling elevator would experience. For the modern reader, doing the same thought experiment with the forces someone would experience in a windowless rocket ship provides the same insight. If someone had their feet on the floor of a rocket ship traveling at constant speed, they would not feel any force. That person would be weightless in space. If, however, the rocket ship accelerated, they would feel a force and their feet would press on the floor of the rocket. Also, if the rocket ship began to approach a planet, like Earth, the person would feel exactly the same force pressing their feet against the floor of the rocket. If the rocket ship had no windows, the person would be unable to tell whether the force was due to the acceleration of the rocket or to the force of gravity from the planet. This thought experiment gave Einstein the idea that gravity might simply be acceleration. If space were bent around objects with large mass, objects approaching the vicinity of the large mass would experience an acceleration and, hence, a force—the force interpreted as the force of gravity. Water skiers, for example, experience the same type of increase in force when a boat that is pulling them turns and their path of travel goes from a straight line to acceleration around a curve. At the time Einstein first conceived of the theory, he did not have the mathematical background to express it quantitatively. Therefore, the next step in his journey was to teach himself the nonlinear geometric constructions that had been developed by the mathematician Bernhard Riemann.

Mathematician and educator Morris Kline (1967) addresses the question of how mathematics can be made more intuitive and more the creation and discovery of the learner. He advocates involving students in the following activities: thinking in physical and geometrical terms, conjecturing and guessing, formulating hypotheses and testing them, and generalizing specific cases. Actual physical problems that call for mathematical expression set the stage for discovery. Kline (6) states that a traditional deductive approach to mathematics, one that modern mathematicians would regard as rigorous, is "meaningless before one understands the ideas and the purposes to which they are put." He asks how discovery can take place when students are required to work with ideas overlaid with sophistication and refinement. The following discussion illustrates a portion of what Kline is advocating.

Calculus came about because of Newton's and Leibniz's desire to determine instantaneous velocity and acceleration. Velocity is defined as the change in distance divided by the change in time: $\frac{\Delta d}{\Delta t}$. Instantaneously, the change in distance and the change in time both equal zero. Zero divided by zero is undefined in mathematics. Let's say that the plot in figure 4.13 depicts distance traveled versus time elapsed.

Using the equation for velocity, we can calculate the velocity between a reference time t_0 and a future time t_3. We do so by subtracting the distance traveled at time t_3 from the distance traveled at time t_0 and dividing the distance traveled by the difference between these two times. This gives us the average velocity between these two times. Please note that this calculation is the slope of the line connecting these two points on

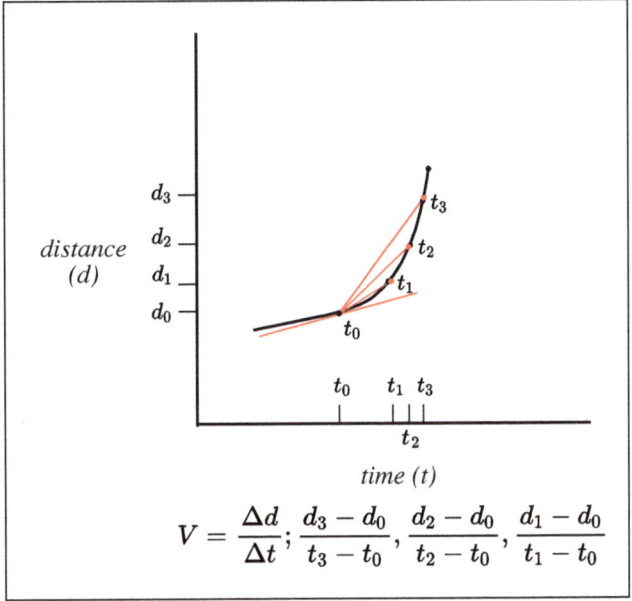

Figure 4.13
Graph of distance traveled versus time elapsed

the curve. We can take a shorter interval of time, or time closer to the reference time, like t_2 or t_1, and make the same calculations. Note that the shorter we make the time interval between the chosen time and the reference time (t_0), the closer we get to the instantaneous velocity, or the velocity at the reference time t_0. We cannot make the time interval 0, because the velocity becomes undefined. We can, however, visually inspect the graph and see that the instantaneous velocity, indeed, has a defined finite value and is the slope of the line tangent to the curve at the point t_0, d_0. To overcome the problem created by dividing by 0, Newton and Leibniz came up with the concept of a limit. The limit of a mathematical expression at a particular value of the independent variable, time in the case of the expression for velocity, is the number the expression approaches as the independent variable approaches that value. The idea of a limit can be illustrated with the following example. Let's consider the following equation:

$$y = \frac{x^2 - 9}{x - 3}$$

We can see that at x equals 3, the denominator becomes 0, and the expression is undefined.

Let's now examine values of the equation as we approach the number 3 from the left side.

$$y = \frac{2.9^2 - 9}{2.9 - 3} = 5.9$$

At $x = 2.9$, the value of the equation is 5.9.

Now let's get a little closer to 3 and put 2.95 into the equation.

$$y = \frac{2.95^2 - 9}{2.95 - 3} = 5.95$$

At $x = 2.95$, the value of the equation is 5.95.

Next let's get even closer and try $x = 2.995$.

$$y = \frac{2.995^2 - 9}{2.995 - 3} = 5.995$$

At $x = 2.995$, the value of the equation is 5.995.

We can see that the closer we get to $x = 3$, the closer the equation gets to the number 6. Although the expression is undefined at $x = 3$, we can say that the limit of the equation as x approaches 3 is the number 6. Using the symbolism of math, this is expressed as

$$\lim_{x \to 3} \frac{x^2 - 9}{x - 3} = 6$$

Using the concept of a limit, Newton and Leibniz defined instantaneous velocity as

$$\lim_{\Delta t \to 0} \frac{d(t + \Delta t) - d(t)}{\Delta t}$$

This equation states that instantaneous velocity is the limit of the equation for velocity as the time increment approaches 0. The preceding equation was generalized to express the immediate rate of change of any dependent variable with respect to the change in an independent variable. It is known in mathematics as the *derivative*. The derivative not only allowed Newton to mathematically express his laws but also opened the door to many future advances in science.

Let's now consider the formal definition of a limit.

Given a function f and the numbers a and L, we say that the limit of $f(x)$ as x tends to a is L if for every positive number ε there is a positive number δ such that $|f(x) - L| < \varepsilon$ whenever $0 < |x - a| < \delta$.

Wow! I believe this definition is consistent with Kline's description of a mathematical idea overlaid with sophistication and refinement. If this is a student's first encounter with the idea of a limit, they would naturally have the following questions: What is this for? What problem does it solve? What exceptions or pitfalls is the wording trying to avoid? How is this used or applied? As Kline (1967) states, understanding this formal definition is greatly enhanced if the answers to these questions are addressed before the student encounters the formal definition. To their credit, most modern textbook authors take students through a few examples of how limits of actual functions are determined, as I have done in the preceding example. The concepts of limits and derivatives are so seminal to an understanding of calculus that I believe even more time should be spent helping students develop an intuitive and physical understanding that answers the preceding questions before introducing the formalities.

Induction and Interpretations of Classical Literature

Another activity that is inductive in nature that students are asked to undertake is deciphering multiple entendre in classic literature. Classic novels are allegories. There is a literal story and a more general depiction and investigation and sometimes a resolution of timeless, universal themes that characterize the nature of the human condition. The literal story is usually an exemplar or prototype of a more general condition, dilemma, conflict, or circumstance faced by humankind. Themes such as destiny versus freedom, power and the corruption of power, class struggles, and the nature and consequences of guilt, revenge, and redemption are explored in classical literature.

To say that students struggle with multiple entendre in literature would be a great understatement. The ability to abstract to the more general theme is completely contingent upon the student's prior experience and knowledge. Like perception itself, where a person is unlikely to perceive something never encountered before, it is unlikely that a student will discern an allegory from a literal story unless their prior knowledge and experience support doing so. For example, during high school, one of my children was assigned the task of reading the short story *Sonny's Blues* by James Baldwin ([1957] 2013) and writing an interpretive essay about it. This autobiographical short story is an excellent depiction of the difficult life circumstances faced by African Americans in late 1940s and early 1950s Harlem. It took a great amount of scaffolding on my part before this seventeen-year-old, raised in middle-class suburbia, could understand what the blues meant to the main character, Sonny. The blues is an artistic effort to make some personal meaning and to create a sense of agency out of a life filled with oppression and pain and feelings of hopelessness and helplessness. It is also a release and catharsis of repressed emotion and pain afflicting the soul. This well-constructed short story is well worth reading and does an excellent job of illustrating the plight of African Americans during this era. My point is that my son's comprehension of the story's meaning required a considerable amount of support. The support came from me, not from his teacher. I think sometimes teachers do not fully understand that simply making things more difficult for students does not constitute a challenging and rigorous education.

The study of classic literature is important. It not only examines ageless themes that are still relevant today but also shows how people in the past lived, what they believed, and why they did what they did. It makes history come alive for the student as the real actions of real people, like themselves, guided by the values and beliefs of the times in which they lived. The caveat for the study of classic literature is that the abstracting process that reveals the allegory should be heavily guided, supported, and directly taught if necessary.

No course covering American literature is complete without covering the work of Herman Melville, one of America's greatest authors. Since his most famous work, *Moby Dick*, is long and difficult to read, teachers often assign the more accessible short novella *Billy Budd, Foretopman*. Billy Budd is a sailor on a merchant ship, *Rights of Man*, who is impressed by the British Royal Navy, which is actively involved in a war with France, to serve on a warship, the *Bellepotent*. Billy is an innocent with no capacity for understanding people who employ deceit, guile, and treachery to accomplish their ends. He is always positive, cheerful, and friendly. Billy sees only the good and positive in other people. Melville structures the story as a classic Greek tragedy and gives Billy a tragic flaw: when he is under stress, Billy stutters and cannot articulate his thoughts. Other than this flaw, Billy is innocent perfection.

The antagonist in the story is Claggart, the warship's master-at-arms. Melville depicts Claggart as the incarnation of evil itself. His treatment of the crew is harsh, brutal, and capricious; he is hated by every sailor except Billy Budd. With time, Billy is loved and respected by his fellow sailors, as well as by the ship's officers. He is promoted from deckhand to foretopman.

As Billy's circumstances improve, Claggart becomes increasingly angry. He is jealous of the treatment accorded to Billy and is frustrated by his inability to dominate Billy with his harsh treatment and punishments. To destroy Billy, he accuses him of organizing a rebellion among the crew. The ship's captain (Vere) calls Billy to his quarters to face his accuser. After Claggart levels his charges, the captain asks Billy to respond. Billy begins to stutter and cannot express himself. Frustrated, Billy strikes Claggart, and he falls; the blow is fatal.

In a lengthy trial, the ship's officers at first want to either dismiss or lightly punish Billy because they all understand Claggart's deceptive, evil, and conniving nature. They cannot believe the rebellion charges, given their prior experience with Billy. To dismiss or lightly punish Billy would be natural or even divine justice before the eyes of God. Claggart deserved his fate. Captain Vere delivers a forceful soliloquy and convinces the other officers that the rule of law, the Admiralty code, must supersede the dictates of the officers' conscience. In accordance with the law, Billy is hanged.

This is the literal story. As in Moby Dick, the sailors and officers in the story are a microcosmic representation of society. The Admiralty code of the Royal Navy is the law by which this society is ruled. The theme that Melville explores within this context is the dialectic between moral sense and action at the level of the individual versus at the level of the institution. Membership in any institution or society requires that individuals sacrifice a portion of their rights and powers to the institution to further the common good. It is the duty of the institution to protect those surrendered rights for all. This is the basic idea of a Social Contract. Policy and rules dictate behavior. Melville illustrates that the stronger and more powerful the institution, the more individuals abrogate their responsibility to one another and the more they fail to take personal action against injustice. Natural justice is replaced by institutional rules. Melville's character Dansker, the oldest and wisest of the crew, laments the fact that he did not speak out to the captain regarding Claggart's cruel and callous treatment of the crew and, in particular, his treatment of Billy Budd. He feels a sense of responsibility for Billy's fate. One interpretation of Dansker is that he represents the typical individual in a strong institution who acts simply to fit in and comply with the requirements of their circumstances. Dansker is a "go along to get along" character who never musters the courage to personally confront evil and injustice. Melville strongly implies that the more powerful an institution, the more disconnect there is between people and their humanity, conscience, and responsibility to others.

Billy Budd is also symbolic of Adam and Eve in the biblical book of Genesis. Claggart is symbolic of the serpent in the garden. For example, when describing Claggart's dead body on the floor of the captain's office, Melville invokes the image of a dead snake. Adam and Eve's original sin is having eaten from the tree of knowledge of good and evil after succumbing to the temptation of the snake. Adam and Eve, like Billy Budd, had no knowledge of evil prior to the act that sealed their fate. Melville seems to suggest that innocence invites its own destruction. To not recognize and confront evil is to be its victim.

There are other allegorical elements in Melville's story, but these two suffice to illustrate my points. I believe in the importance of studying classical literature. The historical context and understanding supplied, the exploration of universal themes that explicate the human condition, and the illustration of literary devices that expand understanding and enrich human communication are all valuable educational benefits. My point with this discussion is that given K-16 students' knowledge and life experience, it is unwise to presume that they will, on their own, flesh out and comprehend multiple entendres and allegories such as those illustrated for Billy Budd. I believe the important parts of the learning experience are exploring universal themes, developing historical knowledge and context, and understanding how literary devices are employed by authors. This implies that guiding and supporting the abstractions required to understand the allegory, or "other story," being told is crucial. If necessary, directly teach and show the parallels. Let students read papers that discuss how scholars have interpreted the work. I believe that reading classical literature should not be an assessment of students' preexisting capacity to decipher multiple entendres.

The argument against my position is that it will stunt students' ability to make an interpretation that reflects their personal meaning. They may generate an insight or create a personal interpretation that is unique and more personally meaningful. I would agree if the principal goal of the reading is the creation of personal meaning. This, however, is rarely the teacher's goal. In my son's case, for example, I believe the teacher wanted him to get more out of *Sonny's Blues* than "glad I don't live in Harlem," his initially derived personal meaning.

Inductive Reasoning

When teachers ask students to write a paper, they will typically remind them to be sure to provide evidence in support of any conclusions they reach in the paper. In the abstract, this directive asks students to produce an argument for their contentions. An argument is a claim that something is the case. It consists of two parts. First is a set of declarative statements, called *premises*, that provide evidence in support of a conclusion. The conclusion is the second part of the argument. To qualify as an argument, the set of statements must be such that one or more of the statements provide support for another statement in the set. The evidence must have a connection to the conclusion. Philosophy students are taught to summarize philosophical arguments by putting them into a standard form. The standard form lists the premises vertically, draws a line below the premises, and then has the logical symbol for "therefore" followed by a conclusion. The following example illustrates this for a simple deductive argument.

If it is not raining and the temperature is above 70°F, then Jim will go to the lake today.

It is raining today.

∴ Jim will not be going to the lake.

I believe this procedure for summarizing an argument should be taught to all high school students.

All high school students are taught the process for producing a four- to five-paragraph argumentative essay. The first paragraph of the essay introduces the topic and presents a thesis or statement that such and such is the case. The next two to three paragraphs provide the justification in support of the thesis. These paragraphs begin with a topic sentence, which is a premise that supports the thesis, and then present data and/or arguments to justify the premise of the topic sentence. This is followed by a paragraph that consists of a refutation of possible counterarguments to the thesis. The final paragraph is a summarization and a restatement of the thesis. The essay has the same structure as a general argument. The parallels are shown here:

Essay	General argument
Thesis	Argument conclusion
Paragraph 2 topic sentence	Premise 1
Paragraph 3 topic sentence	Premise 2
Refutation of counter arguments	
Summary	Restate conclusion

We can see that teaching students the general structure and process for summarization of an argument would be of benefit in helping them develop an argumentative essay. Other essay types that students are asked to produce that have the same abstract structure as an argumentative essay are textual/rhetorical analysis essays and literary analysis essays. In a textual/rhetorical essay, the student analyzes the way the author uses different rhetorical devices, like pacing or hyperbole, to achieve their writing goals. These essays are particularly difficult for students since there are more than one hundred such devices, some of which, like irony, are subtle and sophisticated. Unless the teacher has spent considerable time teaching students to recognize and use such rhetorical devices, the results of these essays are often disappointing. A literary analysis essay is like a textual/rhetorical analysis essay. It looks at story elements such as setting, character, and plot structure and the use of figurative language to explain how these elements serve to convey the theme of the story. An expository essay investigates an idea by evaluating evidence, expounding on the idea, and presenting an argument concerning the idea. Additional essay types are narrative and descriptive essays. These essays are fundamentally a description of something that is worth knowing. As such, coherence and flow within the essay are achieved using other relational mechanisms, such as time, space, or part/whole relationship.

The most common form of inductive reasoning is referred to as simple enumeration. Simple enumeration is the creation of a generalization from a pattern of similarity among objects, actions, and events. A classical example, which is often utilized to characterize and exemplify induction itself, is the statement "All swans are white." The structure of the argument that results in this generalization would be as follows:

Swan A is white
Swan B is white
.
.
Swan Z is white

∴ All swans are white

Like all inductions, this statement is regarded as true until an exception is found. In this case, the exception may be found in the southern hemisphere. Swans in Australia are black. A more correct induction is that all swans are either white or black or some combination of the two colors. This example illustrates the point that induction leads to contingent knowledge. Contingent knowledge is knowledge of how the world happens to be, up until the current time and as far as we know. Whoever first made the statement that all swans are white had likely never been to the southern hemisphere; therefore, as far as they knew and up until that time, their experience supported the induction that all swans are white.

What is called necessary knowledge in philosophy is knowledge the validity of which is ensured by conformance to the rules of formal logic. If the set of beginning postulates are true, then inferences and deductions made according to the rules of formal logic are necessarily true. For example, if it were, in fact, true that all swans are white, then if something is a swan, it is necessarily true that it is white. The idea of necessary truth in any form has been philosophically assailed by philosophers such as Willard Van Orman Quine. Most initial premises in deductive arguments that utilize formal logic are arrived at inductively or are assumed to be intuitively obvious and not in need of proof. For example, Euclid presumed that his five initial postulates, used to formulate geometry, were intuitively true and not in need of proof. In the nineteenth century, mathematicians demonstrated that self-consistent non-Euclidean geometries could be created in which Euclid's initial postulates were false. So much for initial postulates that render absolute truth and knowledge.

The strength of an inductive argument is contingent upon four factors: sample size, sample diversity, sample relevance, and whether all the relevant information was considered. The sample size question for the swan generalization would be, Is the number of swans examined twenty or two hundred thousand? The sample diversity question is, Were swans all over the world examined or just those in New Jersey? The evidence relevance question is, Did we just examine swans or were some large white ducks included in the sample? Obviously, the color of ducks is not relevant to the conclusion. All of the relevant information, color in this case, was considered in making the generalization.

Another type of inductive reasoning is called *statistical syllogism*. This type of reasoning is quite similar to deductive categorical reasoning. The form for this type of argument is shown here:

Most Italians eat pasta.

Luigi is an Italian.

―――――――――――

∴ Luigi eats pasta.

Note that one of the premises is an inductive generalization and that the process infers something about the specific from the general. The use of the word "most" in the first premise is what makes the argument statistical.

As discussed previously, a lecture or reading assignment consists of some combination of descriptions, inductive arguments, and deductive arguments. A common strategy used by lecturers and authors is a process that I will term *induction by analysis*. Analysis is the inverse of synthesis. All the inductive processes that I have discussed so far fit in the category of synthesis: building the general from the specific. Analysis involves breaking something down into its component parts and determining the relationship that exists between those parts. Using the models proposed in this book, the analysis of an object concept would involve determining the defining attributes and characteristics of the object and determining the relationship that exists between them. Analysis of an action concept would involve defining the changes brought about by an action and determining the relationship between them, such as causality.

Authors and lecturers often state a summarizing thesis in their introduction to a topic. The thesis might be that that some object or action constitutes a such and such. For example, some contemporary authors contend that Donald Trump and his followers' actions after Trump lost the 2020 presidential election constituted an attempted coup. These authors typically begin by defining the concept "coup." This definition would consist of listing the concept's attributes/characteristics and the relationship between them. The authors then describe why they feel the contention is justified. The goal is to get the reader to abstract the concrete information and verify that these abstracted elements as well as the relationship between them conform to the definition of a coup. Often, the author will directly argue that the examples do, in fact, justify the characterization and do the abstracting for the reader.

Analysis itself can be used as a teaching model. For example, let's say that I'm teaching a lesson on infinitives and their use in writing. My goal for this specific lesson is the attribute and characteristic that infinitives and infinitive phrases can be used as adjectives, adverbs, and nouns. After stating the goals of the lesson and undertaking some other introductory activity to generate interest, I might proceed as follows:

1. Review required prior knowledge:

    a. Remember that every sentence has a subject and a verb (predicate).

    b. The verb (predicate) specifies a state of being (is, are, was) or an action (gave, went, played) or links the subject to a subject complement that further describes the subject (looks, became).

    c. An action verb that is transitive has an object that receives the action. A transitive verb requires a receiver of the action for the sentence to make sense and to complete a thought.

2. State the rule or portion of the rule that is the goal of the lesson:

    a. An infinitive is a verb with the word "to" added to it (e.g., to sleep, to eat, to spend).

b. Infinitives can also be in phrases where they can be combined with a modifier, an article, and an object that is the receiver of the action expressed by the infinitive. The phrase acts like a noun, adjective, or adverb. Example: "to finish a new book." Note that "a" is the article, "new" is the modifier, and "book" receives the action of the infinitive "to finish"—it is what is finished.

3. Describe the knowledge-construction process:

   a. I want you to <u>analyze</u> a group of sentences by undertaking the following steps:

   1. Circle the infinitive. If the infinitive is a phrase, I have highlighted the phrase for you. I want you think of the phrase as a single unit, like a word.

   2. Find the subject and the verb and put one line under the subject and two lines under the verb. To find the verb, ask yourself what action or state of being is expressed. To find the subject, ask yourself who or what is doing the action or is in the state of being.

   3. If the verb is transitive (requires a receiver of the action to make sense), ask yourself who or what is receiving the action to identify the direct object and put a wavy line under the direct object.

4. Now ask yourself the following questions:

   a. Is the infinitive or infinitive phrase the subject of the sentence; is it the direct object, and does it express a person, place, or thing? If the answer is yes, the infinitive is a noun. Write the word "noun" under the sentence.

   b. Does the infinitive or infinitive phrase describe or modify a noun? Does it describe or explain which one, how many, or what kind? If the answer is yes, the infinitive is an adjective. Write the word "adjective" under the sentence.

   c. Does the infinitive or infinitive phrase describe or modify a verb? Does it answer a question like when, why, how, or for what reason? If the answer is yes, the infinitive is an adverb. Write the word "adverb" under the sentence.

5. Model the knowledge-construction process:

Figure 4.14
Sentence with parts of speech designated

» What action or state of being is expressed? [verb: bring]

» Who is bringing? [subject: I]

» Is the verb transitive? If so, who or what is being brought? [direct object: something]

» Is the infinitive the subject or direct object? [no]

» Does the infinitive describe a noun and describe which one, how many, or what kind? [yes: the infinitive is an adjective describing the noun "something" and answering what kind of something]

Go through the same process with the sentences shown in figure 4.15 to demonstrate an infinitive phrase as an adverb and a noun.

Figure 4.15
Additional sentences with parts of speech designated

6. Pass out a sentence set and a sheet that outlines the analysis process.

7. While students are working, move around the class and provide scaffolding to those needing assistance.

8. Open the class for any questions or discussion, summarize the rule learned, and have students turn in their completed sentence sets.

Note that while the knowledge-construction process is analysis, the model of instruction is direct instruction.

This lesson is very guided. I did this to focus on and facilitate the principal goals of the lesson and to eliminate potential complications and confusion. An important aspect of lesson planning is to make certain there are no rabbit holes or other diversions that will divert students from the primary goals of the lesson. This is the reason, for example, that I highlighted the participle phrase and asked the students to think of the phrase as a unit. This alleviates the problem of identifying the object of the phrase as the object of the sentence. Note also, the reinforcement the lesson provides for previously learned concepts like adverb, adjective, and indirect object. Strong knowledge of the basic parts of speech is crucial to any lesson involving grammar. By applying previously learned concepts, their prior knowledge is strengthened.

The general process for learning by analysis is to state and present the rule and then have students verify it by breaking it down to its elements (attributes/characteristics/changes) and determining the relationship between those elements.

Induction is also a popular academic research paradigm. Let's say you are a business professor and want to make some money to supplement your meager professor's salary. You can select a topic to research that a great number of people outside of academia care about or are interested in. For example, you could investigate what makes a person effective or how a company can make the transition from good to great. The professor's next step is to find examples of people who have been effective or corporations that have made the transition from good to great. After finding these examples, and perhaps some nonexamples, the next step is to examine effective people or great corporations and find out what attributes/characteristics and actions taken they all have in common. As a professor of business, you have a good idea of what to look for. You then create relationships between these attributional elements and abstract the commonalities of your examples to induct the answer to your research question. After your induction, you can publish a book like *The 7 Habits of Highly Effective People* by Stephen Covey or *Good to Great: Why Some Companies Make the Leap and Others Don't* by Jim Collins.

After teaching students the inductive process, a teacher could assign a long-term paper or project that follows the described pattern. At the graduate level, this might be an investigation of several schools that showed success in narrowing the performance gap between students at different socioeconomic levels. What did they have in common? At the high school level, it might be a paper that asks students to discuss why they think that the authors you covered in class are notable and worth the time spent studying them. What positive commonalities make them notable and worth studying?

The last form of inductive reasoning that I would like to cover is called *reasoning by analogy*. This is the process of drawing conclusions from examples based on the similarity between the examples and some other object of consideration. Plato made extensive use of the strategy in his dialogues. The following paraphrased example from the *Republic* demonstrates the process.

The conversation begins with one of the participants, Thrasymachus, putting forth the proposition that a Ruler, insofar as he is a Ruler, always commands for his own self-interest. Socrates asks whether Thrasymachus means a Ruler in the strict (theoretical) sense or the popular (actual Ruler) sense. He responds that he means in the strict sense. Socrates then takes apart Thrasymachus's proposition as follows:

Socrates's question or statement	Group response
In the strict sense, is a physician a healer or maker of money?	Healer
In the strict sense, is a pilot a captain of sailors or merely a sailor?	Captain

Every art (medicine, sailing) has an interest for which it must consider and provide.

The interest of the art is the perfection of it.

In the strict sense, the physician considers not his own good but the good of the patient in what he prescribes.

The pilot or Ruler of the sailors provides for the good of the sail.

∴ Any Ruler, insofar as he is a Ruler, considers not his own interest, but the interest of his subjects.

As the preceding shows, the basic process is to contend that the object of consideration is a member of a class or category. As such, the object shares the attributes/characteristics/relationships of the class or category, and we can make inferences about the object based on its membership.

If we were to disagree with Plato, we would question the premise that the interest of the art is the perfection of it. We all know people who learn occupations and crafts, Plato's arts, simply to further their own self-interest. Remember, however, that Plato's overarching goal is to arrive at perfect, timeless, and universal concepts, not to document actual human practice.

Teachers can use reasoning by analogy as a teaching tool. Students should become familiar with the process because it is often used by authors and lecturers.

To conclude this section, I would like to comment on the teacher practice of casually requesting that students undertake inductions. When assessing students for reading comprehension, for example, it is typical to ask what the main idea, point, or position of the reading is. An assessment of reading comprehension could also ask the student to summarize the reading in their own words. Additionally, it is common for an assessment to ask the student to make an inference or deduction from an inductive generalization that they have hopefully derived from the reading. An example of such a question, following the reading of a brief history of Jane Goodall, might be, "Which of the following statements is not a reason why Dr. Leakey invited Jane Goodall to join his research team in Africa?" This question requires the student to have inducted from the reading the concept "reason why Dr. Leakey invited Jane to join him" and to deduce from this concept which of the multiple choices listed is incoherent with this concept.

Induction is such a natural brain process that I think teachers often take it for granted. Summarizing, obtaining the gist or main idea and formulating conceptual encapsulations of items expressed in the details of a reading, as required by the Jane Goodall question, is not trivial. To summarize or obtain the main idea, students must abstract the details of the reading and place them under the umbrella of a previously known concept or to construct, while they are reading, a previously unknown concept.

As such, the process is highly contingent upon the student's prior knowledge and experience. Does the student have concepts in memory developed to the extent that the attributes, characteristics, and relationships constituting those concepts capture the abstracted details of the reading? Also, how organized and coherent is the reading? Does the author maintain a theme, a consistency between thematic elements, and a logical flow, or is the paper ambiguous and disconnected?

Ely (2005) summarizes the components of reading that must work together to make reading a seamless process that facilitates the construction of meaning.

- Letter recognition
- Grapheme-phoneme correspondence
- Word recognition
- Semantic knowledge of word meanings
- Comprehension and interpretation of texts

The phonological theory of reading asserts that a reader must not only recognize and discriminate letters and letter combinations (orthography) but also correlate these representations with the sounds of spoken language. To read, a child must develop the knowledge that spoken words can be broken apart into elementary components of speech (phonemes) and that the letters in a written word represent the sounds of these elementary components (Shaywitz, Lyon, and Shaywitz 2006). This is the goal when teaching students phonics: creating letter-sound relationships. Creating these relationships speeds reading comprehension because the relationship between words and their meaning is first developed through spoken language. With time and experience, readers can quickly recognize words and go from word recognition directly to the semantic content that composes the word meaning. During the 1980s, a philosophy of reading called "whole language" emerged that attempted to skip steps one (letter recognition) and two (grapheme-phoneme correspondence) and teach students word recognition initially. In schools that adhered to this philosophy, phonics was not taught. The phonics/whole language debate was resolved with the publication of the results of the blue-ribbon National Reading Panel (2000). After reviewing the extensive body of literature on reading instruction, the panel concluded that children who received formal instruction in phonics were able to read more quickly and recognize more words than children who received less explicit instruction were able to. Again, this is likely the case because of the early and strong connection between spoken words and word meanings. Step four, vocabulary development, occurs progressively throughout the student's education. Words codify and represent rules (concepts, theories, generalizations, and principles), and the teaching of consciously constructed rules is the goal of formal education. It is step five, comprehension and interpretation of texts, that, in my estimation, currently receives insufficient emphasis in reading instruction.

As stated previously, a reading typically consists of a mix of descriptions, narratives, inductive arguments, and deductive arguments. Step five is contingent upon not only having a sufficient vocabulary but also having the ability to follow an author's inductive arguments and deductive arguments. I, therefore, contend that directly teaching students the nature and construction of these types of arguments is of great value. Recognizing these arguments and understanding how they are structured and developed is invaluable in reading comprehension and interpretation. When reading texts, for example, students should be able to recognize and differentiate premises, supporting evidence, and conclusions.

A large urban school district in the Dallas–Fort Worth metroplex, whose reading test scores are among the lowest in the state, recently announced that they are going to dramatically increase their teaching of phonics. Good to see that they are at least addressing three-fifths of the problem. It is my contention that step four, semantic knowledge of word meanings, accounts for most of the difference between the early-grade performance of children coming from different socioeconomic backgrounds. A major thesis of this book is that consciously constructed knowledge is enabled by the brain's capacity for symbolic representation through language or mathematics. Words codify and represent rules, which in turn are the structures that represent the organization of an individual's semantic knowledge. When knowledge construction occurs within the brain's working-memory system, it is words that cue the activation of semantic information in long-term memory. As Vygotsky ([1943] 1986) states, thought is not merely expressed in words—it comes into existence through them.

Studies indicate that a vocabulary of between three thousand and four thousand words is required for students to be successful in kindergarten. If one were to go to various sites on the internet that address the size of vocabulary for different age groups, one will find that the average vocabulary of a five-year-old is in fact around three thousand to four thousand words. This is not a coincidence. What is taught in kindergarten reflects many years of experience regarding what a five-year-old is capable of learning. This evolved empirically. It was not the result of any research concerning the vocabulary required by kindergarten curriculum. When I served on the Fort Worth Independent School District Board of Trustees, we had children entering kindergarten with vocabularies of eight hundred to nine hundred words. Most of them had never been more than a mile and a half from where they lived. The vocabulary these students possessed generally related to things necessary to survive difficult living circumstances. Another thesis of this book is that consciously constructed knowledge is built on a foundation of prior understanding. In short, what you can learn is strongly impacted by what you already know. This has been thoroughly discussed and demonstrated in prior sections of this chapter. What this means is that the child who comes from a difficult low socioeconomic environment has a limited number of rules (concepts, theories, generalizations, and principles) with which to comprehend and construct new knowledge. The child with the vocabulary of eight hundred to nine hundred words has only eight hundred to nine hundred ideas that they can use to comprehend what their teacher is saying and asking for and as a foundation for constructing new knowledge and successfully performing learning tasks. It is no wonder that they struggle and quickly fall behind the progress demonstrated by children with the vocabularies of three thousand to four thousand words. A major deficit that results from poverty and difficult living circumstances is the paucity of life experience and lack of development of a conceptual inventory that would support the type of learning that occurs in schools.

If I took a flight to France and watched television for a month in my hotel room, it is unlikely that I would learn to speak French. It is not simply exposure to language that matters. Poor children watch more television than middle-class children do and are, therefore, exposed to many words. The key to learning new words is the idea expressed in the priorly presented quote by Russian author Leo Tolstoy. People need to hear the word in context with other words that they understand, and they need to use the word. If instead I lived with a French family who spoke English and they told me the French word for different objects and actions that I encountered and I then worked to use those words to communicate with them, I would be much more successful at learning French.

A key, then, to narrowing the gap between the performance of children in different socioeconomic groups is to expose them to richer and more diverse life experiences, describe and discuss those experiences with the children, and help them use the words that represent, describe, and explain the experience. Fort Worth, for example, has three art museums, a child-friendly science and history museum, a zoo, a botanical garden, a log cabin village of old historic homes, a concert hall with children's programming, a historically preserved area with daily cattle drives, many fire and police stations, and numerous other venues that are free or low-cost. Taking young children to any of these, taking the time to describe and discuss what they are experiencing, and engaging children in conversation about their experience would greatly increase their vocabulary and conceptual inventory. Even going to a house and garden exposition at the coliseum would be beneficial. Early learning is largely associative. At this stage, language learning and conceptual expansion need not proceed according to some rigorous, research-based process. Simply giving children the experience and expressing the experience in language will work. Perhaps the school district that is increasing phonics instruction needs to couple this with extensive guided field trips.

Federally funded universal pre-K in the United States is currently on the table politically. I certainly support this as a wise investment. I would recommend that in addition to getting a jumpstart on decoding and grapheme-phoneme correspondence, vocabulary building be made an integral part of the pre-K experience. Stories about bears who encounter a young girl in their house or a young girl who encounters a wolf in the woods are charming and fun, but they are not particularly rich in conceptual diversity.

Additionally, I would recommend that research be conducted to determine the specific vocabulary and conceptual inventory that are required for students to be successful in the early grades. I'm going to bet that not all of the three to four thousand words that successful kindergartners know are necessary for success. I think it is the case that if a child has this size of vocabulary, it is highly probable that they will be in possession of those words and ideas that are required for success in kindergarten.

Sometimes, I think educators are their own worst enemies. Many contend that given sufficient resources they can educate all children to the desired level of competence. There is very little empirical evidence to support this conclusion. There is no large urban school district in the United States that has yet been able to bring the performance level of underprivileged children up to the level of more privileged children in suburban schools. This is not due to a lack of effort or poor leadership. I believe considerably more research is necessary to develop techniques and strategies that can bridge the gap. I believe the current knowledge base is insufficient and not yet up to the challenge. The purpose of formal education is to help students enhance their lives. Currently, the percent of students who move beyond the social class that they find themselves in is discouragingly low. This needs to change. The possibility of upward mobility has always been one of the promises of formal education.

Deductive Learning

The value of knowledge in the form of rules is that it enables and facilitates rule-based, higher-order thinking activities like communication, problem-solving, decision-making, strategizing, planning, design, and creation. Fundamental to these activities is the capacity for deduction, or making inferences from rules. In the language section of this book (chapter 3), the hypothesis was developed that the human judgment of logical and true was predicated on whether a proposed relationship between elements was coherent with and could be supported by the semantic features of the respective elements put into relationship. "The boy talked to his friends" can be judged as plausible, possibly true, and logical given the attributes and characteristics (semantic features) of a boy, like the ability to speak, and the semantic features of his friends, like the ability to comprehend speech. The sentence "The rock talked to his friends" is judged to be implausible, false, and illogical, unless we are specifically referencing a Disney cartoon. The semantic features of rocks, like the inability to speak, do not support the proposed relationship.

To support this view of logic and truth, we require a coherent and compatible theory of deduction and inference. The work of Johnson-Laird (1983), Johnson-Laird, Byrne, and Schaeken (1992), and Johnson-Laird and Goodwin (2005) provides such a theory. Their theory is termed *model theoretic*, since deduction proceeds from information derived from mental models of elements put into relationship. Johnson-Laird et al. are not specific as to the nature and origin of the mental models. I am applying their theory to neural representations of object semantic features and relationships and the neural representation of changes in objects and the relationships that connect or account for the changes—my hypothesized two large categories of human knowledge.

The model theoretic approach contrasts with a proof theoretic approach that presumes that deduction proceeds according to independent rules of inference or separately existing logical or syntactic structures. Note that the model theoretic approach eliminates the need to postulate a separately existing logic/syntax processor in the brain. The working-memory system with its capacity to connect, hold, and process several item representations in memory simultaneously and fluidly is what enables a model theoretic mechanism based on the coherence of semantic features. I contend that this approach is more powerful and accurate than processing via a separate logic/syntax mechanism. For example, let's look at the following set of statements:

Osama bin Laden was a Muslim.

The Muslim religion advocates peace and discourages violence.

Therefore, Osama bin Laden was a man of peace.

The first two statements are true; therefore, the rules of formal logic would necessitate that the conclusion is true. Everyone knows the conclusion is false because it is incoherent with all the representations people have in their memory concerning Osama bin Laden, including his orchestration of the September 11, 2001, attacks on the United States. The brain's process of determining logical and true could be characterized as rendering what the weight of the evidence indicates. The human judgment process incorporates considerably more information when making a judgment. Information from all representations in memory can potentially be activated to support a judgment. As such, the human judgment process is more likely to conclude correctly than is a system that processes propositional information according to a collection of fixed rules of logic. Such a system would have to be extremely large to quickly and efficiently process all the propositions that could be constructed from semantic and episodic memory representations relevant to the object of consideration. It would also be considerably slower than a semantic feature processor because processing would be serial and sequential rather than parallel and simultaneous.

Formal logic renders necessary conclusions if the premises that are being processed in accordance with its rules are true. The power of formal logic is that it is independent of the specific content (semantics) of the premises processed. It also renders necessary conclusions versus the more probabilistic conclusions of the human judgment process. However, garbage in, garbage out. If the premises are false, the process has no value. If the brain had a separate logic/syntax processor, how could it determine the veracity, accuracy, or truth of the premises that it processed? Such a mechanism would itself be a logic processor and would render the need for a separate or additional processor redundant and unnecessary.

One additional level of memory representation, the symbolic level, and the evolution of increased working-memory capacity seem to be easier and more plausible evolutionary mutations than the evolution of a logic processor or universal grammar with thousands of rules.

The generalized model of the deductive process as per Johnson-Laird et al. is as follows:

1. Constructing a representation of the premises of the problem.

2. Invoking the representation of the applicable rule.

3. Formulating a semantically coherent conclusion from the representations.

4. Checking for alternative conclusions.

5. If no alternative conclusions are found, considering the collusion to be correct.

Note that this model is coherent with how human executive function operates. Johnson-Laird et al. present the following simple example that captures the essence of the process:

Problem: If there is a circle, what follows?
Rule: If there is a circle, there is a triangle.

Rule model:
Given/model: There is a circle.

Conclusion/deduction: There is a triangle.

The conclusion, or deduction, that there is a triangle follows as semantically coherent with the rule through the comparison of the representation of the rule and the representation of the circumstance to which the rule is applied.

In experiments that test participant performance on tests of abstract logic, when given a rule like, "If there is a circle, then there is a triangle" and the information that there is a triangle, most participants will incorrectly state that there is a circle. The Johnson-Laird et al. model supports this incorrect conclusion. To answer correctly would require a representation wherein there was a triangle and not a circle. As Johnson-Laird et al. state, the problem arises because a direct comparison of semantic features yielding the correct solution requires that the collection of representations exhaustively represents the possible states of the elements involved in the relationship. This is the reason why participants in tests of abstract logic struggle with purely abstract logic but can easily process an inferential relationship like "If struck by lightning, the house will catch fire." In this case, they can access a wealth of episodic and semantic representations that would inform them that house fires can be caused by many different reasons. They would not make the mistake of immediately assuming that because the house is on fire it was struck by lightning. The contrasts between participant performance on tests of purely abstract logic versus logic involved with propositions that have numerous semantic features supports Johnson-Laird et al.'s theory.

As discussed previously, a reading or lecture consists of descriptions, narratives, inductive arguments, and deductive arguments. We can analyze a hypothetical lecture on the basic theory of flight to see how the Johnson-Laird et al. model works in practice. A teacher might present the theory using a deductive argument as follows. I have shown the teacher's argument on the left and a description of the type of information supplied on the right.

Teacher's statements	Type of information
1. When moving air encounters an obstacle, like a building or a wing, its path narrows as it flows around the object.	Physical fact
2. Conservation of mass requires that the amount of air moving past any given point at any given time remains the same.	Rule: conservation of mass
3. Therefore, as the path of flow narrows, the velocity of flow must increase.	Deduction from rule (2) given fact (1)
4. The shape of an airplane or bird wing is such that it narrows the area for airflow above the wing but not below it.	Physical fact

5. Therefore, the velocity of air is greater above the wing than below it.
   Deduction from deduction (3) given fact (4)

6. Conservation of the energy of the air, which consists of its potential energy, expressed in terms of pressure, plus, its kinetic energy, expressed in terms of velocity requires that the sum of the two must remain constant.
   Rule: conservation of energy

7. Therefore, an increase in the velocity of the air above the wing compared with below the wing results in a lower pressure above the wing than below it.
   Deduction from rule (6) given deduction (5)

8. Pressure is the force per unit area that a fluid exerts on its surroundings.
   Rule: definition

9. Therefore, there is a greater force below the wing than above the wing.
   Deduction from rule (8) given deduction (7)

10. By Newton's law, if there is a net force on an object, it will accelerate in the direction of the net force.
    Rule: Newton's law

---

11. ∴ If the net force created by the difference in pressure is greater than the downward force of gravity, then a plane or bird will accelerate upward and fly.
    Final deduction from rule (10) given deduction (9)

A rule can express the relationship between the semantic features or changes in features of a single object/action or among different objects/actions. In the first three statements by the teacher, the semantic feature or fact that the path of the flow of air narrows around an object is connected (related) to the semantic feature that the velocity of the airflow increases. The relationship is one of causality required by the rule of conservation of mass. Referring to the Johnson-Laird et al. model of deduction, we can think of the circle as the narrowing of the path of flow and the triangle as the increase in velocity—two semantic features of the air connected through relationship. Statement four states that the shape of an airplane or bird wing is such that it narrows the area for airflow above the wing but not below it. The statement says that there is a circle.

Then, using the preceding rule, there is a triangle—the velocity of the air above the wing increases compared with the velocity of air below the wing. Note that the rule used to make this inference is a deduction from the rule stated in statement two—conservation of mass. Using this deduction or inference that the velocity is greater above the wing than below it as the new given, the instructor then inputs this given into a new rule that relates velocity to pressure, a new semantic feature. Now think of the increased relative velocity above the wing as the circle and the new semantic feature pressure as the triangle. The rule of conservation of energy states that if there is a circle, an increase in velocity, then there is a triangle, a decrease in pressure. This relationship is also one of causality. The new given, the result of the previous deduction, that there is an increase in relative velocity above the wing states that there is a circle. The rule then renders the deduction that there is a triangle, the pressure above the wing decreases compared with the pressure below the wing. This is the deduction expressed in statement seven that, in turn, becomes the given for the next rule utilized. This pattern continues to the conclusion; each new deduction or inference becomes the given or input for the next rule. This pattern expresses a chain of reasoning and is common to a great many deductive arguments or explanations. In the preceding case, the teacher used two statements of fact and created a chain of reasoning using four rules. This chain allowed the teacher to go from the facts to the conclusion that was the goal of their lesson.

Now let's look at deduction in the context of human executive function and the problem-solving process. Human executive function begins with a goal or a problem to solve. It perceives the givens or current state and then searches long-term memory for rules (knowledge) that will facilitate going from the given state to the desired state. In the case of the "what allows things to fly" problem, the givens are: obstructions decrease the path of fluid flow and a wing is an obstruction such that the area available for flow decreases above the wing but not below it. The next question is, What rules allow us to explain the phenomenon of flight given these two facts? For a student to solve this problem they would have to have the following rules in their long-term memory: (1) conservation of mass, (2) conservation of energy for fluids (Bernoulli's equation), (3) definition of pressure—the relationship between pressure and force, and (4) Newton's law. They would then have to create the chain of reasoning shown earlier, where the givens are input into a rule, a deduction is made, and the deduction made is subsequently put into and used as the given for the next rule. In abstract, the question is, What set of rules when related and connected allows us to go from what we know to what we want to know? What takes us from our current state of knowing to our desired state of knowing? This question and process are manifest in deductive arguments in all disciplines, not only in math and science. In the case of our flight problem, we could go to the result "flight" and work backward. To stay in the air, a bird or plane must be subject to a force that equals or exceeds the force of gravity. What rule relates force and motion? Newton's second law does. For a fluid, how is force characterized? It is characterized by pressure. What connects or relates pressure to velocity of fluid flow? The rule for conservation of energy for fluids, known as Bernoulli's equation, does. What rule relates velocity of fluid flow to area available for flow, the information contained in our givens? The equation of conservation of mass for a fluid does. This completes the chain of rules that allows us to go from our givens to the conclusion that is the solution to the problem or the answer to our question. We have gone from what we know to what we want to know. New knowledge has been created deductively.

Now, let's look at the deductive argument from a student-comprehension perspective. First, the students would have to know or comprehend the semantic features involved in the argument, such as force, pressure, area, and velocity. For a true conceptual understanding, they would also have to have prior understanding of the rules. The relationship expressed between the semantic features would have to make sense to them. For example, total energy consists of potential energy added to kinetic energy. The fact that total energy must be conserved is a brute fact of nature. If kinetic energy increases, potential energy must decrease to keep the total energy, the sum of the two, constant (conserved). The student must understand this if the portion of the argument that involves this rule is to make sense to them. We can see that there is considerable prior understanding required for students to follow and comprehend the deductive argument. Figure 4.16 summarizes the teacher's qualitative explanation. I have shown the chain of connection with arrows as well as the equations that would be required for a quantitative explanation.

Figure 4.16
Schematic of the deductive chain of reasoning

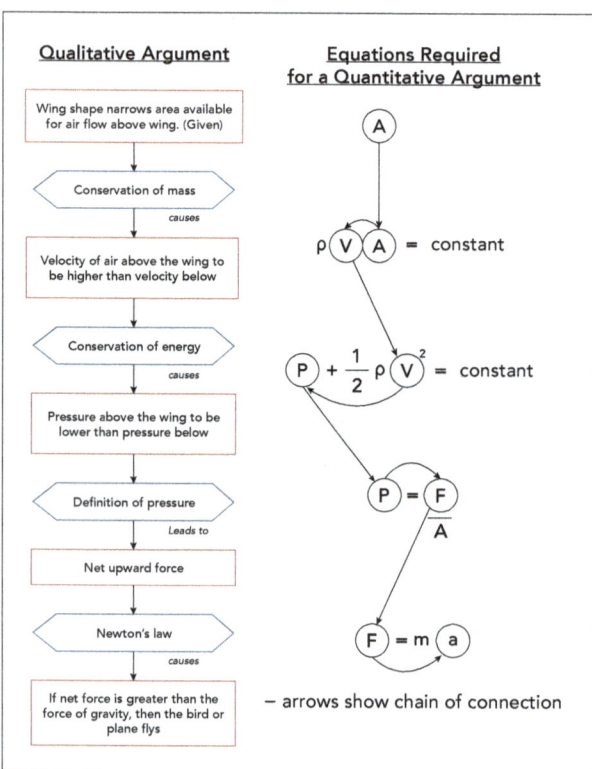

If one is already in possession of a rule, new knowledge is not created using the rule. The statement "The bachelor will not be bringing a wife to the party" provides no new knowledge. The truth of the statement is guaranteed by the definition of "bachelor." The predicate of the statement is contained in the subject. New knowledge is created by combining and relating currently known rules to create new rules. New mathematical theorems, for example, are derived through the combination of existing theorems. The example to follow illustrates the process.

Suppose we are at the point in our knowledge of geometry where we know that the sum of the angles in a triangle equals 180° and that if two angles and the included side, the side connecting the angles, of one triangle are equal to two angles and the included side of another triangle, then the two triangles are congruent. *Congruent* means all the sides and angles are equal. We want to know what is the case if two angles and a <u>non-included</u> side are equal. We can answer this question by combining the two rules that we already know as follows.

Prior knowledge (rules)

1. The sum of the angles of any triangle equals 180°.

2. If two angles and the included side of one triangle is equal to two angles and the included side of a second triangle, then the two triangles are congruent.

Figure 4.17 Givens for two different triangles

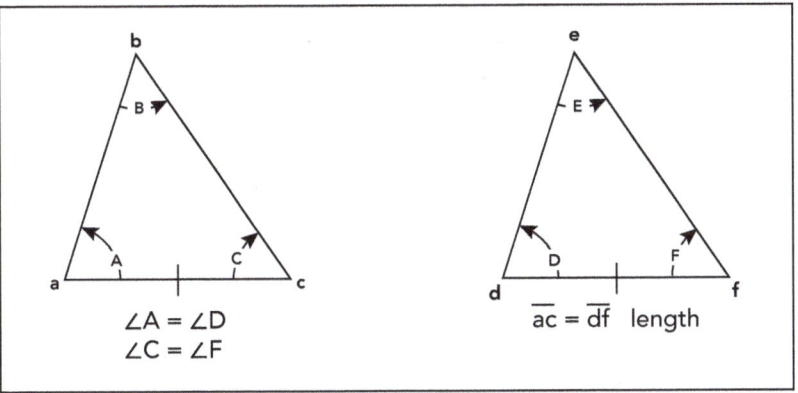

Problem: If two angles of two different triangles and a non-included side are equal, what follows?

Figure 4.18 Givens for two different triangles

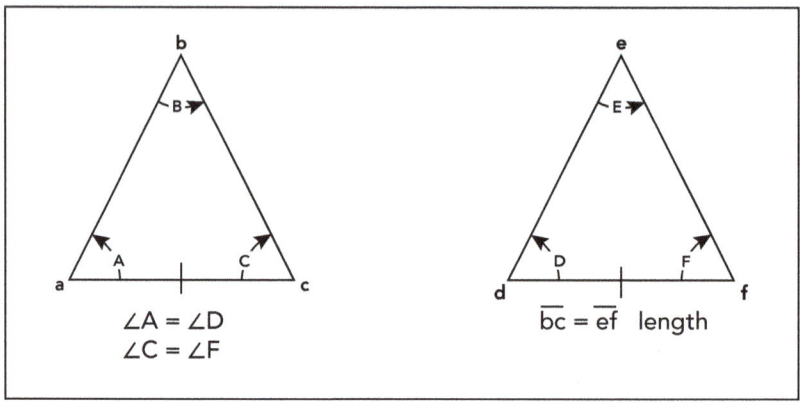

Argument/proof:
1. Angle A equals angle D — given

2. Angle C equals angle F — given

3. Angle B must equal angle E — by rule 1, all angles added together must equal 180°

4. Line segment length from b to c equals the length from e to f — given

5. The two triangles are congruent — by rule 2, since the equal line segments are included between angles equal in both triangles ($B = \angle E$ & $\angle C = \angle F$)

New knowledge (rule) created:
If two angles and the non-included side of one triangle is equal to two angles and the non- included side of a second triangle, then those two triangles are congruent.

The deductive process illustrated in the prior two examples is not confined to mathematics and science. This generalized process occurs in deductive arguments in all disciplines. The example to follow shows how it works in a philosophic argument. To illustrate, we can examine the philosopher Hume's ([1739] 1982) argument that feeling and emotion are the source of human moral and ethical judgments. Hume begins with a rule that defines what reason is.

Rule 1: Reason is the discovery of truth or falsehood in the agreement or disagreement of ideas or to the real existence of matters of fact.

Hume's rule defines the category/class of reason by listing the attributes, characteristics, and relationships of the category: determining whether a relationship between ideas is coherent or verifying that some fact, like the sky is blue, is correct. He then makes a deduction from rule 1.

> Deduction from rule 1: Whatever, therefore, is not susceptible to this agreement or disagreement is incapable of being true or false and can never be the objec of reason.

Here, Hume states a basic rule of logic: if something does not share the attributes and characteristics of a class, it cannot be a member of the class. Hume then states rule 2, which defines another class or grouping and its common attributes—the group consisting of feelings, emotions, and actions.

> Rule 2: Our feelings, emotions, and actions are original facts complete in themselves and imply no reference to other feelings, emotions, or actions.

The common attribute of this categorization or collection is that all elements of it are original facts and realities that are not derived by combination or relationship to other elements of the categorization or collection—other feelings, emotions, or actions. What he means here is that if you are angry, that is a simple fact or reality and not something that is derived by some relationship between other feelings and emotions. Important to Hume's argument is the contention that human actions and motivations are connected to feelings and emotion and not to logic and reason. This contention is made in several sections of the book that contains the argument we are analyzing. Hume's logical constructions are always impeccable. If you want to argue against him, you must question the validity of his premises. Here, I would call into question whether actions were original facts. I can think of some actions that are motivated by logic and reason. From rule 2, he deducted as follows:

> Deduction from rule 2: Therefore, feelings, emotions, and actions are not susceptible to agreement and disagreement and, also, it is impossible that they be pronounced either true or false and either contrary or conformable to reason.

Hume here contends that because feelings, emotions, and actions are original facts and are not derived from a relationship between other feelings, emotions, and actions, they are not a member of the class of things subject to reason and, therefore, cannot be declared true/false or logical/illogical (conformable to reason). Declarations such as true/false or logical/illogical are attributes that belong exclusively to the class reason. Hume then elaborates this deduction as follows:

> Elaboration: Actions, therefore, do not derive their merit from reason nor their blame from contrariety to it.

The final deduction of Hume's argument then is as follows:

Deduction using the result of the prior deduction: Since reason cannot prevent an action by contradicting or disproving of it, reason cannot be the source of moral good or evil.

The implicit, though unstated, conclusion is that feeling and emotion are, by default, the source of moral and ethical judgments. The argument explained in Johnson-Laird et al. terms is as follows:

1. Hume builds a model of logic and reason.
2. Then he builds a model of feelings, emotions, and actions.
3. He juxtaposes and compares the two models.
4. He shows through this comparison that logic and reason cannot be the source of moral judgment concerning actions because there is no common element or connection between the two models.
5. By default, and by reference to other statements in his book, Hume shows that the source of these judgments must lie within the model of feelings, emotions, and actions.

Deductive Learning Models

The three most prominent models of learning in the education literature that I would categorize as predominantly deductive in nature are referred to as *inquiry learning*, *problem-based learning*, and *experiential/scientific method–based learning*. All three models have the same fundamental structure. They begin with some question of interest. The next step is the formulation of a hypothesis or proposed preliminary answer to the question of interest. The hypothesis is typically an inductive generalization of what is currently known about the question of interest or the object of investigation. The hypothesis includes all the elements and the relationships between the elements thought to be relevant and impactful in answering the question of interest or in characterizing the object of investigation. The hypothesis guides the design and planning of the inquiry, experiment, or problem-solving process. The process is then conducted and the results evaluated. Results of the process will either confirm the hypothesis, disconfirm it, or provide the basis for the formulation of a new hypothesis that better explains and describes the results of the inquiry, experiment, or problem-solving process.

The following example illustrates the model for experiential/scientific method–based learning.

1. *Question of interest:* What determines how fast a pendulum swings (its frequency of oscillation)?
2. *Generation of the hypothesis*
    a. Elements (attributes/variables) thought to be impactful:
        1. Length of the pendulum (L)
        2. Weight of the pendulum (W)
        3. Initial angle of release (θ)
    b. Relationship between the elements (hypotheses):
        1. The shorter the pendulum, the greater the frequency
        2. The heavier the pendulum weight, the greater the frequency
        3. The greater the initial angle of release, the greater the frequency

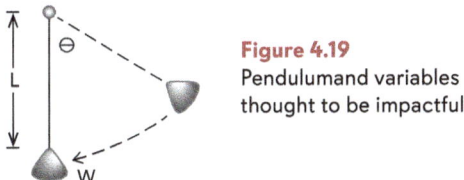

Figure 4.19
Pendulumand variables thought to be impactful

3. *Gathering information* (inquiry, experiment, research process)
    a. Construct a pendulum with string attached to a fixed point and attach a weight to the end of the string (as shown in figure 4.19).
    b. Keep the weight and the angle of release the same and vary the length of the pendulum. Record the number of swings in fifteen seconds. Do this three times.
    c. Keep the length and angle of release constant and vary the weight. Record the number of swings in fifteen seconds. Do this three times.
    d. Keep the weight and length constant and vary the angle of release. Record the number of swings in fifteen seconds. Do this three times.
4. *Organizing information*

Angle: 45°
Weight: 2

Length	Avg. # of swings
30	12
40	11
50	10
60	9

Angle: 45°
Length: 50

Weight	Avg. # of swings
1	10
2	10
3	10
4	10

Weight: 2
Length: 50

Angle	Avg. # of swings
60°	10
45°	10
30°	10
20°	10

5. *Evaluate results—assess hypotheses*
   Only hypothesis 1 is true. The length of the pendulum is the only thing that affects the frequency of oscillation (how fast it moves).

6. *Symbolize and connect to other knowledge*
   Discuss how this result might be related to the concept that falling objects move at the same rate regardless of their weight. Talk about Galileo's experiment in which he dropped heavy objects off the Leaning Tower of Pisa. How might this relate to our experiment?

The next example illustrates the use of the inquiry model of learning. The overarching question of interest is, How was Martin Luther King able to improve conditions for African Americans and help bring about the Civil Rights Act of 1964? The inquiry explores one aspect or dimension of the answer to this question.

1. *Question of interest:* How did Dr. Martin Luther King convince America that the treatment of African Americans violated its founding principles and values, its espoused religious beliefs, and common sense?

2. *Generating hypotheses:*

   a. *Elements*: sources of American values, ideals, and beliefs

      1. Foundational documents - Declaration of Independence, Constitution, Bill of Rights

      2. Christian values - Christian Bible

      3. Common sense - common notions of fairness and decency

   b. Relationships (hypotheses)

      1. The treatment of African Americans violated the democratic ideals that the country was founded on.

      2. The treatment of African Americans violated Christian values and beliefs.

      3. The treatment of African Americans violated common sense and common ideas of decency.

3. *Gathering information:* Read and analyze the following speeches and documents by Dr. Martin Luther King.

   a. Letter from the Birmingham Jail

   b. I Have a Dream

   c. The Death of Evil upon the Seashore

   d. I've Been to the Mountain Top

   e. A Time to Break Silence

4. *Evaluating results:*

   a. Combine evidence from the preceding analysis to deduct whether the initial hypotheses are supported or need to be modified.

   b. Can the hypotheses be generalized into a more comprehensive and larger idea?

5. *Symbolize and connect to prior knowledge:*

   a. Write a six-paragraph essay to summarize the inquiry.

   b. Discuss what it means to "hold someone accountable."

   c. Discuss what it means to be antiracist.

As with induction, which has a forward path (synthesis) and a backward path (analysis), deduction has two paths to a rule. The forward path is the application of logic, and the backward path is termed *Kantian logic* or, alternatively, *abduction*. The backward path asks the question, What rule must inhere for the outcomes or phenomena to be such as they are? The philosopher Charles Sanders Peirce (Hoopes 1991), who coined the term *abduction*, describes the process as follows. If he is an observer in a foreign land who sees an elegantly dressed man on horseback being followed by an entourage that, among other activities, shields the man from the sun with an umbrella, he would abduct that the man is likely the potentate or ruler of the land in which he is making his observation. Note that abduction, which is the twin sister of induction, yields contingent and probabilistic truth, whereas the forward path yields necessary truth if the utilized premises are presumed to be true or justifiably assertable.

Kant ([1781] 1990) accorded the same stature to his abductions as he did to his forward deductions. For example, he surmised that the possibility of perception absolutely demanded a priori conceptions of space and time. Without the ideas of space and time, perception was not possible. An analogy to Kant's position is the assertion in a criminal trial that, given the evidence, a defendant is judged to be guilty of a crime beyond a reasonable doubt. The implication being that it could not have been otherwise. This position is most difficult to justify philosophically. In deference to the philosophic position of functionalism (Fodor and Block 1972), or the idea that the same outcome can be realized in multiple ways, it is safer to ascribe to abduction or Kantian logic a contingent and probabilistic stature on par with that of induction. In a classroom setting, abduction would take the form of some mystery or issue to be resolved by students through the postulation of various rules that could explain the phenomena observed.

The example to follow illustrates how abduction might be used to teach how models of the atom evolved through time. After introductory activities to communicate the goals of the lesson, activate prior knowledge, and generate interest in the lesson, a teacher could proceed as follows:

1. Introduce Democritus and the thought process that led to his theory that matter was composed of atoms.

    a. Democritus thought about cutting something again and again. He thought that eventually you would reach the point where you can no longer divide it. At that point you would have some fundamental entity that was indivisible. This fundamental entity must be the building block from which all things are composed. He called this entity an *atomos*, which is the Greek word for indivisible.

2. Engage students in a similar thought process and have them abduct a conclusion.

    a. Democritus didn't know about the principle of conservation of mass in 400 BC, but you do.

    b. Let's say you have the technology to cut something into pieces as small as you want, even so small that you cannot see the pieces with your eyes. Let's also say that you can cut the object an unlimited number of times. If you can cut the object an unlimited number of times, then, in theory, you could reduce the size to zero or cut it until it didn't exist anymore. This, however, would violate the principle of conservation of mass. You can't turn something into nothing. So, what must be the case to stay compliant with the principle of conservation of mass?

The specific abduction you want the students to make is that to comply with the principle of conservation of mass, there must be a point at which you can no longer cut the object. At that point it is indivisible. For now, we can call what is left an *atom*, or the Greek word for indivisible.

The abduction process consists of presenting the facts, evidence, and applicable known principles relevant to the phenomenon and asking students "what must be the case" for everything we know to be coherent and relate the known facts, evidence, and applicable principles. What rule explains the phenomena observed?

3. Provide the facts, evidence, and applicable principles for the next abduction.

   a. Democritus's idea didn't last very long because it was dismissed by a more influential philosopher, Aristotle, who thought the idea was ridiculous. It wasn't until 1803, or more than two thousand years later, that the idea of atoms was reprised by English scientist John Dalton. Dalton was aware of the work of French scientist Antoine Lavoisier, who formulated the law of conservation of mass. In a chemical reaction, for example, if you combine 2 g of one chemical with 16 g of another chemical, the resulting compound is 18 g—no more, no less. He was also aware of the work of another French scientist, Louis Proust, who formulated the law of definite proportions: if you break a chemical compound into its elements, the masses of the elements will always have the same proportions. For example, if you break water down into hydrogen and oxygen, the ratio of the mass of oxygen to hydrogen will always be the same. Dalton knew of these results as well as the results of his own experiments and came up with another law: the law of multiple proportions.If the combination of two elements results in more than one kind of compound, the ratio of the elements in the different compounds is a small whole number. For example, if you combine tin with oxygen, 2 tin oxides can be produced. The ratio of the mass of oxygen in the two compounds is exactly 2. Combining hydrogen and oxygen can produce water or hydrogen peroxide. The ratio of the mass of oxygen in hydrogen peroxide to the mass of oxygen in water is exactly 2.

   b. Now, let's look at the following situation and see if we can arrive at the same conclusion that Dalton did.

Figure 4.20 Possible combinations of chemicals x and y

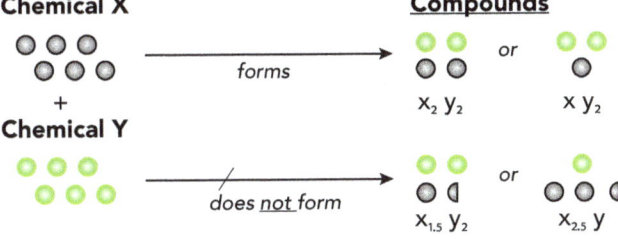

Let's say we have two chemical elements represented by the colored circles and the open circles. The two compounds they form are composed of 2 colored circles and 2 open circles or 2 colored circles and 1 open circle. The ratio of the open circles in the two compounds is 2. It is never the case that the ratio is 1.5 or 2.5. To get that ratio, what would have to happen to the elements represented by the open circles? What must then be true about the nature of the elements represented by the circles?

The abduction we are looking for is that the original elements are composed of something that cannot be split or divided—in other words, Democritus's original idea of the atom. In addition, although the mass proportions of the different elements in the compounds are always the same, as per Proust's law, they are different in absolute quantity. Therefore, the atoms of different elements have different masses and weights. We now have Dalton's model of the atom: indivisible entities with different masses and chemical properties for each element. From the Dalton model, we are now ready to introduce new facts, evidence, and relevant principles that will allow the student to abduct the Thompson model of the atom.

4. Provide the facts, evidence, and applicable principles for the next abduction.

   a. Let's move the clock forward about one hundred years and examine the experiments of British scientist J. J. Thomson. Thomson constructed a device called the cathode-ray tube.

This device consisted of a glass tube with almost all of the air removed. It had two pieces of metal inside separated from each other. One of the pieces of metal had a hole in the middle that could let something pass through. On the other side of the piece of metal with a hole, the glass tube expanded and contained a phosphorescent screen at the end. In addition, at the point where the tube began to expand, there were either plates where a voltage could be applied, and a positive or negative charge created on the plates, or a magnet. The diagram in figure 4.21 shows the device.

Figure 4.21 Thomson's experimental device

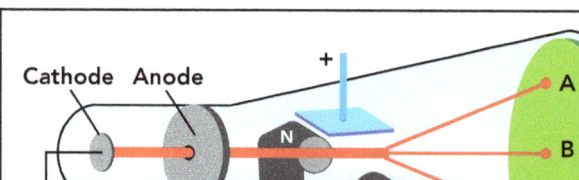

Thompson knew from prior experiments that applying a high voltage between two metal plates in a glass tube with the air removed would produce a ray, or stream of particles. He designed the device to figure out what this ray was. What were the physical properties of the ray? He applied a high voltage to the two metal plates, negative at the plate on one end of the tube, which was called the *cathode*, and positive at the other plate with the hole, which was called the *anode*. The cathode ray began to form and passed through the hole in the second plate. By applying a voltage to the metal plates beyond the plate with the hole, he could move the cathode ray up or down. When the ray hit the phosphorescent screen, it produced a light, so he could see the influence of the voltage. He could also move the ray up or down with a magnet. What he found was that the ray was repelled by the plate with the negative charge and attracted by the plate with the positive charge. He could control where the ray hit the screen by altering the voltage, and hence the charge on the plates. Knowing the voltage and, therefore, the force applied, and where the ray hit the screen, Thompson was able to determine the mass of the cathode ray particles. Now, let's summarize what we know from the experiment.

1. The particles came from the atoms in the negatively charged plate.

2. The particles are attracted to a positive charge and repelled by a negative charge.

3. The particles have mass.

4. Like charges repel, opposite charges attract. [Principle]

5. Before the voltage was applied, the original metal plates were electrically neutral, with no net charge. From facts and principles 1 through 4, what can we conclude about the makeup of the atoms in the metal plate that was the original source of the ray?

What we are looking for with this question is the abduction that the atoms contain negatively charged particles with mass. This is the particle that came to be known as the *electron*.

Now, adding in fact number 5, what else can we conclude about the atom?

The abduction we are looking for with this question is that there must also be something in an atom with an equal amount of positive charge.

After this abduction, the teacher could summarize by reviewing Thompson's "plum pudding" model of negatively charged electrons (plums) scattered in a spherical cloud of positive charge (pudding).

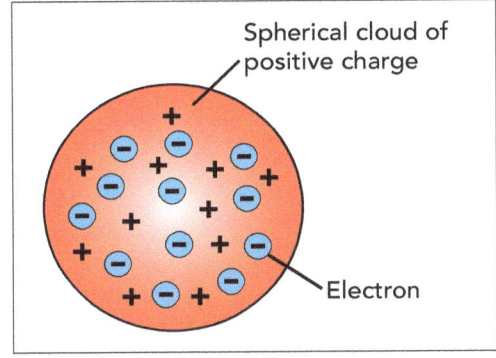

Figure 4.22 Thomson's "plum pudding" model of the atom

In similar fashion, a teacher could continue the story and develop the Rutherford-Bohr model and, ultimately, the quantum mechanical model of the atom. In summary, the process consists of telling the story in a way that reveals the facts, evidence, and applicable principles involved and using questioning to guide the students toward an abduction that develops an explanatory theory that is coherent with the supplied information.

Alternatively, a teacher could readily develop a lecture to present all these models efficiently within an hour. The abductive process described offers the following advantages over a lecture:

1. It simulates the thought process that scientists went through in developing their models.
2. It gives students practice in conducting abduction, an important process in constructing new knowledge.
3. It generates interest and engagement when presented as solving a mystery.

It should be pointed out to students that abduction is the same process used by a detective solving a crime or by a jury trying to determine guilt or innocence. The abductive process can be made interesting and engaging. People enjoy solving mysteries. The trade-off, as with other non-lecture models of teaching, is time and efficiency versus depth of engagement and level of comprehension and understanding.

Research Paradigms

Academic research involves both inductive and deductive processes. It begins with some question of interest. The next step is a literature search to determine what is currently known about the problem or question and what has been published that addresses the research question. A decision must then be made regarding the paradigm under which the research will proceed. Will it be quantitative research, qualitative research, or some mix of the two? If the decision is quantitative, the process proceeds in a manner analogous to the outline presented previously for the deductive learning models. A hypothesis is formulated. The elements thought to be impactful are turned into constructs that can be quantified, and a relationship is proposed between those constructs. The hypothesis drives the research design, and results are typically evaluated using the methods of statistics.

Qualitative research, as it is practiced today in the social sciences, rests on two major presumptions. The first is that many important things in life cannot be quantified or reduced to a number. The second is that a hypothesis prejudices the outcome of the research. The thought is that to form a hypothesis, an investigator presumes to already know what elements are going to be impactful and control outcomes. A hypothesis also presumes some form of relationship between these impactful elements. The qualitative paradigm attempts to collect data from observations, interviews, surveys, and artifacts in a way that does not impose a context or filter of prior beliefs and understandings. The idea is to let the data tell the story and define what elements are impactful and what the nature of the relationship between those elements might be. Various techniques have been developed to obtain these "bias-free and paradigm-free" understandings (Guba 1985; Glesne [1992] 2006).

Both research paradigms have pros and cons. There is merit to the concern that a beginning hypotheses or theoretical framework for research has the potential to limit the scope of the researcher's investigation. The problem is not terminal, however, since failure to confirm a hypothesis can result in a revised hypothesis that better explains the data or in the revelation that other factors not considered may be impactful.

Devotees of quantitative research sometimes claim that qualitative research can be fluffy and unscientific. The real issue, however, is the extreme difficulty of obtaining and analyzing data in a manner that is not influenced by prior understandings and beliefs. I experienced this as a graduate student. The questions I formulated, the interviews I conducted, and the observations I made were of necessity filtered through, influenced by, and interpreted through my prior knowledge and understanding. As discussed in the section on human executive function, a stimulus processed through conscious thought immediately activates the contents of long-term memory (knowledge) relevant to the object of consideration. This, in fact, can be considered the brain's definition of context: those items in memory and those contents of perception relevant to and connected with the object of consideration. The critical question is whether a context-free and prior understanding–free process for collecting and interpreting data is even possible.

The problem is the same as that experienced by the practitioners of the philosophic approach called *phenomenology*. The goal in phenomenology is to obtain a context-free understanding of the world. Various techniques, such as bracketing prior understanding, were developed in order to do so. Early attempts to obtain this kind of knowledge were not particularly fruitful. Again, the problem is the fact that the brain automatically imposes the context of prior knowledge and understanding. This is simply what it does. A pragmatic solution to the dilemma is the approach to phenomenology used by researchers such as Nell Noddings (1992). To examine the nature and meaning of the idea of "caring," Noddings viewed it in multiple contexts, like care between a parent and child, between a teacher and student, and so forth. To develop her definition, she selected those items that appeared in all of the contexts and excluded those that differed between contexts. Her answer is not context-free but what is universal about caring in all contexts.

My view is that both paradigms should be taught to prospective researchers. It is important to understand the advantages and disadvantages of both approaches to research. For example, even if the quantitative approach is used, a preliminary qualitative investigation could be helpful to make sure the hypothesis addressed all the variables that could potentially be impactful.

At this juncture, a rule that is intuitively obvious but should be explicitly stated is presented:

Principle 9: Learning experiences and learning representations (graphs, charts, matrices, models, simulations) must clearly, directly, and comprehensively contain all of the elements (attributes, characteristics, changes, and relationships) necessary for the learner to successfully perform the desired knowledge-construction process.

Principles of Learning Applicable to Deductive Learning

The principles of learning derived from the foregoing and pertaining to successful learning through deduction are as follows:

Principle 10: For a student to successfully perform a deduction, their rule in memory must be sufficiently robust. It must

» Contain all the elements that constitute what is known (givens) and what is desired to be known (inference/conclusion)

» Contain a coherent relationship between these elements (knowns and unknowns)

Principle 11: For a student to successfully use deduction, they must be able to "see" and connect the concrete elements of the problem or activity to the abstract elements of the rule.

Principle 12: For a student to follow or construct a deductive argument, they must be able to discern the common elements that connect rules in a chain of reasoning.

Principle 10 simply states that the student's rule must have all the elements and relationships between those elements required to enable a successful inference, conclusion, or problem solution. The next rule deals with the relationship between the concrete and the abstract. Rules are abstractions, while givens, or what rules are applied to, are invariably concrete. This rule requires that teachers help students connect the concrete and the abstract. They need to help students "see" that the rules are relevant and that the rules can express relationships between concrete items in the real world. This is accomplished by teachers overtly and directly connecting the concrete to the abstract and, also, going from the abstract to the concrete. Moving from examples to summarizing abstractions and then from abstractions to exemplifying real items cannot be overdone.

Reflective Abstraction and Trial and Error

Trial and Error

The trial-and-error process has been an important learning- and knowledge-creation method for humankind throughout history. It is also the way nature learns. The organisms that inhabit Earth today are the products of mutations in those organisms that worked and were adaptive to the contingencies of the changing environments the organisms experienced. In this sense, today's inhabitants of the world represent 4.5 billion years of trial and error. Those species whose mutations were not adaptive are no longer with us.

Early learning is largely associative but also consists of a good measure of knowledge construction through trial and error. From learning how to use their hands and how to walk, to discovering how things in their world work, infants and toddlers learn about their world and how to accomplish their ends by trying out different things and seeing what works.

The most famous practitioner of trial and error as a path to knowledge, discovery, and innovation was inventor Thomas Edison. Edison invented the lightbulb, telephone transmitter, phonograph, movie camera, and alkaline battery and held 1,093 patents in all for his innovations. Trial and error became so closely associated with Edison that it is sometimes referred to as the *Edisonian method*.

Edison's approach was not random and unguided. He examined existing theories relevant to his goals and made educated guesses as to what might work. Edison described his process as follows:

> When I want to discover something, I begin by reading up everything that has been done along that line in the past—that's what all those books in the library are for. I see what has been accomplished at great labor and expense in the past. I gather data of many thousands of experiments as a starting point and then I make thousands more. (Edisonian 2021, 1)

Edison, despite his success, was not without his critics. Nikola Tesla, a trained electrical engineer who worked for Edison for two years, was reported as saying,

> His method was inefficient in the extreme, for an immense ground had to be covered to get anything at all unless blind chance intervened and, at first I was almost a sorry witness of his doings, knowing that just a little theory and calculation would have saved him 90% of his labor. (Willis 2019)

Tesla's critique points out an important aspect of a successful trial-and-error process. To avoid going down too many blind alleys or garden paths, it is important to avail oneself of the concepts, principles, and theories (rules) that bear on and could have relevance to the task at hand. While not being sufficient to provide a direct path to a solution or to the achievement of a goal, theories can be useful in identifying the elements (variables) and relationships that are potentially impactful and that need to be considered. Edison's statement indicates that he researched what others had done before embarking on his own experiments. Apparently, Tesla, an electrical engineer, who would have been more versed in quantitative as well as qualitative theories of electrical phenomena, judged that Edison's use of prior knowledge was insufficient.

Another useful principle in guiding a trial-and-error process is using the procedure of the scientific method of changing one variable while holding the other variables constant. The process in general involves making changes to narrow the gap between outcomes and goals. The path toward continuous improvement can be obscured if more than one variable at a time is changed. The impacts can confound one another. One variable change could result in movement toward the goal while the other could result in movement away from the goal.

Engineers typically use mathematical models of physical processes to guide their design efforts. Mathematical models are, of necessity, often idealizations and approximations of the highly complex physical phenomena they describe. To get a set of equations that can be solved, it is sometimes necessary to limit the number of variables (attribute/characteristics) to those thought to be most impactful and to ignore nonlinear aspects of the phenomena if they are thought to have a small impact. Since the models are idealizations, the final design sometimes must be tweaked and modified using a trial-and-error process to achieve the desired result. In short, even in a rule-driven process that Tesla would endorse, trial and error often plays a role.

Trial and error as a knowledge-construction process does not have to be directly taught; it is instinctive. The process is the final step in the operation of human executive function: comparing outcomes with goals and effecting required compensations. This process is built into the brain. The two steps of using prior knowledge to guide the process and doing the experiments along the lines of the scientific method are, however, procedures that should be taught. The following are two lessons that incorporate trial and error and utilize the two procedures.

The goal of the first lesson is to teach students how to solve algebraic equations using the trial-and-error method and to show how algebraic solutions create efficiency and eliminate the need for trial and error. The equation that students are trying to find solutions for has two variables: x and y. The teacher begins by asking the students to employ the scientific method procedure of leaving one of the variables constant while varying the other variable. In the following example, the teacher instructs the student to fix the y value at 1 and to begin to try different values of x. The student tries $x = 0$ and then $x = 1$. The answers are less than the desired answer of 0, and the larger the x value, the more the answer moves away from 0. The teacher then points out that it looks like the student needs to move in the other direction. The student then moves in the other direction and tries $x = -1$ and $x = -2$. Both answers are greater than 0, and again, the more negative the x value, the more the answer moves away from the desired answer of 0. The teacher points out that the x values that gave an answer closest to 0 were $x = -1$ and $x = 0$. The teacher also points out that since one of the x values gave an answer below the desired value and the other above the desired value, then the correct x value must lie between the two. The student then tries $x = -\frac{1}{2}$ and achieves the desired result. The teacher then asks the student to pick additional y values and use the same procedure to find the corresponding x value that satisfies the equation. Figure 4.23 shows the result for $y = 4$. As a final step, the teacher demonstrates how algebraically solving the equation for y results in an equation that gives the y value directly for each x value that is a solution to the equation without trial and error. She also presents a graph and points out that the resulting equation is a straight line with slope 2 and y intercept 2. When this graph is plotted, all the numbers that are solutions to the original equation can be read directly off the graph. This highlights the idea that a graph of an equation is a visual depiction of all the solutions to the equation.

Construction of Knowledge 195

Figure 4.23a Trialand-error solution of an equation

Trial and Error Equation Solution

- Find Solutions to $y - 2(x+1) = 0$ by trial and error

a. fix y and vary x

@ $y = 1$, try $x = 0$; $1 - 2(0+1) = -1$
          try $x = 1$; $1 - 2(1+1) = -3$

- Wrong direction - moving away from 0
          try $x = -1$; $1 - 2(-1+1) = 1$
          try $x = -2$; $1 - 2(-2+1) = 3$

- Wrong direction again; the closest x's were 0 & -1, so the answer must be between these numbers
          try $x = \underline{-1}$; $1 - 2(\underline{-1}+1) = 0$
                    2 2

This is the solution; $x = \underline{-1}$, @ $y = 1$
                                2

b. Try a different y and vary x again; try $y = 4$

x	y	result
-2	4	6
-1	4	4
0	4	2
1	4	0 Solution ($x = 1, y = 4$)
2	4	-2

Figure 4.23b Algebraic and graphical solution to the equation

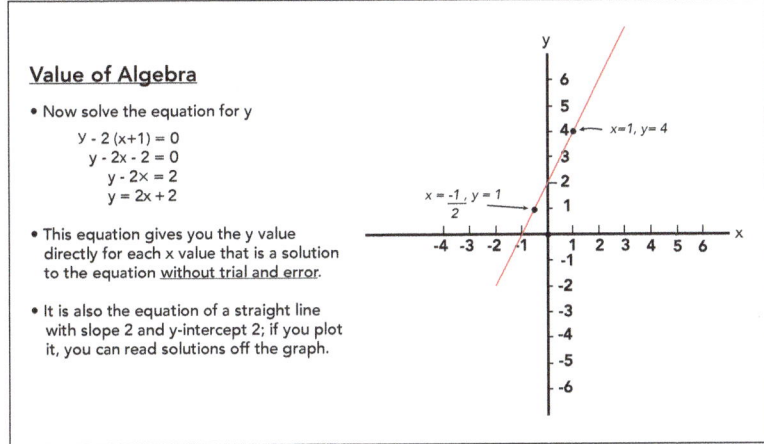

Value of Algebra

- Now solve the equation for y
    $y - 2(x+1) = 0$
    $y - 2x - 2 = 0$
    $y - 2x = 2$
    $y = 2x + 2$

- This equation gives you the y value directly for each x value that is a solution to the equation <u>without trial and error</u>.

- It is also the equation of a straight line with slope 2 and y-intercept 2; if you plot it, you can read solutions off the graph.

Every chemistry student is required to learn the process for balancing chemical formulas. This is a trial-and-error process. The following is a teacher demonstration of the procedure. The teacher begins by telling the students that conservation of mass requires that the quantity of each atomic element must be the same before and after a chemical reaction. The first reaction demonstrated is the combustion of methane. Methane combines with oxygen to form carbon dioxide and water. As shown in figure 4.24, the teacher demonstrates that the elements can be listed vertically with the number of elements before the reaction written to the left of the element symbol and the number after the reaction written to the right. This will help the students see where the balancing is required. In the first step, carbon is balanced but hydrogen and oxygen are not. There are 4 hydrogen atoms before the reaction and 2 after. To balance the hydrogen, we must double the water molecules produced (multiply by 2). We have balanced carbon and hydrogen, but now have 2 oxygen atoms before the reaction and 4 after the reaction. We now must double the oxygen molecules (multiply by 2) before the reaction to get the final balance.

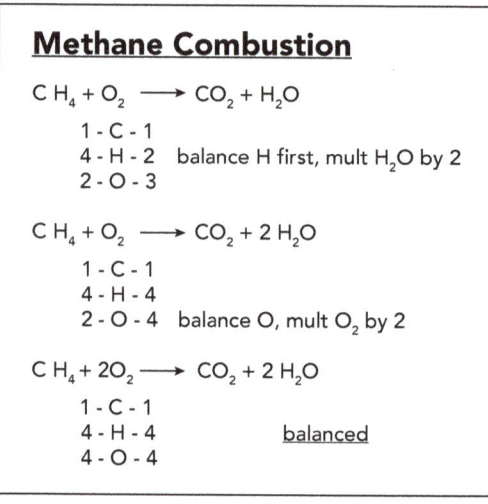

Figure 4.24
Balancing a chemical equation

In the next example there is a twist. When balancing the oxygen, there are 2 molecules of oxygen before the reaction and 7 afterward. The multiplication factor to balance oxygen is 7/2. Another rule must be invoked here: atoms and molecules cannot be split. This rule requires that everything be multiplied by 2 to eliminate the fraction as the final step. We can see from this example that although the process is trial and error, there are two relevant rules—conservation of mass and molecules/atoms cannot be split—that guided the process. As these two examples show, although the fundamental process is trying out different things to solve a problem or achieve a goal, the process is made more efficient by invoking relevant rules and using the procedures of the scientific method.

Reflective Abstraction

In observing children performing the numerous experiments he conducted, Jean Piaget (1985) noticed that to make sense of the outcomes of the experiments, children invariably reflected on their actions and the consequences of those actions. Mental and physical actions, which Piaget termed *operations*, were his units of analysis; meaning that operations were the fundamental construct used to frame and interpret his research results. Note that he expressed his stages of development in terms of the operations (mental and physical) that the child could perform at different stages of development. Piaget's interpreted knowledge-construction device from the results of operations or actions is a process he termed *reflective abstraction*. Reflective abstraction was his model for the construction of all human knowledge.

His model for the construction of causal knowledge using reflective abstraction is as follows. The learner first takes consciousness of the results of their activity and the specific actions that created the results. Actions and their consequences are put into juxtaposition for comparison. The result of this activity Piaget termed *empirical abstraction*. For example, a child in the early stages of development will roll clay in their hands and notice that it gets longer. At a later stage of development, the child will notice that it gets longer and thinner simultaneously and that the two results are reciprocally connected: the longer it gets, the thinner it gets. The empirical abstraction is that rolling clay makes it longer and thinner—a perceptually derived conclusion. The child then reflectively abstracts the operations or actions to summarize them in terms of a rule that is evidenced by the results of their activity. For example, the developmentally early child will report the rule that rolling the clay caused it to get bigger. The more developmentally advanced child will report the rule that the rolling action that caused an increase in length also caused a corresponding or reciprocal decrease in width, noting that the total quantity of clay never changed (idea of conservation being implicit). In the next step of the process, the proposed rule and the predicted consequences of the rule are put into juxtaposition for comparison with actual physical results to check for coherence or, in Piaget's terms, equilibrium.

Piaget points out that reflective abstraction is the product of judgment concerning the nature of the relationships derived from perceptual content. It is the product of thought and not something directly observable. It is an interpretation of the observables. The conservation and reciprocity reported by the older child are judgments that explain, not a simple report of sensory stimulus (clay dimensions). It is the conservation of quantity that brings about and makes necessary the reciprocal relationship between length and width. If the total quantity of clay is conserved, expanding one dimension demands a contraction in at least one of the other dimensions. The observation of dimensional changes is empirical; however, the fact that conservation of quantity requires the change observed is a judgment. Note that this judgment is an interpretation of the nature of the relationship between the empirical contents of the perception. It is the process of creating relationships between perceived attributes/characteristics and changes in them with time.

Piaget provides an example of reflective abstraction derived from a conversation with a friend. The friend reported that as a young child he was amazed by the fact that when he counted pebbles backward and then forward, he got the same answer. If he arranged them in a circle or a square or otherwise grouped them and then counted, he also got the same answer. The individual's thought process was, according to Piaget, reflectively abstracting the rule that addition is commutative and associative. This rule was an interpretation or judgment resulting from the detection of an invariant result consequent to a series of actions. The commutative and associative properties of addition are not directly observable properties but an induction or summarization of a rule derived from judgment of the consequences of actions. Note that, as with inductions that pertain to matters of substance, inductions related to sequences of actions that consistently produce a specific result also involve an invariance construct. In other words, beginning with state A, if a series of actions are undertaken, they will invariably lead to state B. The invariance construct is the basis for the derived rule. Given the rule, it is necessary that a specific consequence or effect follows a specific action or cause. A consequence of the commutative law is that the order of operations in arithmetic does not change the outcome or answer. Similarly, the conservation of the quantity of clay being rolled necessitates that if one dimension increases another must decrease.

Since collective actions can be expressed in terms of causal logic, Piaget theorized that reflective abstraction was the mechanism whereby individuals implicitly acquired the rules of logic evident in thinking. For example, "If I do this and I do that, then the following happens." As discussed previously, causal logic is hypothesized in this model to be an expression of the brain's capacity for consolidating repeatedly experienced invariant sequences in time. I interpret the reflective abstraction, as described by Piaget, to be the backward path that enables the construction of a rule from a successful procedural process. In my proposed model of learning, it is the process whereby a sequence of actions or a procedure is connected to abstract symbolic rules that are expressed through language or mathematics. It is the mechanism that facilitates the application of symbolic rules.

Reflective abstraction is an important instructional tool. When instruction involves carrying out an action sequence, it is of great value for the teacher to ask the studen to reflect on why a specific result inhered or, in other words, to come up with a rule that explains the specific result obtained. Why did this happen? What explains the result obtained? The specific process is precisely as described by Piaget and summarized previously.

Alan Turing, a British mathematician most famous for breaking the code of the Enigma machine, a cipher device used by Nazis during World War II to code communications, developed a hypothetical device that became the intellectual forerunner of the digital computer. This device is known as a Turing machine. A Turing machine has a head that reads symbols on a tape. "Perceiving" the symbol causes the machine to print a replacement symbol on the tape. The symbol printed is contingent upon a state table internal to the Turing machine. The state table is a collection of rules that specify the symbol to be printed on the tape given the perception of a specific input symbol on the tape and given the current state of the machine. The state of the machine is the current rule being executed. Rules that constitute the state table not only specify the symbol to be printed but also change the state of the machine to the subsequent or next rule to be implemented and direct the reading head to the place on the tape to look for the next symbol or input. Repeating the actions described implements the algorithm (Morton 2005). An algorithm is defined as the set of steps to be followed in solving a problem or making a computation. In the abstract, as Dennett (2013) discusses, a Turing machine and a digital computer are equivalent; the digital computer is simply more efficient.

A mathematical theorem called the Church-Turing thesis states that any and all conceivable algorithms can be implemented by a Turing machine. If this is the case, then it also must be the case that a Turing machine contains all the necessary and sufficient components required to implement a procedure, solve a problem, or perform a calculation. We can compare the human process of implementing a procedure, solving a problem, or performing a calculation to the operation of a Turing machine. Let's say that the human has been taught the steps of a procedure, problem-solving process, or calculation or has learned it through trial and error. The representation of the procedure in the human brain is connected to both a goal and previous perceptions of circumstances that invoked and are applicable to the procedure. The head of the Turing machine that perceives the symbol on the tape is analogous to the human perceptual process. The goal of the Turing machine is implicit in the rules of the state table that control its action. For example, a set of Turing machine state table rules designed to perform addition has addition as its implicit goal. In a Turing machine, each subsequent perception of the tape invokes an action (printing a symbol on the tape) in accordance with the state table rule. The machine then moves on to the next rule and place to "perceive" the next input. In the human brain, the steps of a procedure are connected and sequentially carried out without requiring subsequent perceptions. It is, however, sometimes the case that a human will re-perceive or recheck the given circumstances while carrying out the procedure in a manner similar to the Turing machine. The action sequence represented in the brain performs the role of the state table rules of the Turing machine. The human brain has a higher level of processing, or metacognitive ability, to monitor the outcome of each action step and alter the procedure as required. The Turing machine does not.

The advent of the Turing machine, and subsequently the digital computer, gave rise to something called the Turing test. In a Turing test, if a machine performs in a manner that is indistinguishable from the performance of a human being, then the machine must be said to have intelligence. This presumption was challenged by philosopher John Searle (1984) in a famous thought experiment called the Chinese Room. In this thought experiment, an individual in a closed room provides answers to questions written in Chinese. The individual has no knowledge of Chinese but has instructions for generating a series of Chinese symbols that constitute correct answers in response to the questions. From the standpoint of someone outside the room, the answers are indistinguishable from those of a native Chinese speaker. The individual inside the room, however, is simply procedurally responding to perceptual cues in accordance with an algorithm, in the fashion of a Turing machine or digital computer. Searle asked two questions about the situation: Does the person inside the room have any understanding of the Chinese symbols? Does the operation of the Chinese room shed any light on human understanding? He emphatically says no to both questions. If the person in the room could read and speak Chinese, the symbols would carry meaning because they represent things in the world and express some coherent relationship between those things. For the person in the room, the symbols have no meaning and simply cue a process or procedure. Searle's thought experiment demonstrates the value and importance of symbolic representation of processes and procedures. It implies that connecting procedural knowledge to symbolic rule representations is a requisite step for giving meaning to processes and procedures and creating conceptual-level understanding. As discussed previously, many students learn topics like math procedurally without a conceptual understanding of the basis for the procedures they are carrying out. A Turing-machine process of learning procedures that are simply cued by perception and goal suffers from the same problem that behaviorism faced. Human behavior and performance cannot be reduced to actions driven solely by a stimulus or a perception. Behavior is driven by how a person interprets and understands the stimulus or perception.

In trial-and-error learning, an action is evaluated against goal criteria. Contingent upon outcome, a subsequent action is tried or undertaken. Such a process can lead to an action sequence that, given a goal and perceptual cue, leads to a desired outcome without the involvement of a rule or abstract symbolic representation. In Piaget's reflective abstraction, consciousness is invoked to construct symbolically based rules that **serve to explain** how the sequence of actions produced the specific result. This conscious process also serves to abstract the action sequence symbolically. Once abstracted and expressed in terms of a rule, it can also serve to cue the sequence in the future. In the absence of abstraction, a procedural sequence can still be constructed; however, it is cued perceptually and, moreover, consists of a series of connected physical action steps that might contain or express an implicit rule, but such a rule is unconscious and, in pure procedural learning, no rules are ever consciously constructed. The limitation of this type of learning is that it does not provide understanding and meaning, like the circumstance in the Chinese room. The how and why level of understanding is missing. An additional benefit of connecting procedures and actions to symbolic-level representations is that it permits higher-level thinking regarding the procedures and offline processing of procedural knowledge. The person is not simply an automaton responding to perceptual cues from their environment. Conversion into symbolic representation allows people to analyze, modify, plan, and conduct other higher-level thinking with procedural knowledge.

During an initial learning process conducted through conscious processing, the rule serves to facilitate understanding and to create the required connection between perceptual cue, goal, and action sequence. If such an action sequence is sufficiently repeated and is successful in producing a desired outcome, the connection through a rule becomes unnecessary and inefficient. The rule, used in initial construction, is still there as it was a requirement for constructing the sequence initially. It is, however, no longer necessary to consider it to invoke the sequence. It is hypothesized that this is what occurs in expert performance. What was once a conscious rule-driven process has been automated to become an unconscious perceptually driven process. If the rule representing an action sequence has been abstracted through language and symbolically represented, it is always available as an element for use in future cognitive processing. It can be evaluated and expanded and, importantly, as an abstraction, can be utilized outside the domain in which it was developed. Therefore, it is imperative that action sequences and procedures be initially understood as the logically necessary consequences of rules.

The principles of learning pertaining to successful procedural learning and application of rules that follow from the preceding are as follows:

Principle 13: For the learner to successfully create a symbolic rule from a sequence of mental or physical actions requires that they create a relationship involving judgment between the abstracted attributes and characteristics of the consequences or changes brought about by the actions.

Principle 14: Successful application of a rule requires that the learner understands what set of mental or physical actions (process/procedure) are the expression of and the coherent and necessary consequences of the rule. A relationship between the rule and procedure must be created.

Principle 13, pertaining to successful knowledge construction through reflective abstraction, basically states that the consequences of actions must be abstracted into the symbolic representations of language or mathematics and connected to each other by relationships that express a judgment regarding the specific nature of the relationships. These wordy statements have a simpler actualization. For example, the perceived change in dimensions of the clay-rolling experiment is abstracted via language to "the clay gets longer and thinner" and a causal **relationship** involving judgment is made by adding the statement that "the change in dimensions is necessarily reciprocal (longer requires thinner) because the total amount of clay did not change (mass is conserved)."

A more operational articulation of principle 14 for successful application is that the learner must know what the rule tells them to do. What specific mental or physical actions are suggested by and coherent with the symbolically represented rule. For example, for the rule for the slope of a line m = $\Delta y / \Delta x$, the student must know that the rule requires that they obtain two values for y and two values for x and that they need to subtract the y values from each other, subtract the y values, and then divide the results of the y value subtraction by the results of the x value subtraction. These are the actions that the rule expresses and that are coherent with and necessary given the rule.

Figure 4.25 Connecting abstract rules to concrete actions

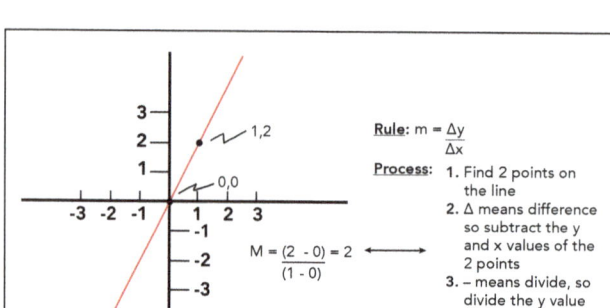

Similarly, knowing Newton's laws is interesting, but to apply them requires that students learn the following process that is coherent with the rules and "what the rules tell them to do." For those not familiar or comfortable with physics, reading the following is not necessary. I have included it to give an emphatic example that simply knowing rules is not sufficient for being able to apply them.

1. Draw a sketch of the problem and write down the known information (givens) and identify what is to be found (unknown—goal).

Figure 4.26 Sketch of the problem and the given

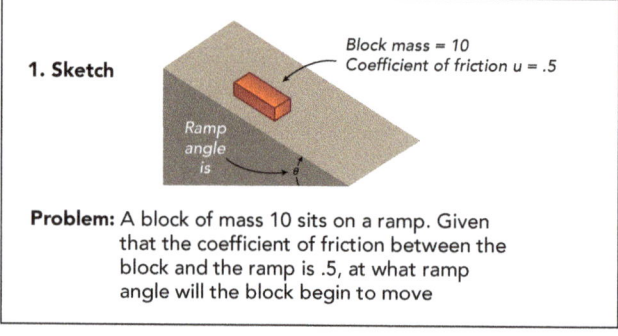

2. Identify all the forces acting on the object and make a diagram. In the diagram, connect arrows depicting the direction of the forces to a central point that represents the object.

Figure 4.27 Diagram of the forces on the object

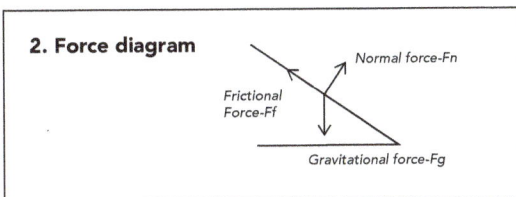

3. Impose a coordinate system on the diagram and resolve the forces into components along each axis. Determine the net forces in the direction of the axes.

Figure 4.28 Imposition of a coordinate system and resolution of the forces along the axes

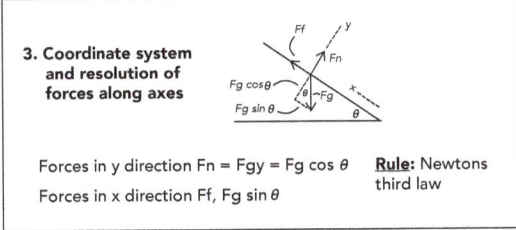

4. Place the net forces in Newton's law for each direction and use algebra to solve the equations.

Figure 4.29 Solution of the problem in abstract terms

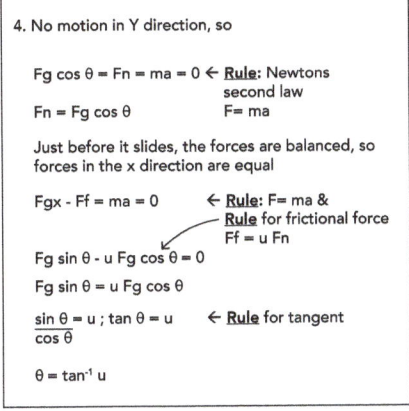

5. Substitute numerical values to obtain the final answer. If required by the problem, use the calculated acceleration to obtain velocity and displacement.

5. Substitute numerical values $\theta = \tan^{-1}(.5) = 26.6°$ A ramp angle greater than 26.6° will cause the block to move.

Figure 4.30
Substitution of numerical values

Note that **the procedure gives meaning to the rule, and the rule gives meaning to the procedure**. When connected, both serve to enhance understanding of each other. This is the learning mechanism for rule learning through reflective abstraction and application.

We can give students the rule for the circumference of a circle, $c = \pi d$, that contains the mysterious element π. Alternatively, we can have them measure the circumference and the diameter of a group of discs of different sizes and have them divide the circumference by the diameter for each disc. Each division will render the number 3.1416. The teacher can then identify this number as π. This gives π more meaning, and students will have the understanding that this constant is what relates circumference and diameter, an important understanding that students will use whenever they deal with anything circular.

The generalized process for reflective abstraction consists of the following steps:

1. Learning the steps of a procedure.

2. Performing the procedure numerous times with concrete elements.

3. Abstracting the concrete elements.

4. Using reflective abstraction to create a relationship between the abstracted elements to create the rule. The rule expresses a judgment about the nature of the relationship between the elements.

For example, in the disc-measurement exercise, the students get concrete numbers for the diameter and the circumference. The exercise demonstrates that the division of the concrete numbers for circumference by the concrete numbers for diameter equals a constant number. The circumference is abstracted into the letter c, the diameter is abstracted into the letter d, and the constant is abstracted into the symbol π. The student can then reflectively abstract that the relationship between these abstractions is $c = \pi d$. The same process would also be used in deriving the abstract rule for the slope of a line.

The following example lesson illustrates the use of reflective abstraction to develop the concepts of metaphor and simile.

1. Begin with an activity to generate interest and define the goals of the lesson.

2. Review required prior knowledge.

3. Model the process:

   a. Decide what you are going to create a metaphor or simile for.

   b. Determine the goal of the metaphor or simile:

      1. Create drama.

      2. Create imagery.

      3. Increase understanding.

      4. Evoke feelings and emotion.

   c. List the attributes, characteristics, and actions associated with the thing you are creating a metaphor or simile for.

   d. Find something that shares those attributes, characteristics, and actions in the abstract. That is your metaphor/simile.

   e. Write a sentence using the metaphor and another using a simile.

Example:

   1. I am going to create a metaphor and simile for a character named Jim.

   2. My goal is to create imagery and avoid a lengthy description of Jim.

   3. Jim is aggressive, large, and powerful. Jim has a beard and long hair. Jim has a gruff demeanor.

   4. What is something that has these traits in the abstract? A **bear** does.

   5. Jim is a **bear** that that should be approached with caution. **Metaphor**
      Jim devoured his food like a **bear**. **Simile**

Example:

   1. I am going to create a metaphor/simile for the character Juliet.

   2. I want to create understanding of how Romeo feels about Juliet.

   3. Juliet warms Romeo's heart. Juliet brightens up his day. Juliet is the energy that motivates and powers Romeo's life.

   4. What warms, brightens, and supplies energy? The **sun** does.

   5. Juliet is the sun. William Shakespeare **metaphor**
      Like the sun, Juliet lights up Romeo's life. **Simile**

The teacher should point out that a simile differs from a metaphor because it uses the words "like" or "as" and expresses a single attribute and characteristic.

4. Present the learning activity. Walk around the classroom and scaffold students requiring assistance.

   a. Have students create a metaphor/simile using the process modeled for the following items:

      1. An interesting person in their life (not a classmate). Create an image of them.

      2. An aspect of their personality or life that they think is complicated. Create an understanding of this.

      3. Something that frightens them. Create feelings and emotions about that thing.

      4. Something they really like. Create drama and excitement about that thing.

      5. Undertake a classroom discussion with students of their metaphors/similes and guide them toward the abstract expression of the process they just completed.

Rule: A **metaphor/simile** compares two unlike things that share abstract qualities in order to create drama, imagery, understanding, and emotion in writing.

Note how the process the students undertook gives meaning and understanding to the abstract expression of the rule. In addition, the abstract expression now directly connects to a process for creating a metaphor and simile.

The next example shows how to teach solving algebraic equations with a single variable using reflective abstraction. I will present only the teacher demonstration portion of the lesson. The teacher uses an old-style balance beam and places an unknown number of marbles in very lightweight small boxes and visible marbles on both sides of the balance beam as shown in figure 4.31.

The teacher then states the goal of the process: to find out how many marbles are in a box by undertaking actions that result in one box on the left side of the balance beam and some number of marbles on the right side. The overarching rule is that whatever we do has to keep the beam balanced. The teacher asks the students to write down the starting situation using the letter B to represent the boxes and numbers to represent the marbles. The starting situation, expressed symbolically, is shown in figure 4.31. The teacher then points out that one box can be taken from each side in order to get marbles only on the right side of the balance beam.

Next, the teacher asks students to subtract 1B (box) from each side of their equation to get the result shown in figure 4.32. Then, the teacher points out that there are still two

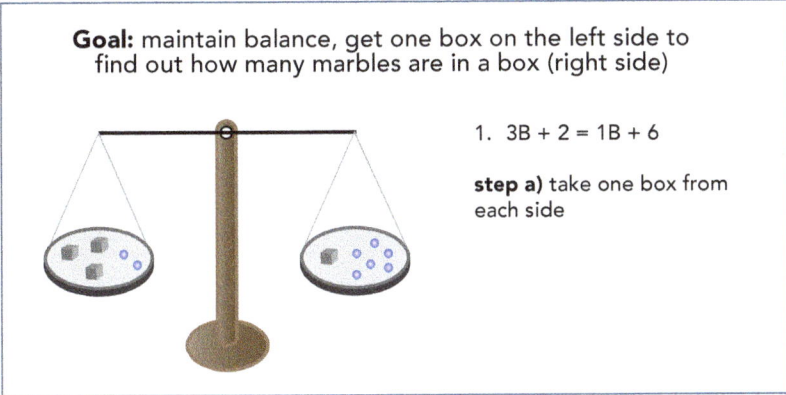

Figure 4.31 Beginning situations—the givens

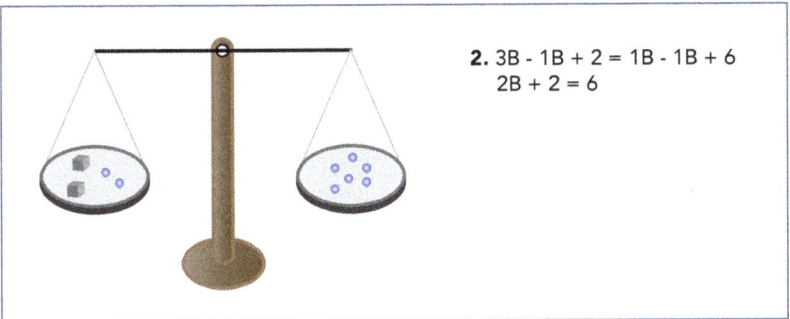

Figure 4.32 Getting only boxes on one side

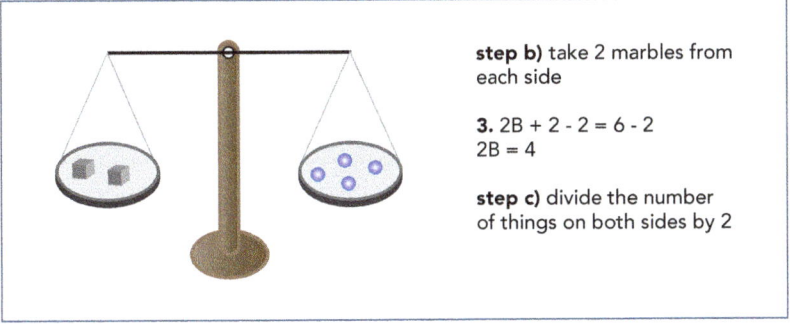

Figure 4.33 Getting only marbles on the other side

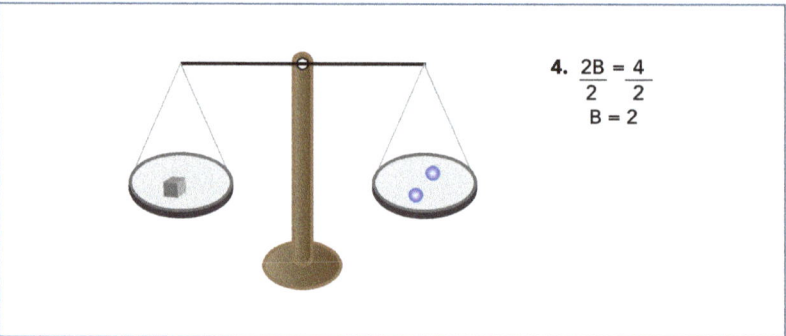

Figure 4.34 Using division to get only a box on one side

marbles on the left side of the balance beam. They can be removed, and balance maintained, by subtracting two marbles from both sides of the balance beam. The teacher then asks the students to subtract two from both sides of their equation as shown in figure 4.33.

Attention is then called to the fact that there are now two boxes on the left side and four marbles on the right side of the balance beam. We can no longer use subtraction. Our original goal was to get one box on the left side of the balance beam and some number of marbles on the right side. To accomplish our goal, we can, however, divide the contents of both sides of the balance beam by two. Physically, this means taking away half of what is on the left side and half of what is on the right side. The teacher then asks the students to divide both sides of their equation by two, as shown in figure 4.34, to get the final answer.

If there are extra balance beams, the teacher can group students and assign them to different balance beams. One student places an unknown number of marbles into the boxes and then sorts boxes and marbles to create a balance on the beam. The remaining students work together as a group and undertake the same process that the teacher demonstrated. They are asked to symbolically record each step taken, as was done in the demonstration. After several rounds, the teacher then engages students in a discussion to summarize what has been done and to articulate the rules learned.

To solve an equation involving one variable, do the following:

1. Perform the same operation on both sides of the equation to maintain equality (balance).

2. Use addition and subtraction to get the variable on one side of the equation and numbers on the other side of the equation.

3. If a multiple or a fraction of the variable remains after the addition and subtraction process, use multiplication and division to get the final answer.

Since the abstract rule here specifies a process or procedure, it is expressed in terms of steps. This lesson not only gives meaning and creates understanding for the abstract process of solving an algebraic equation in one unknown but also directly connects the abstract (variables and numbers) to the concrete (marbles and boxes with marbles). As discussed previously, learning with understanding is enhanced when connecting the concrete to the abstract and vice versa. As shown, reflective abstraction is an important tool not only in teaching abstract rules but also in enabling their application.

Learning through Application

Direct Application

The knowledge and skill requirements of occupations in the economy have always been a driving force in education. The Industrial Revolution of the nineteenth century, and the resulting shift from an agrarian to an industrial economy in the United States, was, in fact, the impetus for the emergence of free public education for all. The demands of the industrial workplace called for employees with basic literacy and numeracy skills. The mission of schools during this era was to teach reading, writing, and arithmetic. In time, continued expansion of industrial activity increased the demand for employees with the knowledge and skill level imparted by a college education. This demand expanded the mission of K–12 schools to prepare at least a portion of their students for success in postsecondary education.

From the end of World War II to the early 1980s, the enormous expansion of the American economy provided industrial jobs for many noncollege graduates with salary levels sufficient to enable a middle-class lifestyle. High school graduates, and even those without a high school diploma, could often find industrial jobs that paid enough to afford a home, two cars, a yearly vacation, modest savings, and the other amenities associated with a middle-class lifestyle in the United States. During this era, K–12 schools functioned as sorting and filtering mechanisms that identified and funneled their most capable and successful students to colleges and universities. Students with higher grades and higher standardized test scores (ACT, SAT) could continue their education after high school. Because of the large number of good-paying jobs for noncollege graduates, there was little social pressure to do otherwise.

Beginning in the 1970s, the industrial world changed dramatically. Technological and transportation advances made it possible to produce high-quality goods and services anywhere in the world. Globalization emerged and many industries moved offshore, where they could take advantage of cheaper labor and less regulation. High-quality goods and services could be produced offshore at lower price levels. Jobs in the United States at middle-class salary levels for those without a college education began to increasingly disappear as considerable industrial activity relocated offshore. Extensive media coverage of these changes, backed by trends, supported the idea in the public consciousness that not having a college degree would consign one to a lower-class life. This upped the ante for K–12 schools. The mission now became preparing *all* students for either a higher-paying job or a college education. In the 1960s through the 1970s, around 45 percent to 50 percent of high school graduates went on to postsecondary education. Currently, the number is around 70 percent, with most of the percentage increase having occurred during the 1980s through 1990s. The number of students who successfully complete their postsecondary education has averaged around 50 percent to 55 percent from the 1960s to the current time.

The emergence of the internet created yet another revolution with as much impact as the Industrial Revolution. From reading, writing, and arithmetic at the beginning of the Industrial Revolution, the demands of the modern workplace became characterized as follows:

1. Efficiently access task- and goal-relevant information.
2. Process the information into usable form.
3. Utilize this processed information to solve problems and achieve goals.

A college graduate in 1950 was in possession of knowledge that others did not possess by virtue of their education. Employers hired such individuals partly because of the secular knowledge that they had accumulated through their education. Today, everyone with a cell phone has access to virtually all the knowledge in the world. The modern mantra has become that it is not what you know but what you can do with what you know, or what you can do with what you can access on the internet. This creates increasing pressure on schools to emphasize the application of knowledge and information. In aggregate, K–12 schools have not yet achieved the goal of preparing all students for success in college, a goal that emerged from economic change in the 1980s. There is also little evidence of increased emphasis on the application of knowledge. There is no doubt, however, that these economic pressures will continue, and schools will be expected not only to improve academic rigor and outcomes but to impart information-processing skills and increase their emphasis on the application of knowledge.

It is not uncommon to have graduates of college professional preparatory programs make statements like, "I did not learn to be a teacher in college; I learned when faced with a classroom full of actual students," or, "I didn't learn engineering until I went to work." The implication in both cases being that what the individuals learned in college was not particularly useful, applicable, or sufficient for professional practice. These individuals felt that demands of the real circumstances they faced were such that they had to develop solutions and responses based on their own logic and reason applied to the circumstances they faced. Having been both an educator and a practitioner in the fields of education, engineering, and business, I can attest to the fact that what they were taught in college was more relevant and useful than the preceding statements would imply.

I attribute these lamentations to several factors. First is the likelihood that the instruction was such, or the student was such, that an abstract, conceptual level of understanding of the content of the instruction was never attained. It is not possible in a school setting to illustrate all the possible applications of an abstract theory. As discussed previously, an abstract, conceptual-level understanding of a theory facilitates the application of the theory in contexts beyond and different from the specific context in which the theory was learned. Example applications in school settings are often idealized for purposes of clarity and direct connection to the principles being applied. Outside of school, applications are messier, more complex, and less directly interpretable as circumstances to which previously learned theories could apply. Therefore, perception of the real circumstance does not easily or directly cue the long-term memory of an applicable principle.

During my graduate studies, I spent some time as a teaching assistant for a veteran professor who taught primarily child development courses. She employed a textbook in each of her classes, but her lectures and instruction did not follow the textbook sequence in any way. When I inquired about this, she provided the following explanation. She said that after teaching the content in textbooks for over twenty-five years, she came to the realization that very little of what she taught found its way into classroom practice. Her thesis to explain this was that none of the material was learned to a level sufficient to give students confidence in applying the presented theories in practice. She said a typical textbook for a child development class contains hundreds of ideas. These ideas are the results of different researchers employing different contexts, paradigms, and units of analysis. There is no such thing as a unified, verified, and universally agreed-upon theory of child development. Textbooks present a buffet of the work of the most important and contributory practitioners in the field. Since the learning of any single practitioner's theory is relatively shallow, students soon forget what they've learned, and the learning experience is simply one of increasing student awareness of child development practices. Students are made aware, for example, that Piaget worked in and made contributions to the field of child development by experiencing a brief summary of his work. Should students ever want to apply any of Piaget's ideas, they would have to study his work in more detail, on their own, at some future time. Given her thesis, the professor elected to spend her classroom time getting students to a level of mastery of what she considered to be the ten to fifteen most important ideas in child development—a level of mastery that would result in the students being confident enough to apply these principles in their classrooms.

The preceding suggests some enhancements to instruction intended to develop the ability to apply theory to practice. The examples used to illustrate application need to be varied and in different contexts. If students are guided and assisted in abstracting the concrete exemplars used in the applications back to the abstract theory (rule), it will strengthen the development of a conceptual-level understanding of the theory and increase the probability that it will be applied in contexts beyond the ones in which it was learned.

Application is a case where less is more. Taking the example of the professor, it is often better to focus instruction and application time on the most important theories and ideas. The key is for students to develop a level of conceptual understanding that gives them sufficient confidence to use these theories and ideas in the high-stakes setting of actual practice. Those working in environments that have proscriptive content-coverage requirements must make decisions regarding what rules are important to master to an application level and what rules they are simply going to make students aware of.

The students I taught who were pursuing a master's degree in education typically had around seven years of experience as classroom teachers. After assigning a research paper to read, I would sometimes have students say that the paper was interesting, but it didn't apply to their students. I would respond that the author of the paper would probably disagree with them, and then ask them to tell me how their students differed from the research participants in the study—to the extent that the author's recommendations and conclusions were inapplicable. The students' responses revealed that they believed their students had unique attributes, characteristics, and circumstances that the research study did not address.

I would then present a short discussion regarding the nature of academic research. To make research and the interpretation of the research tractable, the researcher must limit the number of variables (elements) and the number of relationships investigated to those thought to be most relevant and impactful. If there are fifty items that could have some bearing on outcomes, the number of possible relationships among fifty variables is gigantic. A study to evaluate all fifty impacts is simply not feasible, and the report of such a study would be unreadable. Of necessity, rules derived from research are, therefore, idealized to a degree. They will not address all the circumstances that could be encountered in practice.

I would then have the student tell me whether the variables (impacts) the researcher investigated are manifest in their students and whether it was possible that these variables could be more impactful than the idiosyncrasies that caused them to think that the research was not applicable. The answer was often yes. I then pointed out that the results the researcher obtained might not be precisely replicated with their students because of the differences they identified, but, if beneficial results are likely, they can always tweak or modify the research recommendations to address the idiosyncrasies of their students. Putting students through this process helps to overcome the reluctance some practitioners have to apply theory when the circumstances they face seem to be more complex than what theory addresses. In many cases, what one needs from theory is guidance that is directionally correct and suggests an action that produces a beneficial result, rather than a precise reproduction of research outcomes.

Another application problem arises when a learner cannot see the attributes, characteristics, and relationships of the concrete circumstance in terms of the abstract elements and relationships of the rule. We can illustrate this with a simple example. Students typically learn the Pythagorean theorem in the context shown in figure 4.35. They are given two side lengths and asked to calculate the length of the third side.

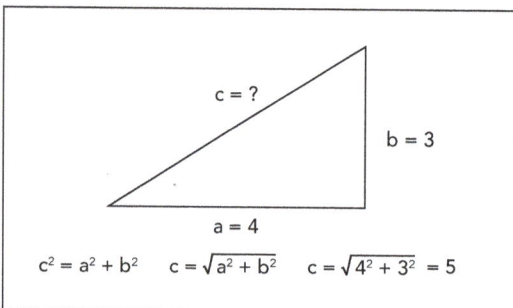

Figure 4.35
Using the Pythagorean theorem to find side length

In the application shown in figure 4.36, to calculate the distance between two points, the student must "see" that a right triangle can be formed using the difference in x values and y values (dotted lines) as the sides. The distance between the points is then the hypotenuse of a right triangle, and the Pythagorean theorem is applicable.

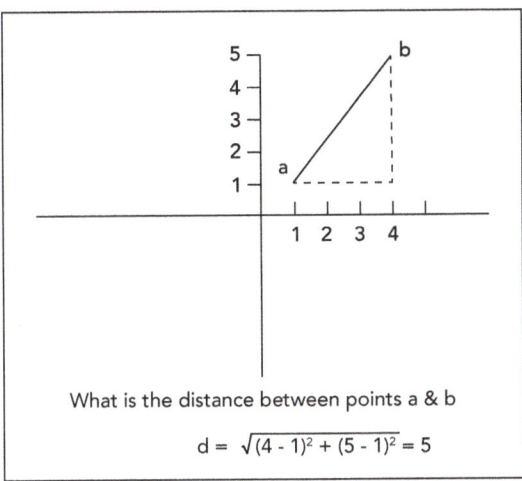

Figure 4.36
Applying the Pythagorean theorem to get the distance between two points length

In the next example, the right triangle is more difficult to "see." As before, the key to applying the rule is connecting the concrete circumstances of the problem to the abstract expression of the rule.

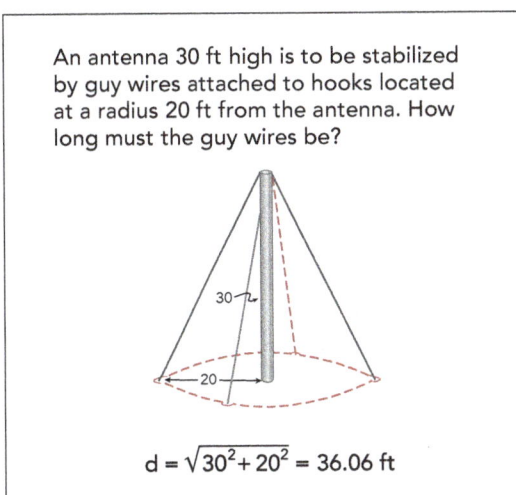

Figure 4.37
Applying the Pythagorean theorem to a practical problem

The last example presents a case where the triangle is even more difficult to "see." The required visualization is that at any level of fill, the distance (radius) from the center of the cone to the edge of the cone, the height of fill and the edge of the cone form a right triangle that is mathematically "similar" to the triangle formed by the known radius of the base, the known height of the centerline, and the edge of the cone. This similarity relationship allows the equation to be reduced to a single variable and enables the solution to the problem. Very few high school students could solve this problem because of the difficulty of seeing the triangles in the concrete circumstances of the problem.

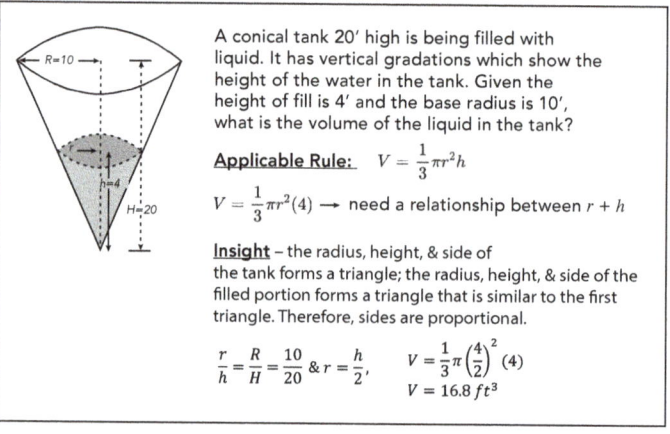

Figure 4.38 Problem where triangular relationships are difficult to see

Seeing the connection between the abstract and the concrete is important in all academic subjects. The following is an example in social studies. The US Congress is currently deliberating the necessity of passing a voting rights act. An interesting applied social studies lesson would be for students to render an opinion regarding the current need for such a law. In looking for theory to help guide them in this process, it is obvious that examining canonical documents such as the Constitution and pertinent literature that explores the rights of individuals in a democracy would be relevant and helpful. It is also obvious that state laws pertaining to voter qualification and voting processes need to be examined, as well as the history of state attempts to restrict voting and advantage certain groups of voters. What is less obvious is that the theory of a social contract is also relevant. Individuals, as participants in the American democracy, give up the right to gather behind closed doors with like-minded individuals to select the leaders of their choice. In exchange for their giving up this right, the central government, through an implied social contract, agrees to protect citizens' right to vote for the leaders of their choice in a free and fair public election open to all eligible voters. Citizens agree to live by the principle of majority rule.

How do we metaphorically help students "see the triangle"? How do we help students understand what rules are applicable to the concrete circumstances of problems and issues they will face in the future? Experience helps. Application is a procedure or series of actions; therefore, the more the process is undertaken, the better the individual gets at it. As with deduction and problem-solving in general, the process involves finding rules that will enable a chain of connection between what is known (current state) and what is desired to be known (goal state). A good conceptual level of understanding of the rule, the ability to connect the concrete to the abstract, and a direct connection between rules and the procedures they suggest and represent are all crucial to the successful application of rules.

The typical application lesson is a follow on after having taught a rule or rules by some other process. This type of lesson teaches the process or procedure, mental or physical, for using the rule to accomplish a goal or to achieve some desired result. The applicable rules relevant to this type of lesson are principles 11, 13, and 14. Principle 11 addresses the requirement to see the concrete circumstances of the situation in terms of the abstract elements of a rule. Principles 13 and 14 incorporate the idea that directly connecting rules and procedures enhances the meaning and understanding of both.

The following example illustrates this type of lesson. Algebra students learn the abstract procedure for solving two linear equations with two unknowns. They are then given sets of equations with two unknowns and asked to solve them using the learned procedure. In addition, the students are typically given word problems to solve that require them to derive and then solve two equations, with two unknowns, that are expressed and embedded in the problem description. As I discovered when serving on the National Assessment of Educational Progress (NAEP) standard-setting committee for mathematics, most students struggle greatly when asked to solve mathematical word problems. It is the conversion from language to mathematical symbolic expression that causes the problem. The following lesson teaches a direct analytical procedure for solving word problems that describe some quantitative relationship involving two equations with two unknowns.

1. Explain the goals of the lesson.

    a. Explain to the students that a word problem expresses a relationship between the quantities of different things. To solve a word problem, we must convert the verbal expressions of quantities to mathematical expressions. The process we are going to learn will help them do that.

2. Model the process with two examples and have students perform the steps as you do them.

    a. Here is the first problem: A food truck sells salads for $6.50 and drinks for $2.00 each. The food truck made $836.50 by selling 209 drinks and salads. How many drinks and salads were sold?

    b. Read the problem carefully. Now reread it, assign variable letters to all the entities, and create the following chart. If the quantity of an entity is given, write it down in the chart. If it is not, put a question mark in the chart. The question marks are the unknowns.

Entity	Variable letter	Quantity
Number of salads	S	?
Number of drinks	D	?
Price of salads	SP	6.50
Price of drinks	DP	2.00
Total sales	TS	836.50

c. Now, write down the relationships between the entities given in the statement of the problem in mathematical terms.

3. The problem states that a total of 209 drinks and salads were sold so: $S + D = 209$.

4. The problem also states that total sales were $863.50. Recall that sales equals price times number sold, so: $TS = S(SP) + D(DP)$.

d. Replace the variable letters with quantity numbers for the entity quantities that are given in the problem description.

$$S + D = 209$$

$$836.5 = 6.5S + 2.0D$$

e. Solve one of the equations for one of the variables.

$$D = 209 - S$$

f. Use this result to replace that variable in the other equation.

$$836.5 = 6.5S + 2.0(209 - S)$$

g. Solve this equation for the remaining variable.

$$836.5 = 6.5S - 2S + 418$$
$$836.5 - 418 = 4.5S$$
$$\frac{418.5}{4.5} = S$$
$$93 = S$$

h. Put this answer into the first equation and solve for the remaining unknown.

$$94 + D = 209$$

$$D = 116$$

i. Problem solved. 93 salads and 116 drinks were sold.

5. Pass out a chart that summarizes the process modeled and ask students to apply the process to a set of word problems. Go around the room and help (scaffold) students requiring assistance.

6. Discuss and summarize the process undertaken.

A word problem discusses a group of entities, expresses a relationship between the quantities of the entities, and gives the value of the quantities for some of the entities. To solve a word problem, we assign each of the mentioned entities a letter designation, write the quantitative relationship specified in the problem, and replace the letter designations with numbers for the quantities given. This will give us two equations with two unknowns that we can solve algebraically.

7. Assign and grade homework.

8. Assess homework and check for understanding.

9. Reteach if necessary.

Contextual Teaching and Learning

Beginning in the late 1980s, there was growing concern that schools were not adequately preparing students for the demands of the modern workplace. Lauren Resnick, in a much-cited 1987 paper, outlined four broad characteristics of mental activity outside of school that stood in contrast to typical schoolwork. One, schoolwork consists of individual cognition versus the shared cognition that occurs outside of school. In a school setting, a student succeeds or fails independently of what other students do. In contrast, most activity outside of school is socially shared. The success or failure of an enterprise depends on the successful interaction of a group of individuals. The aggregate knowledge necessary for successfully accomplishing a goal or task often consists of the collective contribution of individuals with different knowledge competencies. Two, school activities place a premium on pure thought activities—what students can do without the external support of tools and instruments. This contrasts with mental activities outside of schools, where cognitive activity is shaped by and contingent upon the kinds of tools available. The third contrast Resnick pointed out is that symbol manipulation is the primary activity in schools, in contrast to the direct connection with objects and events outside of school. "People often use objects and events directly in their reasoning without necessarily using symbols to represent them" (Resnick 1987, 14). Out of school, since people are continuously engaged with objects and actions that make sense to them, they do not forget what their calculation or reasoning is about. Resnick states that symbolic activities in schools can become detached from any meaningful context. School learning can then become learning symbolic rules and saying or writing things according to those rules. This leads directly to the last difference cited by Resnick, which is related to the transferability of school learning. School learning, by design, is general and nonspecific. Outside of school the requirement exists for situation-specific forms of competence. Resnick states that there is growing evidence that very little of school learning is directly transferable to out-of-school use.

In response to the growing concern about the disconnect between school and work, US secretary of labor Elizabeth Dole appointed a commission in 1990 to determine the skills young people needed to succeed in the world of work. This Secretary's Commission on Achieving Necessary Skills (SCANS) defined five competencies and three foundations deemed necessary for workforce success:

1. Basic skills foundation: reading, writing, mathematical operations, effective listening and speaking skills

2. Thinking skills foundation: creativity, decision-making, problem-solving, reasoning, lifelong learning

3. Personal qualities foundation: responsibility, self-esteem, sociability, self-management, honesty, integrity

4. Information-processing skills: successfully acquiring and using information

5. Systems thinking: understanding and using complex system interrelationships

6. Technology: working with a variety of technologies

7. Resources: identifying, organizing, and allocating resources

8. Interpersonal: effectively working as a member of a team and exercising leadership

While the school-to-work movement was never fully embraced, these concerns and the work done to address those concerns in the late 1980s and 1990s were impactful on schools. Teaching students higher-order thinking skills increasingly became an important goal of educational institutions. Cooperative learning and engaging students in group projects to develop teamwork and leadership skills became increasingly utilized. Schools also increased their use of technology and made efforts to increase students' information-processing skills. Educational approaches such as project-based education and problem-based education emerged. Two of the SCANS competencies—systems thinking and resource allocation—never seemed to find their way into general education. How responsive schools should be to the specific requirements of the workplace is still a matter of great debate. Some believe that imparting a good liberal education that produces generally educated individuals with strong thinking skills should remain the principal mission of schools. Others want more emphasis on the specific knowledge and skills that would prepare students to contend with the emerging realities of the workplace and to obtain higher-paying jobs. The extent to which academic institutions wish to address the disconnects between school and work, such as those delineated by Resnick, or to impart a knowledge and skill set that is more relevant to today's work environment, such as those outlined by SCANS, is a matter for each institution to decide based on their mission and constituencies. If institutions move toward increasing preparation for work, then contextual teaching and learning (CTL) will play a more important role in their pedagogy. It is extremely important that schools maintain a communication link with the employers of their students. For example, school districts sometimes complain that colleges of education are not adequately preparing students for the challenges they will face in their school districts. In response, colleges of education maintain that they give students the foundation necessary to become effective teachers and that school districts are remiss in providing the necessary staff development required to bring their graduates to full competency as practitioners. Better communication and reaching consensus regarding each institution's responsibilities are certainly in order.

Thomas Sticht was an important figure in defining the theory behind contextual teaching and learning. Sticht et al. (1986) cites a study that found young adults required an eleventh-grade general reading level to comprehend, with 70 percent accuracy, material they had no prior knowledge of. Conversely, when given material they had prior knowledge of, 70 percent accuracy was achieved by students with only a sixth-grade general reading level.

Sticht (1999) attributed reading comprehension differences to the dynamics of working memory. Reading with comprehension requires that words read be connected to knowledge in long-term memory to facilitate a coherent interpretation and understanding of a sentence. As a limited resource, if working-memory space is occupied decoding print to speech (phonics) or in working to comprehend an unknown word by comparing it in the context of other words in working memory, sentence comprehension is greatly compromised. Sticht states that comprehension requires automaticity in the decoding aspect of reading (word recognition) and a large body of knowledge relevant to what is being read. Both require a lengthy period of time and practice to develop. He interprets this to be the reason why adults who leave literacy programs with one hundred or so hours of instruction show little improvement in reading comprehension.

During the 1960s, Sticht directed research teams that developed content-based literacy programs for the military services. Literacy programs focused on job-specific content rather than on general topics. For example, those training to be cooks learned word recognition and comprehension by reading cook's materials.

Sticht's teams also had students organize and relate the content of the material read by undertaking activities like drawing pictures of what was read, drawing flowcharts of procedures, and creating lists, outlines, illustrations, and matrices. When compared with students who participated in six-week, full-time general literacy programs, the students in the job content literacy programs made about the same improvement in general literacy, but three to five times the amount of improvement in job-related reading.

As Sticht points out, reading comprehension depends on automatic decoding of print to speech, automatic word recognition, and sufficient inventory of word meanings. Becoming highly literate when beginning with a low level of automaticity and a low baseline of knowledge takes considerable time and practice. There are no real shortcuts or silver bullets. If the goal is to prepare someone for a specific occupation, then reading and learning in context, as described by Sticht, are of great benefit. If the goal is a high general level of literacy, then years of reading broadly across many content areas is necessary.

Sticht's process of having students relate and organize what they had read by creating pictures, diagrams, flowcharts, outlines, lists, and matrices is extremely valuable in comprehending what was read and in creating long-term memories that reflect understanding. This process reflects learning principle 3, which states that learning with understanding is enhanced when students relate and organize the content of a learning experience like reading. Learning is largely the process of creating relationships among the semantic contents of experience, or expressed in neural terms, creating connections between neural representations of the semantic features of experience. The activities performed by Sticht's students serve to make these connections.

Sticht's work shows that reading comprehension requires that the vocabulary the reading utilizes be familiar and previously known by the reader. This in turn requires that teachers pre-read reading assignments to ensure that this will likely be the case.

It does not require any theoretical knowledge to hammer a nail into a piece of wood. This is something that is easily learned associatively through empirical experience. The theory behind what is occurring during this process is that the swing of the hammer gives the mass of the hammer velocity and creates momentum. When the hammer impacts the nail, the speed of the hammer is greatly reduced, and it decelerates. In accordance with Newton's laws, this deceleration creates a force on the nail equal to the mass of the hammer times the rate of deceleration. The surface area of the tip of the nail is small so the tip exerts a large pressure on the wood in contact with the tip and separates the wood, allowing the nail to penetrate the wood.

What benefit does teaching Newton's laws in the context of hammering nails provide? The answer is that the supplied context serves the same role as a metaphor or analogy. It connects something the student knows, hammering nails, to something they do not know, Newton's laws applied to the physics of impacts. Everyone knows that hitting something with an object slows it down and imparts a force. They may not know that the amount of force is proportional to how quickly and to what extent it slows down or that the object hit imparts an equal and opposite force to the thing that is doing the hitting. Everyone knows empirically that punching a pillow will not hurt their hand but punching a concrete wall will. The reason is that the pillow deforms, and the deceleration is considerably less than the almost instant deceleration that occurs when hitting a concrete wall that does not deform. The force the pillow exerts on the hand is, therefore, considerably less than the force the wall exerts. The context of the hammer provides the same benefit that Sticht's reading students received from their prior knowledge of word meanings. A principle of learning for contextual instruction can be derived from this discussion:

Principle 15: Learning in context is enhanced if the learner has prior familiarity and understanding of the objects and actions that constitute the context.

Contextual teaching and learning (CTL) provides several auxiliary benefits. It addresses Resnick's (1987) concern that students often lose sight of what their calculation and reasoning are about. CTL provides a direct connection with and an illustration of how symbolic rules have practical applications.

One of the consistent findings of research on CTL is that it increases learner motivation and engagement. Research by Melanie Rathburn (2015) provides an interesting example. Rathburn used CTL methods to teach a course at Mount Royal University in Canada called Scientific and Mathematical Literacy for the Modern World. She had her students keep a journal of their reflections on the learning experience that consisted of 250-word responses to prompts that she provided. She then analyzed the journal responses using qualitative research methods. One of her findings was a high level of motivation, interest, and enthusiasm for the course content. Students reported that relevant examples motivated them to engage with the material. Many of her students characterized their prior math courses as useless. "'No more does math seem like useless knowledge or stuff I will never use after school' (Student R); 'I was able to actually look at math in a positive light and not assume it's useless' (Student S)" (Rathburn 2015, 9). This is clearly a reflection of Resnick's concern regarding the nature of decontextualized mathematics education as well as an illustration of how CTL addresses this concern.

Rathburn also found that students were relating and connecting her math and science instruction to other academic courses, their personal lives, and even societal/global issues. "'My favorite part of the course was the statistics unit because I feel like it applies to my major and my day-to-day life' (student F)" (2015, 9). Many of the student responses indicated that experiencing the application of the material in context enabled them to build connections, integrate content, and see the broad applicability of the content to numerous aspects of their lives. It appears that the CTL approach was facilitating a generalizing and abstracting process in their minds. They were able to see how they could apply the content in various contexts and see how these different contexts were, in aggregate, related to the abstract rules they were learning. This addresses another of Resnick's (1987) concerns regarding the transferability of school learning to real-world circumstances.

After serving on SCANS with Resnick and Sticht, I was inspired to create pilot applied learning schools employing CTL in the Fort Worth Independent School District, where I served as a board member. We created an applied learning elementary school and, subsequently, an applied learning middle school. Students from the entire school district could apply to attend the schools and were provided transportation. To judge the efficacy of the schools, we selected students by lottery but made sure that the demographics and social circumstances of the students reflected those of the district at large. Teachers applied for positions at the school and received training in CTL methods.

The initial applied learning elementary school, Alice Carlson Elementary, was a mothballed school that had been closed for many years. Among the first projects that students undertook was to design and manage the construction of their own playground. Students also designed their lunchroom and scheduled when each grade went to lunch. Students played a participatory role in many aspects of school life and management.

Alice Carlson Elementary was an exciting and vibrant place. The context in which students experienced academic content was only limited by the teacher's imagination. We experienced the same effect on motivation and engagement that Rathburn and other researchers have reported. Students were highly motivated to learn and highly engaged in the classroom. They were excited to go to school. Disciplinary problems were almost nonexistent.

We learned quickly that all the academic content could not be taught using CTL. Math and science, for example, are sequential and productive disciplines. These disciplines begin with simple concepts that are deductively combined to produce more complex concepts, which, in turn, are deductively combined to produce even more complex concepts. It is virtually impossible to create a series of applied learning experiences that simulate this progression and connection. Where possible and practical, content was taught using CTL. Other content was taught using alternative methods but included an application of the content in a real-world context.

The applied learning schools are still in existence and still very popular. For nineteen years, the schools have substantively outperformed the district average on state accountability tests. For example, at Alice Carlson Elementary, in 2019, 85 percent of the students met state standards for reading, writing, and mathematics versus the district average of approximately 65 percent. In evaluating school performance, it was difficult to isolate the impact of the CTL pedagogy. The schools attracted the more creative and inspired teachers in the district. The principals have been excellent, and the schools enjoy a great deal of parental support. Even children from the poorest neighborhoods had parents who cared enough about their children's education to apply for the schools and adapt to their children enduring as much as a forty-five-minute bus ride to and from school every day. Affective impacts, such as motivation and engagement, also played an important role in enhancing performance.

One thing that was clear, however, was the development of SCANS' type competencies in students. For example, the school district holds an annual conference for area school districts that invites the authors of children's books from all over the country to present and discuss their works with area teachers. The applied learning elementary students are responsible for funding, planning, and managing the conference. With guidance, the students invite the speakers, arrange for their transportation and accommodations, obtain the venue, and create the programming and associated materials. When students took over the conference, funding levels increased. It was difficult for a corporate sponsor to say no to earnest, teary-eyed six-year-olds. The students work as a team and subdivide the responsibilities. Positive peer pressure is at play. Students are loath to drop the ball and let their fellow students down. If stumped by the requirements of an assignment, the students quickly seek help. The importance of the responsibility also keep students motivated, engaged, and on task. They acquire leadership skills and learn how to be constructive members of a team. In addition, participating in projects like the conference increases students' resource-allocation, information-processing, and problem-solving skills.

During my graduate studies, I did work at a large number of schools in the Fort Worth Independent School District. One of the things that was definitely in evidence was stronger-than-average problem-solving skills and a stronger sense of agency and self-confidence in applied learning students when compared with students at other schools. In summary, CTL provides benefits beyond academic content learning. There is a strong case that at least a portion of every student's school experience should be in a CTL format.

Constructing a CTL lesson is straightforward. The teacher must find an application of a rule or procedure to be learned that is a solution to a problem encountered in a real-world setting. The teacher then presents the problem to students and discusses the elements or variables and the relationship between them that must be considered. The rules or processes that solve the problem are then presented and the teacher shows students how they are used to solve the problem. Students then receive an analogous problem or the same problem with the variables altered to solve themselves using the same rules/procedures. In perhaps the most exotic example of CTL in the Fort Worth schools, students went to the Lockheed aircraft manufacturing plant in Fort Worth to learn how long a runway had to be to allow an F-16 fighter jet to take off and land. A Lockheed engineer told them the rate of acceleration of the jet, the speed required for liftoff, and the speed at which touchdown occurred when the airplane was landing. Their instructor showed them how to use Newton's laws to solve the runway-length problem. The students then got to check the answer by watching an actual F-16 take off and land and then measuring the distances. The students then did the calculations themselves for aircraft with different weights and performance parameters. To say the students were engaged and motivated would be an understatement.

Applied Learning and Writing Instruction

In addition to struggling to produce students with sufficient math skills to pursue STEM careers, nationally, K–12 schools have struggled to produce students with sufficient writing skills. The most recent National Assessment of Educational Progress reported that 75 percent of both twelfth- and eighth-grade students lacked proficiency in writing. In addition, 40 percent of the students who took the ACT writing exam lacked the writing skills necessary to successfully complete a college-level English composition class, according to the company administering the test (Goldstein 2017). Difficulty writing is not something new. In 1873, Harvard University initiated a writing requirement as part of its admissions process. When implemented, more than half of the first-year students at Harvard failed the writing examination (Goldstein 2017).

Philosophies of writing instruction have changed over the years and are still a matter of great debate. Prior to the late 1970s, writing instruction emphasized the production of satisfactory finished products rather than emphasizing writing as a process. Students were taught lessons on producing the ideal written product with a strong instructional emphasis on word choice, spelling, punctuation, and grammar. Grammar was taught separately rather than in context with the writing process. It seemed intuitive that students with a strong command of the rules of grammar would become better writers. Students spent considerable time with workbooks and worksheets doing activities like circling adverbs or adjectives, identifying types and categories of phrases and clauses, and diagramming sentences. Instruction was acontextual and focused on grammar as a subject in and of itself. Beginning in 1963 and continuing to the present day, academic papers have been published that conclude that there is no evidence that teaching grammar is a benefit in supporting writing development (Braddock, Schoer, and Lloyd-Jones 1963; Hillocks 1986; Locke 2009). A 2007 study by Graham and Perrin found that isolated grammar teaching was the only instructional practice to have a negative impact on students' writing (Dunn 2017). The following quote from Patricia Dunn, a professor of English at Stony Brook University, sheds light on the reason for these counterintuitive research results:

> However, a technique called sentence combining (where students take a series of short sentences and combine them into longer ones, using a mix of clauses, phrases, and linking punctuation) did fairly well in multiple studies of student writing. In other words, students who did sentence combining (crafting short sentences into longer ones, actively manipulating sections of sentences, rearranging clauses and phrases, adding or deleting modifying words, and punctuating the longer sentence so that it was smooth) saw their own writing improve after this work. But grammar exercises—quizzes on parts of speech, the naming of types of phrases, clauses, and sentences? After those, students' writing got worse. (145)

From the preceding, it is clear that grammar must be taught in context with the writing process to be impactful. In concert with learning principle 14, for the rules of grammar to guide the process of writing, the writing process must be understood as the expression of and the necessary consequences of the rules of grammar. A connection must be directly and overtly made between the rules and the process/procedure of writing. Learners must know "what the rule tells them to do." Students may be able to distinguish between a noun clause and an adjective clause on an examination; however, this does not lead to the ability to combine two short sentences by expressing one as a dependent adjective clause that modifies the noun that acts as the subject of the other sentence. As the quote from Dunn indicates, knowing the rules of grammar can improve writing, but it must be taught in the context of the writing process as an application using contextual learning methods. Grammar needs to be directly connected to sentence production and sentence editing, not taught acontextually as a subject in and of itself.

Grammatical rules manifest in language number in the thousands. Not only are they voluminous but some are quite complex. It has always been a mystery how a five-year-old, who has not learned any formal rules of grammar, can speak in a way that reflects mastery of a great many of the rules. There have been several theories proposed to explain this phenomenon, among them Noam Chomsky's postulation of an a priori grammar built into the cognitive hardware that humans are born with. In other words, according to Chomsky, humans are born with the rules of grammar embedded in the cognitive hardware in the part of the brain that processes language. I have an alternative hypothesis: the rules of grammar are learned associatively. What humans are born with is cognitive hardware that detects and records the invariant patterns in experience. Many of these patterns are learned implicitly without the requirement for conscious recognition and processing.

What a child hears their parents say is, "Jimmy, put your dirty clothes in the hamper." They do not hear, "Hamper, your clothes dirty in put." The five-year-old has heard a great many sentences spoken by others that embed and reflect the rules of grammar. Their brain's capacity for detecting and recording invariant patterns has "taught" them associatively how to relate words verbally to express the contents of their thought.

I have, on occasion, asked my students to write down all the rules of grammar that they can think of. With the exception of students who are English teachers, they typically come up with around four to five rules. In spite of this, most of them produce papers that are grammatically correct and implicitly reflect knowledge of hundreds of rules of grammar. Clearly, this reflects that they have implicit, subconscious knowledge of the rules. When someone writes, they do not think, "I'm going to express this idea using a complex sentence with an independent and dependent clause in which the dependent clause will begin with a relative pronoun and function as an adjective." Writing simply flows from the contents of one's mind. Grammar instruction can and should be an aid in improving writing. It simply must be taught in an applied fashion in the context of producing and editing writing.

Learning to write is also, to a degree, associatively learned. Through reading, learners associatively perceive and mentally record the patterns of word relationships manifest in the reading material. This means that the more students read, the better their writing will become. Having students extensively read increasingly rich and complex text is crucial. Writing is a procedure or process; therefore, the more a student is required to write, the better they will get at it. Like any procedure or process, practice makes perfect. This speaks to the importance of extensive reading and writing experiences as requirements of K–16 education.

Research and academic discourse in the 1970s not only reduced the emphasis on grammar instruction but also changed the emphasis in writing instruction from producing perfect finished products to viewing writing as a process. Donald Murray (1972) was an influential voice in advocating for this change in approach. He stated that holding students to high standards of polished finished writing was unhelpful. Rather than critiquing and correcting students' writing, teachers should show students how to discover and create knowledge through the writing process. Murray's sentiments were echoed by many others working in the field of writing at the time.

The requirement to write produces anxiety and worry in most students. They must simultaneously consider what ideas they want to express, how to organize those ideas, and how to put them into grammatically correct sentences. It was felt by many researchers and teachers at the time that the pressure to produce polished, grammatically perfect sentences was inhibiting student writing and their ability to express themselves in written form. It was also felt to inhibit writing as a knowledge-discovery and creation process. To write about a topic, the writer must mentally organize their thoughts and ideas. If the reader is to comprehend those thoughts, the words, sentences, and paragraphs expressing them must be coherently connected and related. This mental organization increases the writer's understanding and retention of the content of the writing in conformance to learning principle 2. In addition, the writing process stimulates the generation of new ideas or changes in the initial ideas and the relationships between them. It was felt that the emphasis on grammatically correct finished products was a matter of form getting in the way of function.

In response to these concerns, the emphasis in writing instruction shifted from grammar to writing process. Today, most writing instruction proceeds according to what is now formally called Writing Process. Writing Process consists of the following steps:

1. **Pre-writing:** Select a topic, generate ideas about the topic, gather information about the topic, determine what you are going to say about the topic. Strategies for generating ideas include the following:

    a. **Brainstorming:** Make a list of every idea you can think of about the topic—just words and phrases.

    b. **Free writing:**

    - Write about every idea you have concerning the topic for fifteen to twenty minutes without stopping.
    - Don't worry about structure, grammar, or punctuation.
    - Keep your hands moving, write about something, even if ideas don't come.

    c. **Moodling:**

    - Sit quietly with paper and pencil/pen and daydream about the topic.
    - Only write when an idea pops into your mind.

    d. **Research and reading:**

    - Gather information relevant to the topic.
    - Read like a writer: make notes, question and critique the reading, look for patterns.
    - Look for answers to questions.

2. **Organizing and planning:** Connect ideas and create a logical structure for your ideas. How will you explain and support your ideas and connect them to the thesis of your work?

    a. **Graphic organizers:** Use spatial bubble organizer, charts, matrices, and lists. Organize in hierarchical fashion: thesis — main idea — supporting ideas — supporting detail.

   b. **Detailed outline:**

- Hierarchical structure as above.
- Use of verbs: For example, "Industrial Revolution changed the nature of jobs," not simply "Industrial Revolution."

   d. **Drafting:** Get ideas roughly into sentences.

- Let ideas flow into sentences.
- Work through the outline and just write.
- Don't labor over sentences or worry about word choice, grammar, punctuation, and spelling and get yourself stuck.

4. **Revising:** Ask if the text is something readers can relate to and understand?

  1. Think about readers' needs:

- Is the organization and structure sensible to readers?
- Is there sufficient support for the ideas? Or does additional detail need to be added?
- Is the flow of ideas or the argument effective, clear, coherent, and logical?
- Do terms need to be defined for the reader?

  2. Incorporate self-reflection and feedback:

- As one writes, ideas change and new ideas often emerge. Have new ideas or changes been incorporated?
- Has teacher or peer feedback on the draft been incorporated?

5. **Editing:** Get the text in final form.

  1. Check for grammatical correctness, spelling, and punctuation.

  2. Are sentences efficient, effective, interesting, clear, and free from ambiguity and redundancy?

  3. Is the tone and style of the writing appropriate to the audience and purpose?

We can see that the design of the Writing Process reduces writers' anxiety and worry concerning what ideas to express and how to organize them. The Writing Process also does a good job of using writing as a means of knowledge discovery and knowledge construction. It addresses many of the concerns previously expressed by professionals in the field. One possible critique is that there is too little emphasis on the construction of grammatically sound sentences. After going through the process, if students do not have a firm grounding in grammar, spelling, and punctuation, it is still possible that sentences are produced like, "Well machines are good but they take people jobs like if they don't know how to use it they get fired." This sentence was a real submission on the essay section of the ACT test (Goldstein 2017). Standardized college entrance exams like SAT and ACT, as well as state accountability tests and the National Assessment of Educational Progress, grade grammar, punctuation, spelling, and capitalization as well as content. As previously discussed, the results of these tests are quite discouraging. To preserve the benefits of the Writing Process and to address the current shortfalls in student writing, I strongly recommend teaching grammar using application as the knowledge-construction process and embedding it in the context of writing production and editing. The following discussion illustrates my proposal.

If grammar is to be used as a basis for producing and editing writing, young writers must master certain basic concepts. First, they need to know that writing is a way of expressing and recording their thoughts about something to someone who is not usually present. A sentence, which is a combination of words that serve different functions, is the basic unit for expressing a thought. For someone who is not present to understand what they have written, a sentence must express a complete thought. "Once upon a time" is not a sentence. "Once upon a time, I was in kindergarten" is a complete sentence.

Sentences are always about something: a person, place, thing, or concept. As such, a sentence always has a subject. Nouns are words that express a person, place, thing, or concept; therefore, the subject of the sentence is a noun. There are two things that can be expressed about a subject: (1) the state of being or condition they are in or (2) an action they are involved in. Words that express a state of being or an action are called verbs; therefore, every complete sentence has both a noun and a verb.

Students must know all nine parts of speech, their function in a sentence, what ideas they represent, and the questions they answer.

Part of speech	Function/idea	Examples	Question answered
1. Noun	person, place, thing, or concept	cup, computer, dog, Paris	who or what
2. Verb	expresses action or state of being	is, was, hit, run, sing	did what, is what
3. Adjective	describes nouns	blue, smooth	which one, what kind
4. Adverb	describes verbs, adjectives, other adverbs	quickly, slowly	when, where, why how, in what manner, to what degree, under what conditions
5. Determiner	limits or determines nouns	a, the, 2, 12	how many, which, how much
6. Pronoun	replaces a noun	I, she, he	who or what
7. Preposition	relates a noun to other words	to, at, with	where, when, why, how
8. Conjunction	connects words, phrases, and clauses	and, or, when	what else, under what circumstances
9. Interjection	exclamation	oh! hi! well	emotional expression

It is proposed that these parts of speech, their function, their use, and the questions they answer be taught in the context of producing and editing sentences. There are seven basic sentence structures in the English language. A total of 95 percent of all sentences are in one of these forms (Kolln and Gray 2017).

1. Subject	Form of be	Adverbial
The dog	is	in the yard.

2. Subject	Form of be	Subject complement
The sky	is	blue. [adjective that describes subject]
My father	was	a soldier. [noun phrase that renames subject]

3. Subject	Form of be	Subject complement
My brother	looks	tired. [adjective that describes subject]
My sister	became	a nurse. [noun phrase that renames subject]

4. Subject	Intransitive verb		
The man	cried		

5. Subject	Transitive verb	Direct object	
The bat	hit	the ball.	

6. Subject	Intransitive verb	Indirect object	Direct object
The teacher	gave	Juan	the pencil.

7. Subject	Transitive verb	Direct object	Object complement
The coach	called	the effort	outstanding. [adjective]
The teacher	considers	the students	scolars. [noun phrase]

Phrases and clauses that act as the different basic parts of speech can be added to these seven structures to produce more expressive sentences and to produce compound and complex sentences. It is proposed that students be taught to produce sentences using the seven structures initially. For example, to teach structure 2, the teacher could show students pictures of familiar objects, like dogs or cars, and ask them to produce simple sentences that describe the objects. Students would be guided to produce sentences like "The dog is black," "The dog is shaggy," and "The dog is small." The teacher would then point out or develop through questioning the concept that words like "black," "shaggy," and "small" are words that describe nouns. They are called adjectives and answer the questions what kind or which one. The teacher could then show pictures of people in different clothes, uniforms, and settings and ask them to produce sentences that say what occupation the person has. The teacher is guiding the students to produce sentences like "The man is a fireman" or "The woman is a doctor." The teacher could then develop with the students the concept that these sentences are different because the information the sentence provides renames rather than describes the subject, using another noun rather than using an adjective to state a quality (attribute/characteristic) that the subject has. The goal of teaching parts of speech in this manner is to get the student to think that when they have a writing goal like expressing a quality or a characteristic of a noun, they can use an adjective. The adjective tells the reader what kind of thing it is or which one of the things it is. You are trying to connect the rule and the process of producing a sentence; let the rule guide the process rather than have the rule be a stand-alone concept detached from the process of writing and editing. Let's say that the teacher has taught sentence structure 5 by having the students write what a dog was doing in a video—what actions the dog was undertaking. The teacher could then guide students in editing their writing by combining the structure-5 sentences with the ones produced when learning structure 2. For example, instead of writing four sentences like the following:

The dog is small.

The dog is black.

The dog is shaggy.

The dog jumped the fence.

The students could write, "The small, shaggy, black dog jumped the fence." This sentence conveys all the information but is more compact and easier on the reader. These types of applied-learning experiences can be combined with traditional grammar lessons. If they precede the traditional lessons, students will already know how the presented concepts are used and what they are for, and they will have a connection between the rules and the procedure for using them.

The metaphor for teaching grammar in this fashion is "building a house." Creating text can be viewed as using words together to build phrases, combine phrases to produce clauses, combine clauses to produce compound and complex sentences, combine sentences to produce a paragraph, and combine paragraphs to produce a text. After students have mastered the basic sentence types and parts of speech, instruction proceeds to learning how to use phrases as parts of speech to provide additional detail, context, and clarity. Figure 4.39 shows a concept map for phrases.

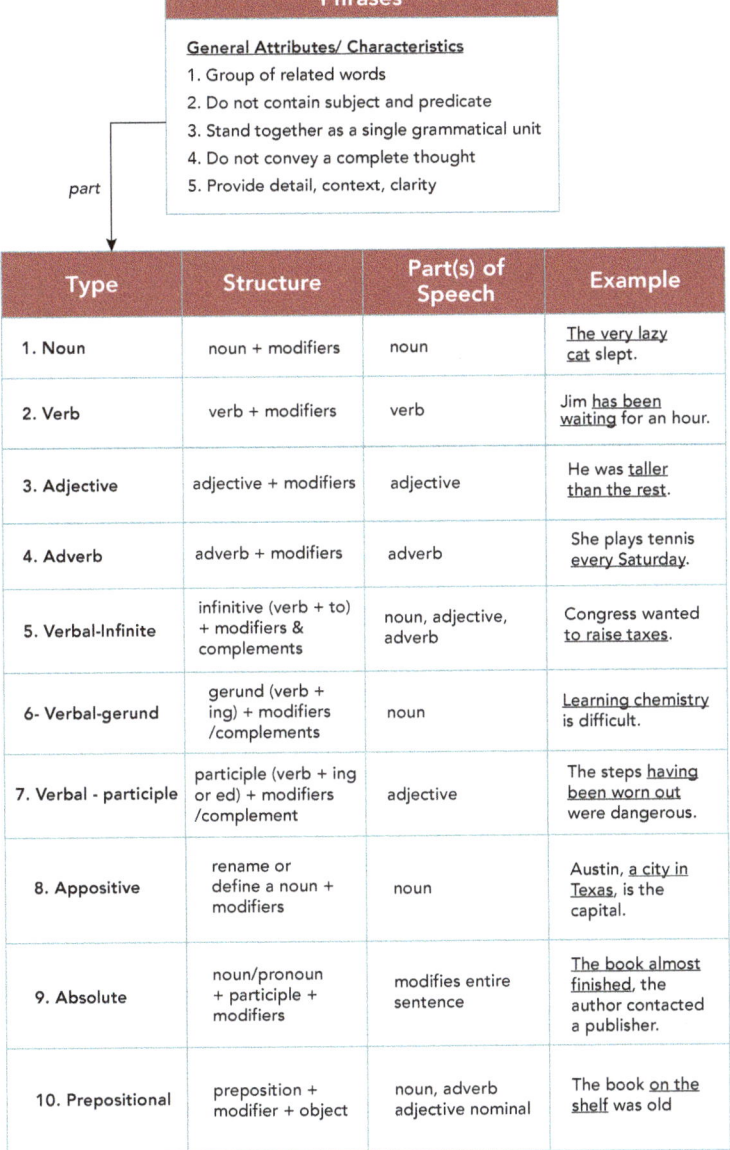

Figure 4.39 Concept map for phrases

Phrases and clauses function as a unit to act as parts of speech like nouns, adjectives, and adverbs. This makes them very useful not only in adding detail, color, context, and clarity to writing but also in improving connectivity and flow between ideas expressed in writing. For example, prepositional phrases not only relate and connect words in a sentence but also connect sentences and even paragraphs. For example, a prepositional phrase in the topic sentence of a new paragraph can connect the sentence to the main or summarizing idea of the prior paragraph.

A good way to teach prepositional phrases is in the context of a valuable editing tool. For example, the following sentences can be connected via prepositional phrases to produce a single sentence that more cohesively describes an event.

Sentence	Information conveyed
1. The picture fell.	Action
2. The picture was on the wall.	Location
3. The picture fell at night.	Time
4. The picture broke Mother's vase.	Action
5. The vase was on the table.	Location
6. The vase broke into small pieces.	Manner

These six sentences can be combined into a single sentence using prepositional phrases. The key to combining the sentences is to identify the type of information conveyed by the sentence. The first and fourth sentences describe an action. As such, the verbs of the sentences can be combined into a compound verb in the final sentence. The second and fifth sentences describe the location of the picture and the location of the vase. Since they describe nouns and answer the question which picture and which vase, they are candidates for expression as a prepositional phrase that acts as an adjective in the final sentence. The third sentence expresses when an action took place and the sixth describes the manner in which the action produced an outcome. They answer when and the manner in which an action took place, and they describe verbs. As such, these sentences can be converted into adverb prepositional phrases describing the action verbs in the final sentence. The final sentence becomes:

During the night, the picture on the wall fell and broke mother's vase on the table into small pieces.

The preceding illustrates the importance of knowing the parts of speech, the functions they serve, and the questions they answer as core concepts that can be used in both producing and editing writing. The thought process that we wish to encourage in students is along the lines of, "I want to express something about the subject of the sentence; therefore, I need an adjective; I can either use a single word, a phrase, or a clause to do that; what I want to say is best said by a clause, so I will write, 'Jim, who is very charming, convinced the salesperson to give him a discount.'" An analogy to this thought process would be, "I want to connect these two pieces of wood and I have a Phillips screw; I need a Phillips screwdriver." In other words, thinking about the rule of grammar I can use as a tool to accomplish my goals.

The following is an example lesson, in CTL format, whose goal is to teach the use of participles and participle phrases. A concept map for participles and participial phrases is shown in figure 4.40.

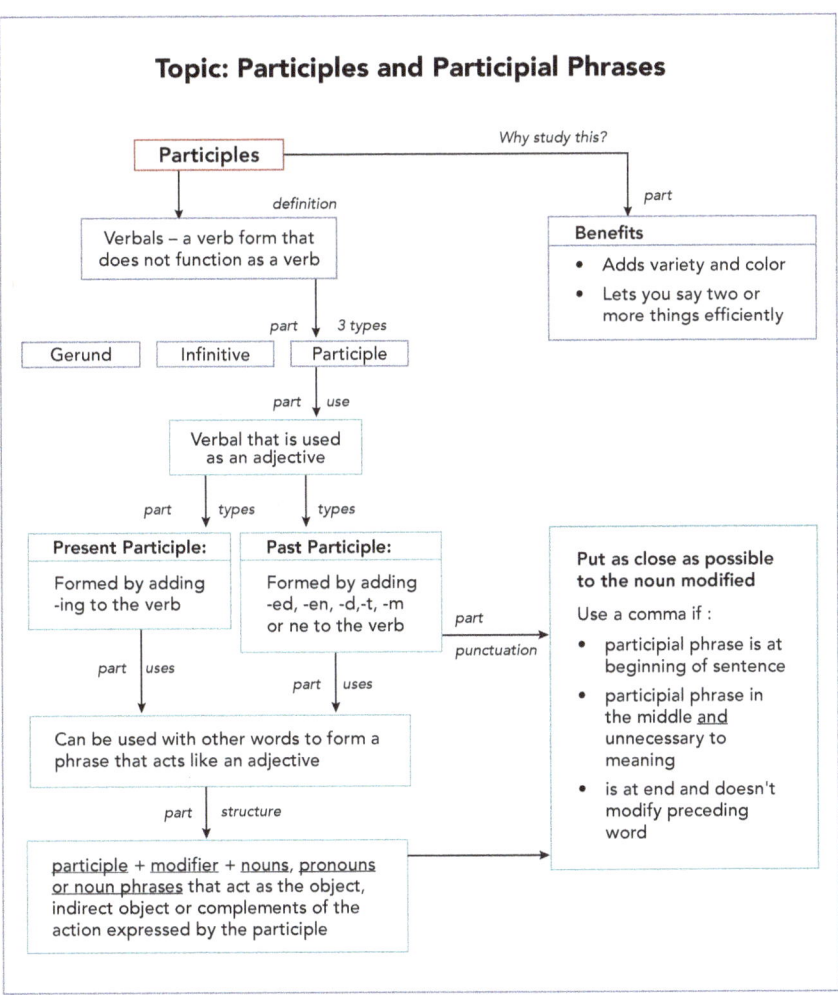

Figure 4.40 Concept map for participles and participial phrases

As with any lesson, it begins with a warm-up whose goal is to activate required prior knowledge and to present the goals of the lesson. Since this is a CTL lesson, it is put into the context of a problem or goal to be achieved in a real-world setting.

You are working in a writing center and a student looking for assistance has given you a narrative about a firefighter named Mandy. Sections of the narrative have short choppy sentences that should be combined to improve connectivity and flow.

The next step is to present the rule or procedure (the objective of the lesson) that solves the problem and achieves the goal.

There are variety of strategies you could use. Let's choose the use of participles and participial phrases. A participle is an adjective that we form from a verb by adding "ing" to a verb. We add "ing" for the present tense. For the past tense we add "ed," "en," "d," "t," or "n." For example, to convert the verb "work" into an adjective in the present tense, called a *present participle*, we add "ing": "working." To convert "work" into an adjective in the past tense, we add "ed": "worked." This is referred to as the *past participle*. We can combine a participle with a modifier and a noun/pronoun or noun phrase to create a participial phrase. This phrase acts as a single unit, in this case, an adjective.

As with any completely new rule introduction, this discussion will not have a lot of meaning for students until they see the new rule used in the context of prior understandings and see how the new rule works. The next step is to give the students some practice converting a list of familiar verbs into present and past participles. Next, we tackle the problem first presented.

The paper we're editing has some of the following sentence sequences that we are going to combine using either participles or participial phrases.

> The firefighters combed through the smoking rubble.
>
> They found guns.
>
> They found an empty gasoline can.

We first look at the verbs in each sentence and convert them into participles. We can choose the verb "found," which occurs in two sentences, and change it into "finding" to create an adjective, or we can choose the verb "combed" and change it into "combing." If we chose "found," the combined sentence would be:

> "<u>Finding guns and an empty gasoline can</u>, the firefighters combed through the smoking rubble."

This reverses the order in which things actually happened, so we choose the verb "combed." The combination would then yield:

"Combing through the smoking rubble, the firefighters found guns and an empty gasoline can."

This is the better choice. Now let's look at another sentence sequence.

The firefighters worked around the clock.
The firefighters finally put out the fire.

Here we have the same issue of the timing of the events. The best choice is to convert the verb "work" into "working" and create the combined sentence:

"Working around the clock, the firefighters finally put out the fire."

Note that in creating both sentences, we kept the direct object and modifiers of the direct object in our final sentence. This created a participial phrase with the former direct object and modifiers becoming the object and object modifiers of the participle. Now let's try another sequence:

Mandy was mud covered.
Mandy was shivering.
Mandy sat hunched over a cup of cocoa.

The first two sentences describe Mandy using adjectives. In fact, "shivering" is already a participle being used as an adjective to describe Mandy. We can use these two adjectives directly to create our combined sentence:

"Shivering and mud covered, Mandy sat hunched over a cup of cocoa."

The last step in a CTL lesson is to have the students apply the rule or procedure themselves on analogous problems or to achieve an analogous goal. Students would be given sentence sequences and asked to combine them using the demonstrated rule and process on sentence sequences like:

The old man sat outside.
The old man was smoking his pipe.

The boys sat by the side of the road.
The boys were gossiping.

Following lessons teaching the construction and use of phrases, the next sequence of lessons would cover the effective use of clauses. This would be followed by lessons on creating good paragraphs and then complete texts. Teaching students to be excellent writers involves more than just being able to craft grammatically correct sentences, knowing the ins and outs of parts of speech, writing simple declarative sentences, and studying the correct construction and use of phrases and clauses. Students need additional lessons on other aspects of grammar, such as subject-verb agreement, parallelism, and coordination. In addition, students should learn how to use different literary devices, how to construct inductive and deductive arguments, how to create rhythm and voice, and a host of other writing strategies. However, mastering parts of speech, simple declarative sentences, and the effective use of phrases and clauses will get them a long way down the road to becoming good writers.

Learning through Dialectic Process and Emergence

What happens when a human being encounters a fact or experiences an event that cannot be explained or understood in terms of their preexisting knowledge and representations in long-term memory? In fact, the fact or event could suggest the opposite or antithesis of what their preexisting knowledge and representations would tell them should be the case. From a neural perspective, the brain's representation of the new fact or event in perceptual-processing circuits has no connection to any representations in long-term memory. As a nonlinear system, the brain is trying to achieve a state of stable equilibrium between the representations in perception and long-term memory. Since it cannot do so, processing stops, and the system is in a state of unstable equilibrium. The individual experiences this state as confusion. Subsequent to this experience, the brain can either temporarily store the new experience and go on to other processing, or if the driving forces are sufficient, as an open nonlinear system, it can undertake the process of self-organization. As discussed in the nonlinear system section of this book, a nonlinear system in this state will undertake various changes in configuration in an attempt to reach a state of stable equilibrium. The brain will try different connection (relationship) possibilities between the representation of the semantic features of the item in perception and the semantic features of the representation of existing rules in long-term memory. If this process is successful, the new fact or experience will be accommodated and a new more expansive rule with altered and expanded relational connections will be created. Self-organization of neural representational circuits is hence a knowledge-construction process. It is my hypothesis that one of the behavioral action sequences that facilitates this process is none other than the dialectic process described by Plato and subsequently by the philosopher Hegel. In general, I believe self-organization is ubiquitous and occurs often when individuals encounter new information or have new experiences that cannot be accommodated using their existing inventory of rules in long-term memory. In young children, the circumstance of new experience requiring the construction of new rules is frequent.

An analysis of the first dialogue of Plato's (1951) *Republic* reveals the fundamental process of behaviorally driven self-organization and creation of new knowledge. As discussed previously, the dialogue begins with Socrates asking the host, an elderly man of wealth, to inductively generalize his past experience and provide the interlocutors with a definition of justice. The host states that because of his wealth, he has had the luxury of always speaking the truth, unlike poor men, who are tempted to lie in order to gain advantage. Also, as an elderly man, he must make preparations for his departure from the earth by returning those things borrowed from others and giving the gods their due before his departure. He summarizes by defining justice as "telling the truth and giving others what is owed to them."

Socrates responds by immediately producing a circumstance where the rule fails, and the antithesis of the rule seems to be the appropriate response to the circumstance. He asks the interlocutors to consider a case where a man fully in control of his faculties deposits his arms for safekeeping with another man. This man subsequently returns to collect his arms but is clearly no longer sane or in control of his faculties. Knowing that the man will likely injure either himself or someone else in his current state of mind, would it be just to tell him the truth and return what is owed to him?

After much discussion, the interlocutors decide to revise their definition to accommodate the circumstance introduced by Socrates. Their new rule is that justice is defined as "doing good to friends and doing evil to enemies." In terms of the mechanisms of the dialectic process, the initial rule, when applied to a sane man, worked and was sufficient. When applied to an insane man, the rule failed and its antithesis seems to be the appropriate response: lie to the individual and do not return his arms. In fashioning a new rule, the prior rule was saved, but the antithesis and the new variable or attribute, sanity, that invoked the antithesis were accommodated by creating a relationship between the thesis of the old rule and the antithesis and making them both subordinate to a new rule at a higher logical level: "do good to friends and do evil to enemies." Telling the truth and returning what is due are doing good to a sane friend, while lying and withholding what is due constitute doing good to an insane friend. The challenge in resolving the impasse was to find a higher-level rule that combined both thesis and antithesis into a logically coherent structure. Under what more general rule are the two seeming opposites both logically necessary consequences? What more general rule or idea can be the connective tissue or, to use nonlinear systems terminology, the control parameter that facilitates the resolution of the conflict and allows the combination of thesis and antithesis. In the case of the preceding dialectic, it was the more general idea of doing good to friends that provided the connection. Note that the failure of the original thesis was brought about by the fact that it did not include or accommodate for the variable of sanity. It was this variable that brought about rule failure. Rule failure typically occurs because there is a variable in the new circumstance, an attribute or characteristic that is not an element of the original rule. A rule can also fail because there is not a relationship between the attributes and characteristics of the new circumstance and those of prior circumstances that were the basis of the original rule that failed. The generalized dialectic process proceeds as follows:

1. The experience of instability or the secession of progress under the original rule.

2. The identification of the variable, attribute, or characteristic in the new circumstance (fact or event) that caused the old rule to fail.

3. The generation of a more general, inclusive concept at a higher logical level that accommodates the variables or elements of the new circumstance and creates a relational structure between these elements and the elements that composed the original rule. This higher-level concept must subsume both thesis and antithesis as logically necessary consequences of the higher-level concept.

It is step three that is the most difficult. In nature, self-organization is a trial-and-error process. This is also the case in the behavioral process of conducting a dialectic. There is no direct analytical way to find the higher-level concept or idea. The key is examining the circumstances that gave rise to the old rule and finding what commonalities or common elements these circumstances might share in the abstract with the new circumstance that brought about the failure of the original rule. Can the elements, attributes, and characteristics of the circumstances that produced the old rule be related to the elements, attributes, and characteristics of the new circumstance in such a way that they express the range of states of a new idea or rule that is more general and inclusive? In what way are they both manifestations of some more general rule at a higher logical level? What more abstract idea includes the elements of the original circumstances that were generalized by the old rule and the elements of the new circumstance that resulted in the failure of the old rule? It also involves determining what relationship can connect these elements in a way that produces a logically coherent new rule that serves to accommodate the idiosyncrasies of the new circumstance while preserving the old rule that applied to priorly experienced circumstances. This is not a trivial enterprise. If it were, I would write a book that describes how to resolve the conflict between progressive Democrats and radical Republicans in the United States.

To give an example of dialectic resolution, pleasure and pain have always been considered as two distinctly different phenomena. The abstract attribute that they have in common is that they both serve to guide an individual toward behaviors that promote their well-being. This is the idea that connects these seeming opposites. Modern researchers working in the field of feeling and emotion understand pleasure and pain as part of an overall system that attempts to guide human behavior in a way that promotes the well-being of the individual.

Steven Pinker has stated that whenever he sees two highly educated and highly intelligent individuals arguing opposite positions, he often suspects that they are arguing the extremes of some principle that exists at a higher logical level. This is a good description of a circumstance in need of dialectic resolution.

The premise of author Thomas Kuhn's (1996) best seller *The Structure of Scientific Revolutions* is that the developmental history of science demonstrates that it proceeds according to some guiding paradigm until this paradigm can no longer explain or account for new experimental evidence. He states this as follows:

When the profession can no longer evade anomalies that subvert the existing tradition of scientific practice—then begin the extraordinary investigations that lead the profession to a new set of commitments, a new basis for the practice of science. The extraordinary episodes in which that shift of the professional commitment occurs, are the ones known as scientific revolutions. They are the tradition shattering complements to the tradition bound activities of normal science. (Kuhn 1996, 6)

The history of the development of Einstein's special theory of relativity illustrates Kuhn's premise and the operation of the dialectic process. Prior to Einstein's theories, scientists took for granted the highly intuitive notion that space and time dimensions were universal: fixed and independent. Classical physics uses space as the fixed context or frame of reference in which events occur; measurements of time are presumed to be the same for all observers. Under this paradigm, if a train is moving toward a tree on the side of the track at 40 mph and you are on the train walking in the same direction that the train is moving at 5 mph, you are approaching the tree at 45 mph; you add your velocity to that of the train. If you are walking in the opposite direction, you are approaching the tree at 35 mph; you subtract your velocity from that of the train.

In 1880, the American physicist Albert Michelson and his assistant, Edward Morley, devised an instrument capable of measuring differences in the speed of light, corrected for the speed of the Earth's rotation. In accordance with classical physics, there should be a variation in the measured speed of light when moving in different directions with respect to the source of the light. As in the train example, the measured speed should be the speed of light plus the velocity of motion when moving toward the source of the light and the speed of light minus the velocity of motion when moving away. Much to Michelson and Morley's shock and dismay, they found no variation in the speed of light. It appeared that the speed of light was independent of the motion of the observer. As with every discovery that violates the prevailing paradigms of the time, these results were dismissed and ignored by the scientific community for over twenty years. It was not until the publication of Einstein's special theory of relativity in 1905 that an explanation for this experimental observation was provided.

As with any deductive derivation, Einstein's theory begins with two postulates. The first postulate is that if two frames of reference (system of spatial coordinates and time) are moving at a constant velocity relative to each other, they are both inertial reference frames in which the laws of physics hold in their usual form. What Einstein is saying is that the laws of physics do not change just because one reference frame is moving away from another at constant velocity. Einstein's second postulate was that the speed of light has the same value in every direction in all inertial frames. As the Michelson and Morey experiment showed, the speed of light is independent of the motion of the observer. Einstein went on to derive the consequences of these two postulates. We can get a flavor of his results by considering the following example of the consequences of these two postulates.

Figure 4.41 Diagram of relativity thought experiment

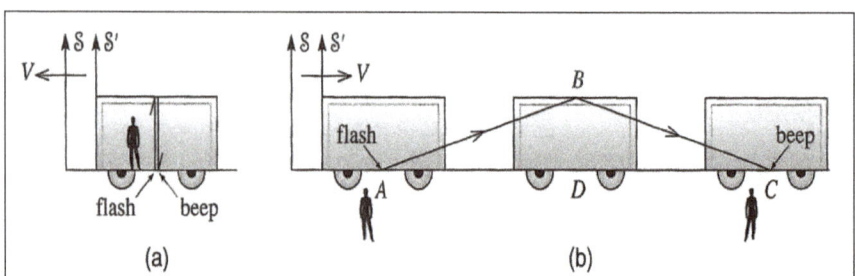

In this thought experiment, we have a person on a train who sets off a flashbulb on the floor of the train. The light travels to the roof where it is reflected and returns to its starting point. When it returns, it strikes a photocell and causes a sound. We want to compare the times between when the flash leaves the floor and when it arrives back, in two different reference frames: the reference frame of the train and the reference frame of a person on the ground observing the event. The laws of physics are the same in both reference frames, so in both reference frames the time required is the distance traveled divided by the speed of light. As per Einstein's second postulate, the speed of light is the same for both observers. However, as can be seen, the distance traveled is longer for the observer on the ground than it is for the observer on the train. Since we are dividing both differences by the same speed of light, the observer on the ground measures a longer time for the event to transpire than the observer on the train does. In other words, time is relative and measurements of time by two different observers moving away from each other at a constant speed will be different. I'll spare the reader the calculation, but if the train is moving at 87½ percent of the speed of light, the time difference will be a factor of 2.

The relativity of time gives rise to something called the *twin paradox*. If there are two thirty-year-old twins and one of them boards a spaceship that travels at 87½ percent of the speed of light to a planet in another galaxy and then returns to Earth twenty years later, the twin who remained on earth will be fifty years old, while the twin who undertook the space travel will be only forty years old. This is indeed a highly counterintuitive result.

The speed of light is the fastest any change can take place. That is why all observers measure the same speed. We can use the analogy of a budget for the interval of time measurement. If you are traveling at a large percentage of the speed of light, there is a limited amount of time left in your time budget in which change can take place. In the limit, as the speed of an object approaches the speed of light, time is undefined. It disappears altogether. A light beam does not experience time.

If we continue to derive the implications of Einstein's postulates, they yield several other emergent consequences. One of them is length contraction. From the perspective of an observer who we can consider to be stationary, the length of an object moving away from them at a constant velocity is shorter in the direction of motion of the object.

For example, if a one-hundred foot-long object is moving away from them at 60 percent of the speed of light, the observer will measure the length of the object to be eighty feet long. As the velocity approaches the speed of light, the length measured will approach zero. Space in the direction of motion is, therefore, also relative. The most profound result of special relativity is the equivalence of mass and energy. Special relativity produced the famous equation $e = mc^2$. Mass produces an enormous amount of energy when converted. This is the basis of the atomic bomb where a chain reaction converts some uranium mass into energy.

There are several things to note about the development of Einstein's theory. First, as with every dialectic, the original rules are preserved. As the first postulate states, the laws of physics remain the same in all inertial frames of reference. Also, relativistic effects, like time dilation (lengthening) and length contraction, are minimal at speeds encountered and experienced in human activities; hence, classical physics accurately describes most of the phenomena in human experience. Dialectic is evolutionary not revolutionary. Second, self-organization and dialectic often produce emergence. Emergence is the phenomenon that nonlinear systems can produce results that are more than or greater than the sum of the parts. Unanticipated new rules and results are produced consequent to and because of the nonlinear combinations and relationships. In the preceding example, combining the laws of physics with the fact that the speed of light is constant in all frames of reference produced the unanticipated emergent result that mass and energy are equivalent and can be converted into each other.

As nonlinear systems grow and become more complex, there are more and more emergent consequences. The behavior and relationships between atomic particles are described by the rules of quantum mechanics. The relationship between atoms can be described by classical physics. The relationship between atomic combinations or molecules brings about the emergent rules of chemistry. If organic molecules combine to produce cells, the combination and relationship of cells produce the emergent rules of biology. We can continue this combination process to ultimately produce the rules of the social sciences that describe relationships between individuals. At each level of combination and relationship there are emergent consequences that cannot be derived from a consideration of the nature of the elements put into relationship. For example, the fact that humans have consciousness cannot be anticipated or derived from the rules of quantum mechanics. The inverse of this process also holds true and demonstrates the limitations of reductionism and analysis of nonlinear systems. If you think the performance of Meryl Streep in a motion picture can be reduced to the actions of the organic molecules that she is composed of, you have missed the point of emergence.

As the preceding discussion illustrates, the progress of science with time can be taught using the dialectic process. The previously discussed example of the evolutionary history of models of the atom is a good candidate for this approach. Hegel viewed human history as one long dialectic. Human societies evolve a culture and set of social behaviors thought to be beneficial and necessary for their collective well-being and survival given the contingencies and conditions of the environment they find themselves in. Conditions change and they find that the old rules no longer work or produce the desired outcomes. A social dialectic ensues, and societies change. Any topic which demonstrates evolutionary change is a candidate for teaching via the dialectic process.

Prospective attorneys are taught the dialectic process in law school as a means of refuting an opposing attorney's argument. Other than this, there are no instructional models in the literature that directly use the dialectic process as a teaching method. To qualify as a dialectic, previously learned rules must be contradicted or otherwise shown to be insufficient. In an educational setting, this must be done with caution. Plato's dialogues themselves illustrate the type of emotional reaction individuals can have when their expressed thoughts and beliefs are contradicted and summarily dismissed. The following is a lesson that teaches the transition in American history from what is called the Gilded Age to the subsequent era of progressivism as a dialectic. The historical information discussed is largely derived from the work of two scholars who specialize in this era, Richard White (2017) and Edward O'Donnell (2015). The description is lengthy and elaborated because we will use this information and background to demonstrate curriculum development in the next chapter.

One of the principal reasons for studying history and teaching it to young people is, or should be, to understand how past generations dealt with the challenges and issues they faced. This will hopefully help the younger generation avoid repeating the mistakes of their forefathers and foremothers. As Winston Churchill said in a 1948 speech to the British House of Commons, "Those who fail to learn history are condemned to repeat it."

An interesting transition in American history that exemplifies Hegel's contention that the progression of history reflects a dialectic process is the transition from the Gilded Age (1868–1900) to the Progressive Era (1900–1920). The term Gilded Age comes from author Mark Twain. Twain's metaphor communicates his view that the wealth and prosperity of the few constituted a thin coat of gold that hid the rampant greed of industrialists, the corruption of politics, and the dismal living conditions of most Americans during that era.

The Gilded Age is also referred to as the Second Industrial Revolution. During this time, the American economy grew at an unprecedented rate and made the United States one of the world's leading economic powers by the turn of the twentieth century. This growth was in large measure driven by technological innovation and progress. The biggest driving force for economic expansion and the source of several fortunes was the development of the American rail system. Locomotive and rail travel were not inventions of the Gilded Age. Before the Gilded Age, however, rail travel was problematic and dangerous. Passengers often sat near a wood burner and had to be careful of sparks landing on their clothing. Engines sometimes exploded before the train reached its destination. Tracks were in different gauges and there were frequent delays while passengers and cargo changed trains. Braking systems were very unreliable, which led to numerous crashes and derailments.

During the Gilded Age, innovations in railroading included larger, more powerful, and reliable locomotives, new types of freight and passenger cars, automatic car couplers, adoption of a standard gauge by virtually all railroads, the creation of four standard time zones across the country to allow trains to run on schedule, and the replacement of iron by steel, which is lighter, stronger, and more durable. The use of steel facilitated the bridging of major rivers and other bodies of water. Importantly, in 1872,

George Westinghouse invented the air brake, which made rail travel safe. The first transcontinental railroad was completed in 1869 and, from this time to the end of the Gilded Age, 170,000 miles of railroad tracks were built and most of the nation's railroad system was in place. Railroads tied the country together and enabled the movement of people and goods across the nation in a relatively quick, efficient, and cost-effective manner.

The construction of the national rail network greatly affected every aspect of American life and economic activity. It led to the development of the West. Thousands of hopeful individuals flocked to the frontier with the hope of making their fortunes by exploiting the untapped resources of the West. New towns and settlements sprang up. It was no longer necessary for each community to be self-sufficient. Whatever a community lacked, it could bring in via the rails. Sales markets for goods went from local to national. For example, midwestern farmers could now ship their produce to East Coast markets. The material needs of railroad development led to the growth and expansion of many other industries, such as steel, machinery, copper, glass, and fossil fuels. It changed the nature of business in general. Raw materials could be brought in and finished products shipped to markets via rail. A great many new economic opportunities were created by the expansion of the rail system.

The railroad business went through the cycle that always occurs when technical innovation creates significant new economic opportunities. The chance for financial gain attracts a lot of people to the space. Significant capital flows in and a great many enterprises form, hoping to exploit the new opportunities. There end up being too many companies fiercely competing and driving prices down to the point to where nobody is making a profit. There are many inefficiencies in the market and a multiplicity of products and services of varying quality result. Not all companies are created equal. Many are poorly managed, are less effective in exploiting the innovation, and are undercapitalized. Undercapitalized means that they have insufficient funds to create and sustain an efficient, viable, and profitable business. A natural Darwinian process then occurs in which the stronger, more capable, better-managed, and better-financed companies survive and the weaker companies die out. This is a natural and healthy process that occurs in free-market systems. The net result of the process is a much smaller group of strong, well-run, and profitable businesses competing against one another. During the Gilded Age, a period when government was not involved in business, certain entrepreneurs took things to the next level, eliminating all competitors using questionable business practices, which today would be considered illegal, and creating monopolies that dominated entire industries.

Americans view competition as a mechanism to ensure fairness in the marketplace. Because of the consolidation of railroad companies, there were often no real competitors in many routes. Railroads could charge different rates to different customers and were not required to publish or reveal their rates. This gave them enormous power to decide economic winners and losers. Even when more than one railroad served the same route, railroads often entered into secret agreements to fix rates and to eliminate other competitors. White provides the following example of how railroads used their pricing power.

In 1883, the Northern Pacific Railway Company raised the rates it charged O. A. Dodge's Idaho lumber company. The new rates left Dodge unable to compete with the rival Montana Improvement Company, reputedly owned by Northern Pacific executives and investors. Dodge knew the game was up. All he could do was ask if they wanted to buy his company (White 2018, 3).

This same strategy was used by John D. Rockefeller to build his oil monopoly. Rockefeller began in the oil industry by building a refinery in Cleveland, Ohio, in 1863. He had twenty-five competitors with refineries in the city. Oil was supplied via rail to these refineries by producers in Ohio and Western Pennsylvania, and refined products were also shipped via rail. In 1871, Rockefeller was able to effect a secret alliance with the three major rail lines that ran through Cleveland to increase their shipping rates to his competitors while paying him "rebates" and "drawbacks." Word of the arrangement got out and Rockefeller was able to buy twenty-two of his twenty-five competitors in under six weeks. Using the rail rate strategy, he was also able strong-arm oil producers into selling their assets at greatly reduced prices. He effectively employed the same strategies in Pittsburgh, Philadelphia, Baltimore, New York, and other refining centers. By 1882, Rockefeller's Standard Oil Company had a near monopoly (90 percent) of the oil business in the United States.

In an ironic twist of fate, the daughter of one of the oil producers that Rockefeller had bankrupted, Ida Tarbell, dedicated herself to researching and studying Rockefeller's business practices. Tarbell revealed the strong-arm tactics, espionage, collusion, bribery, and deceit that were common in Standard Oil's business practices in a nineteen-part series published in *McClure's* magazine. So great was the public outcry in response to her articles that she is credited with being the catalyst for the eventual government breakup of the Standard Oil monopoly.

Building railroads required enormous investments for purchasing rights-of-way over land, constructing railways, and building train engines and railcars. Railroad companies looked to investors for capital and to government for subsidies. Financier J. P. Morgan, who had strong connections to European investors interested in participating in American enterprises, saw financing and consolidating railroads as a great opportunity. His interests went beyond arranging financing for a fee. He was interested in ownership, control, and ultimately monopolization of the industries he financed. Turning an industry into a stable, monopolized, and, therefore, reliably profitable, entity was more alluring to potential European investors. In return for financing, Morgan demanded board of director positions and stock in the enterprises. This allowed him to control management, create efficiency and modernization, and, importantly, effect mergers between the entities that he exerted control over. Morgan's formula for creating monopolies was to buy up smaller companies, lower prices until competitors went bankrupt, buy up bankrupt competitors, create efficiencies and economies of scale, slash the workforces, reduce the wages of remaining employees, and then increase prices to maximize profits. Morgan was instrumental in creating monopolies in the railroad industry, steel industry, banking industry, farm machinery industry, and the electric generation and distribution industry.

In 1870, Andrew Carnegie founded his steel company in Pittsburgh. He adopted the Bessemer process, an innovation in steelmaking, to produce steel more efficiently and cheaply. He also employed vertical integration to make his company even more competitive. Carnegie owned and controlled the mines that produced the raw materials for steel as well as the transportation infrastructure required to bring raw materials to his manufacturing plants and to transport the finished products to markets. These practices gave him a lower cost structure than his competition had. When the price of steel dropped, he was able to buy out his less efficient competitors and build his steel empire. The price of steel still had large fluctuations, and Carnegie Steel Company president Charles M. Schwab talked publicly about the advantages of combining competing companies to rationalize production and stabilize steel prices. In 1901, he orchestrated a secret meeting between himself, Andrew Carnegie, J. P. Morgan, and Elbert Gary that resulted in the formation of US Steel Corporation. This new company combined two major vertically integrated companies, Carnegie Steel and Federal Steel, with three steel-finishing companies, American Tin Plate, American Steel and Wire, and National Tube. The combined companies were capitalized at $1.46 billion, making US Steel the world's first billion-dollar corporation. US Steel controlled 213 manufacturing plants, 1,000 miles of railroad, and 41 mines and employed 168,000 workers. In 1901, the company produced 66 percent of all the steel produced in the United States and 30 percent of the steel produced in the world (Warren 2001).

Inventions and innovations by Thomas Edison and employees of George Westinghouse facilitated the distribution of electric power and light to American cities. Readily available electric power revolutionized every aspect of American life, from factory to home, and created enormous economic opportunities.

Arc lights powered by alternating current (AC) began to be installed in American cities by the late 1870s. These systems employed high voltage, above 3,000 volts, and were used to light streets and factory yards. Edison saw a market for a system that could bring electric lighting into homes and businesses. His system used low voltage (110 volts) direct current to power the incandescent lightbulb that he had invented and to power electric motors, most of which operated on direct current at the time.

J. P. Morgan quickly recognized the potential of electric power. He hired Edison to install electricity and electric lights in his Fifth Avenue Manhattan mansion. Morgan's home became a lab for Edison's experiments and a small generator was installed to power the home's light bulbs. Morgan financed the creation of the Edison Illuminating Company. The Edison Illuminating Company created the world's first power station, and shortly half of Manhattan was connected to electric power.

Westinghouse moved in a different direction. One of the limitations of Edison's low-voltage direct-current system was that electricity could not be transported over large distances. This meant that many power plants had to be constructed in close proximity to customers. Alternating current provided advantages over direct current. It could easily be changed into different voltages using transformers. Using higher voltage allowed an alternating-current system to transmit power over longer distances from more efficient large central generating stations. The higher voltages could then be stepped down with transformers to the voltages appropriate for different applications, like light bulbs and electrical machinery.

Westinghouse purchased the US patent rights to the European Gaulard-Gibbs transformer. He hired electrical engineer William Stanley Jr. to develop the first practical transformer that could be used commercially. He then bought the Consolidated Electric Light Company in 1887 and two additional companies in 1888 to gain control of all the incandescent light patents not controlled by Edison. In addition, in 1888, he licensed Nikola Tesla's US patents for a highly efficient alternating-current motor. This gave Westinghouse all the ingredients necessary for a completely integrated system that was considerably more cost effective than Edison's system.

Edison did not take these developments lying down. He began an aggressive campaign to prove to the public and government officials that alternating current was dangerous and a public hazard. He also sued Westinghouse and other alternating-current competitors for infringing on his patents and worked to push for legislation to limit alternating-current installations.

J. P. Morgan could see the handwriting on the wall. It was clear that Westinghouse, not Edison, was poised to light up and electrify America. He made several unsuccessful attempts to acquire Westinghouse's electric business. In lieu, he merged Edison's electric business with a competitor, Thompson-Houston, which had developed an alternating-current system. Thompson-Houston was expanding their business while trying to avoid patent-infringement conflicts with Westinghouse. They paid a royalty to Westinghouse to use the Stanley alternating-current transformer. The combination of Edison and Thompson-Houston created General Electric, an entity that controlled 75 percent of the electric generation and distribution in the United States. Edison stubbornly refused to abandon direct current and was marginalized and subsequently forced out of General Electric. While Morgan was not able to acquire Westinghouse, he kept pressure on him with patent-infringement lawsuits and governmental roadblocks. He was ultimately able to force a patent-sharing agreement between General Electric and Westinghouse that ended the conflicts and gave Morgan effective control over yet another industry.

Business during the Gilded Age was a brutal affair. With no oversight or regulation, business owners used whatever tactics were necessary to gain power, dominance, and wealth. Moral and ethical considerations were set aside; there was little concern for the welfare of the public and maximizing the bottom line became the only goal. As many journalists of the time documented, bribery, deceit, collusion, espionage, strong-arm tactics, and even violence when considered necessary were commonplace in business activity at the time. The press called wealthy industrialists of the era "robber barons" and insinuated that behind every great fortune there was a great crime.

To further their financial ambitions, businessmen of the Gilded Age became heavily involved in politics. Government was viewed as a source of capital and regulations/laws that could advantage one competitor over another. Businessmen found candidates to run for office, financed their political campaigns, and used bribes and kickback arrangements to obtain government grants and legislation favorable to their business objectives. For example, it was reported in the press that the Central Pacific Railroad had paid over $500,000 in political bribes between 1875 and 1885. The Pennsylvania Railroad had an office in the state capitol building. Their chief lobbyist was known as the fifty-first senator. In all, governments gave railroad companies $150 million and two hundred million acres of land.

Political corruption was rampant from the local level to the federal level. At the local level, political machines were dominant. These machines rigged elections and operated patronage systems. In return for bribes and kickbacks, they awarded lucrative contracts to businesses and awarded high-paying public offices to loyalists. The political machine in New York City, Tammany Hall, headed by Boss Tweed, is estimated to have siphoned off between $45 and $200 million of city funds before Tweed was ultimately convicted of 204 counts of fraud. Political machines existed in most major cities. For example, Boss Ruef ran San Francisco and Tom Dennison ran Omaha.

State governments were similarly compromised. At the time, state legislatures elected US senators. By controlling state legislatures, business interests could, in effect, control the US Congress. In addition to obtaining grants and favorable legislation, businessmen used inside knowledge of public works to successfully speculate on land.

Even the office of president of the United States was compromised. After the financial Panic of 1893, President Grover Cleveland had to borrow $65 million of gold from J. P. Morgan to keep the federal government afloat. Morgan, Rockefeller, and Carnegie financed the political campaign of Cleveland's successor, William McKinley. McKinley outspent his opponent by a multiple of five to one. Because of corruption at the local level, how one voted during the Gilded Age was public knowledge. Many workers voted for McKinley because they feared losing their jobs if they voted for his opponent.

In all, it was felt by many that business had converted America from a representative democracy to a veritable oligarchy. Former president Rutherford B. Hayes commented in 1886 that the country had changed from a government of, by, and for the people to a government of, by, and for the corporations. Journalists routinely wrote that the American government was of Wall Street, by Wall Street, and for Wall Street. Many lamented that the nation had lost its democratic character and had reverted to an old European system of haves and have-nots fixed into unchangeable social classes.

It was clear who the beneficiaries were of the great expansion of the American economy during the Gilded Age. At the turn of the twentieth century, the top 1 percent of Americans owned 51 percent of the country's wealth. The bottom 44 percent owned a paltry 1 percent. Of all Americans, 40 percent earned below the poverty level of $500 per year and 90 percent earned less than $100 per month. To earn these meager wages, workers had to labor twelve hours a day and six days a week. There were no vacations, no benefits, no workers' compensation for employees injured on the job, and no retirement benefits. Workplaces were often crowded, unsanitary, and dangerous. In 1882, an average of 675 people a week were killed in work-related accidents. Mines, steel mills, and railroads were particularly dangerous workplaces. In 1893, 1,567 railroad workers were killed and 18,887 were injured on the job.

Since industries were largely monopolized, there was no place to go if workers were unhappy with their pay and working conditions. Many monopolies entered into secret agreements not to hire one another's workers. Attempts at unionization and collective activity by employees were dealt with harshly. One of the things that enabled the exploitation of workers was an enormous influx of immigrants to the United States during this period. If a disgruntled worker left, they were easily replaced. Instead of using skilled craftsmen who performed multiple functions, work was subdivided into simple manual tasks that required very little training or knowledge. To make ends meet, sometimes entire families went to work. Women were paid half of what men were paid, and children typically received around 27¢ per day.

Living conditions for America's workers were also poor. Two-thirds of the population of New York City lived in tenement apartments, many of which were unfit for human habitation. Thousands roamed the streets at night. Jacob Riis's book *How the Other Half Lives: Studies among the Tenements of New York* revealed to the public the dreadful conditions of tenement life: people living in dark, cluttered, and unsanitary conditions. Many health problems resulted, and it is estimated that as many as a million people died of preventable diseases during the Gilded Age.

By the turn of the twentieth century, things had reached the breaking point. Between 1880 and 1900 there were thirty-seven thousand strikes by workers. Strikes were becoming increasingly violent, and many deaths had resulted. Journalists began to write that the nation was close to class warfare. Some even suggested that a Marxist revolution of the working class against the industrialist class was imminent. The tide of public opinion was going against the industrialists. Investigative journalists, writers, and photographers, who were called muckrakers, revealed to the public numerous examples of corporate malfeasance, political corruption, and social injustice and described the dreadful working and living conditions of workers. For example, the book *The Jungle* by Upton Sinclair revealed the deplorable and unsanitary conditions of the Chicago stockyards and meat-packing industry and shocked the public. His book is considered to have been instrumental in bringing about the Meat Inspection Act and the Pure Food and Drug Act in 1906. The latter act created the federal Food and Drug Administration (FDA).

A growing number of ministers, priests, and rabbis were proponents of what has been called the Social Gospel. They worked to arouse the social conscience of their congregations. The idea that people should concern themselves about the welfare of others and that to some extent we are our brothers' keepers began to replace the "every man for himself" mantra and social Darwinism of the Gilded Age.

Academics and professionals also turned against the industrialists. A new generation of economists, political scientists, and sociologists began to undermine the philosophical foundations of laissez-faire—the idea that there should be no interference by government in the affairs of business and society. A new school of social workers went into slums to discover and report the extent of human suffering found.

Together, these forces combined to raise public consciousness and convince most Americans that the status quo could no longer continue; dramatic societal change was necessary. The nation was founded on the ideal that every vote mattered, that the results of elections reflected the will of the people and could be expected to result in benefits to the population at large. Government should be of the people, for the people, and by the people, not an oligarchy controlled by a handful of super wealthy industrialists. The conditions during the Gilded Age also called into question the nation's foundational belief that in America everyone, no matter how humble their origins, could achieve upward economic mobility and a measure of success. Someone should be able to start a business and succeed based on the merit of the business without having to worry about being crushed by a monopoly employing unethical business practices or being impeded by a corrupt government controlled by the monopolies. The circumstances of the Gilded Age called into question the idea that America was a meritocracy, or even a representative democracy.

Wealthy industrialists like Morgan, Vanderbilt, Carnegie, and Rockefeller had enormous wealth and power. However, there is strength in numbers. When the sentiment of the majority became that current conditions were no longer tolerable, change began to occur. Importantly, the industrialists lost the support of the middle class.

The roots of the ideology prevalent during the Gilded Age can be traced back to economic philosopher Adam Smith. In his 1776 book *The Wealth of Nations*, Smith proposed the idea of enlightened self-interest. He stated that the baker does not produce and sell a loaf of bread because he wants to help the butcher. He does it to make a profit. In turn, the butcher sells the baker a pound of meat to make a profit. Both parties act out of self-interest and both benefit and prosper as a result. Smith contended that everyone acting for their own self-interest would bring about the greatest prosperity for all. He coined the phrase "invisible hand" to describe the benefit that all received in an economy driven by self-interested parties. Smith also believed there should be no government involvement in or regulation of the economy. He thought the role of government was education, defense, public works, protection of private property, and punishment of crime.

Smith's ideas of enlightened self-interest and no involvement by government in economic activity was reinforced by an ideology promoted during the Gilded Age called social Darwinism. Social Darwinism was an application of Charles Darwin's scientific theories of evolution and natural selection to the evolution of human society. British social philosopher Herbert Spencer was its first and most ardent proponent. Spencer believed that competition was the "law of life" and that it resulted in the "survival of the fittest." He argued that wealth and power showed signs of fitness and the superiority of wealthy and powerful individuals. In his view, the poor were poor because of their laziness, stupidity, and immorality. For Spencer, the evolution of social classes was the natural order that resulted from competition and that this sorting of individuals according to "fitness" should not be disrupted by government action. He opposed laws regulating housing, sanitation, working conditions, and health conditions because they interfered with the rights of property owners. To him, government aid only encouraged laziness and vice. Unlike Darwin, Spencer believed that people could genetically pass on what they had learned in life. The fittest would pass on industriousness and the ability to accumulate wealth to their children, while the unfit would pass on laziness and stupidity.

Spencer's views were echoed and supported by American sociologist William Graham Sumner. Sumner argued that millionaires were the product of natural selection. He held a strong laissez-faire position, arguing that government had absolutely no role in the functioning of the economy. He believed that charity to help the poor only encouraged them to breed and create more poor people who would produce a weaker, less competitive society. Sumner contended that social progress depended on the fittest families passing on their wealth. Numerous American businessmen adopted the views of Spencer and Sumner as "scientific proof" of their superiority over the masses and as justification for their accumulated wealth and power. These views also justified their indifference toward the circumstances of their employees. They were sometimes used as an argument against paying higher wages.

These ideologies helped to produce, or at least rationalize and support, the social and economic circumstances that prevailed during the Gilded Age. As discussed previously, they produced highly unstable social and economic conditions for the nation. Continuation under these premises was untenable and put the nation at risk of a revolution. Rather than revolution, what occurred was an altered view of the role of government and a more humane view of social relationships and obligations. Laws to correct society's ills replaced "survival of the fittest." The view became that government could play a role in improving the lives of citizens and in transforming society. Through judicious application of laws, regulations, incentives, and punishments, government could guide human behavior toward more constructive and equitable outcomes. Government needed to play a role in regulating business, keeping markets free, and protecting democracy.

The progression from the Gilded Age to the Progressive Era also reflected the dialectic process in the sense that what was good and what worked in the Gilded Age was retained. It was evolution not revolution. Journalists, academics, and religious leaders did not give up on free enterprise, free markets, and capitalism. It was felt that this economic system still offered the best opportunity for social progress, upward mobility, and prosperity. The robber barons had simply corrupted the system with their unscrupulous practices. With appropriate governmental regulation of business activities, the economic system could be restored to health. Similarly, Americans did not give up on their form of government. New laws simply had to be put into place to ensure that government reflected the will of the people and allowed for equal democratic participation.

A proposed method for teaching this era in American history is as follows. The story of the Gilded Age could be developed through a combination of selected readings, video material, and lectures. The big ideas in the content from these sources could be structured and organized according to the following summarizing propositions:

- Technological innovation drove a substantial increase in new business activity and materially changed both the nature of business and the lives of the citizenry.

- Because of prevailing social philosophies/ideologies and a lack of government involvement, a small group of industrialists were able to create monopolies and corrupt governments.

- This resulted in the creation of large fortunes for these industrialists but also resulted in low wages, dismal living and social conditions, and an end to prospects for upward mobility and the chance for prosperity for most Americans.

- An unstable social, economic, and political condition resulted, and the status quo could not continue.

After having developed the story of the Gilded Age, the teacher would then engage the class in a dialectic process. The rules that prevailed during the Gilded Age were enlightened self-interest, no involvement by government in business or social circumstances, and "survival of the fittest." These rules facilitated economic growth and the emergence of the United States as one of the world's leading economic powers. It also resulted in untenable social and economic conditions for a majority of the population. What rule or rule changes would preserve economic growth but resolve the social impasse and instability present at the end of the Gilded Age—an instability that created the possibility of revolution? Students would be directed to think in terms of the role of government and changes in people's attitude regarding their responsibility to one another. In the previous Plato's dialogue example, the missing variable that brought about rule failure was sanity. In the Gilded Age circumstance, the rules were problematic because they did not account for, nor could they address, the unethical and unprincipled manner in which some individuals behaved—behavior that was justified and rationalized by the ideology of self-interest and social Darwinism.

After the students have developed their new rules, the teacher would then cover the actual events that transpired during the Progressive Era. The students could compare their dialectic results with the new ideologies that emerged during this era and the events they inspired. The events of the Progressive Era would then make all the sense in the world to students from a causal perspective. They would understand the following:

- The actions of Theodore Roosevelt:
  » Using the office of the president as a bully pulpit to rally public opinion and spur Congress to pass reform legislation
  » Reviving the Sherman Antitrust Act of 1890, which Cleveland and McKinley refused to enforce, to break up the railroad, beef, oil, and then tobacco monopolies
  » Securing passage of the Hepburn Act in 1906, which enlarged and strengthened the Interstate Commerce Commission and gave it the authority to regulate and make transparent the rates charged by railroads
  » Intervening on behalf of the United Mine Workers in their strike against Pennsylvania coal operators
  » Securing passage of the Meat Inspection Act and the Pure Food and Drug Act
- Progressive reforms under President Taft:
  » Passing the Sixteenth Amendment to the Constitution establishing an income tax
  » Passing the Seventeenth Amendment to the Constitution establishing the direct election of US senators

- » Expanding the jurisdiction of the ICC to regulate telephones, telegraphs, and radio
- » Establishing the Children's Bureau to eliminate child labor and to improve health care
- Continued reforms under President Woodrow Wilson:
  - » Passing the Federal Reserve Act in 1913 to regulate banking and establish the Federal Reserve System
  - » Passing the Federal Trade Commission Act, which established the FTC and its role in stopping unfair, deceptive, or fraudulent practices in the marketplace
  - » Passing the Clayton Act in 1914 to strengthen antitrust regulations and establish that employee unions were not a restraint of trade
  - » Passing the Nineteenth Amendment to the Constitution giving women the right to vote
  - » Passing the Adams Act, which limited the workday for railroad workers to eight hours
- The emergence of young idealistic leaders at the state level, such as Robert La Follette in Wisconsin, Charles Evans Hughes in New York, and Hiram Johnson in California, who implemented practices such as direct primary elections, initiative, referendum, and recall to help restore democracy to state government
- The establishment of the National Municipal League to unite reform groups across the country and facilitate the overthrow of corrupt governments in New York City, Baltimore, and Chicago
- The establishment of laws and regulations at each level of government to increase protections for workers, improve public health and education, prevent child labor, extend charitable services to the poor, restrain big business, and make politics more democratic

Students should understand that societal change through dialectic process does not necessarily occur. If pressures continue to build during a time of social instability and there is no change or path to progress, the system can move from instability directly into a state of chaos. The state of chaos for a social nonlinear system is revolution or war. There are many examples in history where a dialectic did not occur, and social conditions moved from instability directly to revolution or war. Another scenario is also possible if the power of the existing regime is sufficiently great. A regime can maintain its power and suppress dissent by controlling the media and other sources of information, restricting the public's ability to meet and congregate, and severely punishing all dissenters. Such social/political systems remain unstable but can sometimes last for lengthy periods.

As discussed previously, an important reason for studying history is to inform the present and to provide knowledge that could be useful in helping to forge a better future. Contemporary journalists and historians are questioning whether the current times are a second Gilded Age. As with the first Gilded Age, technological advances created a boom in economic activity and resulted in an enormous transfer of wealth. The invention of the internet and digital computer, and other digitally based technologies, have dramatically changed the nature of business and everyday life. Originally, tens of thousands of business enterprises emerged to take advantage of the economic opportunities provided by these new technologies. While there are still many companies exploiting these technologies today, a small number of companies have created virtual monopolies in different areas of the technologies. For example, Amazon dominates retail sales over the internet, Alphabet (Google) dominates internet search, and Meta-Platforms (Facebook) dominates social media. The combined market value of Apple, Microsoft, Alphabet, Amazon, Meta Platforms, Tesla, and Nvidia (chip maker) is 27 percent of the total value of the S&P 500. European regulators have found several of these companies to be in violation of their antitrust laws and have levied large fines. In addition, several European countries have passed laws to limit their power and influence.

The founders of these corporations have net worths that rival those of Carnegie, Vanderbilt, and Morgan. As in the Gilded Age, the economic benefits of the new technologies have not been widespread. Based on data from the Federal Reserve Bank of St. Louis, from 1989 to the third quarter of 2021, the net worth of the top 1 percent of Americans increased from 23 percent to 32 percent of total national net worth, while the net worth of the bottom 50 percent decreased from 3.7 percent to 2.4 percent. During this same time, the top 1 percent went from receiving 17 percent of the total income received in the United States to 23.5 percent, while the income of the bottom 50 percent declined from 9.8 percent to 3.6 percent of total income. The US Government Accountability Office (GAO) recently reported to Congress that 40 percent of American workers earn below $16 an hour, or an average of $17,950 per year. Of these workers, 83 percent qualify for government entitlement programs such as Medicaid, TANF, and food subsidies. While these statistics are not as dire as those of the Gilded Age, the trends are alarming and have generated considerable political discourse and activity concerning the growing income and wealth disparity in the United States.

The final part of the proposed lessons on the Gilded Age and the subsequent Progressive Era should be to contrast and compare this time with the present time. In what ways are they similar and in what ways are they different? Are there lessons from the historical period that are applicable to today's circumstances? One difference to note is that today's Progressives are advocating more radical changes to the nation's economic system than Progressives in the past did. This has made it very difficult for them to get the support of a majority of Americans for their agenda. Connecting the historical era to the current time will allow students to better understand the relevance of studying history.

This lesson also provides an opportunity for students to examine the nature of ideology. The question students should ask about any ideology espoused by a social or political group is the extent to which it is based on valid philosophical arguments that reflect sound logic and reason, valid scientific facts and principles, the results of honest scholarship and inquiry, and a true rendering of historical facts and events. Is this the basis for the ideology or is it simply a rationalization or set of beliefs that if acted on would give advantage and preference to one social/political group over another? Is the ideology a reflection of Schopenhauer's contention that humans do what they want to do and then invent philosophies and theories that justify and rationalize their actions? Is the ideology a reflection of the philosopher Foucault's contention that historical eras evolve a set of beliefs or "epistemes" that serve the self-interest of those in power rather than reflect any underlying truth or reality?

Ideologies are often concocted as a means of gathering a following. There is strength in numbers. If a political/social group can develop an ideology that serves the needs or desires of a significant number of people, they can use it as a tool to increase their numbers and their political power. A true rendering of history reveals that the desire for wealth and power in individuals and groups is the driving force behind a great number of historical events.

A word of caution is in order regarding the questioning of ideology by students. For many people, their ideology is part of their personal identity. Questioning their ideology is interpreted as a personal attack. In this era, as with prior eras, attacking sacred cows is often dangerous. University professors enjoy the privilege of academic freedom championed and protected by their institutions. As the current school board wars concerning COVID-19 policy and the teaching of critical race theory demonstrate, the commitment to academic freedom does not necessarily extend to public K–12 institutions. Educators examining current ideologies with students should, therefore, proceed with caution and an understanding of the context they find themselves in.

While social studies is particularly amenable to being taught through the dialectic method, numerous other topics can be taught using this approach. The following illustrates a lesson to teach determining the volume of different types of objects using the dialectic method.

---

1. Define the goals of the lesson and do an activity that generates interest in the content.

2. Model the process for determining the volume of a rectangular solid (box).

    To determine the volume of the rectangular solid, we multiply the width of the solid times the height and the length.

    $$V = whl$$

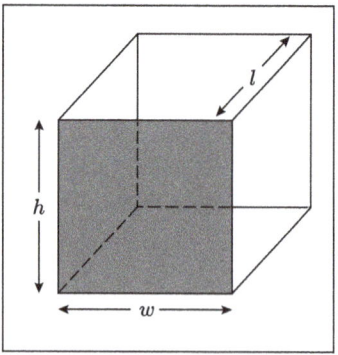

Figure 4.42 Diagram of a cube and its characterizing dimensions

3. Present a circumstance in which the rule fails.

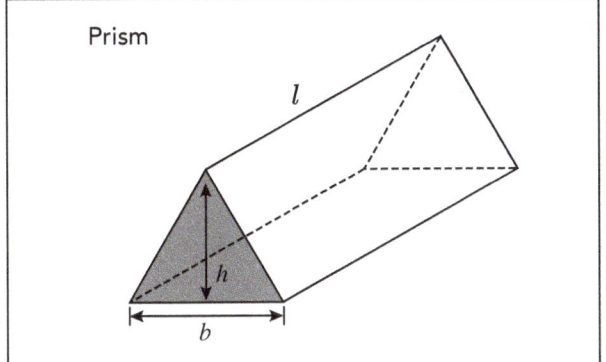

Figure 4.43 Diagram of a prism with characterizing dimensions

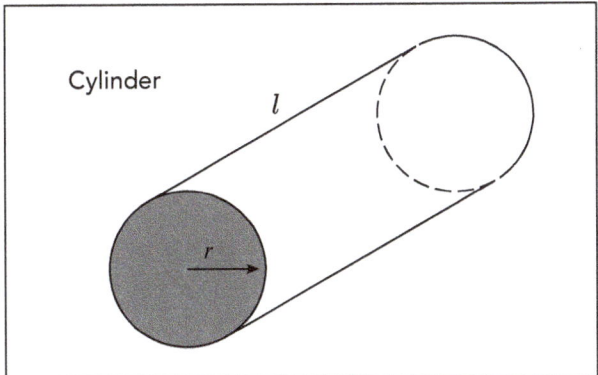

Figure 4.44 Diagram of a cylinder with characterizing dimensions

Can we use the formula for the volume of a rectangular solid for the preceding two figures?

> No. The width of the prism varies from bottom to top, and the cylinder is not characterized by a height and width, so the formula is not applicable.

4. Guide the students in using the dialectic process to develop a new, more comprehensive rule that still works for the old circumstance but accommodates the new circumstances.

> Compare and contrast the old and new circumstances: What is the same, what is different?

The length dimension is the same.

The width and height dimensions do not characterize the new figures, a new idea that unites these differences is required.

5. Is there an idea at a more abstract and higher logical level that unites the original characterization, accommodates for the different characterizations present in the new figures, and makes both an expression of the range of conditions of the new idea?

> The length multiplied times the width of the original formula expresses the area of the face of the figure. The face of the new figures is a triangle and a circle. We know formulas for the area of a triangle and circle. The idea that unites the different characterizations is area. We can now derive a more inclusive formula for volume:
> $$V = area \times length$$
> The formula for the volume of a prism is then: $V = \frac{1}{2} bhl$
> The formula for the volume of a cylinder is: $V = \pi r^2 l$

6. Next, have students derive the formulas for additional geometric figures, such as the one in figure 4.45, using the higher-level formula of area times length.

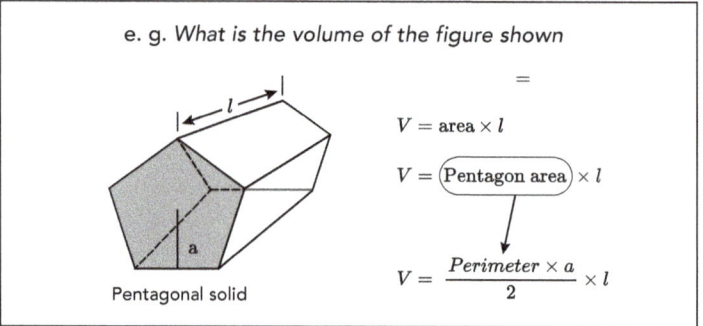

Figure 4.45 Derivation of the formula for the volume of a pentagonal solid

The preceding lesson is relatively simple. The value of teaching the content through the dialectic process is giving students practice using this important problem-solving and knowledge-construction process. Consideration of the foregoing yields the following principle of learning:

> **Principle 16**: When their current inventory of rules fail, learners can construct new rules by discerning the cause of rule failure (missing elements/variables and relationships) and finding a more abstract concept that unites the circumstances that were the basis of the old rule and the new circumstances that resulted in rule failure and makes them the range of conditions of the more abstract concept.

A Note on Creativity

An experience that some college graduates have after spending seventeen years of their life in school preparing to be a teacher, an accountant, or an engineer is hearing a recruiter say that the person they are interested in hiring is someone who can "think out of the box." It took seventeen years for them to learn the box, so it can be frustrating to hear that the recruiter places limited value on their accomplishment. What the recruiter should have said is that they are interested in someone who can use the contents of the box in creative and innovative ways. The contents of the box being the knowledge and skills students learned in school. Creativity and innovation have always been prized, but today's economic circumstances have placed an even greater premium on individuals who demonstrate these skills. Some states, like Oklahoma and Massachusetts, have even included creativity in their state K–12 academic standards.

The theory of knowledge proposed in this book provides some insight into what constitutes creativity. Knowledge of an object is knowledge of its defining attributes and characteristics, the relationship between them, and the relationship between the object and other things in different contexts. Related to objects, creativity involves seeing previously overlooked or deemphasized attributes and characteristics, seeing a different relationship between them, or seeing a different relationship between the object and other items in different contexts. Creativity involves re-perceiving an item and seeing something more or something different. As discussed previously, conscious thought has a subject and, more often than not, a goal. The goal or subject of thought controls the focus of attention and perception toward goal- or subject-relevant attributes and characteristics. It also controls which portions of long-term memory are activated and brought into consciousness. In other words, it imposes a context, and only context-relevant perceptions and ideas enter consciousness. Some researchers refer to this process as cognitive inhibition. Creativity researcher Shelley Carson believes that cognitive disinhibition, or the ability to decrease cognitive filtering and allow more information into conscious awareness, is the key to creativity. As she states,

> We think that reduction in cognitive inhibition allows more material into conscious awareness that can be reprocessed and recombined in novel and original ways, resulting in creative ideas. (Carson 2014, 32)

Carson's theory is supported by the work of other researchers. Thompson-Schill, Ramscar, and Chrysikou (2009) asked research participants to tell them a common and then an unusual use for ordinary items they presented to them while their brains were being scanned. They found that participants who were able to come up with creative and atypical uses for the objects showed minimal activity in the prefrontal cortex areas of the brain associated with cognitive control. They concluded that less filtering of knowledge and experience allowed their research participants to consider a greater variety of possible answers. Some researchers have theorized that creative individuals may be those who are better able to regulate their cognitive control system.

Even if you are not an individual with the capacity to regulate your cognitive control system up or down, you can increase your creativity by invoking different contexts or looking at things in several contexts. An exercise that is done in many creativity workshops and seminars is an example of this process. It involves seeing a lemon or other common object in different contexts. To most people, a lemon is simply a flavoring for food or drink. When they encounter a lemon, this context is immediately invoked, and their lemon thoughts are about how they might use the lemon to add flavor. Now imagine that you are trapped on a deserted island that happens to have a lemon tree. What alternative uses are there for the lemons? What attributes and characteristics of a lemon might be useful in helping you to survive on this island?

The juice of a lemon is acidic. As such, lemon juice can be used as a disinfectant to clean and sanitize. On a deserted island, someone could use it to clean and treat small wounds or to clean and disinfect food preparation and consumption utensils. If meat sources on the island are tough to chew, they can be tenderized as well as flavored and preserved by marinating them for a while in lemon juice. Bugs and insects are repelled by lemon juice, so it could be used as a bug repellent. Being acidic, lemon juice can also be used to dissolve things.

If you squeeze the exterior of the lemon, it will yield an oil. This oil can be used as a lubricant as well as a preservative for wood that protects it from aging and drying. If you dry the peeled skin of the lemon in the sun and then crush it into a powder, the lemon powder can be used in a variety of ways. It could be combined with sea salt produced by evaporating seawater to produce a scrubbing agent or to spice and flavor food like fish. The smell of lemon products is very pleasant, so they can also be used as a deodorant. The skin of the lemon is impermeable, so after removing the pulp, which is edible and can be used as a food item, the lemon can serve as a small drinking cup.

The weight and size of the lemon makes it easy to throw. If no rocks or seashells are immediately available, lemons can be thrown at small varmints to keep them away or thrown at a tree to try to dislodge an out-of-reach item in the tree. A lemon would be less damaging to the item than a rock. The skin of the lemon is also deformable. A pile of hollowed out lemons placed in a carved-out depression could serve as a temporary mattress for sleeping.

The preceding creative process involves recognizing attributes and characteristics of the lemon beyond those considered when thinking about the lemon in the context of a food or drink flavoring. The context of survival on a deserted island helped to create a focus on a more fundamental and wider view of the attributes and characteristics of a lemon. The newly focused-on attributes and characteristics, like acidity, then suggested the various alternative uses for the lemon. New and unique relationships were created between the lemon and other items. It isn't immediately obvious that creating a lemon juice barrier around your stored food will keep ants away.

Changing one's context or perspective can reveal what might have been overlooked, glossed over, taken for granted, or assumed when developing a theory or concept. It can be used as a strategy to expose the limitations of existing concepts and theories and to develop new concepts, theories, and applications.

Knowledge of an action or event consists of knowing the consistent and invariant changes that occur in the attributes and characteristics of objects and the relationship that connects or brings about the change. A creative reinterpretation of actions and events, therefore, involves seeing new or different changes and reexamining and rethinking the nature of the relationship that connects or brings about the change. One way of reexamining the nature of change is to examine it under the lens of the dynamics of a nonlinear system. Because of the newness of nonlinear systems theory and the greater difficulty of analyzing and comprehending nonlinear change, a great deal of theory presumes linear relationships between the elements that are components of the theory. One of the attributes of a nonlinear system is multiple realizability. There are often multiple paths that lead to the same or similar outcome. In addition, it is important to recognize that all things organic enter into nonlinear relationships. Scientific progress has been made by rethinking changes as nonlinear in nature. For example, the dominant model for the progression of cancer was a single path involving specific genetic mutations. The latest research has shown that epigenetic factors arising from gene-context (environment) interactions can lead to multiple pathways. This realization has improved cancer prevention and treatment (Rose, Rouhani, and Fischer 2013).

An underrecognized consequence of using statistical methods in evaluating research is its linearizing effect. Statistics deals with averages. While it is important and valuable to know and explain what happens on "average" and what the average path of change is, analyzing the reasons for individual variability can lead to creative insights. There are often detectable patterns in collective individual variability. Modern "big data" analysis techniques can facilitate finding such patterns.

In nonlinear systems, context (environment) is a critical factor in determining outcomes. As with developing creative insights pertaining to objects, examining the nature of change in different contexts can lead to new insights.

Another path to creative insight involves abstracting something to a higher logical level. As the saying goes, "the devil is in the details." This adage expresses the idea that an overarching theory is often simpler than the details that it summarizes or explains. If you are stuck in the trees, the path out may be to think in terms of the forest. The modern history of the International Business Machines company (IBM) illustrates this process. During the 1970s, IBM dominated the market for digital computers. It supplied almost 70 percent of the mainframe digital computers purchased in the world. Its flagship IBM 360 and 370 computers, nicknamed "Big Blue," set the industry standard for computers. I recall seeing an IBM 370 when I went to work for Exxon in 1971. It was a sight to behold. It occupied half of a floor of the office building in which I worked. Its disk drives seemed to be the size of Volkswagen Beetles and its enormous tape drives looked like many large bookcases placed side by side. The large central processing unit was a flurry of rapidly blinking lights. Little did IBM realize, at the time, that two young engineers working in a garage in California were creating the seeds of their undoing and an end to their dominance. IBM was forced to begin producing personal computers and to compete with upstarts like Apple. In the beginning, they viewed personal computers as an annoyance and a distraction from their main business of producing mainframe computers. To shorten the time to market for their personal computer, IBM contracted with Microsoft to create its operating system and with Intel to create its processor rather than creating proprietary hardware and software. This proved to be their undoing. It paved the way for the rise of competing PCs and the creation of hundreds of billions of dollars of market value outside of IBM. By 1993, IBM was on its knees financially, having lost $16 billion between 1991 and 1993. IBM fired its CEO and replaced him with Louis Gerstner in April 1993. Gerstner undertook numerous strategic changes to restore IBM, but one of the most important was thinking at a higher logical level and understanding that IBM was not, in the abstract, in the mainframe computer–making business but in the information-processing business. He repositioned IBM as a company that could provide integrated information-processing solutions to its customers. IBM's solutions could employ other companies' products as well as their own. Gerstner was able to restore IBM to financial health. To this day, providing integrated technology solutions for corporations, academic institutions, and other customers remains an important line of business for IBM.

Many business historians feel that the motion picture industry in the 1940s and early 1950s was similarly shortsighted. During this era, movies were dominant as the entertainment of choice for most Americans. Because the industry viewed itself as a producer of motion pictures rather than the provider of entertainment, a more abstract idea at a higher logical level, the industry completely missed the opportunities provided by the emergence of television. Conversely, the Mars corporation has always understood that it was not in the candy bar–making business, it is in the sugar-dispensing business. Human beings have a limited daily desire and demand for sugar-based foods. As such, Mars understands that they compete not only with other candy manufacturers but also with soft drink makers, pastry and cake makers, and other producers of sugar-based products. You can see this acknowledgment in their advertising, which extols the unique characteristics and attributes of their product versus competing sugar-based products. If you are hungry and in need of a quick burst of energy, you can take a Snickers bar out of your pocket and eat it. It is not handy to carry a cake or even a can of Coca-Cola in your pocket.

A similar strategy that relies on abstraction to a higher logical level is to abstract your problem to a higher level and see if the problem so abstracted has been addressed and solved in another discipline. Even if the other discipline has not completely solved the problem, it may have solved an aspect of it that can assist you in solving the problem in your discipline. Interdisciplinary thinking has led to some important advances. For example, the key to solving the climate change problem is understanding the ways that individuals and institutions interact with the natural world. Principles from the field of biological ecology, when abstracted, could provide energy producers and distributors insights regarding how to adapt and create equilibrium with the rapidly changing environment they find themselves in. One of the keys to surviving in business is often finding your "ecological niche" in the business space. In general, solving the climate change problem is going to involve knowledge from a variety of disciplines. Note that, in the abstract, this creative strategy also involves changing contexts.

The dialectic process previously discussed is also a creative process. This idea is contained in the adage that "necessity is the mother of invention." Overcoming the failure of existing knowledge to provide solutions through dialectic is another source of innovative solutions.

The easiest way to help students think creatively about content is to have them examine it from a variety of perspectives or in different contexts. For example, having students read original source material that expresses the experiences of an enslaved person, a plantation owner, Confederate and Union soldiers, and politicians from both the North and the South would give students a more creative understanding of the American Civil War than could be obtained by simply reading a textbook.

A Note on Technology

Today's teachers have access to a variety of technologies to assist them in their efforts. How can teachers and administrators decide which of the many available technologies should be employed? Involving students with technology is a learning experience just like any other classroom activity. As such, the value and efficacy of technologies can be evaluated using the principles of learning derived in this book.

An important consideration for educators is the impact of technology on students' motivation and desire to learn. Many offerings available on the internet can be interesting, motivating, entertaining, and well produced. I have used internet video segments to introduce or embellish topics in an effort to stimulate interest, to show relevance and importance, and to generally enhance motivation for learning.

Technology can also increase access. For example, it is not likely that your school budget would be sufficient to take your students to the Louvre in Paris. Not a problem. The Louvre has a wonderful website that not only allows students to view the collection but also offers strong educational features that bring the history, importance, and artistic methods and techniques used to produce different works in their collection to life. If you have a virtual reality headset, they have a virtual reality experience that gives a detailed view of Leonardo da Vinci's painting process and shows how this process brought the *Mona Lisa* to life. The MonaLisa–Color by Number app can also be downloaded on a smart phone. Needless to say, the technology experiences offered here are more engaging and motivating than simply showing slides and lecturing.

During my career in teaching, I had limited luck getting notable figures to visit my classroom in person. With the advent of software like Zoom and Microsoft Teams, I had much better luck getting them to give me twenty to thirty minutes of their time to speak to my students remotely. Hearing from the source or person directly involved added a new dimension to the learning experience.

Not all digital offerings are created equal. My two youngest children attended a high school that used software to teach precalculus. A teacher was available to answer questions, but the software presented the content as well as assigned and graded homework and tests. Both students absolutely detested the experience. They came away thinking mathematics was drudgery and that it certainly wasn't anything they wanted to do for a living. For someone who began their career as an engineer, hearing this from my children was like having a dagger plunged into my heart. After trying the software myself, I had empathy for their sentiments. The program had several pernicious features that converted a subject I love, mathematics, into the twelve labors of Hercules. I can remember nights when my children insisted that I teach the chapter so they could avoid the software. They got to the point where they did not care about learning concepts and theorems, they just wanted to learn the algorithms and procedures for getting answers so they could do well on the homework and the tests. This anecdote is an example of another principle of learning:

Principle 17: You cannot teach someone something they do not want to learn; creating motivation for learning is important.

Technology does not do affect. It doesn't take a personal interest in students. It doesn't offer empathy, understanding, and encouragement. It is imperative that teachers understand how the technology is going to interact with their students. Is it motivating and energizing? Or does it make learning a chore?

As previously discussed, a crucial aspect of helping students construct knowledge is scaffolding their efforts. The key to scaffolding is recognizing what students require to be successful. Where are the shortfalls? What needs to be supported? The current state of artificial intelligence is not sufficient to allow programmed instruction to do this effectively. Some software addresses frequently asked questions or often encountered problems, but this falls short of addressing an individual student's unique needs. Until the artificial intelligence embedded in instructional software advances to the point to where it can adequately address student scaffolding needs, the promise of digital instruction will not be fulfilled.

Another important question pertaining to the use of technology is whether it assists the construction of knowledge or replaces it. I was among the first generation of engineers to receive training in programming digital computers and using them to solve engineering problems. During my first year of work, the local chapter of the Society of Petroleum Engineers invited a retired Shell Oil Company researcher to speak. This person had derived, in the 1930s and 1940s, some of the most important equations used by petroleum engineers. The content of this gentleman's speech was surprising. He contended that digital computers were going to destroy the practice of engineering. He was certain that engineers, such as me, were going to "turn into monkeys that simply fed data into computers and blindly accepted the results." If we did not manually do the calculations, as he had done in his career, we would lose all sense of the reliability and practicality of the results of the computations. The computers would separate us from reality. As a product of the new digital age, I, of course, scoffed at his conclusion and thought of him as simply a luddite trying to throw a monkey wrench into the wheels of progress.

His speech did, however, have an impact on me. Not wanting to turn into a "monkey," I made certain that I knew exactly what algorithms the computer program was employing and what assumptions were embedded within the algorithms. This knowledge would allow me to evaluate the practicality and reliability of the answers the computer was giving me and not to simply become someone putting data into a "black box" and blindly accepting answers. This was possible in the 1970s and 1980s; it would be most difficult to do today given the enormous complexity of many programs. It is still possible to have at least a qualitative understanding of what a program is doing and how it is doing it. The most important questions for educators to ask are how their students are going to interact with the software and whether the software helps students construct knowledge or is simply a "black box" that students get answers from that replaces the need to construct knowledge.

I once viewed a demonstration of presentation software that allowed a fourth grader to put together a multimedia presentation on the Holocaust that would have made Steven Spielberg envious. The result was impressive, but the cognitive activity required to build the presentation was embedded in the program's artificial intelligence software. The child did little more than choose among the software's very poignant suggestions. The program didn't teach students how to create presentations, it created presentations for them. The software would be very handy for a busy business professional, but it was not a learning tool.

Software is available that does support the construction of knowledge. Physics simulations are an example. I viewed a physics simulation of a skateboarder on a half-pipe. The simulation had three meters that the student could view that showed the velocity, the potential energy, and the kinetic energy of the skater as she moved up and down the half-pipe. Students could clearly see how potential energy was at a maximum and velocity was at a minimum at the top of the half-pipe. They could also see how the potential energy was converted into kinetic energy as velocity increased when the skater moved down the half-pipe, reaching a maximum at the bottom. They could then see how this relationship reversed with velocity decreasing and potential energy increasing as the skater moved backed up the half-pipe. The student could then add friction between the wheels of the skateboard and the half-pipe and see how the friction ultimately dissipated the system's energy. The meters had the effect of reducing the requirement for students to hold a lot of information in short-term memory to build the relationships between potential energy, kinetic energy, and velocity. In this way, they aided the knowledge construction process rather than replaced it. This example demonstrates my final principle of learning:

Principle 18: Technology employed in the learning process should aid knowledge construction, not replace it.

Applications

Educator's Toolbox

This final chapter shows how to apply the foregoing to create lessons, audit and improve lesson plans created by others, and create blocks of curriculum. To facilitate the goals of this chapter, it is helpful to create what we can call an *educator's toolbox*. The toolbox contains the following:

- a summary of the theory of knowledge
- a list of relationship types
- the schematics of knowledge structures
- a summary of knowledge-construction methods
- the first principles of learning
- an inventory of activity verbs associated with knowledge-construction methods

Theory of Knowledge Summary

Knowledge of rules—the concepts, principles, theories, and generalizations that represent the brain's organization of experience—consists of the following elements:

Objects/phenomena: abstracted, similar, and invariant attributes and characteristics of a group of entities and the relationship between those attributes and characteristics

Actions: abstracted, similar, and invariant changes in the state of objects/phenomena with time and the relationship that connects or accounts for those changes

Procedures: an invariant sequence of actions, coherent with and the necessary consequences of a rule, that lead from the current state to a desired state

For convenience, let us define an additional element, which is a composite of prceding elements:

Events: combinations of objects involved in actions that are similar and invariant across multiple instantiations

The definitions of meaning/understanding, and teaching are as follows:

Meaning/understanding: creating a relationship that achieves semantic coherence (logical closure) between the items put into relationship

Teaching: helping students create relationships that give meaning to and provide understanding of the content of their experience; helping students connect the dots of experience

The operation of the mind on rule-based knowledge or logic and reason is defined as follows:

Logic/reason: the process of creating relationships between the brain's representations of the items (object/phenomena, actions) put into relationship that achieves coherence (logical closure) between the semantic features of those items put into relationship

As teaching is defined as the process of helping students create relationships that give meaning and provide understanding of the content of a learning experience, the following summarizes the types of relationships that can be created:

Table 5.1 Types of Relationships that Can Be Created

Question answered	Relationship type	Description
1. What?	State of being—existential	(a) Relationships between attributes and characteristics of objects
		(b) Relationships of parts to wholes
		(c) relationships of item to contexts
2. When?	Temporal	Relating points in time
3. Where?	Spatial	Relating positions in space
4. Why?	Causal	Relating causes to effects

continues

Question answered	Relationship type	Description
5. How?	Action nature	Relationships of manner, extent, and degree
6. How much?	Quantitative	Relationships of amount and size
7. Necessary?	Logical	Relationships created through logical connectives: and, or, not, if/then
8. Why care?	Feeling/emotion	(a) Relationships of value—important/unimportant (b) Relationships of valence—positive/negative, good/bad

Figure 5.1 shows schematics of the basic elements of knowledge (object/phenomena and actions).

Table 5.2 Five Fundamental Processes for Constructing Knowledge

Knowledge construction process	Forward path	Backward path
1. Induction	Synthesis	Analysis
2. Deduction	Logic	Abduction/Kantian logic
3. Reflective abstraction	Trial and error	Reflective abstraction
4. Application	Procedural learning	Contextual learning
5. Dialectic	Dialectic process	Dialectic process

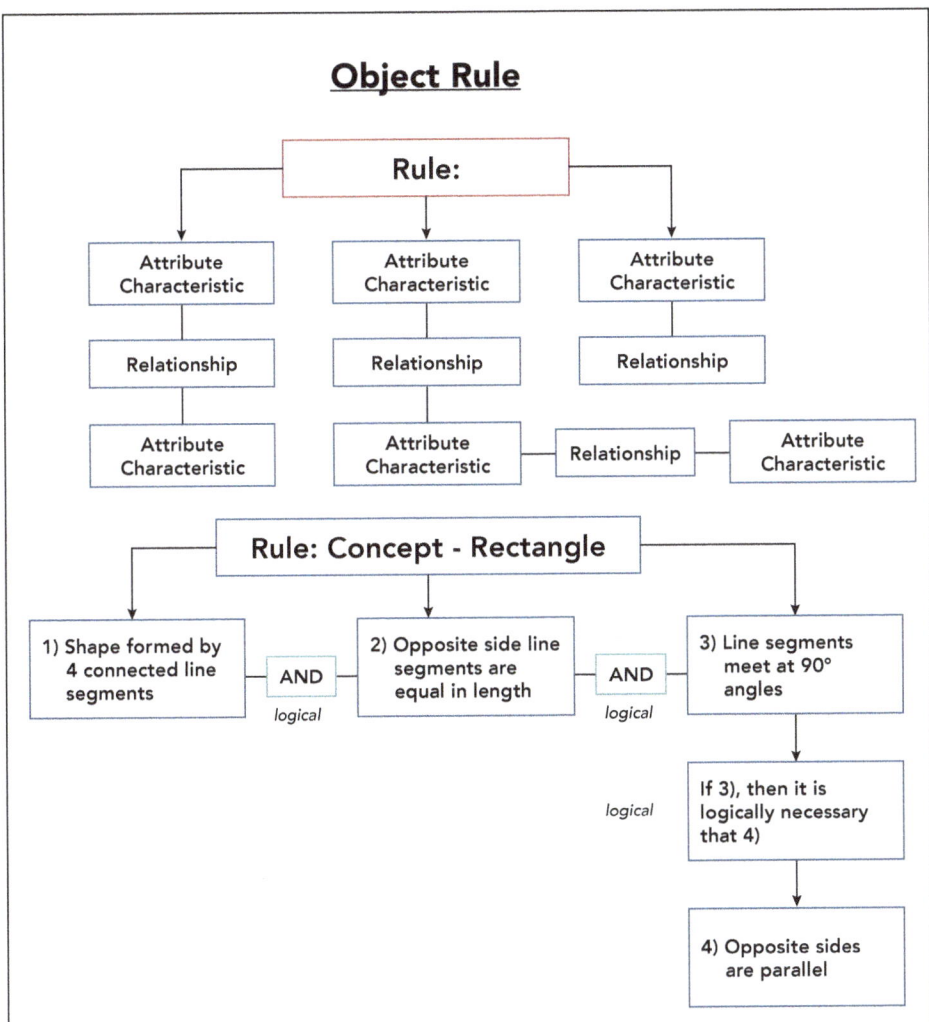

Figure 5.1a
Schematic of the rule structure for objects/phenomena

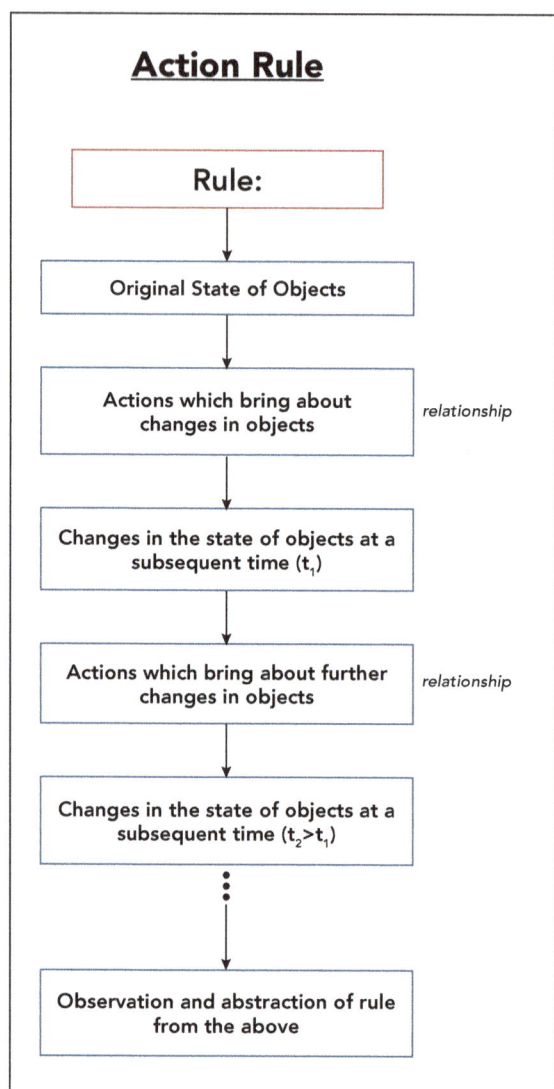

Figure 5.1b
Schematic of the rule structure for action rules

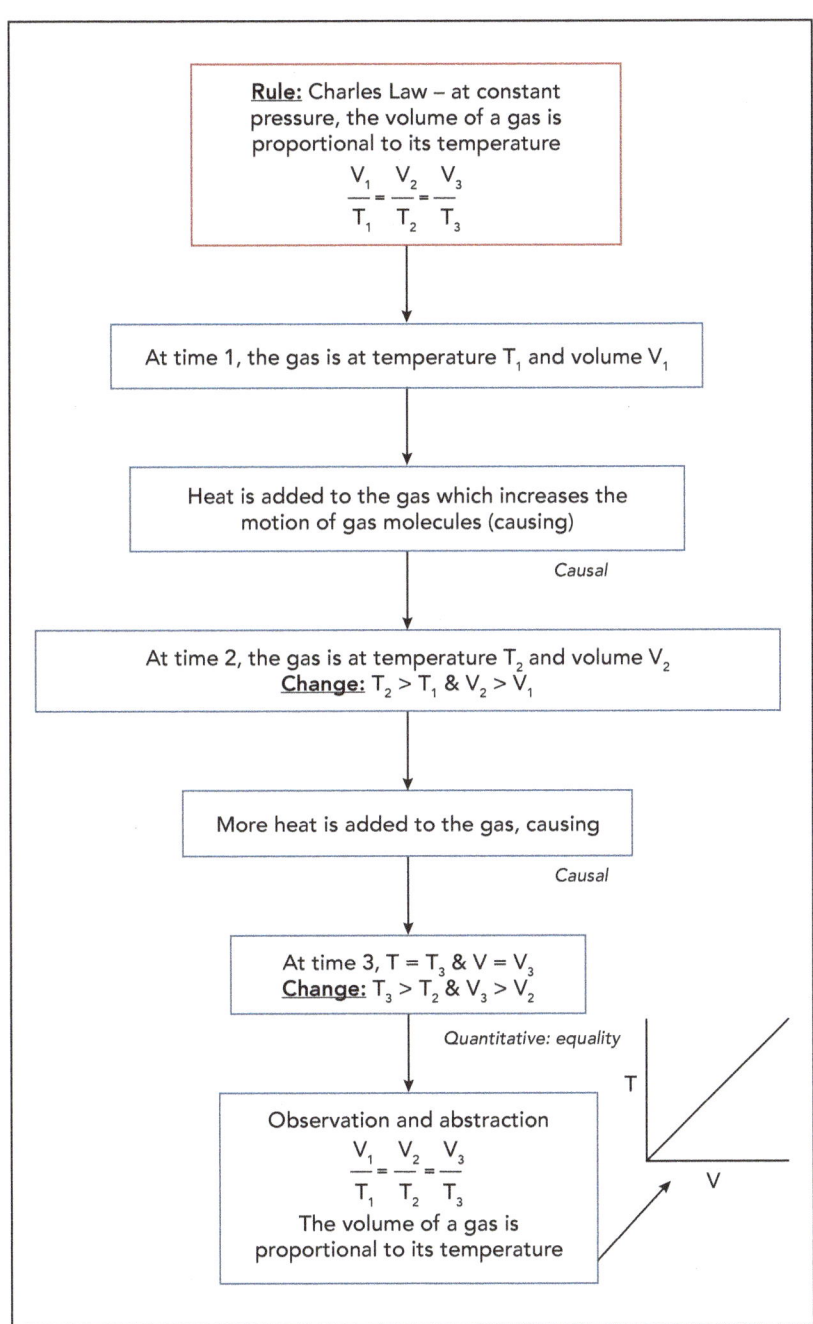

Figure 5.1c
Schematic structure for Charles's Law

First Principles of Learning

General Principles

Principle 1: New knowledge is constructed by the individual, from their experience, and built on the foundation of prior understanding.

Principle 2: Individuals remember and recall best what they understand best. Understanding involves finding a coherent pattern of connection and relationship between the semantic features of objects, actions, and events.

Principle 3: Learning and recall are enhanced by experiences that maximize the number of connections and the strength of the connections between the brain's representations of the semantic features of objects, actions, and events:

- linking new content to prior understandings
- experiencing content in multiple modalities and in multiple contexts
- experiencing deeper, more elaborated processing of content that focuses on meaning and understanding—finding the pattern of organization and order within content
- experiencing repeated exposure to content

Principle 4: Learning is enhanced when instructors augment through scaffolding the human executive processes that learners engage when processing content.

Principle 5: Instructors should be careful not to overload working memory. Learners should be allowed to reach logical closure on a presented concept before proceeding to the next.

Principle 9: Learning experiences and learning representations (graphs, charts, matrices, models, simulations) must clearly, directly, and comprehensively contain all of the necessary elements (attributes, characteristics, changes, and relationships) necessary for the learner to successfully perform the desired knowledge-construction process.

Principle 17: You cannot teach someone something they don't want to learn; creating motivation for learning is important.

Principle 18: Technology used in the learning process should aid knowledge construction, not relace it.

Principles Pertaining to Inductive Learning

Principle 6: To successfully induct an object rule, the learner must "see" and comprehend the attributes and characteristics of a collection of objects that are similar and invariant across the collection and that distinguish the collection from other objects. They must also "see" and comprehend the nature of the relationship that connects those attributes and characteristics.

Principle 7: To successfully induct an action rule, the learner must "see" and comprehend the invariant changes in object attributes and characteristics brought about by actions and the invariant relationship that connects or brings about the changes.

Principle 8: Rules developed in one context or domain can be transferred to another if

- they are abstracted to more general, higher-level rules
- the new domain or context is understood as a circumstance to which the more general, higher-level rules are applicable

Principles Pertaining to Deductive Learning

Principle 10: For a student to successfully perform a deduction, their rule in memory must be sufficiently robust to

- contain all the elements that compose what is known (givens) and what is desired to be known (inference/conclusion)
- contain a coherent relationship between these elements (knowns and unknowns)

Principle 11: For a student to successfully use deduction, they must be able to "see" and connect the concrete elements of the problem or activity to the abstract elements of the rule.

Principle 12: For a student to follow or construct a deductive argument, they must be able to discern the common elements that connect rules in a chain of reasoning.

Principle of Reflective Abstraction

Principle 13: For the learner to successfully create a symbolic rule from a sequence of mental or physical actions requires that they create a relationship involving judgment between the abstracted attributes and characteristics of the consequences or changes brought about by the actions.

Principles of Applied Learning

Principle 14: Successful application of a rule requires that the learner understands what set of mental or physical actions (process/procedure) are the expression of and the coherent and necessary consequences of the rule. A relationship between the rule and procedure must be created.

Principle 15: Learning in context is enhanced if the learner has prior familiarity and understanding of the objects and actions that compose the context.

Principle of Learning through Dialectic Process

Principle 16: When their current inventory of rules fail, learners can construct new rules by discerning the cause of rule failure (missing elements/variables and relationships) and finding a more abstract concept that unites the circumstances that were the basis of the old rule and the new circumstances that resulted in rule failure and makes them the range of conditions of the more abstract concept.

Inventory of Active Verbs Associated with Knowledge-Construction Methods

Inductive Learning

break down

collect, compare, compile, compose, connect, contrast

describe, diagram, differentiate, distinguish

gather, generalize

identify

label, list

map

name

observe, organize, outline

paraphrase, point out

select, sort, summarize

relate

Deductive Learning

conclude, compute

deduce, defend, demonstrate

explain

hypothesize

illustrate, infer

justify

predict

validate

Applied Learning

apply

convert

design, develop, devise

employ

formulate

plan, prepare, produce

solve

transfer

use

Dialectic Process

appraise

critique

differentiate

extend

reconfigure, reformulate, re-relate, resolve

Creating and Designing Lessons and Instructional Experiences

The vast majority of lessons involve teaching rules and procedures for using rules. The first step in designing such a lesson, using the theories developed in this book, is to define the structure of the object/phenomena rule or action rule. A procedure is a sequence of actions; therefore, it has the same structure as an action rule. The schematics at the beginning of the chapter can be used to express and define the structure of the item to be learned. Learning principle 1 states that learning with understanding requires that the student **construct** the desired knowledge on the foundation of prior knowledge and understanding. The schematic expression and definition of the structure of the rule or procedure to be learned show the construction that students will have to make. This schematic will also be used to choose the method of knowledge construction that will be utilized. It is the blueprint of your lesson plan.

The first example that I will use to illustrate the process of lesson design is teaching the procedure for testing a hypothesis using a sample mean. This is the first topic taught in inferential statistics. Inferential statistics is the process of using sample information to make inferences about a population. An example application of the procedure would be an investigator who wants to judge the impact of some action taken on a population. The technical term for the action is a *treatment*. For example, the Centers for Disease Control (CDC) might want to know the impact of vaccinations on the number of people hospitalized after contracting the virus that causes COVID-19. It is often too costly and/or too impractical to collect and evaluate data for an entire population. In such cases, representative random samples are collected, and conclusions are drawn about the state of the population from sample data using the methods of inferential statistics.

The rule that is the basis for the process of using sample means to reach conclusions about a population is the central limit theorem. Shown in figure 5.3 is a schematic that shows the structure of the rule.

It is important that every teacher learns to become a reflective practitioner. This means analyzing how successful your past teaching was. It involves observing students apply the rules and procedures taught, evaluating their performance on formative assessments, and analyzing the questions they have and the assistance they require when utilizing the knowledge. This analysis will provide vital information that can be used to improve and enhance future lessons.

I have never taught a class in statistics. I have taught classes where students had to utilize statistical methods. The questions that students have asked and the assistance that they have required informed me that very few of the students had a conceptual understanding of the central limit theorem and how this theorem facilitates the procedure that connects sample data to population data. Questions I have gotten include the following:

Applications 275

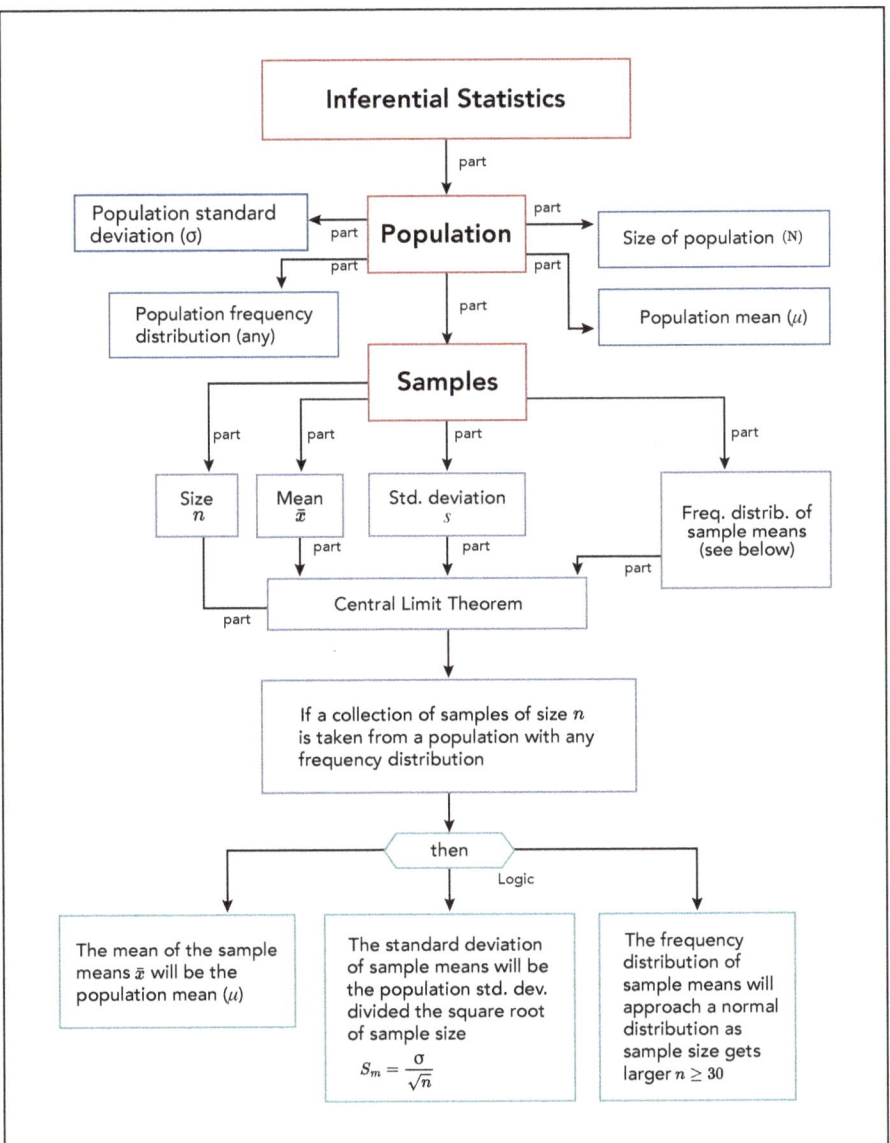

Figure 5.3
Rule structure for the Central Limit Theorem

- Why are we testing the null hypothesis and not directly testing the alternative hypothesis?
- When we tested for the likelihood of something being the case, we used the standard deviation. Why are we now dividing the standard deviation by the square root of the sample size?
- Why does rejecting the null hypothesis automatically mean that the alternative hypothesis is true?
- What does "alpha error" mean?

A conceptual understanding of the central limit theorem provides an answer for each of the preceding questions.

The expression *conceptual level understanding* is frequently used by educators. We can examine the meaning of this term in the context of the proposed theory of knowledge. In the proposed theory, **understanding** is defined as the creation of a relationship that achieves semantic coherence (logical closure) between the items put into relationship. Learning principle 1 states that **knowledge with understanding** must be actively constructed by the student. As the word *theorem* implies, the central limit theorem can be mathematically derived. The derivation, however, involves mathematics beyond what a student in a first statistics course would know. The theorem is, therefore, simply presented to students: for any population with mean μ and standard deviation σ, the distribution of sample means for sample size n will have a mean of μ and standard deviation of $\frac{\sigma}{\sqrt{n}}$ and will approach a normal distribution as n approaches infinity. The theory simply presented becomes what I call *received wisdom*. The implicit communication to the student being "trust me, what I'm presenting is the case and is true." Since received wisdom is not constructed or developed by the student, by necessity, it must be memorized to be retained.

If a concept is actively constructed by the student and becomes part of their symbolic or rule-based knowledge inventory, it is connected through the construction process to other symbols and rules in their mental inventory. Regrettably, this is not the case with memorized knowledge or received wisdom. If the received wisdom is not repeatedly used, it will disappear from memory because of a lack of connection to other items in memory that are periodically and regularly activated. Another problem that frequently occurs is that students, who have a lot of experience with mathematics courses, understand that what will be tested will be an application of the process derived from the theory. This means that learning the procedure or algorithmic steps involved in applying the theory is all that is required to do well on the test. A conceptual understanding of the theory is not required. In addition to the memory retention issues, if knowledge is not conceptual in nature, there is no chance that it can be used outside the context in which it was learned. It does not have the "portability" that conceptual knowledge does. To provide an analogy, suppose I've only experienced one dog in my life. If I experience numerous dogs, I can abstract the similar attributes and characteristics of the dogs in all the dog experiences to form the concept of a dog. With this concept, I can make inferences about dogs or do hypothetical thinking about dogs. If I have only one dog experience, the dog has meaning only in the context in which this experience occurred.

Since deduction is precluded as a knowledge-construction method because of mathematical complexity, I've chosen to teach the theorem using reflective abstraction, which is induction of a rule from a sequence of learner actions. Learning principle 6, pertaining to inductive learning, states that the learner must "see" and comprehend the parts or elements of an inducted rule (for example, attributes/characteristics) and the relationship between them. The parts or elements of the central limit theorem, as shown on the rule schematic, are the size, mean, standard deviation, and nature of the distribution of parameter values of the population and the sample. The student should be familiar with the concept of a frequency distribution as a graph or table that shows the fraction of a population that has a particular parameter value. They should also be familiar with a normal distribution, which is a particular type of frequency distribution with fractional values that peek at the mean of the population values and are distributed symmetrically around the mean in a bell-shaped fashion.

Students at this stage of the course should have mastered mean and standard deviation. They would have had experience using the normal distribution; however, their understanding might still be tentative. Considering this, it would be helpful to have the students do a simple problem that requires the use of a normal distribution.

After a short video intended to generate interest in the lesson topic that perhaps demonstrates the benefits and importance of inferential statistics, students should be presented with a problem to solve individually, such as the following one.

Female height in the United States is normally distributed. The average height of women is 64.5 inches with a standard deviation of 2.5 inches. What percentage of women in the United States are taller than 5'10" (70 inches)?

As the students work on the problem, the teacher should move around the room and offer any assistance the students might require. This will allow the teacher to determine how well the students have mastered the elements that they will need to know to successfully perform the inductive generalization that the lesson requires. Activating and monitoring the strength of required prior knowledge is always good practice.

In the next part of the lesson, the student will construct the central limit theorem using the method of reflective abstraction. This theorem is valid for any type of population distribution. We can, therefore, apply it to populations whose distributions are familiar and well known to students. It will be applied to dice and coins. One die has six possible "parameter values" that it can take on: 1, 2, 3, 4, 5, and 6. Each value is equally likely, so the frequency distribution is uniform, with each value occurring one-sixth of the time. The mean of the values is 3.5, and the standard deviation, or the average amount each value differs from this mean, is 1.7.

The teacher will have the students conduct an experiment. They are going to throw a die a certain number of times (n) and average the numbers that come up. This represents a single sample, and the average is the sample average. They are then going to repeat this process of throwing the die n times some specified number of times. For example, roll the dice twenty-five times ten times, in other words, ten trials (samples) of twenty-five rolls. This will give them ten sample averages. In this example, ten is the number of samples with each sample being of size n = 25. If the teacher is having the students physically roll the dice, they will have to limit the number of times the process is repeated, in the interest of time. I, therefore, recommend using technology to do the dice rolling. For example, you can find dice simulations on the internet that allows students to set the number of roles n and the number of times n rolls is done (number of samples). The applet does the rolling, displays the sample average of the n rolls for each specified number of times, and computes the overall average and standard deviation of the sample averages. Conveniently, the applet also shows a graph of the frequency distribution of the averages for each trial compared with a normal distribution. The teacher's instructions to the students should ask them to take note of how close the distribution of sample averages is to a normal distribution for each value of n roles. The pattern you want them to detect, shown schematically in figure 5.4, is that the larger n gets, the closer the distribution of sample averages gets to a normal distribution.

The teacher then asks the students to fill out the table (table 5.3) to record and process the results of their experiment. I have filled out the table using actual data obtained from the referenced applet.

Table 5.3

Number of trials of n rolls = 1000 (number of samples)	Mean of the sample means	Standard deviation of sample means	Square root of sample size	Calculation
n (size of sample)	$\overline{\overline{X}}$	σ_m	$\sqrt{n}$	$\sigma_m \sqrt{n}$
5	3.491	.770	2.236	1.72
10	3.503	.541	3.162	1.71
15	3.489	.450	3.873	1.74
20	3.493	.388	4.472	1.73
25	3.501	.342	5.000	1.71

The next step is to guide the students through the reflective abstraction process.

1. Compare the mean of the population (3.5) to the mean of the samples for each value of n. (The observation you are looking for is that they are very close to equal.)

2. Now let's express this outcome with symbols:

$$\mu = \overline{\overline{X}}$$

3. Next, compare the multiplication of the square root of the sample size times the

Applications

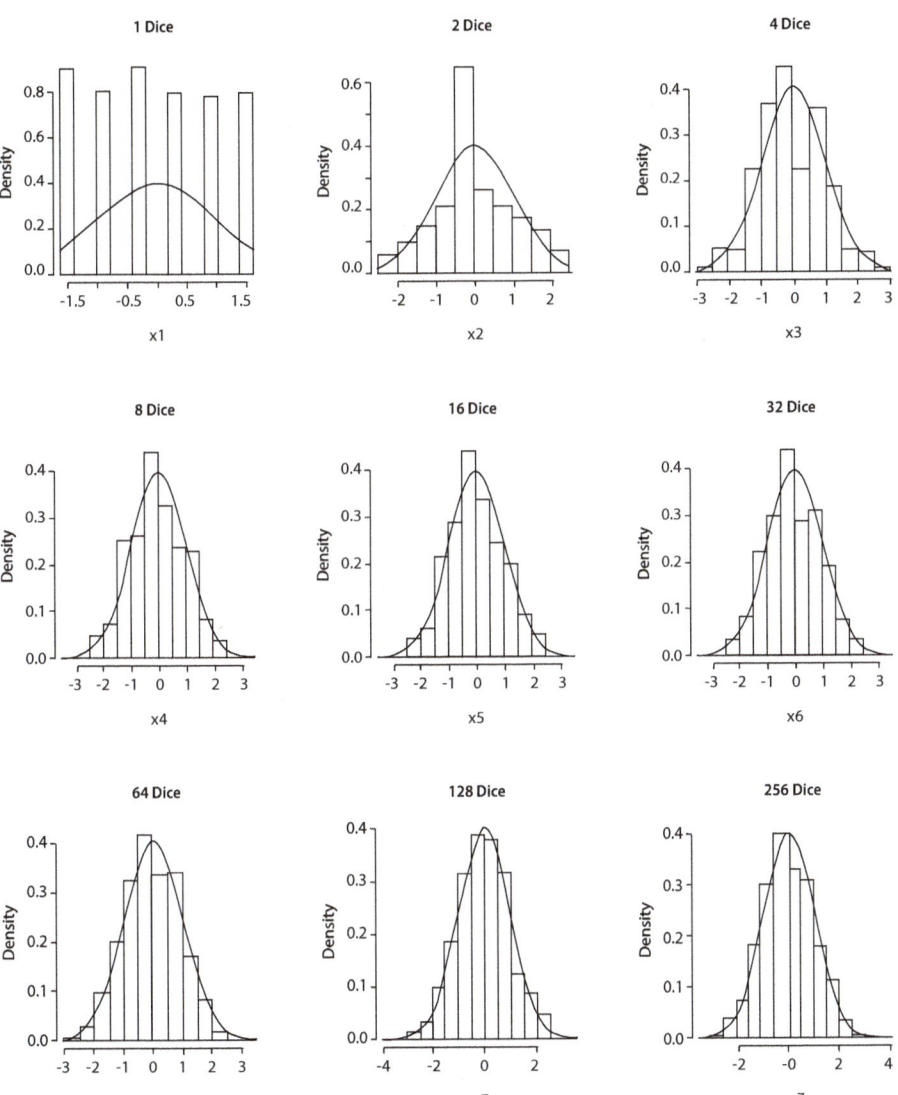

Figure 5.4 Distribution of Sample Means

standard deviation of the sample means obtained for each value of *n* (last column). (The observation that you are looking for is that they are all very close to the population standard deviation of 1.7.)

4. This gives us a relationship between the population standard deviation and the standard deviation of the sample means for each value of n. Let's express this in symbols:

$$\sigma = \sigma_m \sqrt{n} \text{ or }$$
$$\sigma_m = \frac{\sigma}{\sqrt{n}}$$

5. Now let's summarize what the experiment showed:

- The mean of the sample means equals the mean of the population.
- The standard deviation of the sample means equals the population standard deviation divided by the square root of the sample size.
- The larger the sample size *n* gets, the closer the distribution of the sample means gets to a normal distribution. These results express what is known as the central limit theorem.

6. Next, we're going to look at the results of another experiment. This experiment involves tossing coins. For a coin, we can call getting tails "0" and getting heads "1." The mean is then .5 and the standard deviation, or the average of how much each value varies from the mean, is .5. We are not going to flip the coins; we will only process the form that shows the results of the experiment. (The filled-out form is shown in table 5.4.)

7. Does this experiment show the same pattern of relationship between sample and

Table 5.4

Number of trials of n rolls = 1000 (number of samples)	Mean of the sample means	Standard deviation of sample means	Square root of sample size	Calculation
n (size of sample)	$\overline{\overline{X}}$	σ_m	$\sqrt{n}$	$\sigma_m \sqrt{n}$
1	.486	.5051	1	.505
10	.510	.1609	3.162	.509
100	.495	.0506	10	.506

population means and standard deviations that the prior experiment did? Does it conform to the central limit theorem? (Expected answer is yes.)

8. (Now provide the students with some "received wisdom.") As the preceding indicates, the central limit theorem can be applied to any type of population distribution.

What was demonstrated by the preceding exercises was that the central limit theorem applies to coins and dice. Mathematics is required to prove that it necessarily applies to any and all distributions. Given the fact that the students saw it work for two different distributions, they will view the conclusion in step eight as plausible and consistent with their experience.

At this juncture, we can review the learning activities done so far to see if they comply with the principles of learning. Since we identified and checked the necessary prior knowledge for the lesson, and the knowledge of the central limit theorem was "constructed," we have complied with principle 1. During the reflective abstraction lesson, students created a coherent relationship between the elements of the central limit theorem, so principle 2 was complied with. The students had extended engagement with content in an elaborated exercise involved with making connections, so the exercises comply with principle 3. The teacher provided necessary scaffolding, so principle 4 was addressed. Students were not required to hold many items in working memory and the learning representations were complete and sufficient, so principles 4 and 9 were complied with. Hopefully, the introductory video helped with principle 17. The technology employed aided the knowledge-construction process rather than replaced it. At this stage, it is preferable to have students use a printed normal distribution table to be compliant with principle 18. An advanced calculator, like a TI-84, Excel, or a statistical processing program could have been used; however, at this stage of learning, this is too much of a black box that students feed data into and get answers from. Once students have a conceptual understanding, these technologies can be used to save time and create efficiency. Lastly, principle 6 for induction and principle 13 for reflective abstraction guided the design of the lesson and were, therefore, complied with.

The next phase of the lesson is to derive the process for testing a hypothesis from the central limit theorem using deductive learning. The teacher will guide the students through the deduction as follows:

1. The central limit theorem relates the statistics and distribution of sample means drawn from a population to the statistics and distribution of the population.

2. If we are treating a population and expecting a change in some population parameter, like test scores, and we collect a sample from the treated population, does the central limit theorem directly tell us anything about the changed population?

Table 5.5

Relationship parameter	Relationship	Sample means
Size	N	n
Mean	μ	equals $\bar{X}$
Standard deviation	σ	equals $\sigma_m \sqrt{n}$
Distribution	Any	Normal

Desired answer: no. It relates the sample means and the sample standard deviation to the mean and standard deviation of the original population before treatment.

3. Given this, can we use it to determine whether the parameter mean we obtained after the treatment shows a "significant" change resulting from the treatment?

Desired answer: the central limit theorem would tell us the likelihood that the sample mean obtained after treatment could have been obtained from the original population before treatment; in other words, the likelihood that no significant change occurred as a result of the treatment.

4. Let's define what we mean by significant. What the central limit theorem will tell us is what fraction of sample means from the original population have a mean higher or lower than some specific value. We define "significant" by setting a percentage or fraction that the likelihood of the sample mean obtained after treatment must be lower than—a threshold. For example, if we want to be 95 percent certain that a significant change has occurred, we set 5 percent, or the fraction .05, as the threshold for significance. This means there must be only a 5 percent chance or less that the treated sample mean could have been obtained from the original untreated population and indicate that the treatment did not produce a significant change. The threshold selected, for example, the fraction .05, is called the alpha level. If there is, say, only a 2 percent chance that a sample mean after treatment could have been obtained from the untreated population, then we would make the judgment that a significant change has occurred. If there is, say, a 10 percent likelihood, then we would say the change was not statistically significant.

5. Therefore, what we are testing using the central limit theorem is the likelihood that no significant change has occurred. This is called the null hypothesis. It is expressed symbolically as:

$H_o : \mu_H = \mu$ (The mean of the population parameter is the same before and after treatment.)

It could be the case that the treatment makes matters worse, and the parameter moves in the other direction. To account for this, the null hypothesis, when an increase in the parameter value is expected, is expressed as follows:

$H_o : \mu_H \leq \mu$ (The mean of the treated population parameter is less than or equal to the mean of the untreated population parameter.)

When a decrease is expected, it is expressed as:

$H_o : \mu_H \geq \mu$ (The mean of the treated population parameter is greater than or equal to the mean of the untreated population parameter.)

6. If the likelihood that a treated population sample mean is less than the alpha level, .01, .025, .05, etc., then the sample mean is judged to represent a significant change and what is called the *alternative hypothesis* is accepted. This is expressed symbolically as:

$H_a : \mu_H > \mu$ (For an expected increase)

$H_a : \mu_H < \mu$ (For an expected decrease)

$H_a : \mu_H \neq \mu$ (For an expected change in either direction)

After the hypotheses are set up, the procedure for testing them directly follows from the central limit theorem. We determine the likelihood that the sample average obtained from the treated population could have been obtained from the original untreated population. The sample means of the original population are normally distributed. The normal distribution chart is typically expressed in terms of standard deviations. The number of standard deviations a statistic is from the mean is called the *z-score*. We, therefore, need to determine how many standard deviations the treated sample mean is from the original untreated population mean. This is done with the following formula. Recall that the standard deviation for sample means is the population standard deviation divided by the square root of the sample size.

$$z = \frac{\bar{X} - \mu}{\frac{\sigma}{\sqrt{n}}}$$

For example, let's say that we have a company that has SAT test preparation centers scattered across the United States. The company wants to know whether its new instructional strategy is successful in increasing SAT math scores. The national mean and standard deviation of math scores for the SAT test is 500 and 100 respectively. They have randomly selected twenty-five students to evaluate their new strategy. A pretest of the students showed the same mean score and standard deviation as the national averages. After receiving instruction using the new strategy (the treatment), the students averaged 540 on a posttest. Is this a statistically significant improvement? The hypotheses are

$H_o : \mu_H \leq 500$

$H_o : \mu_H > 500$ (For an expected increase)

The z-score for this problem is

$$Z = \frac{540 - 500}{\frac{100}{\sqrt{25}}} = 2.0$$

The next step is to set the certainty level (alpha level). Let's say we want to be 95 percent certain that the average score of 540 indicates a significant improvement. The alpha level is, therefore, .05. We now go to the normal distribution table (table 5.6) to determine the fraction of average scores of twenty-five students drawn from the original untreated population that could be at this level (540, z = 2) or higher.

Table 5.6 Normal distribution table Z versus fraction of samples mean below this Z value

Z	0.00	0.01	0.02	0.03	0.04	0.05	0.06	0.07	0.08	0.09
1.5	0.4332	0.4345	0.4357	0.0437	0.4382	0.4394	0.4406	0.4418	0.4429	0.4441
1.6	0.4452	0.4463	0.4474	0.4484	0.4495	0.4505	0.4515	0.4525	0.4535	0.4545
1.7	0.4554	0.4564	0.4573	0.4582	0.4591	0.4599	0.4608	0.4616	0.4625	0.4633
1.8	0.4641	0.4649	0.4656	0.4664	0.4671	0.4678	0.4686	0.4693	0.4699	0.4706
1.9	0.4713	0.4719	0.4726	0.4732	0.4738	0.4744	0.4750	0.4756	0.4761	0.4767
2.0	0.4772	0.4778	0.4783	0.4788	0.4793	0.4798	0.4803	0.4808	0.4812	0.4817
2.1	0.4821	0.4826	0.4830	0.4834	0.4838	0.4842	0.4846	0.4850	0.4854	0.4857
2.2	0.4861	0.4864	0.4868	0.4871	0.4875	0.4878	0.4881	0.4884	0.4887	0.4890
2.3	0.4893	0.4896	0.4898	0.4901	0.4904	0.4906	0.4909	0.4911	0.4913	0.4916
2.4	0.4918	0.4920	0.4922	0.4925	0.4927	0.4929	0.4931	0.4932	0.4934	0.0436
2.5	0.4938	0.4940	0.4941	0.4943	0.4945	0.4946	0.4948	0.4949	0.4951	0.4952
2.6	0.4953	0.4955	0.4956	0.4957	0.4959	0.4960	0.4961	0.4962	0.4963	0.4964
2.7	0.4965	0.4966	0.4967	0.4968	0.4969	0.4970	0.4971	0.4972	0.4973	0.4974
2.8	0.4974	0.4975	0.4976	0.4977	0.4977	0.4978	0.4979	0.4979	0.4980	0.4981
2.9	0.4981	0.4982	0.4982	0.4983	0.4984	0.4984	0.4985	0.4985	0.4986	0.4986
3.0	0.4987	0.4987	0.4987	0.4988	0.4988	0.4989	0.4989	0.4989	0.4990	0.4990

The chart indicates that .4772 (fraction) of the samples could be between the mean (z = 0) and a z-score of 2.0. Since, in a normal distribution, half of the scores are above the mean and half are below the mean, this means that .5 − .4772 = .0228 (fraction) of the sample means from the original untreated population could have this z-score or higher. In other words, there is only a 2.28 percent possibility that a mean of 540 could have been obtained from a sample of twenty-five students drawn from the original untreated population. Since our alpha level is .05, we reject the null hypothesis and accept the alternative hypothesis. Our conclusion is that we are 95 percent certain that a statistically significant improvement was achieved with the new instructional strategy. Note that there is still a 2.28 percent chance we are wrong.

The preceding illustrates the final step in the hypothesis-testing process: comparing the fraction of samples from the original untreated population that could have attained that score and the z-score of the sample. If the posttest score mean was 530 rather than 540, the preceding process would yield a z-score of 1.5 and a likelihood of obtaining the score from the untreated population of .0668, or 6.68 percent. In this case, since our certainty level is 95 percent, we would accept the null hypothesis and conclude that a statistically significant improvement did not occur. In situations where we are expecting a reduction, since a normal distribution is symmetric about the mean, we can use the same chart and simply consider the z to be negative. For example, a z-score of −1.5 would indicate that 6.68 percent of the samples drawn from the untreated population could have the parameter (i.e., mean) value or lower. To accept the alternative hypothesis, the fraction, or percent, would have to be lower than the alpha level we chose. If we are assessing whether a statistically significant change (either increase or decrease) resulted from a treatment, the same process is used; however, the alpha level is divided by two. The statement would then be that we are 95 percent certain, for example, that a statistically significant change, either positive or negative, occurred.

The final step is to have the student draw a sketch that summarizes the results of the process. Such a sketch is illustrated in figure 5.5.

Figure 5.5 Sketch that summarizes results

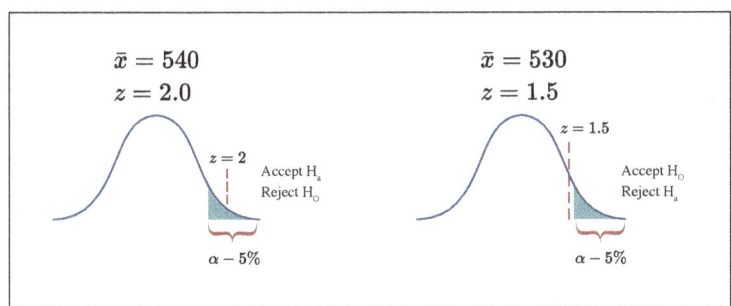

All procedural learning should be followed up with applications. In this case, students should be given a homework assignment that consists of a set of problems that are solved using the procedure. Learning principle 11, for deductive learning, is also applicable to applications. Students must be able to connect the concrete elements of a problem to the abstract elements of a rule. They should be able to move between the concrete and the abstract. For hypothesis-testing problems, this is typically not a concern because the statement of the problem provides a direct explicit connection between the two. The untreated population mean and standard deviation, the sample size and mean, and the alpha level are usually explicitly stated.

The lesson construction process can be summarized and generalized as follows:

1. Select the rule or process to be taught and define it using a rule schematic. This will define the elements, like attribute/characteristics and relationships that constitute the rule or procedure and that will need to be prior knowledge; it will also illustrate the knowledge construction the students will need to undertake—the relationships they will need to make to achieve learning with understanding.
2. Select one of the nine knowledge-construction methods that will be employed in the lesson.
3. Use the principles of learning to design the knowledge-construction process and learning experience. Use both the general principles and the ones specific to the knowledge-construction method.
4. Confirm that your final design conforms to the learning principles.
5. Determine where students may need to be scaffolded to successfully make the required constructions.

For example, in the hypothesis-testing lesson, experience tells me that I may need to scaffold students in setting up the hypotheses and in getting comfortable deciding when to accept and when to reject hypotheses. I, therefore, need to be prepared to scaffold these activities.

The next example shows the design process for a topic from language arts. Novels, movies, and television shows usually tell a story. These stories follow a narrative structure that allows the reader/viewer to understand what is happening and what it all means. The next example lesson design is intended to teach students the basic structure of a story.

This topic has a good hook that can be used to generate interest and motivate learning. As Kahneman (2011) states, the human mind has a special aptitude for the interpretation of stories. Whether you are a teacher, a scientist, or a business executive, the ability to put your message in the form of a story will increase the recipient's comprehension and, interestingly, retention of the communiqué. Catherine Cote (2021), in a Harvard Business School *Business Insights* blog post, states that many companies are including data storytelling as a required skill in analyst job descriptions, and others hire for data storytelling positions to supplement their data analytics teams. The ability to tell a good story that communicates your message is an important and valuable skill to learn.

One of the important considerations in lesson design is thinking about what enduring understanding or lifelong skill you want students to develop through the lesson. A first lesson in story structure is usually taught in the higher elementary grades or in middle school. As such, it is unlikely that many of the students who experience the lesson will become literary scholars. All of them, however, will benefit from the ability to craft a good story from their experience. It is, therefore, more important, at this level, to focus on understanding how to use a story structure to communicate than to analyze and subdivide the events of a complex novel into story structural elements. If the design

Applications **287**

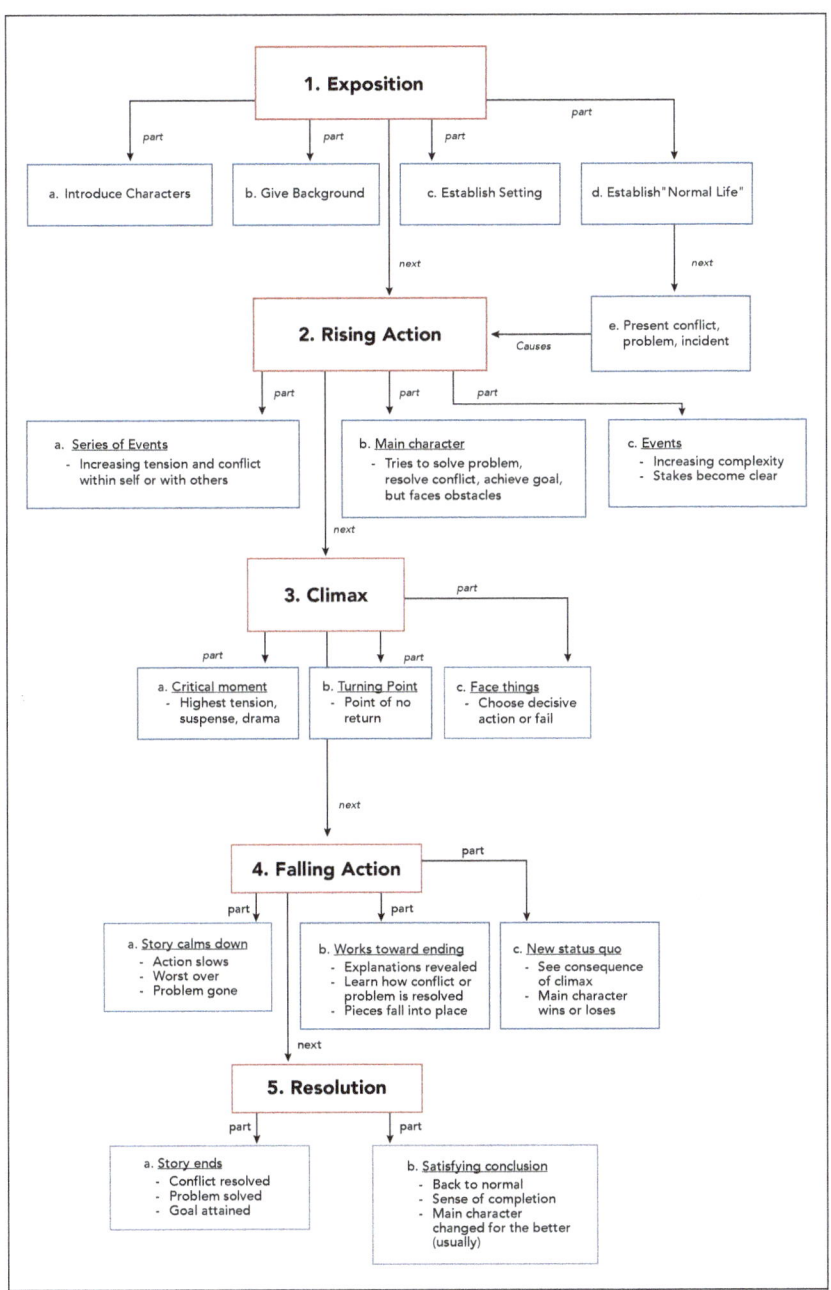

Figure 5.6 Rule structure of a story

was for college students taking a literature class, then the focus would be subdividing a novel into structural elements. These considerations should be one of the guides for lesson construction and design.

With this in mind, we proceed to the first step in lesson design, defining the rules/procedures schematically. The structure of a story is schematically shown in figure 5.6.

The next step in the design process is to select the knowledge-construction method. The structure of a story is not the logically necessary consequence of any set of rules, so deductive methods are not applicable. It is also not the result of the failure or inadequacy of any rule, so dialectic methods can be ruled out. While there will be an application in the lesson, and the application will involve using a procedure, teaching story structure through reflective abstraction or application would be cumbersome, inefficient, and time-consuming. This leaves inductive methods as the only practical choice. Synthesis can be ruled out because it is highly unlikely that students will produce the desired knowledge structure from an examination of example stories. This leaves analysis as the most practical and efficient knowledge-construction method.

The form of analysis that I will employ can be called *guided analysis*. I will present the rule and then demonstrate how an example story exemplifies the rule structure—how it conforms to the rule structure. As with synthesis, unguided analysis, where students would break several stories down into parts, determine the relationship between these parts, and then find the commonalities between the structure of the different stories, would be time-consuming and unlikely to produce the specific knowledge structure I want students to learn.

Learning principle 1 and principle 6 (which is pertinent to inductive learning) require that students have prior knowledge and understanding of the elements (parts) and relationships that will be used in the knowledge-construction process. This is evaluated by reviewing the rule schematic. Student should be familiar with concepts like character, setting, background, "normal life," conflict, problem, goal, and event. They will not know or understand exposition, rising action, climax, falling action, and resolution. Understanding these concepts and their relationship is the goal of the lesson and is to be taught. These concepts will take on meaning as students conduct the knowledge-construction process. The proposed lesson would be structured as follows:

1. Discuss the importance and value of storytelling.
2. Pass out copies of the story structure schematic to students.
3. Have students read "Goldilocks and the Three Bears."
4. Discuss the first element of story structure: exposition. Every story begins with a description of the characters involved in the story, the setting where the story takes place, and other background information that helps the reader better understand the events that take place in the story. A long story, like a novel, can also give the reader some history and reveal character traits, personalities, personal values, and the motivations of the characters in the story. The exposition also establishes the characters' "normal life."

5. Show how the beginning of "Goldilocks and the Three Bears" exemplifies this. In the first part of the story, the author introduces us to the characters, the setting, and the characters' "normal life." We have Goldilocks, a young girl with golden blond hair who lives at the edge of a forest and likes to wander through the forest looking for adventure. We are told she is curious and does not have the "best manners in the forest."

   There are also three bears: a huge Papa Bear, a medium-size Mama Bear, and a small Baby Bear who live in a cottage in the forest. "Normal life" for the bears is for Papa Bear to make a hot pot of porridge for the bears to eat every morning and for the bears to go into the woods to pick berries to put on the porridge, while the porridge cools down enough to eat. "Normal life" for Goldilocks is wandering through the forest in search of adventure.

6. Call attention to the event that creates a problem or conflict. The exposition ends with an event that disrupts normal life by creating a problem or conflict. In our story, the problem is caused by Goldilocks entering the bears' cottage while they are out picking berries, after she looks into the window and doesn't see anyone inside.

7. Explain that what comes next in a story is called "rising action" and describe what happens in this part of the story. After the event that disrupts "normal life," there are a series of events that lead to and set up what is called the "climax," where the problem or conflict comes to a head and must be confronted and resolved. In our story, after Goldilocks enters the cottage, she finds three bowls of porridge and tastes all three. She finds Baby Bear's porridge the most satisfying and eats it all up. She wanders through the house and finds three chairs that she tries out. Again, she finds Baby Bear's chair the most satisfying and starts to bounce in it. This causes the chair to break into pieces. Goldilocks is now tired and goes upstairs to find three beds. The big bed is too hard, the medium-size bed is too soft, but the small bed is just right. She lies down on the small bed and falls asleep. Notice how, as the rising action proceeds, Goldilocks keeps creating a bigger problem. She ate Baby Bear's porridge, broke his chair, and then fell asleep in his bed. This is a characteristic of the rising action part of a story. Each succeeding event increases the tension and makes the problem or conflict worse. The bears arrive back at the house. They discover that someone has been eating their porridge. Baby Bear's porridge was completely gone. They then go to their living room and find that someone has been sitting in their chairs. Baby Bear's chair has been broken into pieces. The story conveys the sense that the bears are getting increasingly angry that someone has entered their house and taken liberties with their possessions. Again, we can see how the rising action steadily increases the tension and intensity of the conflict or problem and sets up the climax.

8. Explain and illustrate with the example the next element of the story structure—the climax. The hungry and angry bears march up the stairs and notice that some one has been sleeping in their beds, and Baby Bear finds Goldilocks fast asleep

in his bed. This leads to the climax, the point in the story where the conflict or problem comes to a head and must be confronted directly. This is the point of no return, where decisive action must be taken. It is the point of highest drama and suspense. In our story, Goldilocks is awakened and sees three hungry, angry bears staring at her. She screams and runs out of the house.

9. Explain and illustrate falling action. Falling action is the point of the story where things slow down. The reader or viewer learns how the conflict or problem is resolved. Explanations are revealed and things fall into place. In the Three Bears story, we are told that Goldilocks never returns to the home of the three bears. She does, however, often daydream about the delicious bowl of porridge, the perfect little chair, and the comfortable bed.

10. Explain and illustrate the final part of a story—the resolution. The resolution to a story ends it. The conflict is resolved, the problem is solved, or the goal is attained. Things get back to normal and the reader or viewer gets a sense of completion. In the story read, the falling action and resolution are short and lumped together. We are given the sense that everyone's life went back to normal. The author tells us that Goldilocks often dreams about and fondly remembers the experience, so we are left to wonder whether she learned the lesson that bad things can happen when you invade someone's privacy and take liberties with their possessions.

11. In the next step of the lesson, you divide the class into pairs and give each pair a short fairytale to read, like "Cinderella," "The Frog Prince," or "Hansel and Gretel." You ask the students to subdivide the assigned story into the five parts shown on the schematic, like you did with the "Goldilocks and the Three Bears" story. You could pass out a form with the five parts listed and blank space provided to make notes and comments or to list events. To help them make the subdivisions, you should give them the following clue. The easiest things to identify in a story are usually the incident, conflict, or problem that disrupts "normal life" and the climax, where things come to a head. The disrupting event is the end of exposition. The rising action is what happens between this point and the climax. What happens after the climax is the falling action and then the resolution.

12. After the pairs have completed their work, call on each pair to present one of the parts of the story. Ask one group to present their exposition, another to present their rising action, and so forth. Alert the students before they begin their evaluation that they need to be prepared to answer two questions: Why did they choose to put particular events and descriptions into the specific story element categories? And how do these events reflect the characteristics listed for the category in the schematic you passed out?

13. As stated previously, an important goal of the lesson is to help students put a message they want to communicate into the form of a story to increase understanding and retention of the message. To facilitate this goal, give students the following writing assignment:

14. Write a story, using the schematic as a guide, of some important event in your life. This should be something that disrupted your normal life, led to a series of other events, and ended in a climax where you had to take decisive action to resolve a problem, end a conflict, or achieve a goal.

I would advise that this assignment be done in a portfolio fashion. Three rounds of submission would be best. The first round is turned in, the teacher makes comments and corrections, the student incorporates the advice and makes changes, and then the revised paper is turned in. This process is repeated a second time, and then the student turns in their final paper. Note that the portfolio strategy follows an apprenticeship model and has the same abstract structure as a master craftsman helping an apprentice create some desired product.

In the instructions for the assignment, the student should be told to first identify the event that altered normal life and to then identify how the matter was finally resolved—the climax. Remind the students that the reader will need background to understand the characters involved, the setting, and what constitutes normal life. This will be their exposition. After describing the catalyst that disrupted normal life, the student should write about the sequence of events that led to the climax. This will be the hardest part for the student. Creating rising action that has an interesting causal chain—increasing tension, drama, and complexity—is what differentiates a writer who sells three hundred books from one whose novel reaches the *New York Times* best seller list. This is an art and not a science. It is a skill that comes with time and practice. This is the segment of the story that will most likely receive the most comments from the teacher. The falling action and resolution should be written next. These story parts also will likely require student revision. Some students will think their story ends with the climax.

The next phase of lesson design is to check whether the lesson conforms to the principles of learning. Conformance to principles 1 and 6 has already been addressed. I believe the combined lesson conforms to principles 2, 3, 9, and 17. It is sufficiently elaborated, involves constructing relationships that create meaning, and has motivating elements. Principle 4 is addressed in the portfolio segment of the assignment. Principle 5 was the driving force behind using children's fairytales, rather than using *Anna Karenina* or *Wuthering Heights* as the examples. Many of the fairytales will be familiar to students and, therefore, already be in long-term memory. There are a limited number of events in each story, so working memory will be taxed less than if the story were longer and more complex. The writing assignment is an application. The portfolio process addresses the connection of rules to actions as is required by principle 14. By making the assignment about a personal experience, principle 15 for applications was addressed. Scaffolding will occur in the portfolio process, so the final step of the design process is addressed.

When I taught lesson design to graduate students, I received comments like, "I teach five different lessons every day, five days a week, for nine months; there is no way I can use a process this complicated for every lesson I teach." Similarly, school principals I have taught comment that they have forty-some teachers who teach five lessons a day. How could I possibly expect them to evaluate lesson plans in this manner? My response is as follows:

1. After you have done this process eight to ten times, the principles of learning and knowledge-construction methods will be part of your long-term memory and second nature to use. You can then simply sketch the rule or procedure elements and relationships and go directly to writing lesson plan steps.

2. I am a pragmatist. If what you're currently doing works, don't "fix it." Use the method when your assessment outcomes are inadequate or disappointing.

Auditing and Improving Existing Lessons

The educator's toolbox can be used to audit and improve existing lessons or lessons created by others. The generalized process is as follows:

1. Read the lesson plan.

2. Identify the rules and/or procedures the lesson is trying to teach.

3. Create a schematic or sketch of the rule or procedure; this will identify the elements, the relationships, and the knowledge construction the students will have to make to create learning with understanding.

4. Go back to the lesson plan and highlight or underline in one color the active verbs that describe learning actions the students are asked to undertake and, in another color, the learning actions the teacher is undertaking.

5. From the statements regarding student actions undertaken, interpret the type of knowledge construction method that the student actions imply or suggest. It is sometimes a case that a lesson has students engage in activities where no knowledge is constructed. In other cases, it is the teacher who is doing all the knowledge construction. Detecting this is the reason for highlighting the teacher action The active verbs section of the educator's toolbox can be used to help identify the knowledge-construction method intended.

6. Use the principles of learning to evaluate the adequacy of the student knowledge-construction activities specified by the lesson.

7. Use the principles of learning to rectify, enhance, and improve the student knowledge-construction.

The first lesson plans that we will evaluate using this method are the first two days of a six-day block of instruction intended to teach eighth-grade students the structure of an atom. These lesson plans were taken from a state curriculum guide available to all school districts within the state. These guides are typically used by smaller school districts whose budgets cannot support curriculum development staffs. The lessons proceed as follows:

1. Show students the video clip: "Powers of 10." (Available on YouTube.)
2. Prior to watching the clip, ask about the levels of structure in the universe.
3. Ask students to recall that atoms are the building blocks of matter. As the clip is shown, discuss the relative change in size as it zooms in to the smaller units.
4. Have students identify at which point they no longer can see objects with only their eyes (surface of the oak leaf).
5. Explain that from this point on they will need to use tools. Have the students list tools we use to magnify objects. These tools allow us to see things as small as one picometer. From this point on, objects are too small to be seen with or without tools. Ask:

    - How did scientists know about the structure of the atom before the electron microscope was invented? (Answers may vary.)
    - What evidence indicates matter is made of atoms? (Answers may vary.)

6. Have students complete a KWL chart about atoms in their journals.
   Ask: What is an atom?

The goal of this segment of the lesson is not a rule that can be constructed; it is a fact that can take the form of a rule and can be used to make an inference or deduction.

> Fact: At different scales or distances from an object, our senses render a different image of what an object is (attributes/characteristics and the relationship between them). Or, in eighth-grade terms, at different scales we experience different things.

"Powers of 10" is an excellent video clip that begins with the depiction of a couple having a picnic in a park in Chicago. It then scopes out in increasing powers of 10 and shows the city of Chicago, the United States, the world, the solar system, the Milky Way galaxy, and collections of galaxies. It then moves in the other direction in decreasing powers of 10 to arrive back to the couple and continues to decrease powers of 10 to show the surface of an oak leaf, cells, molecules, atoms, and then a nucleus with an electron cloud.

As can be seen from the blue-highlighted actions the students are asked to undertake, this lesson does not actively involve students in constructing knowledge. They are asked to recall and list prior knowledge, identify a visual observation, and complete a chart that, at this stage, simply documents prior knowledge. The "Powers of 10" video clip is both clear and dramatic in presenting an experience that would allow students to implicitly induct the fact that at different scales we experience a different reality and, therefore, get a different impression of what things are—what they are made of and how they are constituted. The problem with implicit inductions and deductions that students may make when experiencing something like a video is that they are invisible to the teacher and there is no way of knowing whether the students are, in fact, making the desired inductions and deductions that the teacher desires.

The teacher asks the students four questions that they will not have the answer to regarding (1) the levels of structure in the universe, (2) how scientists knew about the structure of the atom before the electron microscope, (3) what evidence indicates matter is made of atoms, and (4) what an atom is. The purpose of the six days of instruction is to provide answers to these questions. Why ask them at this stage of instruction? It is common practice in science education to ask these types of questions up front. The idea is that they will generate curiosity and interest in finding answers to the questions. I think this is bad practice. I believe asking these types of questions up front makes students feel dumb and inadequate. Humans naturally presume that if someone asks them a question, they expect them to have the answer to their question. Questions like this also make science seem like some mysterious and extremely difficult enterprise. If you remember the lesson in the previous chapter that teaches the structure of the atom, you will recall that the answer to what evidence indicates matter is made up of atoms is quite complex. An eighth grader would not have a clue what the answer to this question is.

I think the "Powers of 10" video is a good start. I would eliminate the rest of the lesson steps and replace them with an explicit inductive generalization activity conducted in a question-and-answer format. I would ask the students to think of being in a spaceship that is entering the solar system and flying toward the Earth. I would then replay the segment of the "Powers of 10" video that depicts the solar system and freeze it at the level where the Earth is shown from space. I would then ask the following questions:

1. This is the world you live in. At this scale, what do you see the Earth to be? What attributes and characteristics can you perceive? (Expected answer: "A big blue sphere.") Next, I would forward the video and freeze it at the level where some of the physical features of the Earth were visible. I would then ask the following question:

2. Now at this scale, what does the Earth look like to you? What features of the Earth can you see? (Expected answer: "I can see mountains, valleys, plains, rivers, lakes, oceans, and cities.")

I would do one more iteration at a closer scale and then guide students toward an inductive generalization.

3. Next iteration.

4. Inductive generalization: So, let's summarize what we just experienced. We can say that at different scales we experience different _____ [Desired answer: "Things."]

5. Restate the generalization in the way you want students to think of it. So, what something is—its parts and the relationship between those parts—changes when we experience that something at different scales.

6. Now play the video down to the scale of the electron cloud. This will reinforce the generalization that was just made. Stop the video at this level and make the following comment:

"Scientists who developed our understanding of atoms could not view or experience them at this scale. We will see in the next exercise how they came to an understanding of the structure of an atom."

The next segment of the lesson supplied by the state proceeds as follows:

1. Create a series of sealed boxes with an object inside, like a smaller box, a baseball, a golf ball, or a box of pins.
2. Divide the class into groups of four students and distribute a box to each group.
3. Explain the activity to students and have them record observations in their journals.
4. Monitor each group and provide feedback.
5. Check students' observations and conclusions about the object's shape and size.
6. Accept all reasonable answers.
7. Ask students what tools might make their task easier.

    The rule that this lesson intends to teach is nothing less than the principle of abduction, or Kantian logic: What must be the case for outcomes or produced phenomena to be such as they are?

    When something cannot be directly observed, we can hypothesize about its nature by evaluating the outcomes and phenomena that it produces and then ask the question: What must be the nature of the thing that produced these specific results?

    As with the segment before, the students are not actively and explicitly constructing this knowledge. The method of knowledge construction here is reflective abstraction. The students are expected to implicitly generalize and induct the actions they are undertaking into the preceding rule. This is not an uncommon attribute of many lesson plans. Students are engaged in activities and the assumption is they will somehow implicitly perform the desired induction, deduction, or reflective abstraction to arrive at the rule that is the goal of the lesson. In this segment, the only explicit learning activities are manipulating the box, recording observations, and guessing what's in the box. I doubt that they will reflectively abstract the desired rule from this activity. They certainly will not gain an appreciation of the power and general applicability of the rule. The preceding activity violates principle 13 for reflective abstraction. To conform to this rule, the concrete actions and the relationship between them would have to be abstracted and connected. I would replace the seven steps listed earlier with the following deductive learning (abduction) activity:

1. We are going to play a game called "What is it?" I'm going to give a member of the class a card with clues written on it. They're going to give you one clue at a time and ask you to guess what the item is.

   The clues will describe what the item can do or what outcome it can produce. [Example cards]

What is it? Lightning	**What is it? A boat**
1. It produces a loud noise.	1. It can allow people to get in it.
2. It can create damage.	2. It can allow people to sit in it.
3. It produces a flash of light.	3. It moves.
4. It only happens on cloudy, rainy days.	4. It can take people from Miami to Jamaica.
	5. It moves slower than an automobile.

2. Lead students through the abstraction of the concrete elements and relationships to generate the rule.

   - Notice that we got a series of clues about what the item could do or the outcomes it could produce. You kept those clues in memory to see what they added up to. In the case of lightning, adding up the first three clues was not enough to decide what it was. It could, for example, have been lightning or a bomb. It was the final clue that enabled you to decide between these two choices. The same was true for the boat, it wasn't clear until the last clue.

   - The general process you undertook can be summarized as evaluating the outcomes or phenomena that something produces and asking yourself the question, "What must be the nature of the thing that produced these specific outcomes or phenomena?" In other words, What is it?

3. Explicitly relate this rule back to the previous exercise. Remember, we said that the scientists who developed our understanding of atoms could not view and experience them at their small scale. How they developed their understanding was by looking at the phenomena and outcomes that atoms produced and asking themselves the question, "What must be the nature of atoms, their attributes, their characteristics, and the relationship between them to produce the results we are experiencing in our experiments?"

This process is called *abduction*. It is a very important form of reasoning. The next day's class, as described in the state curriculum, proceeds as follows:

1. Using reference materials, have groups research various atomic models (Bohr, Rutherford, Thomson, Dalton, and de Broglie and Schrödinger).
2. Have students create a semantic feature map in their journals. As each group discusses their models, the class will fill in the map.

	Protons	Neutrons	Electrons	Distinct nucleus	Electron cloud
Bohr					
Rutherford					
Dalton					
Thomson					
De Broglie and Schrödinger					

3. Discuss with the class the features of the parts of the atom. Ask:

   a. What are the subatomic parts of an atom? (protons, neutrons, and electrons)

   b. Where are the protons located in an atom? (nucleus)

   c. What electric charge do protons have? (positive)

   d. Where are the neutrons located in an atom? (nucleus)

   e. What electrical charge do neutrons have? (neutral)

   f. Where are the electrons located in an atom? (outside)

   g. What electrical charge do electrons have? (negative)

The rule schematic for this lesson is shown in figure 5.7.

Step one of this lesson requires groups of students to research the five different models of the atom that evolved in time and to make a presentation of their findings to the class. Asking students to conduct research and create a presentation of their findings can be a rich learning experience. Creating a presentation requires the student to relate, organize, and articulate the contents of a topic in a coherent and comprehensible fashion. As has been discussed, creating coherent semantic relationships is the heart of learning with understanding. However, asking middle school students to conduct unguided research is a bad idea. Students should have been given research guides that

Figure 5.7 Rule structure for an atom

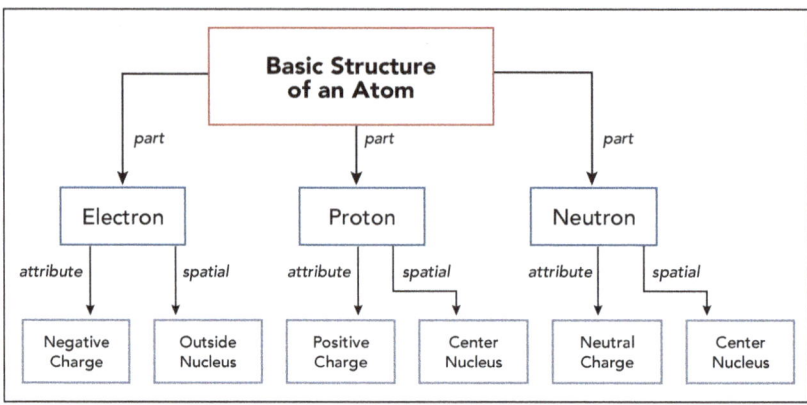

define the goals of the research and direct them to age-appropriate materials. For many of today's middle school students, the phrase "research this" is synonymous with "Google this." Most of the listings on Google will not be comprehensible to the students. This is particularly true for the quantum mechanical de Broglie/Schrödinger model.

As the rule schematic shows, the goals of the lesson are fairly modest. They are the three basic components of an atom, their relative location with respect to each other, and their electrical charge. It is important to the goals of the lesson that the students present the parts, relative location, and charge valence that their researched model includes and demonstrates. The students, therefore, should have been given a presentation guide that tells them what you expect them to discuss regarding the model they researched.

More than anything, the lesson structure proposed is a missed opportunity. The history of the development of models of the atom is a rich story that demonstrates how science works and how scientific progress is made with time and the discovery of new experimental evidence that must be accounted for. An entire class was spent developing the concept that things are different at different scales and the concept of abduction or Kantian logic. These concepts are never again used or referred to in all six days of instruction. Good curriculum ties covered concepts together. Those covered earlier become the building blocks for increasingly complex and comprehensive concepts and principles that follow. This practice was not in evidence in this block of instruction. Chapter 4 illustrates how the history of the development of models of the atom can be taught through abduction/Kantian logic. Teaching the topic through the dialectic method would also be a good choice.

The last two examples involved completely redoing the lessons. If you are in an educational leadership role and reviewing a great many lesson plans, you simply do not have the time to redo a great number of them. Those that are passable may only require a quick fix. That will be the approach taken with the next lesson plan. It comes from an educational website and has the goal of teaching fifth graders how to draw inferences from reading material. It proceeds as follows:

- We all draw inferences. We do it every day when we are listening to someone speaking, when we are reading, and when we are watching other people.
- An inference is a conclusion that we make using things that we already know (prior knowledge) and new information.
- An example of an inference is a mother giving her child blueberries to try. The child puts the blueberry in its mouth, chews it, and then spits it out. The mother can infer that the child does not like the blueberry.
- Sometimes when we are reading, the text does not tell us exactly what we need to know. When that happens, we need to draw an inference.
- A good strategy for drawing inferences is to think, "It says, I know, so . . ."
- When you do this, it helps you to think about what the text is telling you and what you already know. You are then able to draw in inference.
- Now, you're going to read a few paragraphs from a book. After you have finished reading, there are questions for you to answer. Remember to use the inference strategy and remember how to quote a text.
- Does anyone have any questions?

Hatchet
by Gary Paulson

He could not at first leave the fire. It was so precious to him, so close and sweet a thing the yellow and red flames brightening the dark interior of the shelter, the happy crackle of the dry wood as it burned, that he could not leave it. He went to the trees and brought in as many dead limbs as he could chop off and carry and when he had a large pile of them, he sat near the fire—though it was getting into the warm middle of the day, and he was hot—and broke them in small pieces and fed the fire.

I will not let you go out, he said to himself, to the flames—not ever. And so he sat through a long part of the day, keeping the flames even, eating from his stock of raspberries, leaving to drink from the lake when he was thirsty. In the afternoon, toward evening, with his fire-smoked beard and his skin red from the heat, he finally began to think ahead to what he needed to do.

He would need a large woodpile to get through the night. It would be almost impossible to find wood in the dark, so he had to have it all in and cut and stacked before the sun went down. Brian made certain the fire was banked with new wood, then went out of the shelter and searched for a good fuel supply. Up the hill from the campsite the same windstorm that left him a place to land the plane—had that only been three, four days ago?—Had dropped three large white pines across each other. They were dead now, dry and filled with weathered dried dead limbs.

Questions:

1. How do you think Brian felt because of the fire?

2. Which sentence was most useful in helping you figure that out?

   a. "I will not let you go out, he said to himself, to the flames—not ever."

   b. "He would need a large woodpile to get through the night."

3. Why was that sentence useful in drawing an inference about how Brian felt?

4. Find and quote a sentence that helps you understand how Brian got to where he is.

In the mini-lecture, the teacher makes the point that the reading material doesn't always tell the reader exactly (explicitly) what they need to know. When this happens, readers need to make an inference. She then gives them some "received wisdom" in the form of a simple procedure that involves thinking to oneself, "It says, I know, so . . ." Students are then given a few paragraphs to read and some questions to answer about the paragraphs. The intended knowledge-construction method is application. It is hoped that students will learn the procedure by applying it to obtain answers to the questions.

Let's examine the lesson by placing ourselves in the position of the student answering the questions. What we need to know that the text doesn't exactly tell us is "how Brian felt because of the fire." The second question provides a clue as to the sentence most helpful in answering this question. The procedure the student would undertake is, "It says, 'I will not let you go out, he said to himself, to the flames— not ever,' I know _____, so . . ." It appears that the student will need a theory (rule) that explains how a person who is stranded in an unknown environment reacts to objects that have familiarity and usefulness and can be controlled by the person. These object attributes tend to lessen anxiety and the sense of helplessness that results from the situation that Brian is in. Alternatively, knowledge of why humans have historically taken comfort and solace in campfires and fireplaces that provide warmth, light, and protection from animals that tend to avoid fires might also be helpful. What is the likelihood that a fifth grader would have such knowledge? I think there is little or no likelihood. The lesson violates learning principle 1, the requirement for having the prior knowledge necessary for the knowledge-construction process.

The goal of the lesson is teaching inference not literary interpretation. In agreement with principle 15 for applied learning, a quick fix is to give students reading material over a topic they are more familiar with and have a lot more "I knows" in their mental inventory. Getting students proficient at making inferences will require considerably more instruction than this simple lesson provides. As promised, I will not redesign the lesson completely. Another quick fix to strengthen the lesson would be to modify the procedure for making an inference as follows:

- Sometimes when we are reading, the text does not tell us exactly what we need to know. When this happens, we need to draw an inference.
- A good strategy for making inferences is to ask yourself the following questions:
  » What do I want to know?
  » What information am I given?
  » What knowledge do I have that connects and relates what I am given to what I want to know?
- For example, we talked about the mother who gave her child blueberries to eat, and the child spit them out. We are given the fact that the child spit the blueberries out. We want to know why? We know that children spit out foods they don't like, so we can **infer** that the child did not like the blueberries. Notice how our knowledge connected the information given to what we wanted to know.
- Now let's practice using this procedure on some inference questions:
  » **Given** information: The rowboat sank, and the boy swam to shore.
  » **Want to know**: Why did the rowboat sink?
  » **Knowledge**: Boats with holes in them sink.
  » **Inference**: There must've been a hole in the boat.

The "patched" lesson now better conforms to the principles of learning. The students are actively involved in the learning process, and the engagement with the procedures are more extended and elaborated. After practicing on a few inference exercises, the students are now more likely to reflectively abstract the rule and successfully use it on a set of paragraphs that cover a topic they are more familiar with and have better knowledge of.

Curriculum Design

One of the most popular and widely used curriculum development frameworks today is the Understanding by Design framework developed by Grant Wiggins and Jay McTighe (2005). This framework is supported by and available through the Association for Supervision and Curriculum Development (ASCD).

Understanding by Design's popularity stems from several important features of the framework. First, as its name implies, it is focused on deep learning that produces conceptual-level understandings. It strives to instill enduring conceptual structures with lasting value. It incorporates best practice findings from educational research and other related fields. It is also the curriculum development framework that is the most coherent with the theories and practices that are developed in this book. As such, it was the framework I typically taught my students.

Another feature that has made it popular is the reversal of the order of development of curriculum. Traditional frameworks begin with a specification and definition of learning goals and objectives, proceed to lesson development, and then to assessment. In Wiggins and McTighe's framework, the order is defining and developing learning goals and objectives, developing assessments that will confirm that those goals have been met, and then using the assessments to guide lesson design. The order is reversed. Today's public school educators live in an environment driven by state accountability tests. Wiggins and McTighe's approach is, therefore, more compatible with this type of environment than are traditional curriculum-development frameworks.

I will not attempt to teach the Learning by Design framework in this book. I will only sketch its elements and focus on how the theories and practices developed in this book can be made compatible with this framework.

Stage I of their curriculum development process is to identify the desired results—the educational goals and objectives. What should students know and be able to do? Educational goals and objectives can come from a variety of sources, like institutional needs and requirements, societal demands and goals for education, and regulatory agency specifications. For public schools in the United States, they come from the state. They can be the Common Core State Standards adopted by forty-one states or the standards developed independently by the other nine states. Private K–12 schools in the United States develop educational goals and objectives based on the skills and knowledge they believe are required for success in colleges and universities. University professors are free to set their own learning goals, as are institutional and corporate trainers. At this level, professional accreditation requirements often play a role; for example, the passing the Bar exam to practice law or fulfilling CPA-certification requirements to be an accountant.

The first step of Wiggins and McTighe's process is the conversion of these broad standards and specifications into what they call Big Ideas, Essential Questions, and Enduring Understandings. Big Ideas are the essential abstract concepts that serve to organize, summarize, and make coherent the collection of discrete knowledge and skill elements that compose a topic. In their words, the Big Ideas are the conceptual Velcro that connects these elements into a larger intellectual framework. They help to develop a coherent curriculum and are abstract enough to transfer to other contexts.

Wiggins and McTighe state that every academic field can be defined by the Essential Questions it attempts to answer. These Essential Questions also serve to frame and organize content. They are an interrogation of content that leads students to make connections and inferences that promote learning with understanding. They are intended to push students toward the essence or heart of the topic. They can also be used to direct inquiry and other forms of deductive learning.

Big Ideas and Essential Questions are brought together with the expression of Enduring Understandings. These are complete sentences that express a proposition of significance regarding the topic. They are answers to Essential Questions and what the teacher wants students to know about the Big Ideas. The Enduring Understandings must be constructed by students. They are not received wisdom. As previously discussed, if they are to "endure" in memory, they must be acquired through an active knowledge-construction process. As with Big Ideas and Essential Questions, a goal of Enduring Understandings is summarization of important strategic principles and skills with transferability beyond the context in which the Understandings were learned.

In the previous chapter, I presented a detailed discussion of the Gilded Age of American history. Part of my purpose was to provide background and context for what follows. The following is an example of a proposed set of Big Ideas, Essential Questions, and Enduring Understandings that could be used to develop curriculum to teach this segment of American history.

Big Ideas

- Impact of technological innovation
    - » on business
    - » on society
- Competition versus monopoly
    - » income/wealth distribution
    - » working and living conditions
- Impact of government action or inaction
    - » on business activity
    - » on the social and economic conditions of citizens
- Democracy versus oligarchy
    - » preserving democracy
    - » corruption
- Social instability
    - » sources
    - » manifestations (unions, strikes, violence)
- Forces for change

- » strength in numbers/balance of power
- » free press—journalism
- » religious, academic, and social leaders
- Impact of ideologies—social philosophies
  - » Social Darwinism
  - » laissez-faire
  - » the individual versus the collective
- Social evolution versus revolution (dialectic versus chaos)

Essential Questions

- What changes in economic activity and the life circumstances of citizens did technological innovation bring about?
- What conditions allowed monopolies to form?
- What benefits did monopolies bring about and what societal problems did they create?
- How did government impact or not impact business activity?
- How were industrialists able to corrupt and control government?
- How did the emergence of monopolies and other factors lead to the prevalent dismal living and working conditions and the social instabilities that these conditions brought about?
- What turned the tide against the industrialists and began to bring about change?
- What impact did prevailing ideologies and worldviews have in creating or supporting the conditions prevalent in the Gilded Age?
- How and why did these ideologies and worldviews change?

Enduring Understandings (Topical)

1. Technological innovation drove a substantial increase in new business activity and materially changed both the nature of business and the lives of the citizenry.
2. Because of the lack of government involvement, and with support from prevailing social philosophies and ideologies, a small group of industrialists were able to create monopolies and corrupt governments.
3. This resulted in the creation of large fortunes for these industrialists but also resulted in low wages, dismal living and social conditions, and an end to prospects

for upward mobility for most Americans.

4. Unstable social, economic, and political conditions resulted, and the status quo could no longer continue.
5. A change in the balance of power resulted in a dialectic process that culminated in peaceful, constructive change that preserved democracy and the American economic system and averted revolution and large-scale violence.

Enduring Understandings (Abstract)

1. Technological innovation drives substantial changes in the lives of citizens and significant changes in business activity.
2. Lack of government response to change and ideologies and social philosophies that advantage one group over another can lead to the dominance of the few over the many.
3. This can lead to social instabilities and conditions that many find no longer tolerable.
4. At an instability, collaborative and constructive change must occur or the system will become chaotic in nature.
5. Change that preserves what was good in the old system but accommodates new circumstances and rectifies the problems of the old system can occur.

Wiggins and McTighe recommend that the Big Ideas, Essential Questions, and Enduring Understandings be abstract, overarching, and general enough to be transferable and applicable to contexts outside the context in which they were learned. Above, I have shown both topical Enduring Understandings that connect directly to the content and more abstract and overarching Understandings. The more abstract Enduring Understandings can create a bit of a dilemma. If they are overly abstract, the students may have difficulty understanding how they connect back to and summarize the concrete content that they experienced. Each abstract rule expressed in these three categories will have to be constructed by the student to achieve learning with understanding and facilitate consolidation into long-term memory, and thus be enduring.

Topical Enduring Understanding 2 states that "because of a lack of government regulation and involvement, and with support from prevailing social philosophies and ideologies, a small group of industrialists were able to create monopolies and corrupt governments." The statement is supported by and directly connected to the content students will experience. The more abstract version of this Enduring Understanding is "lack of government response to change and ideologies/social philosophies that advantage one group over another can lead to the dominance of the few over the many." The astute student may realize that I have given them only one example where this occurred. I am generalizing a sample of one into a very significant conclusion. Other students may struggle to understand how the statement directly connects to and generalizes what they have learned, given its high level of abstraction. As a history teacher, I would know that there are other historic periods that demonstrate and justify the statement presented. Students, however, would have to experience an explicit inductive generalization process where conditions in different historic periods were abstracted and generalized into the statement for it to be adequately justified and understood as a rule with general applicability. This is something to keep in mind when developing Enduring Understandings statements. Also, not every topic taught can be generalized into universal, multicontext applicable rules. For these topics, the Big Ideas, Essential Questions, and Enduring Understandings can be only topical and a direct summarization of content.

Stage II of Wiggins and McTighe's curriculum development process is to create the assessments where students will demonstrate their knowledge of the Big Ideas, the answers to the Essential Questions, and their attainment of the Enduring Understandings. There are three major questions an educator needs to answer when designing an assessment (Wiggins and McTighe 2005):

1. What kind of evidence will you need to make the judgment that your learning goals have been achieved?

2. What attributes and characteristics in students' assessment performance should you examine to determine the extent to which your goals were met? (This lead to the development of criteria, rubrics, and exemplars of desired performance.)

3. Are your assessments a valid and reliable way of judging student knowledge and skill?

The secret of assessment is that demonstration of knowledge involves the exact same processes that creation of knowledge involves: induction, deduction, reflective abstraction, application, and dialectic. Reflective abstraction and dialectic are rarely used, but induction, deduction, and application are common. The following is a series of examples that demonstrate this point. In addition to these knowledge demonstration processes, some test questions simply require recall of facts, or what we might call descriptive or definitional knowledge. This type of knowledge is typically tested through true or false and fill-in-the-blank types of questions as shown here:

True or false: A prepositional phrase functions like a part of speech.   T   F

Fill in the blank: _____ are words that modify or describe nouns.

Multiple-choice questions can require a recall of facts or descriptive knowledge but often require one of the knowledge-creation/knowledge demonstration methods, as illustrated in the following example. I have indicated the test question and the rules required to answer the question.

Which of the following involves a chemical change?
Rule: a chemical change involves a change in the chemical composition of a

substance. A physical change involves a change in appearance or state but not a change in chemical composition.

a. souring milk

b. cooking an egg

c. baking a cake

d. none of the above

e. all of the above

This question requires students to use the inductive process of analysis. They must decide if souring milk, cooking an egg, and baking a cake result in a change in the chemical composition of the substance. It is analysis because they are determining if the example complies with the rule for a chemical change.

In Wiggins and McTighe's process, the assessment drives and defines the instruction. For example, if the preceding question is used on a test, it indicates that the teacher will have to make sure that students understand that the addition of heat to a chemical compound can bring about either a physical or a chemical change. The key to differentiating is whether a change in chemical composition occurs when heat is added. Students tend to think that a chemical change requires the addition of another substance or chemical. The lesson should cover all the ways in which chemical changes can occur.

The next test question is a common way of assessing whether students inductively generalized rules from a reading or a lecture.

Which statement best summarizes the circumstances present in the early years of Rome?

a. Rome had to fight many battles to survive.

b. Rome was initially dominated by other civilizations.

c. Rome had to develop a unique economy to survive.

d. Rome enjoyed strategic advantages that helped it to develop and prosper quickly.

Rule: Rome enjoyed strategic advantages that helped it to develop and prosper quickly. This rule is an inductive generalization of the following facts from the reading or lecture:

a. Rome was near a source of water and on arable land.

b. Rome was far enough away from the sea to be invisible to hostile foreign vessels but close enough to conduct trade.

c. Rome had more technically advanced neighbors to the north and south from which it learned a great deal.

The preceding question requires students to inductively generalize (induction—synthesis) details from a reading or lecture. The capacity to inductively generalize and thereby organize the details of content into summarizing concepts (rules) is a crucial skill for all students to acquire. Instruction should, therefore, demonstrate and develop this capability, require students to undertake it, and give students sufficient practice employing it. As discussed previously, when reading and lecture learning was covered, students should know and be clear on what rules you expect them to construct from a reading or lecture. These expectations should be explicit.

The next question requires students to undertake both the deduction—logic and application—procedural knowledge demonstration processes.

Your friend has a bracelet that is supposed to be solid gold. List the steps below that you would take to prove or disprove that it is solid gold.

1.

2. _____

3. _____

4. _____

Rules required:

1. Density is equal to mass divided by volume.

2. All substances of the same chemical composition have the same density.

3. Object submerged in water will displace an amount of water equal to their volume.

4. Mass equals weight divided by the acceleration of gravity.

This question requires knowledge of four rules, the ability to create a chain of logical connection between the rules, and the ability to develop and apply a procedure using the concrete particulars given in the problem. The solution might proceed as follows. From rule 2, the student could deduct that they could determine whether the ring was solid gold by comparing the ring's density to the known density of gold. The next step is to connect this deduction (in a chain of reasoning) to rule 1, which specifies how density is determined. The student would then deduct from this rule that they needed a method of obtaining the volume and mass of their friend's ring. Rule 3 suggests a procedure for determining volume. To develop this procedure from the rule, the student must think of a process or set of actions that "are the coherent and necessary consequences of the rule" (learning principle 14). In other words, they need to think, "What does this rule tell me to do?" In this case, it might be to drop the ring into a graduated cylinder of water with a narrow radius that will allow them to read the increase in volume after dropping the ring into the cylinder. The only thing missing now is the mass of the ring. The student should know that they can measure the mass of the ring using a scale. If they don't have a mass scale, they can use an ordinary scale to measure the weight and then divide the result by the acceleration of gravity (rule 4). The final step is to go back to rule 2, calculate the density using the rule, and then compare the result with the known density of gold. As the preceding demonstrates, this is not an easy problem. The student needs to know four rules, employ (demonstrate) learning principles 10, 11, and 12 to successfully perform the required deductions, and use learning principle 14 for application to develop the procedure.

The preceding illustrates several important points. Analyzing the requirements to successfully complete an assessment doesn't necessarily directly suggest the knowledge-construction method to be used to teach the rule. It does show the knowledge demonstration methods students will have to employ to successfully use and demonstrate their knowledge of the tested rules. Teaching a rule, particularly if the rule is received wisdom, does not automatically impart knowledge of how to use the rule to accomplish a goal—how to deduct from the rule or how to apply it. This must be also taught. What analysis of the assessment tells you is what the lesson must include beyond simple knowledge of the rule. It could be the case that induction is the most efficient and direct way to teach a rule. However, if the assessment requires that the student deduct from the rule or apply it, then this must also be part of the instruction. The student will need both knowledge concerning how this is done and experience doing it.

For those operating in an environment where they are judged by student performance on high-stakes accountability tests, the questions in the accountability test should be part of the phase 2 process. The next example illustrates how this can be done.

One semester, the principal of a high school in the most economically disadvantaged area of Fort Worth was one of my students. As a class exercise, he let us evaluate his students' performance on the state accountability test for Algebra 1. We specifically examined a set of questions that virtually all of his students got wrong. The test questions concerned how the graph of a function is impacted by adding a constant to the function, adding a constant to the argument of the function, or multiplying the function by constant. The applicable rules are shown in the following example.

The principal informed us that his students come to him with poorly developed arithmetic skills. As a result, the head of his math department worked with teachers to make

Figure 5.8 Impacts on the graph of a function of different algebraic actions

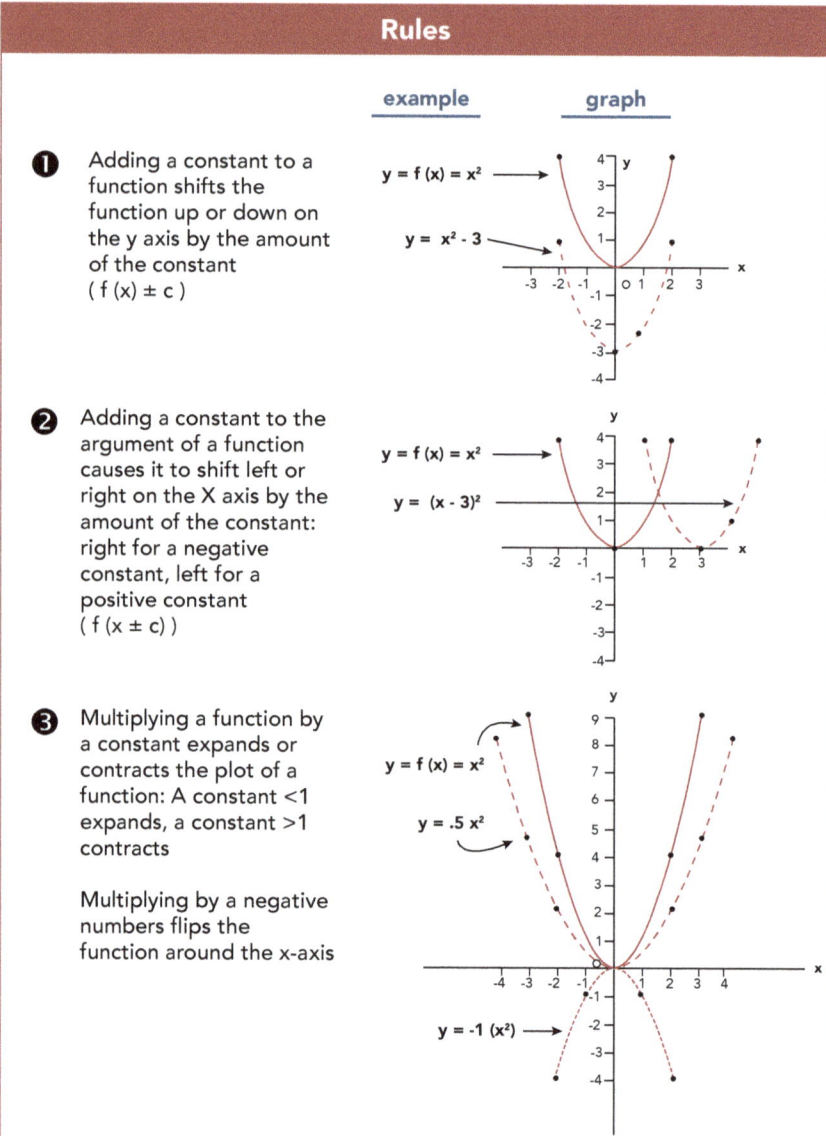

the curriculum centered around the use of a graphing calculator to solve problems. The way students learned the preceding rules was by entering the basic function in their calculator and then entering the function modified by either adding a constant, adding a constant to the argument, or multiplying by a constant. The graphing calculator showed the original unmodified plot juxtaposed against the plot of the function modified in one of the preceding ways. The students learned the rules through the process of reflective abstraction. They observed the consequences of their actions and abstracted rules, like adding a positive constant shifts the graph up.

The students had in fact learned the basic rules in this manner. This was evidenced by the fact that almost all of them correctly answered questions like the following:

1. If we add 5 to a function, it will:

   a. shift the plot of the function 5 units to the right

   b. shift the plot of the function 5 units to the left

   c. shift the plot of the function 5 units up on the y axis

   d. shift the plot of the function 5 units down on the y axis

All the students, however, were unable to solve a problem like the following:

1. Which function is represented by the graph shown below?

   a. $y = x^2 - 2x + 5$

   b. $y = 2x^2 - 5x + 1$

   c. $y = 2x^2 - 8x + 6$

   d. $y = x^2 - 2x - 2$

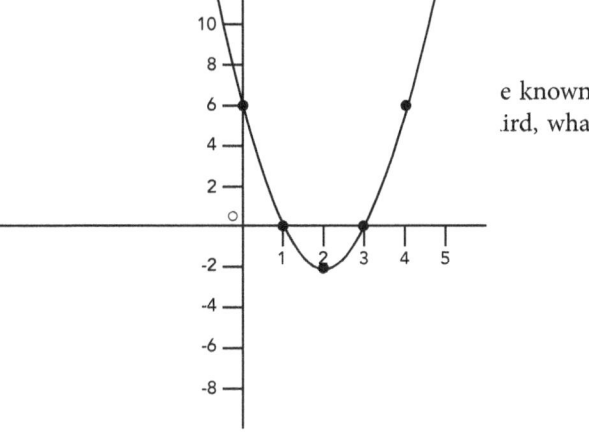

Let's examine the problem   e known;
second, what knowledge den   ird, what

the implications are for instruction.

The three aforementioned rules must be known. As can be seen, knowledge of these rules will not lead directly to a solution to the problem. There is a missing rule that the students did not know. All of the multiple-choice options are parabolas. Anything of the form $ax^2 + bx + c$ is a parabola. The next required rule that the students did not know was that any parabola can be expressed in the form $y = k(x \pm l)^2 \pm m$, where k, l, and m are constants. If they know this rule, they can get l and m directly from the graph using the three rules they know. The graph is shifted down 2 units, so $m = -2$. The graph is shifted right 2 units, so $l = -2$. The equation that results when we plug these two values into the form of the equation for a parabola is

$$y = k(x - 2)^2 - 2$$

We now have only one remaining unknown to determine to get the expression for the parabola and have our answer. The student must make the observation that to solve the preceding equation for k they need concrete values for x and y. They then need to make the deduction from the rule for a graph that a graph shows the y value for every value of x. That being the case, they can pick an x value and the graph will tell them the corresponding y value. For example, let's pick $x = 1$. At this value of x, the graph shows us that $y = 0$. We can now put these values into the equation and solve for k.

$$0 = k(1 - 2)^2 - 2$$

$$0 = k - 2$$

$$2 = k$$

The equation of the parabola is then:

$$y = 2(x - 2)^2 - 2$$

Multiplying the right side out, we get:

$$y = 2x^2 - 8x + 6$$

So, the correct answer is c.

We identified the missing rules; now let's identify the required knowledge demonstration methods.

1. Connecting the missing rules to the known rules requires the deductive process of connecting rules in a chain of reasoning—principle 12 (deduction).

2. Getting information from the graph to put into the missing rule for a parabola required connecting the concrete information on the graph to the abstract rule—

principle 11 (deduction).

3. Getting the required x and y values needed to solve for the last unknown required a deduction from the rule that defines what a graph is and required students to know "what the rule told them to do"—principles 10, 11, (deduction), and 14 (application) were required.

In summary, this analysis informs the teacher that lessons must do the following:

- Develop knowledge of the missing rules.
- Develop the ability to make deductions and inferences from the rules.
- Be able to connect the rules in a logical chain of reasoning.
- Develop the ability to connect concrete data to the abstract rules.
- Know what processes and procedures are the expression of and logical consequences of the rules (know what the rule tells them to do).

We can see from the preceding how assessment can assist and guide the lesson construction process. The analysis indicated that instruction needed to include a significant application segment that involved students in the deductive activities required in the application of the rules. The applications should first be demonstrated by the teacher using "think aloud" modeling of the required deductive processes and students should receive guided practice conducting the rule application procedures. Of course, lessons should include construction of the missing rules that the students required to successfully perform the assessment.

Another popular form of assessment is requiring students to write an essay or paper in response to a prompt or set of instructions. As discussed previously, an essay or paper requires the student to structure and organize their understandings into a connected, coherent, and logically organized exposition of their knowledge. A paper or essay can include descriptive content covering factual information, inductive arguments, and deductive arguments. As such, the same analysis demonstrated earlier is in order when evaluating the implications of a writing assessment on the requirements of preceding lessons. The two fundamental questions are: What rules does the learner need to know and understand? And what knowledge demonstration methods does the assignment require?

To provide an example, I have shown the following guidelines for a writing assessment that could be used for the Gilded Age block of instruction.

> I have listed below what I believe to be the five most important "lessons" to be learned from a study of the Gilded Age. For each of the five "lessons," I want you to compare and contrast the events and circumstances of the Gilded Age with the current times—what some call the Information Age. For example, "lesson" 1 states that technological innovation drives substantial changes in the lives of citizens and substantial changes in business activity. I want you to tell me what

events and circumstances in the Gilded Age justify this conclusion. Next, I want you to do the same for the current time period (Information Age). Then compare and contrast these two time periods in the context of the "lesson" statement. How are these time periods the same and how are they different? When you have evaluated all five "lesson" statements in this fashion, I want you to tell me what recommendations you would give to today's policymakers to support constructive evolutionary change and avoid revolutionary change.

This is a long and difficult assignment as specified. If used, it might be beneficial to present it at the beginning of the block of instruction and specify successful completion of the assessment as the goal of the instruction. The students could begin work on the assignment after the teacher had covered each of the "lessons" and students felt comfortable with their understanding.

The assigned paper requires the induction-analysis method to justify the statements for each age and to compare and contrast the ages. It requires the induction-synthesis and deduction-logic methods to develop the policy recommendations. This means that the lessons need to involve the students in using these methods to process lesson content and develop their understanding. Another consideration is the student's ability to handle an assignment at this level. From experience, I would say that this assignment would work for AP American history or a college-level American history class. A simplified and more directive version would likely be required for other American history students.

The portfolio method can serve as both a knowledge-construction strategy and an assessment tool. This method has students submit an assignment, receive teacher feedback, and then resubmit the assignment after incorporating the teacher's feedback. There can be more than one cycle of submission and feedback. The strategy is analogous to an apprenticeship model. As discussed previously, the key to success here is the quality of teacher feedback. For example, it must be specific, and the student must clearly understand what they must do to comply with the teacher's recommendations expressed in the feedback. As with other forms assessment, the portfolio assessment process should be evaluated in the context of the rules and knowledge demonstration methods required for successful performance. Note that all formative assessments done before the final assessment can be considered to be learning experiences. They involve the same processes in demonstrating knowledge that are used in constructing knowledge. Formative testing can be learning.

Another type of assessment that can serve as both an assessment and a learning experience is performance assessment, or what is sometimes called *authentic assessment*. Wiggins and McTighe (2005) refer to this as demonstrating the ability to "do" the subject. The ideas to simulate the kind of work done by people who routinely employ the knowledge in their jobs. It is essentially both applied learning and the testing of application abilities.

Wiggins and McTighe present the acronym GRASPS as a design guideline for this type of assessment.

G - goal of the assignment

R - role you're playing

A - audience you're producing the product for

S - situation you're addressing

P - product you're producing

S - standards you must adhere to

An example assessment of this type is illustrated here:

You are a member of the staff of the Council of Arts and Letters. The council has announced that they will be building a Hall of Fame in Cleveland, Ohio, that will honor the works of notable US authors and artists. As a person with knowledge of American literature, you have been asked to submit a nomination for an author to be admitted into the Hall of Fame. Submit a nomination paper and create a presentation for the board of directors of the council that presents your rationale for recommending the author and your analysis of the author's contribution to US literature.

In this assessment, the **goal** is recommending a specific author for recognition and induction into the Hall of Fame. The student's **role** is that of an expert on the staff who is qualified to make the requested recommendation. The **audience** is the council's board of directors. The **situation** requires the student to have knowledge of the rules that specify the attributes, characteristics, and relationship between those attributes and the characteristics that make a novel exceptional, classic, and important enough for generations of readers and students to experience and study. Why *Huckleberry Finn* and not *Captain Underpants*?

In this assignment, the student must utilize the knowledge demonstration method of induction analysis to convince the audience that the author's novels comply with the rules that define classical, exceptional, and important literature. The **product** is a written recommendation and a presentation. Producing the product requires that the student organize their oral and written descriptions, inductive arguments, and deductive arguments into a connected and coherent structure that flows logically. The **standards** for the assignment would likely be a teacher-supplied rubric that tells the student the criteria the teacher will be utilizing to grade their paper and presentation.

As with the prior examples, the assessment informs instruction. The students will need rules they can use to analyze an author's works to determine whether they meet the requirements of an enduring and important classic. This implies that classroom instruction should include an inductive generalization/synthesis of these rules. Rather than simply covering different authors, lessons should include comparing, contrasting, and generalizing the works of different authors to create an understanding of what constitutes an enduring classic. If this is not done in the classroom, the student will have to do this on their own to successfully complete the assessment. If students develop the rule on their own, the teacher needs to understand that the students' "enduring classic" rules may be substantially different from those rules developed and recognized by literary scholars. There is a world where *Captain Underpants* is more highly regarded than *Huckleberry Finn*—for example, the world of middle school students.

In addition, the student should develop and have experience using the induction analysis knowledge demonstration process. Lessons should involve this process as applied to the evaluation of literature, as it will be crucial for successfully performing the assessment.

The next and final stage of Wiggins and McTighe's curriculum development process is the creation of lessons. Knowledge of the learning goals articulated in terms of Big Ideas, Essential Questions, and Enduring Understandings and the requirements imposed by the assessments guide the construction of the lessons. The overall process is designed to comply with a cardinal rule of curriculum development: align the learning goals to the assessment and the assessment to instruction.

Chapter 4 and the first part of this chapter extensively cover the lesson design process, so I will end the discussion of curriculum development here.

My parting comment is that whether you are a parent or a volunteer tutoring or reteaching a student, a classroom teacher, a corporate or institutional trainer, or an administrator guiding teachers, I commend you and thank you for your efforts. You are giving your students one of the greatest gifts that one human can give another: the gift of knowledge and skill! I earnestly hope that the contents of this book will assist you in those efforts.

Reference List

Ausubel, D. P. 1963. *The Psychology of Meaningful Verbal Learning*. New York: Grune and Stratton.

Ausubel, D. P. 1968. *Educational Psychology: A Cognitive View*. New York: Holt, Rinehart, and Winston.

Ausubel, D. P. 1977. "The Facilitation of Meaningful Verbal Learning in the Classroom." *Educational Psychologist* 12 (2): 162–78.

Baddeley, A. D., and G. Hitch. 1974. "Working Memory." In *Recent Advances in Learning and Motivation*, edited by G. Bower, 47–90. New York: Academic Press.

Baldwin, J. (1957) 2013. "Sonny's Blues." In *Literature: Portable Anthology*, edited by J. Gardner, B. Lawn, J. Ridl, and P. Shakel, 250–75. Boston: Bedford.

Barclay, J., J. Bransford, J. Franks, N. McCarrell, and K. Nitsch. 1974. "Comprehension and Semantic Flexibility." *Journal of Verbal Learning and Verbal Behavior* 13 (4): 471–81.

Bateson, G. (1979) 2002. *Mind and Nature: A Necessary Unity*. Cresskill, NJ: Hampton Press.

Bear, M. F., B. W. Connors, and M. A. Paradiso. 2007. *Neuroscience: Experiencing the Brain*. Baltimore: Lippencott, Williams, and Wilkins.

Bereiter, C., and S. Engelmann. 1966. *Teaching Disadvantaged Children in the Preschool*. Upper Saddle River, NJ: Prentice Hall.

Braddock, Letter R., L. Schoer, and R. Lloyd-Jones. 1963. *Research in Written Composition*. Urbana, IL: National Council of Teachers of English.

Braine, M., and D. O'Brien. 1991. "A Theory of If: A Lexical Entry, Reasoning Program, and Pragmatic Principles." *Psychological Review* 98 (2): 183–203.

Braman, D., and D. M. Kahan. 2006. *Overcoming the Fear of Guns, the Fear of Gun Control, and the Fear of Cultural Politics: Constructing a Better Gun Debate*. Washington, DC: George Washington University Faculty Publications.

Bransford, J. 1979. *Human Cognition: Learning, Understanding, and Cognition*. Belmont, CA: Wadsworth.

Bransford, J., and M. K. Johnson. 1972. "Contextual Prerequisites for Understanding: Some Investigations of Comprehension and Recall." *Journal of Verbal Learning and Verbal Behavior* 11 (6): 717–26.

Brewer, W., and J. C. Treyens. 1981. "Role of Schemata in Memory for Places." *Cognitive Psychology* 13 (2): 207–30.

Brophy, J. 1998. *Motivating Students to Learn*. Boston: McGraw Hill.

Brophy, J., and T. Good. 1986. "Teacher Behavior and Student Achievement." In *Handbook of Research on Teaching*, 3rd ed., edited by M. C. Wittrock, 328–75. New York: Macmillan.

Capra, Fritjof. 1996. *The Web of Life*. New York: Doubleday.

Cohen, E., and D. A. Smith-Gold. 1978. "Your Students' Cognitive Functioning: Important Factor in Readiness to Learn." In *Proceedings of the Annual Conference of Western College Reading Association* 11 (1): 31–34. Oxfordshire: United Kingdom

Conway, M., G. Cohen, and N. Stanhope. 1992. "Why Is It That University Grades Do Not Predict Long-Term Retention?" *Journal of Experimental Psychology: General* 120:382–84.

Cote, C. 2021. "Data Storytelling: How to Effectively Tell a Story with Data." *Business Insights* (blog), Harvard Business School. https://online.hbs.edu/blog/post/data-storytelling.

Craik, F. I. M., and E. Tulving. 1975. "Depth of Processing and the Retention of Words and Episodic Memory." *Journal of Experimental Psychology: General* 104 (3): 269–94.

Damasio, A. 1994. *Descartes's Error*. London: Vintage Books.

Damasio, A. 2003. *Looking for Spinoza*. New York: Harcourt.

Damasio, A. 2010. *Self Comes to Mind: Constructing the Conscious Brain*. New York: Pantheon Books.

Deacon, T. W. 1997. *The Symbolic Species*. New York: W. W. Norton.

Dehaene, S. 2007. "A Few Steps toward a Science of Mental Life." *Mind, Brain, and Education* 1 (1): 28–47.

Deledalle, G. 2000. *Charles S. Peirce's Philosophy of Signs*. Bloomington: Indiana University Press.

Dennett, D. 2013. *Intuition Pumps and Other Tools for Thinking*. New York: W. W. Norton.

Derrida, J. 1976. *Of Grammatology*. Translated by G. Spivak. Baltimore: Johns Hopkins.

Descartes, R. (1641) 1952. *Meditations on First Philosophy*. Translated by E. Haldane and G. Ross. Chicago: Encyclopedia Britannica.

Dewey, J. 1933. *How We Think*. Boston: D. C. Heath.

Diana, R. A., A. P. Yonelinas, and C. Ranganath. 2010. "Medial Temporal Lobe Activity during Source Retrieval Reflects Information Type, Not Memory Strength." *Journal of Cognitive Neuroscience* 22 (8): 1808–18.

Dunn, Patricia A. 2017. "Teaching Grammar Improves Writing." In *Bad Ideas about Writing*, edited by Cheryl E. Ball and Drew Loewe, 144–49. Morgantown: West Virginia University Libraries Digital Publishing Institute.

Durant, W. (1926) 1961. *The Story of Philosophy*. New York: Simon and Schuster.

Edisonian. 2021. "The Edisonian Approach: What It Is and How Edison Used It." Thomas Edison and the Invention of the Lightbulb. https://edisonian.weebly.com/the-edisonian-approach.html.

Eggen, P. D., and D. E. Kauchak. 2006. *Strategies and Models for Teachers*. New York: Pearson.

Einstein, A. (1949) 1979. *Autobiographical Notes*. Translated by P. Schilpp. Chicago: Open Court.

Ely, R. 2005. "Language and Literacy in the School Years." In *The Development of Language*, edited by J. B. Gleason, 395–443. New York: Pearson.

Evans, J. S. B. T., and A. Feeney. 2004. "The Role of Prior Belief in Reasoning." In *The Nature of Reasoning*, edited by J. P. Leighton and R. J. Sternberg, 78–102. New York: Cambridge University Press.

Evans, J. S. B. T., S. E. Newstead, and R. M. J. Byrne. 1993. *Human Reasoning: The Psychology of Deduction*. London: Erlbaum.

Ewing, J. C., D. D. Foster, and M. S. Whittington. 2011. "Explaining Student Cognition during Class Sessions in the Context Piaget's Theory of Cognitive Development." *NACTA Journal* 55 (1): 68–75.

Flavell, J. H. 1963. *The Development Psychology of Jean Piaget*. New York: Van Nostrand and Reinhold.

Fodor, J. A., and N. Block. 1972. "What Psychological States Are Not." *Philosophical Review* 81 (2): 9496.

Fodor, J., and J. Pylyshyn. 1988. "Connectionism and Cognitive Architecture: A Critical Analysis." *Cognition* 28 (1–2): 3–71.

Foucault, M. 1972. *The Archeology of Knowledge*. New York: Pantheon Books.

Fuster, J. 2009. "Cortex and Memory: Emergence of a New Paradigm." *Journal of Cognitive Neuroscience* 21 (11): 2047–72.

Gagne, R. M. 1985. *The Conditions of Learning*. 4th ed. New York: Holt, Rinehart and Wilson.

Gazzaniga, M. S. 2011. *Who's in Charge?: Free Will and the Science of the Brain*. New York: HarperCollins.

Gazzaniga, M. S., R. B. Ivry, and G. R. Mangun. 2009. *Cognitive Neuroscience: The Biology of the Brain*. New York: Norton.

Gick, M., and K. J. Holyoak. 1980. "Analogical Problem-Solving." *Cognitive Psychology* 12 (3): 306–55.

Gilhooley, K. J. 1988. *Thinking: Direct, Undirected and Creative*. 2nd ed. New York: Academic Press.

Gleick, J. 1987. *Chaos: Making a New Science*. New York: Viking Penguin.

Glesne, C. (1992) 2006. *Becoming Qualitative Researchers*. Boston: Pearson Education.

Glisky, E. L., M. R. Polster, and B. C. Routhuieaux. 1995. "Double Dissociation between Item and Source Memory." *Neuropsychology* 9 (2): 229–35.

Goldstein, D. 2017. "Why Kids Can't Read." *New York Times*, August 2, 2017.

Greene, J. D., L. E. Nystrom, J. M. Darley, A. D. Engell, and J. D. Cohen. 2004. "The Neural Bases of Cognitive Conflict and Control in Moral Judgment." *Neuron* 44 (2): 389–400.

Greene, J. D., R. D. Sommerville, L. E. Nystrom, J. M. Darley, and J. D. Cohen. 2001. "An fMRI Investigation of Emotional Engagement in Moral Judgments." *Science* 293 (5537): 2105–08.

Griggs, R., and J. R. Cox. 1982. "The Elusive Thematic Materials Effect in Wason's Selection Task." *British Journal of Psychology* 73 (3): 407–20.

Guba, E. G. 1985. "The Context of Emergent Paradigm Research." In *Organizational Theory and Inquiry: The Paradigm Revolution*, edited by Y. S. Lincoln, 79–104. Beverly Hills: Sage.

Gutek, G. L. 2009. *New Perspectives on Philosophy and Education*. Columbus, OH: Pearson.

Haidt, L. 2013. *The Righteous Mind*. New York: Vintage Books.

Haken, H. 1981. *The Science of Structure: Synergetics*. New York: Von Nostrand Reinhold.

Hebb, D. O. 1949. *The Organization of Behavior*. New York: John Wiley and Sons.

Hillocks, G. 1986. *Research on Written Composition: New Directions for Teaching*. Urbana, IL: ERIC Clearing House on Reading and Communication Skills.

Hoopes, J. 1991. *Peirce on Signs*. Chapel Hill: University of North Carolina Press.

Hume, D. (1739) 1982. *Treatise of Human Nature*. Chicago: Encyclopedia Britannica Press.

Hunter, M. 1982. *Mastery Teaching*. El Segundo, CA: Instructional Dynamics.

Hyde, T. S., and J. J. Jenkins. 1969. "Differential Effects of Incidental Tasks on the Organization of Recall of a List of Highly Associated Words." *Journal of Experimental Psychology* 82 (3): 472–81.

Jankowsky, J. S., A. P. Shimamura, and L. R. Squire. 1989. "Source Memory Impairment in Patients with Frontal Lobe Lesions." *Neuropsychologia* 27 (8): 1043–56.

Jasper, H. H. 1995. "A Historical Perspective: The Rise and Fall of Prefrontal Lobotomy." *Advances in Neurology* 66:97–114.

Johnson-Laird, P. 1983. *Mental Models*. Cambridge: Harvard University Press.

Johnson-Laird, P., R. Byrne, and W. Schaeken. 1992. "Propositional Reasoning by Model." *Psychological Review* 99 (3): 418–39.

Johnson-Laird, P., and G. Goodwin. 2005. "Reasoning about Relations." *Psychological Review* 112 (2): 468–93.

Joyce, B. R., M. Weil, and E. Calhoun. 2009. *Models of Teaching*. Boston: Allyn and Bacon.

Kahneman, D. 2011. *Thinking, Fast and Slow*. New York: Farrar, Straus and Giroux.

Kant, I. (1781) 1990. *The Critique of Pure Reason*. Translated by J. Meiklejohn. Buffalo: Prometheus Books.

Kant, I. (1783) 1950. *Prolegomena to Any Future Metaphysics*. Translated by L. Beck. Indianapolis: Bobbs-Merrill.

Kelso, J. A. 1995. *Dynamic Patterns: The Self-Organization of Brain and Behavior*. Cambridge: MIT Press.

Klein, S. B., K. Rosendahl, and L. Cosmides. 2002. "A Social Cognitive Neuroscience Analysis of the Self." *Social Cognition* 20 (2): 105–35.

Kline, M. 1967. *Calculus: An Intuitive and Physical Approach*. New York: John Wiley and Sons.

Kolln, M., and L. Gray. 2017. *Rhetorical Grammar*. Boston: Pearson.

Kuhn, T. 1996. *The Structure of Scientific Revolutions*. 3rd ed. Chicago: University of Chicago Press.

Lakoff, G., and M. Johnson. 1980. *Metaphors We Live By*. Chicago: University of Chicago Press.

LeDoux, J. 1996. *The Emotional Brain: The Mysterious Underpinnings of Emotional Life*. New York: Simon and Schuster.

LeDoux, J. 2002. *Synaptic Self*. New York: Viking.

Locke, J. (1689) 1959. *An Essay Concerning Human Understanding*. New York: Dover.

Locke, T. 2009. "Grammar and Writing: The International Debate." In *The SAGE Handbook of Writing Development*, edited by R. Beard, J. Riley, and M. Nystrand, 182–93. London: Sage.

Magliaro, S., B. Lockee, and J. Burton. 2005. "Direct Instruction Revisited: A Key Model for Instructional Technology." *Educational Technology Research and Development* 53 (4): 41–55.

Marzano, R. J. 1998. *A Theory Based Meta-Analysis of Research on Instruction*. Aurora, CO: Mid-Continent Research for Education and Learning, ERIC Document Reproduction Service No. 427 087.

Masters, K. 2013. "Edgar Dale's Pyramid of Learning in Medical Education: A Literature Review." *Medical Teacher* 35 (11): 1584–93.

Maturana, H. R., and F. J. Varela. 1998. *The Tree of Knowledge: The Biological Roots of Human Understanding*. Boston: Shambhala.

McClelland, J. L., and D. E. Rumelhart. 1986. *Parallel Distributed Processing: Explorations in the Microstructure of Cognition*, Vol. 2, *Psychological and Biological Models*. Cambridge: MIT Press.

Miller, G. A. 1956. "The Magical Number Seven, Plus or Minus Two: Some Limits on Our Capacity for Processing Information." *Psychological Review* 63 (2): 81–97.

Milner, B. 1995. "Aspects of Human Frontal Lobe Function." *Advances in Neurology* 66:67–84.

Mitchell, J. P., M. R. Banaji, and C. N. Macrae. 2005. "General and Specific Contributions of the Medial Prefrontal Cortex to Knowledge about Mental States." *Neuroimage* 28 (4): 757–62.

Montaldi, D., T. J. Spencer, N. Roberts, and A. R. Mayes. 2006. "The Neural System That Mediates Familiarity Memory." *Hippocampus* 16 (5): 504–20.

Morton, P. A. 2005. *A Historical Introduction to the Philosophy of Mind*. Ontario: Broadview Press.

Murray, M. M. 1972. "Teach Writing as a Process Not Product." *Leaflet* (November): 11–14.

National Reading Panel. 2000. *Teaching Children to Read: An Evidence-Based Assessment of the Scientific Research Literature on Reading and Its Implications for Reading Instruction*. Washington, DC: National Institute of Health, National Institute of Child Health and Human Development.

Noddings, N. 1992. *The Challenge to Care in Schools*. New York: Teachers College Press.

Noddings, N. 2012. *Philosophy of Education*. Philadelphia: Westview Press.

O'Donnell, E. T. 2015. *Henry George and the Crisis of Inequality: Progress and Poverty in the Gilded Age*. New York: Columbia University Press.

Papineau, D. 2009. *Western Philosophy*. New York: Sterling.

Parkin, A. J. 1984. "Levels of Processing, Context, and Facilitation of Pronunciation." *Acta Psychologia* 55 (1): 19–29.

Pascarella, E., and P. Terenzini. 1991. *How College Affects Students*. San Francisco: Jossey-Bass.

Piaget, J. 1952. *The Origins of Intelligence and Children*. New York: International Universities Press.

Piaget, J. 1985. *The Equilibration of Cognitive Structures*. Translated by T. Brown and K. J. Thampy. Chicago: University of Chicago Press.

Piaget, J. (1970) 2006. *A Child's Conception of Movement and Speed*. Translated by G. E. T. Holloway and M. J. MacKenzie. Abingdon, UK: Routledge.

Pinker, S. 2007. *The Stuff of Thought: Language as a Window into Human Nature*. New York: Viking.

Plato. 1951. *The Republic*. Translated by F. M. Cornford. New York: Oxford University Press.

Poincaré, H. (1912) 1987. *Probability Calculus*. Paris: Jacques Gabay.

Pojman, L. P., and L. Vaughn. 2011. *Classics of Philosophy*. Oxford: Oxford University Press.

Prigogine, I. 1997. *The End of Certainty*. New York: Free Press.

Putnam, H. 1975. "The Meaning of Meaning." In *Language, Mind, and Knowledge*, edited by S. K. Gunderson, 131–93. Minneapolis: University of Minnesota Press.

Ranganath, C., and R. S. Blumenfeld. 2005. "Doubts about Double Dissociation's between Short- and Long-Term Memory." *Trends in Cognitive Sciences* 9 (8): 374–80.

Rathburn, M. K. 2015. "Building Connections through Contextualized Learning in an Undergraduate Course on Scientific and Mathematical Literacy." *International Journal for the Scholarship of Teaching and Learning* 9 (1): 1–14.

Reisberg, D. 2010. *Cognition: Exploring the Science of the Mind*. 4th ed. New York: W. W. Norton.

Resnick, L. B. 1987. "Learning in School and Out." *Educational Researcher* 16 (9): 13–20.

Rips, L. 1990. "Reasoning." *Annual Review of Psychology* 41 (1): 321–53.

Rorty, R. (1989) 2006. *Contingency, Irony, and Solidarity*. New York: Cambridge University Press.

Rose, L. T., R. Rouhani, and K. W. Fischer. 2013. "The Science of the Individual." *Mind, Brain, and Education* 7:152–58.

Rosenshine, B. 1971. *Teaching Behaviors and Student Achievement*. London: National Foundation for Educational Research.

Russell, B. 1919. *Introduction to Mathematical Philosophy*. New York: Macmillan.

Russell, B. 1945. *The History of Western Philosophy*. New York: Simon and Shuster.

Schopenhauer, A. (1819) 1958. *The World as Will and Representation*. Translated by B. Payne. New York: Dover.

Schwartz, D., M. Weaver, and S. Kaplan. 1999. "A Little Mechanism Can Go a Long Way." *Behavioral and Brain Sciences* 22 (4): 631–32.

Scott-Kakures, D., S. Castagnetto, H. Benson, W. Taschek, and P. Hurley. 1993. *History of Philosophy*. New York: HarperCollins.

Searle, J. 1984. *Minds, Brains, and Science*. Cambridge: Harvard University Press.

Shaywitz, B. A., G. R. Lyon, and S. E. Shaywitz. 2006. "The Role of Functional Magnetic Resonance Imaging in Understanding Reading and Dyslexia." *Developmental Neuropsychology* 30 (1): 613–32.

Shimamura, A. P. 2000. "The Role of the Prefrontal Cortex in Dynamic Filtering." *Psychobiology* 28 (2): 207–18.

Sloman, S. A. 1996. "The Empirical Case for Two Systems of Reasoning." *Psychological Bulletin* 119 (1): 322.

Sontag, F. A. 1988. *A Kierkegaard Handbook*. Atlanta: John Knox Press.

Squire, L. R. 1992. "Memory and the Hippocampus: A Summary of Findings from Rats, Monkeys, and Humans." *Psychological Review* 99 (2): 195–231.

Stanford Encyclopedia of Philosophy. 2021. "Rationalism vs. Empiricism." https://plato.stanford.edu/entries/rationalism-empiricism.

Stanford Encyclopedia of Philosophy. 2022. "Kant's Categories." https://plato.stanford.edu/entries/kant-categories.

Sticht, T. G. 1999. "The Theory Behind Content-Based Instruction." *Focus on Basics* 1 (D).

Sticht, T. G., L. A. Armijo, N. Koffman, K. Roberson, R. Weitzman, F. Chang, and J. Morocco. 1986. *Teachers, Books, Computers, and Peers: Integrated Communications Technologies for Adult Literacy Development*. Monterey, CA: US Naval Postgraduate School.

Taba, H. 1966. *Teaching Strategies and Cognitive Functioning in Elementary School Children*. Cooperative Research Project 2404. San Francisco: San Francisco State College.

Thompson-Schill, S. L., M. D'Esposito, G. K. Aguirre, and M. J. Farah. 1997. "Role of Left Inferior Prefrontal Cortex in the Retrieval of Semantic Knowledge: A Reevaluation." *Proceedings of the National Academy of Sciences* 94 (26): 14792–97.

Thompson-Schill, S. L., M. D'Esposito, and I. P. Kan. 1999. "Effects of Repetition and Competition on Activity in Left Prefrontal Cortex during Word Generation." *Neuron* 23 (3): 513–22.

Thompson-Schill, S. L., M. Ramscar, and E. Chrysikou. 2009. "Cognition without Control: When a Little Frontal Lobe Goes a Long Way." *Current Directions in Psychological Science* 18 (5): 259–63.

Tolstoy, L. 1903. *Pedagogicheskie statii* [Pedagogical Writings]. Moscow: Kushnerev.

Tulving, E. 1983. *Elements of Episodic Memory*. Oxford: Oxford University Press.

Vygotsky, L. (1934) 1986. *Thought and Language.* Translated by A. Kozulin. Cambridge, MA: MIT Press.

Wagner, A. D., D. L. Schachter, M. Rotte, W. Koutstall, A. Maril, A. M. Dale, B. R. Rosen, and R. L. Buckner. 1998. "Building Memories: Remembering and Forgetting of Verbal Experiences as Predicted by Brain Activity." *Science* 281 (5380) 1188–91.

Warren, K. 2001. *Big Steel: The First Century of the United States Steel Corporation, 1901–2001.* Pittsburgh: University of Pittsburgh Press.

Wason, P. 1968. "Reasoning about a Rule." *Quarterly Journal of Experimental Psychology* 20 (3): 273–81.

Wheeler, M. B., S. E. Peterson, and R. L. Buckner. 2000. "Memory's Echo: Vivid Remembering Reactivates Sensory Specific Cortex." *Proceedings of the National Academy of Sciences* 97 (20): 11125–29.

White, R. 2017. *The Republic for Which It Stands: The United States during Reconstruction and the Gilded Age, 1865–1896.* London: Oxford University Press.

White, R. 2018. "For Tech Giants, a Cautionary Tale from the 19th Century Railroads on the Limits of Competition." *Conversation*, March 6, 2018. https://theconversation.com/for-tech-giants-a-cautionary-tale-from-19th-century-railroads-on-the-limits-of-competition-91616.

Wiggins, G., and J. McTighe. 2005. *Understanding by Design.* Alexandria, VA: ASCD.

Willis, I. 2019. *The Edisonian Method: Trial and Error.* New York: Springer.

Wong, K. F., and X. J. Wang. 2006. "A Recurrent Network Mechanism of Time Integration in Perceptual Decisions." *Neuroscience* 26 (4): 1314–28.

Woolfolk, A. 2007. *Educational Psychology.* Boston: Pearson.

ABOUT THE AUTHOR

Steffen E. Palko spent 34 years in the energy industry and co-founded XTO Energy, which became an S&P 500 company in 2006. Beginning in 1986, he served in a variety of educational leadership roles at the national, state, and local level. After obtaining a Doctorate in Education, he spent 12 years teaching in TCU's College of Education.

www.ingramcontent.com/pod-product-compliance
Lightning Source LLC
Chambersburg PA
CBHW042146160426
43202CB00023B/2987